MOVEMENT DISORDERS
A Neuropsychiatric Approach

MOVEMENT DISORDERS

A Neuropsychiatric Approach

JAMES B. LOHR, MD
ALEXANDER A. WISNIEWSKI, MD

Foreword by Dilip V. Jeste, MD

THE GUILFORD PRESS
New York   London

This book was written by James B. Lohr and Alexander A. Wisniewski in their private capacity. The views expressed herein do not necessarily reflect those of the National Institute of Mental Health.

© 1987 The Guilford Press
A Division of Guilford Publications, Inc.
200 Park Avenue South, New York, N.Y. 10003

Printed in the United States of America

Last digit is print number: 9 8 7 6 5 4 3 2 1

LIBRARY OF CONGRESS CATALOGING IN PUBLICATION DATA

Lohr, James B.
  Movement disorders.

  (Foundations of modern psychiatry)
  Bibliography: p.
  Includes index.
  1. Movement disorders.   2. Neuropsychiatry.
I. Wisniewski, Alexander A. II. Title. III. Series.
[DNLM: 1. Movement Disorders.   WL 390 L833m]
  RC385.L64   1987   616.7′4   86-27163
  ISBN 0-89862-176-3

To our wives, Melodie and Roma

Foreword

A field of rapidly increasing scientific interest has been that of movement disorders. While conditions such as Parkinson's disease have been known to clinicians for a long time, the recent "epidemic" of drug-induced movement disorders, such as tardive dyskinesia, has served to highlight the importance of studying movement from several different perspectives. Understanding abnormal involuntary movements in a patient requires basic knowledge of the neuroanatomy, neurophysiology, pharmacology, neuropathology, as well as psychopathology of movement disorders. It is improper to classify movement disorders, like many other conditions, as psychiatric *or* neurologic disturbances. A truly neuropsychiatric approach is essential for both research and clinical purposes.

This monograph by Drs. James Lohr and Alexander Wisniewski is aimed at just such a goal, bringing together relevant information on diverse aspects of normal and abnormal movements. The early chapters provide a groundwork for understanding the fundamentals of movement. This information is utilized in later chapters on individual movement disorders. The last section, dealing with aspects such as sleep and handedness in relationship to movement disorders, is unique, since these topics are rarely covered in books on disturbances of movement.

The authors have done an excellent job of putting together this timely book, which should interest clinicians as well as students and researchers in the neurosciences.

Dilip V. Jeste, MD

Acknowledgments

We would like to acknowledge the artistic aid of Jeffrey Aarons and Nancy Bishop, who beautifully executed the complex schematic diagrams in the book. We would also like to thank Dilip Jeste, MD, who read the manuscript and offered many helpful suggestions. Our grateful appreciation goes to Seymour Weingarten, Editor-in-Chief, and Judith Grauman, Editorial Supervisor, of The Guilford Press, for their assistance and seemingly limitless patience. Finally, we would like to thank Melodie A. Lohr, MSN, who coauthored Chapters 1 and 25, read and edited every chapter, and patiently endured the many months of writing and rewriting. Without her support, this book would undoubtedly be simply a fond wish.

Preface

Psychiatry and neurology were not always the separate disciplines they are today. In the 1800s famous neurologists like Charcot and Janet were quite concerned with phenomena, such as hysteria, that largely fall under the aegis of psychiatry in modern medicine. Similarly, great psychiatrists such as Morel, Kahlbaum, and Kraepelin had often received extensive neurological training, and conceptualized major mental illnesses as being fundamentally neurological diseases.

The 20th century has witnessed a schism of these two medical sciences, with resultant confusion in diagnosis and treatment. This confusion is perhaps most pronounced in the areas in which psychiatry and neurology strongly overlap, and one of the most important of these areas is the domain of movement disorders. The various abnormalities of thought, affect, and behavior that characterize psychiatric disorders frequently have important motor manifestations that are often similar to, if not identical with, motor problems occurring in neurological disorders. Tics, hypokinesia, and stereotypies are but a few examples of clinical signs found in both psychiatric and neurological illnesses.

We chose to write this book in response to what we perceived as a deficit in the current neuropsychiatric literature. Although many volumes have been written on different aspects of neuropsychiatry, none, to our knowledge, offers a comprehensive unified neuropsychiatric discussion of motor disorders. We believe that a book that does do so can offer the clinician an important source of information on a subject only incompletely covered from solely a neurological or psychiatric point of view.

The main focus of this book is diagnosis of movement disorders. Many movement disorders are quite complex and confusing, and we believe that correct identification requires an understanding of both the pathophysiological basis and the history of motor disorders. We have correspondingly devoted considerable space to both these aspects. Although treatment issues are not the primary focus of this book, they are discussed where appropriate, especially in the more poorly understood movement disorders.

This book is divided into three main sections. Section I is an introduction to the field of movement from a historical and physioanatomical point of view. In Section II a compendium of different signs and symptoms of disordered movement is offered, and this section is in turn divided into four parts. The first part is a discussion of hyperkinetic disorders, reviewing focal and multifocal disorders of random excessive movement (Chapter 3), generalized disorders of excessive movement (Chapter 4), simple repetitive movements (Chapters 5 through 7), and complex repetitive movements (Chapter 8). Chapters 3 through 8 involve spontaneous movement disorders, in contrast with Chapters 9 and 10, which concentrate on reactive movement disorders—that is, those that are dependent on some type of environmental stimulation. Chapter 11 is a discussion of myoclonus, which can be focal, multifocal, generalized, spontaneous, or reactive. The second part of Section II reviews signs of decreased movement, and the third part reviews disorders of muscular tone. The last part is a discussion of disorders of complex motor performance, including disorders of facial expression, apraxias, and disorders of gait. Finally, Section III offers a discussion of special topics in neuropsychiatric movement disorders, including Tourette's syndrome, catatonia, hysteria, neuroleptic medications, sleep, handedness, and aging. The last chapter offers a discussion of some future directions in the interface of disorders of thought and movement.

We hope this book proves beneficial to clinicians and researchers in neurological and psychiatric disciplines who have an interest in disorders of movement.

James B. Lohr, MD
Alexander A. Wisniewski, MD

Contents

C. Disordered Muscle Tone

D. Disordered Complex Motor Performance

SECTION III. SPECIAL TOPICS IN
NEUROPSYCHIATRIC MOVEMENT DISORDERS

AN INTRODUCTION
TO MOVEMENT

CHAPTER ONE

A Brief History of Disorders of Movement

WITH MELODIE A. LOHR

OVERVIEW

The progress of medicine has ebbed and flowed with the tides of civilization. Yet man's desire for understanding has driven both civilization and medicine gradually forward in spite of many false starts and setbacks. One of the simplest means of understanding the complexities of the world is through magic and mythology. Complicated events are comprehensible by way of what Sir James Frazer (1890) has called imitative and contagious magic. The power of this means of understanding lies in its ability to "explain" virtually everything in a simple way. Thus, the movements of men and society mirror the movements of the cosmos, and disturbances in these motions may be attributed to the unseen forces connecting the bits of the universe. This way of thinking can hold great sway even over more enlightened individuals today, and was probably predominant in the minds of nomadic tribes that periodically invaded or passed through civilized nations in large numbers throughout history.

The early civilizations arose with the appearance of agriculture, and over time grew large enough to necessitate specialization of labor, one form of which became the practice of medicine. The stability of a city made such advances as writing possible, so that detailed observations of different maladies could be kept over time, which perhaps led in turn to the development of a different form of medical thought, one based more on systematic and critical observation than on magical thought: the beginning of medical science.

The stability and wealth of civilizations attracted hordes of barbarous tribes that periodically invaded cities and empires. These tribes were eventually assimilated, of course, and there appears to have arisen after each major invasion a curious blend of the more advanced "scientific" type of thought with the more primitive "magical" type. This process occurred many times throughout history whenever there existed vast outreaches of primitive peoples strong enough to overrun the polities of the time. It appears that the more advanced and complex was the civilization that was invaded, the more systematized and complex was the blend of magical and scientific thinking that ensued. The simple mythologies of outlying tribes poured into the vast edifices of great civilizations and took on immense proportions, as was reflected in religious thought. In its explanatory power early science was, in comparison with religion, relatively limited. The greater predictability that science afforded was eventually recognized as an important political tool, however, and so science began to flourish in the Renaissance.

It is against this panoramic backdrop that the history of medicine unfolded. Modern medicine developed along with modern science, and clinical categories multiplied as theories were made to fit the observations, rather than the other way around. It was not until the 19th century that the four humors of ancient science finally evaporated, and the medieval demons were cast out. Throughout the history of medicine, disorders of movement have held a special place, for they are among the most striking of all aberrant medical conditions. Echopraxia, a complex tic, and a cataplectic fit have all demanded attention and explanation. The attention, however, was not always benign, and the explanation not always rational, as we shall see in the following survey.

PRECIVILIZATION

What little is known about the illnesses that existed before the advent of writing has had to be deduced either from indirect evidence or from comparisons with primitive tribes that exist today. One must exercise caution in extrapolating from disorders of existing primitive tribes to those of prehistoric tribes, though, because many conditions are present in the uncivilized peoples of modern times that appear to have no parallel in civilized cultures, in particular such disorders of movement as *latah* or *amok* (Ackerknecht, 1959, 1982a). It is therefore only a guess whether movement disorders in early man resembled these or other conditions in existence today. Movement disorders certainly existed in prehistory, but were probably thought to be the result of the influence of spirits, demons, or gods—a common explanation even today for phenomena that are not readily understandable.

Cro-Magnon people may have employed magic as the main form of medical treatment, and perhaps some of the statuettes and carvings that date this period were created largely to relieve afflictions (Knight, 1980). The treatment of disorders of movement was very likely not always harmless symbolic manipulation, however, for we know that all over the world in prehistoric times a practice existed that might be considered one of the earliest forms of neurosurgery—trephination. The exact reasons why early men ground or chopped out pieces of skull is unknown. Some have advanced the idea that trephination was performed after head injury, perhaps as a therapeutic measure to relieve increased intracranial pressure. Although there is some evidence for this (Horrax, 1952), it seems more likely that this practice was also couched in the supernatural, the opening the skull being believed to release malevolent spirits (O'Conner & Walker, 1951). These operations could very well have been performed to treat a variety of movement disorders, especially epilepsy, as well as other problems, such as headache or psychosis. The ancient Greeks trephined for epilepsy, and Herodotus reported that the Libyans did also; and trephination for such symptoms as vertigo and psychosis was reported up until the early 1900s. So it seems reasonable to conclude that prehistoric man opened the skull to treat similar conditions (O'Conner & Walker, 1951). Of course, this does not imply that precivilized people had any notion that the brain is instrumental in these conditions, but is instead probably reflective of some magical significance the head was thought to possess (Hays, 1963).

EARLY CIVILIZATION

The Edwin Smith Papyrus contains the earliest known descriptions of the brain and spinal cord, and of illnesses related to them. The existing papyrus, written about 1700 B.C., is actually an incomplete copy of a manuscript written over a thousand years before, perhaps by the famous Egyptian priest and physician Imhotep, purportedly the architect of the Great Pyramid and physician to Pharaoh Yoser around 2800 B.C. Descriptions of the convolutions of the brain and the meninges (or, more likely, just the dura) can be found in this document, along with accounts of hemiplegia and possibly seizures following head injury, and paraplegia following neck injury. In addition, the Edwin Smith Papyrus, along with the Ebers Papyrus, have been thought to contain "representations of alcoholic reactions, senile deteriorations, melancholia, and hysterical reactions, the latter [of which] have been viewed as contagious at times" (Schneck, 1960, p. 10).

In spite of this knowledge, the brain itself was little reverenced. For example, before embalming, the brain was pulled piece by piece through the nose, in contrast to the great care given to the heart and other visceral organs (Woollam, 1958). Also, this early advancement in medical understanding did not lessen the importance of rites, incantations, and other supernaturally based practices in ancient Egyptian medicine (Ghalioungui, 1963).

GREECE AND ROME

The conceptual transition from the viscera to the brain as the seat of the soul took place gradually. The Egyptians, as already mentioned, considered the viscera and especially the heart as most important, whereas Mesopotamians and Etruscans regarded the liver as the essential organ of life. In general, in different cultures there was a shifting trend from liver to heart to brain as the seat of the soul. One hypothesized reason for this is the relative ease with which the cavities housing these organs are surgically penetrated:

. . . the abdomen, the thorax, and the cranium . . . were "invaded" in the order mentioned, perhaps because the abdomen was easily broached by both the enemy's knife and the surgeon's scalpel, while the thorax and the cranium, protected as they are by a wall of bone, were hard to reach by either one. . . . Parallel to the surgical fear of opening the great cavities of the body, there developed the idea—basic to Neurology and Psychiatry—of locating the seat of life in each one of them in turn. The first chosen, by the pre-Homerics, was the abdomen and its large viscera, particularly the liver, which because of its size and fullness with blood was taken as the seat of the soul; later in Homeric times, the heart was considered the seat of life and of the passions; and, finally, post-Homeric physicians deemed the brain to be animated with the magic breath that nurses the fire of life. (Marti-Ibanez, 1959, p. 9)

Ancient Greek medicine reached a pinnacle during the Golden Age, primarily through the efforts of Hippocrates and his school (around 400 B.C.). Critical observation and reasoning in medicine would not again reach an equivalent height for almost 2,000 years. There was little mind–body dualism in Greek thought (Ackerknecht, 1959), and diseases today classified as "mental" were usually grouped with other diseases. The major movement disorders of the time—epilepsy, apoplexy, and paralysis—were localized to the brain and spinal cord, just as most important "mental" disorders were. The uterus continued to remain the seat of hysteria, however, as it had in ancient Egypt. Other movement disorders no doubt also existed, but were probably included either in the disorders mentioned above or in one of the three main categories of mental diseases—phrenitis, mania, and melancholy. The rarer movement disorders were probably either not recognized or were ignored, in part because the ancient Greek physicians were interested less in differentiating diseases than in assessing symptoms as a guide to the general health of the patient. Furthermore, some diseases (such as Alzheimer's or Parkinson's disease), because they usually become manifest only at ages beyond the life span typical during most of history, were probably rarely observed.

Another reason for the neglect of certain more chronic illnesses (which many movement disorders are) was the peripatetic nature of Greek physicians. Their livelihood in a new city depended on success, not failure, and chronic diseases afforded less opportunity for cure than did acute ones. This also helps explain the considerable importance of prognosis to the Greeks (Ackerknecht, 1982a).

The physicians of the Hippocratic school were humoralists, adherents to the doctrine that health depends on a balance of the four humors: blood, phlegm, black bile, and yellow bile, associated, respectively, with the heart, brain, spleen, and liver. This notion, originated by Empedocles, dominated medical thought for over 2,000 years.

Although the Hippocratic school was clear about considering illnesses such as epilepsy (often called the Sacred Disease) as nothing more than illnesses, and rejected any magical component, later Greek and Roman physicians by and large admitted a certain amount of the supernatural into their conceptions of health and disease (Ackerknecht, 1982a). Nevertheless, many advances were made, especially in neuroanatomy, with such discoveries as the venous sinuses and motor and sensory nerves by Herophilus (around 250 B.C.), and descriptions of the cerebral ventricles, pineal and pituitary glands, spinal ganglia, and seven of the 12 cranial nerves (actually 11 were described, but some in combined form) by Galen (131–201 A.D.) (Wechsler, 1963; McHenry, 1969). Most of these findings were made by observation of the brains of oxen and other animals (Woollam, 1958), although Herophilus possibly vivisected criminals. The fluid-filled ventricles assumed great importance for centuries as the seat of higher mental functioning, in keeping with the doctrine of the four humors.

MIDDLE AGES

With the fall of the Roman Empire in 476 A.D. the progress of medicine came to a virtual standstill. Rome still cast its shadow over civilization in medieval times, or at least over what civilization existed after the influx of Goths, Huns, and other tribes from the north. There followed more than one attempt to re-create the cohesiveness and splendor of the Roman Empire, mainly as a result of the centralization of the Catholic Church in Rome. The spirit of Rome survived not only politically, but also medically. The ideas of Galen, the last great Greco-Roman physician, were maintained virtually unchanged through the Middle Ages, except that as time passed they became steeped in mysticism as they spread to areas where primitive thought still reigned. It is possible to look at this period as a time when ancient Mediterranean culture swallowed up the rest of Europe, a time of education of Western man that took over a thousand years. In the Middle Ages, medical progress was slowed, but did not cease.

Although most physicians of this time adhered to Galen's notions of treatment of the ill, two significant schisms in medicine occurred. One was the transfer of surgical practice to barbers, and the second was the transfer of mental illness from the domain of physicians, to that of priests (Ackerknecht, 1982a). Many mentally ill persons were no longer considered "ill" but, rather, "possessed." It is likely that disorders of movement were very important in this regard, because nothing bespeaks so much of a man possessed as do movements beyond his control. In particular, epilepsy, chorea, and perhaps also myoclonus and tics were probably looked upon this way. The Middle Ages were a time of such crowd-frenzy phenomena as St. Vitus's dance, or the dancing mania (Schneck, 1960). Although some individuals afflicted with the dancing mania were possibly suffering from choreiform disorder (as Sydenham described later) or from manic excitement, the large outbreaks of this phenomenon in the 14th century appear to have been some form of "mass hysteria," a clinical state shrouded in ignorance even today (Temkin, 1971). These episodes of "epidemic chorea" were possibly a psychological reaction to the plague, and certainly must have looked like demonic possession in full swing. It is worth noting that such medieval ideas have not completely disappeared from modern popular reactions to movement disorders, as evidenced by the fact that Tourette's syndrome is still occasionally called by some the "devil's disease."

Some people with these and other movement disorders were possibly burned as witches during the early Middle Ages, but the wholesale slaughter really began after the papal sanction of a book published in 1486 by two Dominican monks, Heinrich Kramer and Jakob Sprenger, entitled the *Malleus Maleficarum* or *The Witches' Hammer* (Zilboorg, 1941). This notorious book went into great detail on how to identify witches, with numerous descriptions of their supposed acts and atrocities, many of which were of a sexual nature. Many of the cases mentioned appear to have affected individuals suffering from seizures, mutism, and hysteria, along with other movement disorders. The book was a tremendous success (possibly in part due to the recent invention of the printing press), and it influenced the world for the next 200 years. The content of this book is, in itself, not as surprising as the time it appeared—the beginning of the Renaissance, when advances in medicine were just beginning to be made in the field of anatomy, and traditional Galenic concepts were being criticized for the first time in a thousand years. In view of this, the *Malleus Maleficarum* may be seen as one of the last worldwide manifestations of primitive magical thinking, which was eventually to succumb to the onslaught of the scientific revolution.

RENAISSANCE

The emergence of medicine as a science took place slowly, and only gradually were the shackles of medieval thought cast off. The greatest physician of his time, Paracelsus (Theophrastus Bombastus von Hohenheim, 1493–1541), rejected the humoral theory of illness, considered some of the mentally ill to be diseased rather than possessed, and once again stressed the importance of Hippocratic empiricism. Nevertheless, he strongly held beliefs in the supernatural nature and treatment of many afflictions (Ackerknecht, 1959). Still, in spite of the strong supernaturalism of the 16th century, physicians such as Paracelsus, Cornelius Agrippa (1486–1535), and Johann Weyer (1515–1588) denounced the idea that aberrant behavior invariably meant possession or witchery, and it is with them that mental diseases were again reclaimed by medicine, allowing psychiatry to progress (Ackerknecht, 1959).

The rebellion against Galenic tradition first became strong in Italy, especially in the field of anatomy. Leonardo da Vinci (1452–1519) made wax casts of the ventricles, and Andreas Vesalius (1514–1564), Eustachius (1522–1574), and Fallopius (1523–1562) began intensive anatomical studies of the brain (Wechsler, 1963). Vesalius made such outstanding cross sections of the brain that Garrison (McHenry, 1969) considered the 15 diagrams from the seventh book of *De Humani Corporis Fabrica* (1543) to be among the greatest neuroanatomical drawings ever produced. The gain in anatomical knowledge eventually led to great strides in the understanding of physiology, with Variolus (1530–1589) proposing the brain tissue itself and not the ventricles as the seat of the soul, and Jean Fernel (1497–1558) stating that muscles—and not nerves as had long been believed—were the actual organs of movement (Wechsler, 1963). Fernel also initiated the concept of reflex action, believing that not all movements are under the control of the will. The increase in anatomical knowledge also led to a rebirth of surgery as a medical specialty in the 16th century, although neurosurgery had made some progress in the Middle Ages (Horrax, 1952).

17TH CENTURY

By the 17th century the humoral theory of disease was finally fading. Instead there was a slow shift in focus toward localized pathology as the cause of various diseases. Thomas Willis (1621–1675), in addition to describing myasthenia gravis and dementia paralytica, was one of the first great cerebral localizationists (Isler, 1968), and believed that hysteria was a nervous disease. Hysteria appears to have been exceedingly common through most of history, and remained so through the early part of the 20th century. (In fact, some physicians today believe it to be very common still) (Weintraub, 1983). In the 17th century, Thomas Sydenham (1624–1689) diagnosed hysteria in fully half of his nonfebrile patients, making up one-sixth of his total practice (Ackerknecht, 1959). The diagnosis of hysteria seems to have incorporated in large part what are now referred to as conversion disorders. Sydenham was also one of the founders of the idea that disease entities could be differentiated and catalogued just as animals and plants had been. Important in this regard was his use of quinine to treat malaria, perhaps the most prevalent disease of the time. Not only did this represent one of the first forms of specific chemotherapy, but it also allowed for the distinction between malarial and other types of fevers (Ackerknecht, 1982a). Diagnosis by pharmacological means has become an important tool in many diseases, especially major mental illnesses. Sydenham also described the choreiform disorder that now bears his name.

The 17th century witnessed other advances in the clinical neurosciences. Johann Jakob Wepfer (1620–1695) further strengthened the localizationist perspective when he showed—utilizing careful postmortem dissection—that many cases of stroke and apoplexy were due to cerebral hemorrhage (McHenry, 1969). In addition, the great physician Sylvius (Franciscus de le Boë, 1614–1672) described the lateral cerebral fissure that now bears his name, and noted that some tremors are always present, whereas some appear only with movement (McHenry, 1969).

So we see that the 17th century saw the beginnings of a change in the conception of illness, from the holistic and humoralistic approach that had dominated for thousands of years (in which symptoms served as a guide to the health status of the whole patient) to a syndrome- and disease-oriented approach to the patient. And with the new concepts of localizationism, medicine witnessed the beginning of another important trend of the future—specialization.

18TH CENTURY

The 18th century is commonly called the Age of Enlightenment, and with it an explosion in medical knowledge occurred. In 1761, Giovanni Battista Morgagni (1682–1771) published his monumental work *On the Sites and Causes of Diseases*, further expanding the localizationist doctrine. Luigi Galvani (1737–1798) and Alessandro Volta (1745–1827) discovered the electrical properties of nerves and muscles. Peter Paul Molinelli (1702–1764) reported on the crossed innervation of the nervous system, and Sir Charles Bell (1774–1852) and François Magendie (1783–1855) discovered the pure motor function of the anterior roots of the spinal cord (Wechsler, 1963; McHenry, 1969). Of great importance was the description of reflexes by Marshall Hall (1790–1857), built upon the ideas of Robert Whytt (1714–1766) and others, which was to serve as a cornerstone for neuropsychiatric theories in the future, such as those of Griesinger and Pavlov (Riese, 1959; Ackerknecht, 1959; Clarke & O'Malley, 1968).

The severely mentally ill had suffered much at the hands of the medieval man, and the general pessimism about their treatment in the 17th century led to many of them being locked up and mistreated (Kraepelin, 1918, 1962). With the Enlightenment, the chains were removed and, just as the less severely mentally ill (most of whom were called hysterical or hypochondriacal) had been accepted back into medicine in the 16th and 17th centuries, so the more severely mentally ill were reaccepted in the 18th (see Ackerknecht, 1959).

19TH CENTURY

In spite of the progress in the anatomical and physiological basis of movement that had occurred up to the 19th century, the semiology of nervous disorders, as Garrison pointed out (McHenry, 1969), did not change very much. "Paralysis" still subsumed most movement disorders other than epilepsy; and epilepsy and other disorders of excessive movement such as chorea were not very carefully differentiated (McHenry, 1969). As the doctrine of localizationism spread, hope for understanding motor disease in the 19th century rose, and clinical description and differentiation of movement disorders expanded remarkably.

In the first half of the 19th century, France was the center of medicine in Europe. Phillipe Pinel (1745–1826), one of the great physicians of his time, pressed for the localization of diseases to be taken from the level of "organ" to that of "tissue" (Ackerknecht, 1982a). He and his student Jean Etienne Esquirol (1772–1840) did much to advance the clinical descriptions of psychiatric diseases as well, and were probably the first to separate the epileptics from the insane in mental hospitals (Pinel, 1962; McHenry, 1969).

Localizationism as a tool for understanding was brought to bear on many brain diseases. Franz Josef Gall (1758–1828) was one of the first to do this. Although he was an excellent brain anatomist, his ideas on phrenology led to ridicule from the scientific community. Later descriptions of localized brain pathology in aphasia (or aphemia, as it was originally called) by Paul Broca (1824–1880) were much more successful, and led to great expansion in the study of brain localization (Riese, 1959).

The localizationist perspective was not always helpful in understanding some illnesses, for in many cases no specific organ or tissue pathology could be found. In some of these difficult cases another diagnostic technique did prove useful, a technique whereby diseases were identified by the co-occurrence of sets of symptoms and signs (Wechsler, 1963; Ackerknecht, 1982a). One of the most important uses of this technique led in 1817 to the classic description by James Parkinson (1755–1824), of the shaking palsy, the name of which he Latinized to *paralysis agitans*. In his famous essay, Parkinson described most of the predominant features of the disorder, with the exceptions of rigidity and dementia (Critchley, 1955).

A similar approach was taken by the French physician Jean Alfred Fournier (1832–1914) when he recognized that tabes dorsalis and general paresis of the insane were different manifestations of the same disease (Wechsler, 1963). The elucidation of the different forms of neurosyphilis in the 1860s was one of the most important events in the history of neuropsychiatry because an organic etiology was found for what was perhaps the most prevalent major mental illness of the time, general paresis of the insane. Other motor symptom-complexes with psychiatric components were also recognized later in the 1800s, such as the syndromes described by George Huntington (1850–1916) and Georges Gilles de la Tourette (1857–1904) that today carry their names.

In the last half of the 19th century the center of medicine shifted from France to Germany. Germanic thought during the first half of the 18th century was imbued with romanticism, and neuropsychiatry made little progress until the advent of Wilhelm Griesinger (1817–1868) and his influential book *Pathologie und Therapie der Psychischen Krankheiten*, which went through numerous editions (Ackerknecht, 1959). Adapting many ideas from the French, Griesinger recognized the brain as the seat of mental disorders as well as of many neurological disorders. He based his theories on Bell's and Magendie's discoveries of motor and sensory tracts, and on Marshall Hall's theory of reflexes. Griesinger was thus a localizationist, but he firmly believed that many diseases, especially mental ones, did not allow for easy understanding in terms of brain pathology. Thus, Griesinger became an exponent of psychological causes for many illnesses, and emphasized the interrelationships between psychological and physical causes. He placed psychological pain along with physical pain as sensory phenomena that, through complicated sorts of reflex mechanisms, result in motor or "willed" behavior. Disturbances in willed behavior could lead to an absence (stupor) or an excess of motor activity (Ackerknecht, 1959; Griesinger, 1965).

Griesinger was interested in the anatomical basis of diseases, but recognized that diseases could have multiple etiologies. He developed a kind of "ego psychology" to understand some of the complex interactions that go to make up mental aberrations, and discussed the ways that disturbed emotions can both cause and be caused by somatic illnesses. Griesinger anticipated behaviorism, the concept of the unconscious, and ego psychology, and attempted to unify these with the latest neurophysiological observations of motor and sensory tracts and of reflexes. As Ackerknecht (1959) points out, he deserves to be called the father of neuropsychiatry.

Many advances were made in the basic sciences in the 1800s. Of great importance was the development of cell theory, by Matthias Schleiden (1804–1881) and Theodor Schwann (1810–1882), that eventually led to the creation of neuron theory. Organic chemistry was born, as was germ theory, and the new basic science techniques of microscopy, bacteriology, and chemistry led to greater understanding of many nervous-system diseases. It was hoped that all diseases of the nervous system would be understood by these means, and would reveal their nature to careful analyses, just as neurosyphilis had.

One physician who believed this was Karl Ludwig Kahlbaum (1828–1899). He became a proponent of the symptom-complex approach to understanding disease entities, whereby the course of characteristic symptoms is carefully followed in many afflicted individuals, eventually leading to the description of the complete clinical entity (Kahlbaum, 1973). Kahlbaum based his approach on that used in the unraveling of the different manifestations of neurosyphilis, and he believed that his newly described clinical entity, catatonia, represented a disease whose pathology would eventually be discovered. Emil Kraepelin (1855–1926) adopted the same technique to separate and classify the serious mental illnesses into categories still recognized today, and incorporated Kahlbaum's catatonia into his own descriptions of dementia praecox (Kraepelin, 1919/1971).

Unfortunately, the underlying pathology of these and other mental illnesses continued to remain refractory to all the new techniques of medical analysis. This was especially true of hysterical phenomena, which drew great interest from the neurological community at the end of the 19th century. Jean Martin Charcot (1825–1893), after spending many years making important contributions to neurology (such as the differentiation of multiple sclerosis and Parkinson's disease), in later years turned his attention to hysteria and ways of separating hysteria from other conditions, such as epilepsy. However, unlike other nervous-system disorders such as meningitis, brain and spinal-cord tumors, syringomyelia, peripheral neuropathies, vitamin-deficiency states, and even epilepsy, which were yielding their secrets to biological methodology, the underlying basis of hysteria and other mental disorders was not forthcoming.

20TH CENTURY

By the end of the 19th century disorders of the nervous system could be separated into two groups: those in which the new basic science techniques resulted in greater understanding, and those that remained a mystery. Into this arena entered Sigmund Freud (1856–1939), whose theories eventually led to the field of psychiatry's becoming more psychologically based and to a partial rift between the disciplines of psychiatry and neurology.

Freud, like Griesinger, was initially interested in physiological causes of mental disease, and he too realized that such an approach at that time was not very fruitful. So he also turned to a more psychological approach, developing his famous theories about unconscious conflict and repression that led to a much greater understanding of hysterical phenomena. Freud had become interested in hysteria with Charcot, but Freud's ideas extended far beyond this one clinical problem. Freud's theories, in either the original or in one of many modified forms, were eventually adopted by most psychiatrists, resulting in a selective concentration on the psychological basis of mental illness, with little attention paid to the physical basis. When Eugen Bleuler (1857–1939) applied the ideas of Freud to Kraepelin's concept of dementia praecox, renaming these disorders "schizophrenias" (Bleuler, 1911/1950), psychiatry and neurology separated even further.

Meanwhile, neuroscience research continued to expand: X-rays were discovered by Wilhelm Konrad Roentgen (1845–1943) in 1895, the electroencephalogram was invented in 1929 by Hans Berger (1873–1941), vitamins were identified and characterized between the years of 1906 and 1912, and Paul Ehrlich (1854–1915) advanced chemotherapy with his sidechain theory and his specific antisyphilitic drug, compound 606—salvarsan. These advances and more were applied quite successfully to a host of neurological diseases, while psychiatric illnesses remained enigmatic. Nevertheless, in the early years of this century the break between psychiatry and neurology was probably more appearance than reality, for many major psychiatrists were well-grounded in neurological diseases, and the outbreak of sleeping sickness—von Economo's encephalitis—at the end of World War I created differential diagnostic problems both for neurology (with postencephalitic parkinsonism resembling Parkinson's disease) and psychiatry (with some postencephalitic states resembling schizophrenia). Samuel Alexander Kinnier Wilson's (1878–1936) elucidation of hepatolenticular degeneration (McHenry, 1969) had a similar effect.

Within the last thirty to forty years the expanding fields of neurochemistry, neuropharmacology, psychopharmacology, neuroradiology, and others have begun to shore up the rift between the fields of mental and neurological disease. The discovery of the efficacy of the phenothiazines, antidepressants, and lithium for schizophrenia and the affective disorders, along with the discovery of L-dopa as a treatment of Parkinson's disease marked the rise of the expanding field of neuropsychopharmacology, which is proving so fruitful not only in the treatment but also in the understanding of neuropsychiatric disorders, including movement disorders. The rapidly progressing field of psychosomatic medicine is also bringing neurology and psychiatry closer together (Ackerknecht, 1982b).

Knowledge has increased at so fast a pace that it is impossible to give credit to the work of all those who have contributed, and recent history is of course always the most difficult to put into perspective. It does appear, however, that there is a trend toward the reunification of psychiatry and neurology, or at least recognition that there are many areas in which a combined neuropsychiatric approach is more helpful than an isolated perspective. And it is in this spirit that this book was written.

CHAPTER TWO

An Overview of the Anatomical and Physiological Basis of Movement

This chapter is intended to be a short reference survey of the pertinent anatomy and physiology involved in the production of movement. It is not meant to be a detailed review of the basis of movement, but rather a conceptual guide for the clinician when considering movement disorders. We have divided this chapter into two main parts. The first part contains a brief survey of the structure and function of those parts of the brain that appear to be most intimately associated with the production of movement and maintenance of posture. The second part offers some general principles to be considered when approaching movement disorders from a neuropsychiatric point of view.

THE STRUCTURE AND FUNCTION OF THE NERVOUS SYSTEM IN RELATION TO THE PRODUCTION OF MOVEMENT

Movement refers to a change of the position of an object in space, and in the case of human beings, could include not only walking or waving an arm, but also the beating of the heart, the peristalsis of the intestines, or even the motion of organelles within cells. However, when considering the phenomenon of movement and its disorders, many investigators tacitly limit the term "movement" to changes in position of the body and its parts brought about by striated muscles. This roughly corresponds to movement that is supposedly under voluntary control, but also includes some movements that are outside of conscious awareness, such as postural adjustments. Although there is a large neuropsychiatric interface involving movements subserved by smooth and cardiac muscle, in this book we focus on disordered movement subserved predominantly by striated muscle.

The underlying basis of movement is so complex that it may be helpful to view the nervous system as composed of a number of interacting subsystems, each of which contributes to particular aspects of movement. Many different ways of subdividing the function of the nervous system have been proposed, but the profuse intricacy of the interconnections between different areas of the brain and spinal cord makes any subdivision somewhat artificial and simplistic. In general, though, most investigators recognize the existence of three large brain systems that govern movement. These three are known as the (1) pyramidal system, (2) extrapyramidal system, and (3) cerebellar system. A fourth system, involving reflex mechanisms in the spinal cord, is also important, and in this book it will be considered along with the pyramidal system, with which it is closely associated. In the remainder of this part of the chapter we present discussions of the structure and possible functions of each of these systems.

Pyramidal System (Figure 2-1)

Structure

This system receives its name from the medullary pyramids through which the pyramidal tract runs. The pyramidal system is the one most crucial for the execution of fine voluntary movements and runs from the cerebral cortex through the spinal cord to the motor neurons. It also makes synaptic contact with other neurons in the spinal cord. The extrapyramidal and cerebellar systems seem to exert much of their influence through this pathway (Brodal, 1981).

THE CEREBRAL CORTEX

The Primary Motor Cortex and Its Connections. Beginning at the top of the brain we find the primary motor cortex, which roughly corresponds to the precentral gyrus and to the area 4 of Brodmann, but probably extends beyond these regions (Brodal, 1981). Of the approximately one million fibers in the pyramidal tract, most appear to be axons of pyramidal cells in layer V of the cerebral cortex. Three or four per cent of the axons in the pyramidal tract (about 30,000 fibers) appear to arise from giant pyramidal or *Betz cells*. These cells are thought by some to be similar to the other pyramidal cells but to have axons that extend to the lower part of the spinal column, and thus to possess correspondingly larger cell bodies (Lassek, 1940, 1941; Brodal, 1981).

The primary motor cortex is organized in several ways, including columnar and somatotopic patterns of organization. The *columnar organization* of the primary motor cortex is thought to allow for amplification of incoming sensory impulses, as well as provide for more efficient inhibition of surrounding cortical areas. Related to this inhibitory function is the finding that as many as 100 pyramidal cells may have to fire to evoke a movement (McGeer *et al.*, 1978). In the *somatotopic pattern of organization* cortical neurons

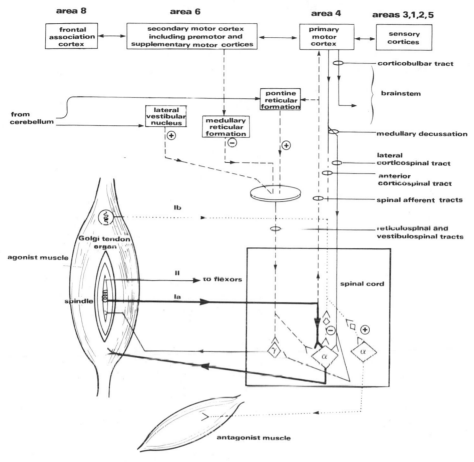

Figure 2-1. Pathways of the pyramidal system along with selected spinal and supra-spinal reflexes. Bold lines indicate the myotatic monosynaptic reflex, dotted lines the inverse myotatic reflex, and dashed lines certain long-loop reflexes thought to be important in the maintenance of posture and tone. *Ia, Ib,* and *II* refer to muscle afferent fibers, α and γ to motor neurons. $\oplus$ and $\ominus$ refer to excitatory and inhibitory pathways, respectively.

located in a lateral-to-medial direction control muscle groups located in a rostral-to-caudal direction. Within this pattern, larger areas of cortex appear to be devoted to control of muscles necessary for fine movements (such as finger and tongue muscles) than for coarse movements (such as trunk and leg muscles).

Although the primary motor cortex mediates most movement, it does not seem to directly govern coordinated purposeful action (Brodal, 1981). It does, however, appear to contain codes for the force of a movement and the rate of change of the force of a movement (Hepp-Reymond & Diener, 1983) as well as codes for the direction of a movement (Georgopoulos *et al.*, 1983). The rate of discharge of pyramidal tract neurons is also related to the force required to maintain a fixed posture (Evarts, 1969).

The primary motor cortex is the beginning of the major common pathway in the central nervous system for the control of many movements— in particular, fine movements. Nerve impulses from the extrapyramidal and cerebellar systems, from the periphery, and from other cortical areas influence the firing of primary motor cortex neurons. In fact, 20 to 50 milliseconds before any evidence of muscular contraction appears, pyramidal tract neurons begin firing, and neuronal activity in the basal ganglia and deep cerebellar nuclei precedes even this (Ghez, 1981a). The connections between the cortex, the basal ganglia, and the cerebellum will be discussed later.

The Premotor Cortex. Lying directly in front of the primary motor cortex (area 4) is the premotor cortex (area 6), which has reciprocal connections with, and is the major cortical input area to, the primary motor area. In contrast to the primary motor cortex, the premotor cortex does appear to govern more complex motor tasks, especially those associated with vision (Porter, 1983b). The premotor cortex receives major projections from the *prefrontal cortex* (area 8), which in turn receives important projections from occipital, parietal, and temporal areas.

The Supplementary Motor Cortex. This area of cortex, which lies in front of the primary motor cortex on the medial aspects of the cerebral hemispheres, is considered by some to be a part of the premotor cortex, although its function appears to be somewhat different. It seems to be important in the performance of motor tasks that require bilateral and especially bimanual activity (Porter, 1983a). It may also be important in the control of postural reflexes, as excitation of this area can produce a pattern of extension and flexion in the limbs that resembles locomotory postural reflexes (Penfield & Jasper, 1954). There are important projections from the supplementary motor area to the primary motor cortex.

The Sensory Cortex. The primary sensory cortex also contributes to the pyramidal tract. In fact, there is no sharp line of distinction between the primary motor (area 4) and the primary sensory areas (areas 3, 1, and 2). Some investigators actually speak of a *sensorimotor cortex*, which contains both the primary motor and primary sensory areas. Another sensory cortical area, area 5 of Brodmann in the parietal lobe (which subserves more complex sensory associative functions), projects to the primary motor cortex and is also possibly important in the production of movement.

Probably all of the above areas of cortex manifest a somatotopic pattern of function to some degree, with the most inferior portions of the pertinent gyrus representing the muscles of the face and tongue, and, in general, as one moves superiorly and across the gyrus, muscles from further down the body are represented. However this is not as clear for the premotor and supplementary motor cortices as for the primary motor and sensory cortices. Also, in the primary motor cortex the functional representation of different bodily areas does not appear to be rigidly fixed, but may vary according to changes in the relative excitability of different but overlapping groups of pyramidal tract neurons that occur with different movements (Brodal, 1981). It should be noted that the right and left primary motor cortices are connected through the corpus callosum in a homotypic fashion, but only for the face, trunk, and proximal extremity areas, and not for the distal extremity areas. This possibly allows for better individual control of the hand and finger muscles (Ghez, 1981b).

THE PYRAMIDAL TRACT

The cell bodies of the neurons that form the pyramidal tract are found almost entirely in the cortical areas that lie to either side of the central sulcus, including areas 1, 2, 3, 4, and 6 of Brodmann. These neurons are called *upper motor neurons*, and their axons project to the striatum, thalamus, brainstem, and spinal cord. In doing so they pass on each side through the corona radiata, the posterior limb of the internal capsule, the middle two-thirds of the cerebral peduncle, the pons, and the medullary pyramid. At the medullary decussation, most of the axons cross to the opposite side of the spinal cord and form the *lateral corticospinal tract*. The uncrossed axons form the *anterior corticospinal tract*.

As the pyramidal fibers run from cortex to spinal column, there is a 180° rotation of the somatotopic organization. In the cortex the representation of upper body structures is more lateral, whereas lower body structures are represented more medially. In the spinal cord and much of the brainstem, the opposite is true, with upper body structures being more medially represented. If viewed from above, this pattern of rotation in the left hemisphere would appear to be in a clockwise direction.

The Lateral Corticospinal Tract. The term "corticospinal tract" is considered to be synonymous with the term "pyramidal tract." They are not really the same, though, as the corticospinal tract is only a part of the pyramidal tract, which also contains fibers that exit in the brainstem. The lateral corticospinal tract appears after the medullary decussation and gradually becomes smaller as it descends in the spinal cord, with about half of the axons terminating in the cervical region, 20% in the thoracic region, and the remaining 30% in the final portion of the cord. Approximately 10% of the axons synapse directly on α-motoneurons, while the rest synapse on other neurons in the cord.

The Anterior Corticospinal Tract. This tract is formed from the remaining undecussated portion of the pyramidal tract and appears to terminate before reaching the end of the thoracic area of the cord. It is involved with innervating motor neurons to neck, trunk, and proximal upper extremity muscles (Carpenter & Sutin, 1983).

The Corticobulbar Tract. The corticobulbar tract is closely related to the pyramidal tract and innervates motor nuclei of the brainstem. It is not usually considered to be a part of the pyramidal tract because it terminates before reaching the medullary pyramids. It runs through the anterior portion of the posterior limb of the internal capsule and the medial part of the middle two-thirds of a cerebral peduncle, and terminates either in the reticular formation or on specific bulbar motor nuclei. At this point it innervates the motor nucleus of the *trigeminal (V) nerve* (mostly crossed innervation), the nucleus of the *facial (VII) nerve* (largely crossed to lower facial muscles, crossed and uncrossed to upper facial muscles), the nucleus of the *spinal accessory (XI) nerve* (mainly uncrossed, or possibly doubly crossed), and the nucleus of the *hypoglossal (XII) nerve* (crossed and uncrossed).

THE LOWER MOTOR NEURONS AND SPINAL REFLEXES

Although not directly a part of the pyramidal system, the local spinal motor control systems will be considered here because of their close association with the pyramidal system.

The Lower Motor Neurons. The lateral corticospinal tract contains nerve fibers that synapse directly on the two types of motor neurons, α and γ (also known as lower motor neurons). The large α-fibers innervate the main mass of muscle cells, directly causing the contraction of muscles. The smaller γ-fibers innervate the contractile portions of the muscle fibers that lie within muscle spindles.

Muscle Spindles. Muscle spindles are encapsulated, fusiform structures that lie in parallel with the muscle cells forming the bulk of the muscle. Each spindle contains two types of fibers, called *intrafusal muscle fibers.* The larger of the two are *nuclear bag fibers*, and the smaller are *nuclear chain fibers*, both of which are so named because of the way the nuclei are distributed in them. Both of these fibers have contractile portions that are innervated by γ-motoneurons. In fact, there may be two types of γ-motoneurons, one to each type of intrafusal muscle fiber. The γ-efferents to many nuclear bag fibers (dynamic γ) are important in spinal reflexes involving the velocity of stretch of the muscle, and the γ-efferents to the nuclear chain fibers (static γ) are important in spinal reflexes involving the amount of stretch (Lance & McLeod, 1981; Brodal, 1981).[1]

Muscle Afferents. The muscle spindle is an important structure for relaying back to the central nervous system information on the length of the

---

[1]In actuality, there are probably two types of nuclear bag fibers, one that is controlled by dynamic γ-fibers and responds to the velocity of stretch (bag_1 fiber) and one that is controlled by static γ-fibers and responds to the length of stretch (bag_2 fiber) (Boyd et al., 1977). The γ-system is so complex and poorly understood that here it can be considered in a cursory fashion only. For further information the reader is referred to Matthews (1981).

muscle and the velocity of contraction. This information is relayed from the muscle spindle through two main types of afferent fibers, Ia and II. Group Ia fibers have endings that wrap around the body of both the nuclear bag and, to a lesser extent, nuclear chain muscle fibers (these endings are also called *primary* or *annulospiral endings*). Group II fibers are much smaller than Ia fibers, and have irregularly branched endings on nuclear chain and nuclear bag fibers (these endings are also called *secondary* or *flower-spray endings*). It is possible that the Ia fibers carry information about the velocity of stretch (largely from the nuclear bag$_1$ fibers), whereas the group II fibers carry information about the length of muscle, or the amount of stretch (largely from the nuclear bag$_2$ and nuclear chain fibers) (Lance & McLeod, 1981; Brodal, 1981). Ia fibers also carry information about the amount of stretch.

Other important afferents from the muscular system include *Ib afferents* from *Golgi tendon organs* which lie in tendons and in muscle bellies near the musculotendinous junctions. The Golgi tendon organs require a much greater degree of muscular stretch to start firing than do the muscle spindles and are important in the production of the clasp-knife reflex described later.

Monosynaptic Stretch Reflex.[2] Briefly and in a highly simplified way the basic spinal reflex system controlling the length of a muscle may be thought of as functioning in the following manner (we shall ignore the functioning of the γ-fibers for the moment):

1. Corticospinal neurons cause α-motoneurons to fire, resulting in contraction of muscles.
2. The muscle shortens, causing a relaxation of the tension in muscle spindles.
3. The primary or annulospiral endings wrapped around the middle of the nuclear bag and chain fibers sense this relaxation, and decrease the impulses through the Ia and II fibers.
4. Some Ia fibers synapse on the α-motoneurons to the originating muscle (the only known monosynaptic reflex in humans), and the decrease in Ia firing causes a decrease in α-firing, which relaxes the muscle.
5. The relaxation of the muscle causes the spindle to stretch, increasing the firing of Ia afferents and increasing the output of α-motoneurons again, causing the muscle to contract again.

Thus, it can be seen that if the γ-system is ignored, the muscle tends to assume a given contractile length. When the γ-system is included in the

---

[2]The monosynaptic stretch reflex, because it is confined to a spinal cord segment and is short-latency, is also called a phasic stretch reflex. It is sometimes referred to as M$_1$ because its short latency makes it the first response to appear on electromyography (EMG) after a muscle is stretched (myotatic reflex response).

analysis, the fact that the γ-fibers can control the amount of stretch of the spindle fibers apart from that caused by the muscle stretching means that the γ-fibers may help control the length of contraction of a muscle. This is sometimes called γ-bias and is probably mediated by static γ-fibers. A similar system may be in operation for the control of velocity of muscular contraction (by dynamic γ-fibers) and it appears that the length and the velocity of muscular stretch may be controlled independently by different regions in the central nervous system (Lance & McLeod, 1981; Brodal, 1981). However, it does not appear that the γ-system is responsible for initiating movements, in that the α- and γ-fibers seem to be activated simultaneously (known as α-γ-coactivation), and there is a time delay involved with impulses traveling through the γ-loop (γ-fiber → spindle → Ia fiber → α-fiber) as compared to the direct α-stimulation. Nevertheless, the γ-system control probably does closely follow up the initial α-contraction of muscle, and possibly assists in the control of the length and velocity of change of the muscle stretch as the muscle contracts. Thus, when the load on the muscle varies, the γ-system allows for fine constant adjustment of the muscular contraction (McGeer et al., 1978). Such considerations are important in understanding motor phenomena such as rigidity (see Chapter 16).

　　Other Segmental Spinal Reflexes. Apart from the γ-loop there are other important circuits involving the spinal cord and the periphery. For example, the firing of spindle afferents, in addition to causing α-motoneurons to agonist muscles to fire, usually also causes an inhibition of firing in α-motoneurons to antagonist muscles. When Golgi tendon organ fibers (Ib) fire, they inhibit firing in the originating α-motoneurons (but only with a large amount of muscle stretch or tension) and cause firing in α-motoneurons to antagonistic muscles. This is in a sense the opposite of the way muscle spindles work, and is called the *inverse myotatic reflex*, sometimes also called the *clasp-knife reflex*. Finally, group II afferents, along with group III and IV afferents (which are largely responsible for carrying information about pain from deep muscle and cutaneous receptors) are sometimes collectively called *flexor reflex afferents* (FRA) because stimulation causes contraction of the main flexor muscles of the body. This forms the basis of withdrawal responses to pain in animals (Meinck et al., 1983). Actually, in man the response is flexor in the lower limbs and probably extensor in the upper limbs, possibly related to the assumption of upright posture in man (Lance & McLeod, 1981).

　　Long-Latency Spinal Reflexes. The reflexes discussed above are sometimes also called *short-latency* or *phasic* reflexes, because they are localized to fast-conducting circuits within segments of the spinal cord. These short-latency reflexes usually last 50 milliseconds or less. There appear to be, in addition, other reflexes involving motor efferents and afferents, in which the time it takes for the circuit to be traversed is considerably longer (greater than 50 milliseconds). These are known as *long-latency reflexes*. Some investigators have proposed that long-latency reflexes are the result of information from muscle afferents being transmitted to higher centers through ascending spinal pathways in the dorsal columns (Marsden *et al.*, 1983b). In this view, long-latency reflexes are considered to travel through several different levels in the brainstem, possibly even traversing the cerebral cortex. Such long-latency reflexes are sometimes termed *long-loop reflexes*. Some long-latency reflexes do appear to be long-loop reflexes, including the tonic stretch reflex (which influences muscle tone) and postural reflexes, which will be discussed later (Nashner, 1976; Lance & McLeod, 1981). Some important pathways involved in the mediation of certain long-latency reflexes, especially the tonic stretch reflex, are shown in Figure 2-1.

In the case of other long-latency reflexes, the evidence for long-loop involvement is less clear. For example, it has been observed for a number of years that, after the initial short-latency response (M_1 response) following muscle stretch, there may be a later response occurring after 50 milliseconds or more (Tatton & Lee, 1975). This has been termed the long-latency component of the stretch reflex (M_2 response), and some investigators have described an M_3 response as well. Some researchers (e.g., Marsden *et al.*, 1983b) have argued that this long-latency stretch reflex is a long-loop reflex, with the increased delay being due to the time it takes for the impulse to travel through the brain, perhaps even through the cerebral cortex (sometimes called "transcortical" reflexes). More recently, investigators have argued that the long-latency component of the stretch reflex is delayed because it is carried by slower group II (instead of group Ia) afferents from the muscle (Cody *et al.*, 1986). Whatever the mechanism, this long-latency component of the stretch reflex is believed to be important in the underlying pathophysiology of parkinsonian rigidity (see Chapter 16), although it is not clear if abnormally increased long-latency responses are sufficient to explain the rigidity.

Function

The main function of the pyramidal tract appears to be the mediation of voluntary movements, especially fine voluntary movements of the distal extremities involving flexor muscles.[3] In addition, the extrapyramidal and cerebellar systems exert much of their control over complex movements through the pyramidal system.

The function of the localized spinal reflexes varies, and to a large extent depends upon the involvement of higher nervous-system structures. The

---

[3]Pure pyramidal tract damage is rare in man, as it can occur only with lesions of the medullary pyramids. In this condition, fine voluntary motor control is lost, hypotonia appears, and a Babinski sign is evident. However, true spasticity and hyperreflexia do not develop (Brodal, 1981). It is unclear exactly what areas must be damaged for spasticity to occur.

localized spinal reflex arcs are short-latency and are termed phasic reflexes. When the higher nervous-system structures are involved the reflexes may become long-latency. For example, the stretch reflex may be either a phasic one (as seen in a tendon jerk) or a tonic one (as seen in rigidity), and a given reflex arc may be involved in one or the other response, depending upon the involvement of supraspinal structures. This switching from a phasic to a tonic reflex may be accomplished centrally by a process of presynaptic inhibition (Lance & McLeod, 1981). The phasic characteristics of spinal reflexes represent the simple machinery involved in keeping muscle lengths relatively stable and avoiding co-contraction of agonists and antagonists. The tonic characteristics show the involvement of supraspinal mechanisms which contribute to muscular tone as well as to posture.

Extrapyramidal System (Figure 2-2)

Structure

At best, "extrapyramidal system" is a vague term. It has been used to include almost every area of the brain, apart from the pyramidal system, that has anything to do with movement—including, at times, the cerebellum, the basal ganglia, the substantia nigra, the red nucleus, and the reticulo- and vestibulospinal tracts, along with many other structures. Some researchers, such as Brodal (1981), have advocated abandoning the term altogether. However, the term appears to have some clinical utility, primarily because the motor function of these regions is so poorly understood. Although lesions in different parts of the extrapyramidal system produce a wide spectrum of clinical pictures, these differ considerably from those produced by lesions in the pyramidal system. Thus, the use of the term "extrapyramidal" has some utility in describing not so much which motor problems exist, but which ones do not. Nevertheless, some relatively specific functions have been attributed to different areas of the "extrapyramidal system," which we shall explore in this section.

In this book, "extrapyramidal system" will refer to the system composed of the basal ganglia (caudate, putamen, and globus pallidus), the subthalamic nucleus, the substantia nigra, and their connections. Although some spinal cord tracts, such as the vestibulospinal and reticulospinal tracts, are sometimes also said to be "extrapyramidal," these are more closely related to the cerebellum, and will be considered in the next section of this chapter.

THE BASAL GANGLIA

The basal ganglia form the largest subcortical mass of grey matter in the cerebral hemispheres. They consist of the *caudate nucleus*, the *putamen*, and the *globus pallidus* or *pallidum*. Some authors have grouped the claustrum,

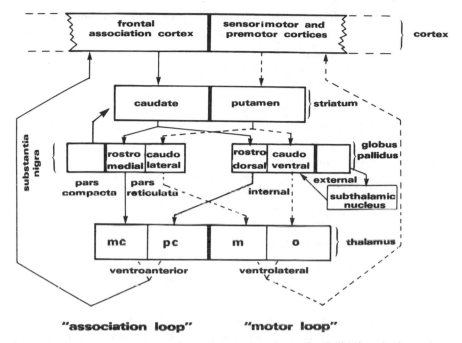

"association loop"   "motor loop"

Figure 2-2. Important pathways involving the basal ganglia. Solid lines indicate the corical–basal ganglia loop involving frontal association cortex, sometimes called the "association loop." Dashed lines indicate the cortical–basal ganglia loop involving motor cortex, sometimes called the "motor loop." The nigrostriatal tract from the substantia nigra parts compacta runs to both the caudate and putamen. In the thalamus, *mc* and *pc* refer to the magnocellular and parvocellular parts of the ventroanterior nucleus, respectively, and *m* and *o* refer to the medial and oral parts of the ventrolateral nucleus, respectively. (Adapted in part from DeLong *et al.*, 1983.)

thalamus, and amygdala with these nuclei; others have included the substantia nigra and the subthalamic nucleus. Table 2-1 illustrates the various ways subcortical structures have been grouped together in the past. As is easily observed, some confusion as to appropriate terminology exists. In this book, "basal ganglia" refers to caudate, putamen, and globus pallidus, and these three are considered to be highly associated with the subthalamic nucleus and the substantia nigra.

The caudate and putamen are histologically similar, and appear to be functionally similar also. These two nuclei constitute the main "receiving station" or afferent system of the basal ganglia. The caudate and putamen receive projections from nearly all cortical regions in a somatotopic pattern. In addition to this somatotopic or mediolateral pattern of projection to the basal ganglia, there is a rostrocaudal pattern of projection from the cortex, with the sensorimotor and premotor cortices projecting largely to the putamen, and the frontal association pathways projecting to the caudate (DeLong

Table 2-1. Various Ways the Subcortical Nuclei Have Been Grouped Together in the Past

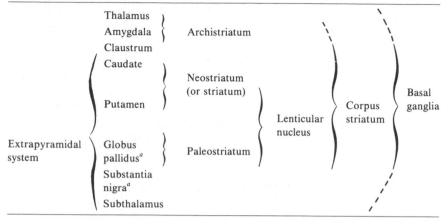

[a] Sometimes the globus pallidus and pars reticulata of the substantia nigra are collectively called the pallidum, but most of the time the term "pallidum" refers solely to the globus pallidus.

et al., 1983). Thus, the two-dimensional organization of the cortex around the central sulcus is preserved in the projection pattern to the striatum (caudate and putamen). The striatum also receives input from the substantia nigra (important in Parkinson's disease) and from the intralaminar thalamic nuclei.

The major outflow tracts from the striatum are to the globus pallidus (mainly internal portion) and the substantia nigra (mainly pars reticulata). Just as the caudate and putamen are histologically and functionally similar, so are the globus pallidus and the pars reticulata of the substantia nigra. Again, a somatotopic arrangement appears to hold in these outflow tracts, as well as the rostrocaudal cortical pattern. The caudate projects predominantly to the rostrodorsal section of the globus pallidus and the rostromedial section of the substantia nigra, whereas the putamen projects largely to the caudoventral section of the globus pallidus and the caudolateral section of the substantia nigra (DeLong *et al.*, 1983). The globus pallidus and substantia nigra both project back to the ventroanterior and ventrolateral sections of the thalamus and finally back to the cortex (mainly back to the premotor cortex, area 6). There is evidence that some degree of somatotopic organization as well as cortical rostrocaudal organization (two dimensions across the cortical surface) may persist through the entire circuit of cortex → striatum → globus pallidus and substantia nigra → thalamus → cortex (DeLong *et al.*, 1983).

Substantia Nigra. The pars compacta of the substantia nigra provides an important fiber tract to the striatum, the nigrostriatal tract, which is dopaminergic. Parkinson's disease—and especially the hypokinesia of Parkinson's disease—is thought to be related to the impaired function of this structure (Schultz *et al.*, 1983).

Subthalamic Nucleus. One final important connection of the basal ganglia is with the subthalamic nucleus, or *corpus Luysii.* This nucleus receives fibers from the external segment of the globus pallidus and possibly also from cortical regions, and sends fibers back to the internal segment of the globus pallidus. Dysfunction in this circuit results in the clinical syndrome of hemiballismus.

Neurotransmitters in the Extrapyramidal System. A considerable amount is known about the neurotransmitters involved in the various basal ganglia pathways. Glutamate appears to be important in the corticostriatal pathway as an excitatory transmitter, whereas dopamine is an inhibitory transmitter[4] in the nigrostriatal pathway. Most of the numerous small interneurons of the striatum appear to employ acetylcholine as an excitatory neurotransmitter. Many of the fibers from the striatum to the globus pallidus and the substantia nigra contain γ-aminobutyric acid (GABA) as an inhibitory transmitter. Other neurotransmitters, such as norepinephrine, serotonin, met-enkephalin, substance P, and cholecystokinin also seem to be involved in basal ganglia pathways, but are not yet as clearly defined. (See Table 2-2 for details.)

Limbic Striatum. The *nucleus accumbens septi* is a large cell mass that lies between the septal region and the striatum. This nucleus, along with a few nearby structures including the olfactory tubercle and the bed nucleus of the stria terminalis, are sometimes referred to as the *ventral* or *limbic striatum.* Stevens (1973, 1982) has pointed out that there are many parallels between neuronal circuits involving the striatum proper and those involving the limbic striatum. For example, the neocortex projects to the caudate and putamen in a manner similar to the projection of the amygdala, hippocampus, and pyriform cortex to the nucleus accumbens. Also, the dopaminergic tract from the substantia nigra pars compacta projects to the striatum just as the dopaminergic tract from the ventral tegmental area projects to the nucleus accumbens. There are also parallels between the outflow tracts of the basal ganglia and the limbic striatum, with the main outflow projections of the basal ganglia being through the globus pallidus and the substantia nigra pars reticulata to the thalamus, while one of the main outflow tracts of the limbic striatum is through the substantia innominata to the thalamus, hypothalamus, habenula, and ventral tegmentum.

Recent evidence indicates that portions of the limbic system may project directly to the striatum proper. These include the hippocampus, amygdala, and cingulum (Nauta, 1982). Interestingly, the projection of these areas is to the segment of the striatum that is also predominantly innervated by the frontal association cortices rather than the motor cortex. There is also little

---

[4]There is some evidence that dopamine may be excitatory at times (see Groves, 1983).

Table 2-2. Neurotransmitters Believed to Be Important in Pathways Involving the Basal Ganglia[a]

Pathway	Neurotransmitter	Possible associated clinical condition
Cortical output		?Huntington's disease
Cortex → striatum	GLU	
Striatal connections		Huntington's disease
Striatal interneurons (aspiny)	ACh, SS, GABA, neurotensin, TRH	
Striatum → lateral GP	GABA, enkephalin	
Striatum → medial GP	GABA, SP	
Striatum → SNr	GABA, dynorphin, SP	
Pallidal output		Progressive supranuclear palsy,
GP and SNr → thalamus	GABA	multisystem atrophies, dystonias
Thalamic output		
Thalamus → cortex	Not known	
SNc connections		Parkinson's disease
SNc interneurons	?GLY	
SNc → striatum	DA	
SNr → SNc	GABA	
Striatum → SNc	SP	
Raphe → SNc	5-HT	
Locus ceruleus → SNc	NE	
Subthalamic connections		Hemiballismus
Lateral GP → subthalamus	GABA	
Subthalamus → GP	?GABA	
Cortex → subthalamus	?GLU	
Other connections		
nbM → cortex, hippocampus	ACh	Alzheimer's disease
Ventral tegmental area → prefrontal cortex, nucleus accumbens	DA	Schizophrenia

Note. Explanation of abbreviations: GP, globus pallidus; SNr, substantia nigra pars reticulata; SNc, substantia nigra pars compacta; nbM, nucleus basalis of Meynert; GLU, glutamate; ACh, acetylcholine; SS, somatostatin; TRH, thyroid releasing hormone; SP, substance P; GLY, glycine; DA, dopamine; 5-HT, serotonin; NE, norepinephrine.
[a]Also see Young and Penney (1984) and Beart (1984).

evidence for reciprocal connections between the limbic system and striatum, with the projections being directed almost exclusively one-way from limbic system to striatum (Nauta, 1982).

The intermediate position of the limbic striatum between the "limbic system" and the "extrapyramidal system" makes it an important structure in the consideration of neuropsychiatric movement disorders.

Function

The basal ganglia are very important structures from a neuropsychiatric viewpoint. For example, many disorders involving the basal ganglia, such as Huntington's and Wilson's diseases, have associated psychiatric problems. Also, there are implications of basal ganglia dysfunction in psychiatric disorders such as schizophrenia (Lidsky *et al.,* 1979).

The function of the basal ganglia is not completely understood. Some functions have been proposed based on observations of patients with Parkinson's disease. Thus, the basal ganglia have been thought to play an important part in the initiation of movement (Rolls, 1983), in the speed of execution of movement (Evarts *et al.*, 1981), and in a number of postural reflexes (Martin, 1967). In addition to these functions, Marsden (1982a) has advanced the hypothesis that the major function of the basal ganglia is the "automatic execution of learned motor plans" (p. 539), whereby the basal ganglia are responsible for running motor programs sequentially or simultaneously, resulting in a complex action. For a patient with disease of the basal ganglia, running a series or combination of motor programs, such as are involved in standing up and shaking hands at the same time, would be very difficult (Schwab *et al.*, 1954). If this hypothesis is correct, the basal ganglia function at a very high level in the organization of movement. The relationship of motor planning function of the basal ganglia to the other functions just mentioned, especially postural reflexes, is not clear.

The basal ganglia also have an influence on muscular tone. Although it was once thought that this influence was mainly indirect, involving the cerebral cortex and its influence on tone, there is evidence that output from the globus pallidus may be able to influence tone more directly through connections with the reticular formation and, in particular, the reticulospinal and vestibulospinal tracts. The globus pallidus has been proposed to be important in the pathophysiology of dystonias (see Chapter 15).

Cerebellar System (Figure 2-3)

Structure

The cerebellum is a large structure that occupies most of the posterior cranial fossa and is attached to the brainstem by three large pairs of fiber bundles, known as the *cerebellar peduncles.* These include: (1) the *superior cerebellar peduncle* (also known as the *brachium conjunctivum*), which is an efferent fiber bundle projecting from the cerebellum to the midbrain and thalamus; (2) the *middle cerebellar peduncle* (or *brachium pontis*), which is an afferent fiber bundle to the cerebellum; and (3) the *inferior cerebellar peduncle* (or *restiform body*), which contains both efferent and afferent fibers. The cere-

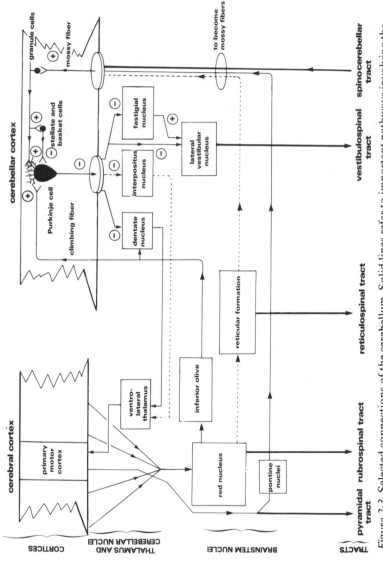

Figure 2-3. Selected connections of the cerebellum. Solid lines refer to important pathways involving the lateral cerebellum and dotted lines refer to the additional connections involving the intermediate cerebellum. Bold lines indicate important efferent and afferent spinal cord tracts. Also shown is a small schematic diagram of the cellular structure of the cerebellar cortex. $\oplus$ and $\ominus$ refer to excitatory and inhibitory pathways, respectively.

bellum is a bilaterally symmetrical structure with many transverse convolutions or folia running along the surface. Five convolutions are deep enough to be called fissures. Two of these fissures, the *primary fissure* and the *postero-lateral fissure*, divide the cerebellum transversely into three lobes, an *anterior,* a *posterior*, and a *flocculonodular lobe*. The cerebellum is also divided longitudinally into a midline strip called the vermis, with two cerebellar hemispheres on either side and two *intermediate zones* between the vermis and each of the cerebellar hemispheres. Each of these longitudinal regions of cerebellar cortex projects to deep cerebellar nuclei, with the hemispheres projecting to the dentate nuclei, the intermediate zones projecting to the *interpositus nuclei* (*globose* and *embolliform nuclei*), and the vermis projecting to the *fastigial nuclei*.

Three different functional divisions of the cerebellum, which largely conform to some of the anatomical divisions just mentioned, are often recognized (Lance & McLeod, 1975, 1981):

1.   The *vestibular loop* consists predominantly of reciprocal pathways between the flocculonodular lobe (*archicerebellum*) and the vestibular nuclei. The connection here is through the inferior cerebellar peduncle.

2.   The *spinal loop* (see Figure 2-3) consists of a circuit beginning with the afferent spinocerebellar tracts (which carry information from Ia and Ib fibers and flexor reflex afferents) that project to the anterior lobe and the median portion of the posterior lobe (*paleocerebellum*). These fibers enter the cerebellum as mossy fibers. The paleocerebellum then sends somatotopically organized projections to the lateral vestibular nucleus, both directly and through the fastigial nucleus, forming a loop from spinal cord to cerebellum and back to spinal cord. (This loop influences the vestibulospinal tract, which will be discussed later). In addition to the direct pathway from spinal cord to paleocerebellum, there is an indirect pathway through the olivary nuclei involving the spino-olivary and olivocerebellar tracts. This indirect pathway terminates as climbing fibers in the cerebellum. Another major group of efferents from the cerebellum to spinal cord consists of fibers that mainly pass through the fastigial nucleus to the reticular formation (and influence the reticulospinal tract, also to be discussed later) (see Figure 2-3).

3.   The *cortical loop* consists of fibers from the cortex that pass to the pons, red nucleus, and inferior olive, and from there to the more lateral areas of the cerebellar hemispheres (*neocerebellum*) to enter the cerebellum as mossy fibers. The cortical fibers largely originate from the primary and secondary motor areas and the sensory areas. It is important to note that there is little, if any, input from higher-level association areas of the cerebral cortex to the cerebellum (Wiesendanger, 1983). The main outflow pathway from the lateral cerebellum is through the dentate nuclei, which projects to the red nuclei and ventrolateral thalamus and then back to the cortex, primarily the primary motor cortex (area 4). There are differences between the cortical loops involving the intermediate and lateral cerebellum. These are shown in

Figure 2-3. These differences relate to different functions of the intermediate and lateral cerebellum, which will be discussed later.

CELLULAR CONFIGURATION

The cellular make-up of the cerebellar cortex is much more stereotyped for the different cerebellar cortical areas than is seen in the cerebral cortex. In simplified terms, there are two main inputs, *mossy fibers* and *climbing fibers*, both excitatory, and one main output, which is from *Purkinje cells* and is inhibitory. The mossy fibers, which provide information from cortex and muscle afferents, are excitatory to *granule cells* (and deep cortical nuclei). The granule cells are excitatory through parallel fibers to *stellate* and *basket cells*, which, in turn, are inhibitory to Purkinje cells. The climbing fiber input to Purkinje cells is simpler, being directly excitatory (and also excitatory to deep nuclei). The Purkinje cells are inhibitory to deep cerebellar nuclei. The deep cerebellar nuclei can be both inhibitory and excitatory. There are also two circuits involving Golgi cells: one that involves stimulation of the Golgi cells by granule cells and is inhibitory to granule cells (a negative-feedback circuit) and another that involves stimulation of Golgi cells by mossy fibers and is also inhibitory to granule cells. These two circuits allow for sharpening of the input both to granule cells and to Purkinje cells. (For a general review, see Eccles, 1973.)

RETICULOSPINAL AND VESTIBULOSPINAL TRACTS

These two spinal cord tracts are sometimes called "extrapyramidal tracts" because they influence motor function but are separate from the pyramidal tracts. However, to call them "extrapyramidal" leads to a possible supposition that these tracts are closely related to the "extrapyramidal system" or the basal ganglia, whereas they are closely related to the cerebellum.

The *reticulospinal tracts* (see Figure 2-1) arise in the reticular formation of the brainstem. The reticular formation has been divided into two areas in terms of its influence on motor functions. One has been termed the *medial reticular (or medullary) extensor inhibitory area*, which, when stimulated, has been shown to inhibit extensor reflexes. The other has been called the *lateral reticular (or pontine) extensor facilitatory area*, which has been shown to facilitate extensor reflexes. Both of these areas exert influence on α- and γ-motoneurons, but usually in a balanced fashion. The extensor facilitatory area receives much of its excitatory input from ascending pathways in the spinal cord, whereas the extensor inhibitory area receives much of its excitatory input from the cerebral cortex. Mesencephalic transection thus significantly decreases the influence of the extensor inhibitory area on α- and γ-motoneurons to a much greater extent than it does that of the extensor facilitatory area, and this results in an extensor posture, called *decerebrate rigidity* (which is actually more akin to spasticity). γ-Motoneurons to extensor muscles, being smaller than α, are excited more than α, so that this type of rigidity is sometimes called γ-rigidity and is relieved by sectioning the dorsal roots.

The *vestibulospinal tract* probably arises from the lateral vestibular nucleus in the brainstem, and travels down the anterior part of the ipsilateral half of the spinal cord. The lateral vestibular or *Deiter's nucleus* has important connections with the cerebellum, and, through the vestibulospinal tract, is excitatory to α- and γ-motoneurons. If this nucleus is destroyed, decerebrate rigidity is abolished, probably because the lateral reticular extensor facilitatory system alone is not enough to maintain the spasticity. In fact, Deiter's nucleus is a powerful excitatory force to both α- and γ-motoneurons, and is generally under inhibition by the cerebellum. If the cerebellovestibular inhibitory connections are interrupted, however, the excitation of Deiter's nucleus proceeds unchecked, causing *α-rigidity*. α-Rigidity, unlike γ-rigidity, is not relieved by sectioning the dorsal roots.

Function

There appear to be two main functions of the cerebellum. The first function, which is mediated in large part by the vestibular and spinal loops and the intermediate cerebellum, concerns the updating and coordination of signals to muscles involved in ongoing activity and in posture. The second function, which appears to be subserved by the cortical circuit and lateral cerebellum, concerns motor programming (but probably only so much as it involves the detailed instructions important to the immediate execution of a movement, and not in the sense of motor planning as described in the previous section).

GENERAL ISSUES IN THE PRODUCTION OF MOVEMENT

The remainder of this chapter is devoted to some general issues involved in the production of movements by the central nervous system. It is divided into three sections. The first section considers the concept of hierarchical control in the motor system. The second section offers a review of different types of concerted movements. The final section of this chapter deals with the neuropsychiatric interface in the control of movements. (See also Chapter 27.)

Hierarchical Control in the Motor System

The various components of the motor system are sometimes placed in an order that corresponds to the complexity of the motor functions that are subserved by them. The lower components of the motor system, such as simple spinal reflex mechanisms, are thought of as being under the control of higher components, such as the pyramidal system. Although this is an over-simplification, there are some situations in which a hierarchical conception is helpful, as is discussed below.

The *spinal cord reflexes* are at the lowest level of organization within the motor hierarchy. These include the myotatic, inverse myotatic, and certain other reflexes previously mentioned. Some of these reflexes are simple feed-back circuits, and control from higher structures is often achieved through what is called *biasing* or *gating* the reflex. This control occurs through interneurons in the spinal cord that receive impulses from fibers of the pyramidal, vestibulospinal, and reticulospinal tracts, as well as others. It is through these gating or biasing circuits that the muscular tone is set, which is very important for the maintenance of many postural functions. As men-tioned earlier, reflexes may be of short or long latencies and in some patho-logical conditions are *released* from higher motor control. Reflexes in many cases are also closed-loop feedback circuits, and the afferent component of such circuits is thought to exert a modulating control important in the performance of slow *ramp movements*. (These movements contrast with fast *ballistic movements*, which appear to be more the result of the motor control programs [open-loop circuits] discussed next).

At a higher level than the reflexes are the *motor control programs*. Motor control programs differ from simple reflexes in that the output of a reflex is graded in correspondence with the amount of input, whereas the output of a motor control program is either all or none; that is, there are no quantities in between (Lance & McLeod, 1975). In the past it was believed that simple rhythmical activities such as those involved in locomotion were the result of sequential activation of different spinal reflexes. However, it is now believed that in the case of locomotion, and probably in many other cases of rhythmic movements, the control is via a central motor program. In many animals the control center for locomotion appears to be located in the spinal cord, but this is not true in man. Besides locomotion, many other concerted muscular activities are probably directed by central programs located in the spinal cord, brainstem, cerebellum, and possibly even the basal ganglia and cortex. Sometimes motor programs are spoken of as being *pathologically released* from control of higher brain areas. The release of a motor program is not always easy to differentiate from the release of a reflex. For example, it is not clear whether a pathological grasp reflex represents the release of a true reflex as opposed to the release of the first part of a motor control program for grasping (such a program would lie dormant in man, but could be important for lower primates). Another example involves the rela-tionship between postural reflexes and motor control programs. The distinc-tion here is sometimes difficult, as some postural reflexes are actually antici-patory in nature and thus are generated in advance of movements caused by a disturbance (Marsden *et al.*, 1981b). Although there is evidence that anticipatory postural reflexes are dependent on proprioceptive feedback, it can be seen that pathological conditions that release parts of motor programs might be difficult to differentiate from those that disturb postural reflexes. This is discussed further when chorea and athetosis are considered later in this volume (Chapter 3).

Higher still than *motor control programs* are what Marsden (1982a) has called *motor plans*. In considering motor plans we move beyond simple concerted muscular contractions and into complex goal-directed patterns of movement, often called *actions*. As an example of a motor plan, Marsden (1982) considers the act of writing a signature. Regardless of whether one writes a signature on a piece of paper or on a blackboard, the signature, except for size, looks the same. This is in spite of different muscles' being activated in the different writing positions. Thus, a motor plan controls the execution of motor programs, according to the dictates of the will. According to Marsden (1982) motor plans are executed by the basal ganglia, but it is not known where they are stored.

At the highest level we find the *motor idea* or the *willed action*. The exact location of the highest centers for the volitional control of movement are not known, but are probably cortical. Between ½ second, and 1 second before the execution of a voluntary movement a slowly increasing negative potential becomes evident on EEG over the precentral and parietal regions of the brain, bilaterally. This is called the *Bereitschaftspotential* (Deecke *et al.*, 1969) or readiness potential, and is believed to originate predominantly in the motor cortex, but probably involves other brain areas as well. That the readiness potential is associated with voluntary movement is clear from the fact that it is absent in the case of passive movement. What the readiness potential actually represents is unclear, but it is present in patients with Parkinson's disease and thus is not completely dependent on the intact functioning of the basal ganglia (Marsden, 1982a). If it indeed does represent some kind of cortical preparatory state for voluntary movement, it would be interesting to assess patients who may suffer from disorders of willed movement, such as catatonia or compulsive disorders, for abnormalities of the readiness potential. Interesting in this regard is the finding of no readiness potential in Tourette's patients prior to the onset of a tic, but an apparent potential when these patients mimic their tics voluntarily (Obeso *et al.*, 1982). The creation of a willed action involves the participation of memory, as well as an analysis of the current environment of an individual. The totality of the action carried out by the motor plans, motor programs, and reflexes for a given specific environmental circumstance at a given time may be called the *behavior* of the person.

The above discussion represents many widely accepted ideas relating to the hierarchical control of movement. However, it has been noted that the execution of even relatively simple movements would require a vast system of motor control programs and feedback circuits. In response to this, an alternative theory that invokes a minimum number of executive instructions has been proposed (Kugler et al,. 1980; Kelso et al., 1980; Green, 1982). This theory involves geometrodynamic considerations and views coordinative structures as energy-dissipative structures. Groups of muscles are considered to have characteristics of nonlinear oscillators, like a spring. These characteristics put constraints on the degrees of freedom of a coordinated movement by themselves, without necessitating higher control mechanisms. Higher mechanisms merely tune the necessary oscillators, and the movement is carried out not only because of information sent to the muscle groups from higher structures, but also because of information inherent in the muscle system. Cyclical activities, such as locomotion, would occur as the result of tuning individual oscillators so that one large oscillation (say, walking) is achieved. And the switch from walking to running would not need a new central program, but would follow automatically when muscular power increases to a critical point. Similarly if a movement such as touching the tip of one's nose is being carried out and a sudden load is put on the arm, the mechanism by which the finger still correctly touches the nose lies within the nonlinear oscillatory characteristics of the group of muscles involved, and not in a neural closed-loop feedback mechanism. Another illustrative example is the case of *Lithobius*, a centipede, which walks like a insect when all but three pairs of legs are removed and like a quadruped when all but two pairs are removed (Kugler et al., 1980). Recent studies have indicated, however, that although these geometrodynamic considerations may be important in large, relatively coarse movements, accurate motor control is still dependent on intact somesthetic feedback from the periphery (Sanes & Evarts, 1984; Sanes et al., 1984).

Patterns of Concerted Movement

Any single given movement does not occur in isolation but, rather, is accompanied by the contraction of many muscles that serve to facilitate and stabilize the movement. Movements therefore involve a pattern of muscular contraction. There are several different types of patterns that will be considered here, including movement synergy, associated movement, coordinated movement, and posture.

Synergy

Motor synergy has been defined in several ways. In its broadest definition it refers to the total coordinated activity of all the muscles necessary for a motor act. Its most restrictive definition, and the one we prefer, is the contraction of muscles that aid in the efficient performance of a movement but are not absolutely necessary for the completion of the movement.[5] For example, if the hand is flexed at the wrist and a fist is made, it will be noticed that along with the curling of the fingers into the fist, there is also an extension of the wrist. This wrist extension is not absolutely necessary for the production of a fist, but aids in the production of a more efficient fist (for whatever purpose). By this definition, another example of synergistic movements would be the swinging of the arms when walking, which, although not necessary for locomotion, make it more efficient. It is not clear, however, whether this is a movement synergy of the same type as that just mentioned.

Associated Movement

This term has also been defined in several ways. It has been considered to be synonymous with synergy. It has also been used to define certain movements that are not normally present but that occur in certain pathological states, such as mirror or adventitious movements. Finally, it has been used for normal movements that are accessory to a given movement but are neither necessary for nor add to the efficiency of the movement. In this book, we use the term in these last two senses. An example of a normal associated movement would be stretching the arms while yawning, a phenomenon that often occurs in exaggerated form in hemiplegic limbs. Associated movements are sometimes also called *synkinesias*. The absence of associated movements may also be pathological. For example, when sitting, there is a certain amount of shifting of position and leg-crossing that is often noticeably absent in conditions such as Parkinson's disease.

Coordinated Movement

The term "coordination" is used in this book to refer to the simultaneous and sequential contraction of all involved muscles in such a manner as to produce a smooth and efficient movement. Some have called this "synergy," but we prefer to use the term "synergy" in the more restricted sense defined above.

Posture

Posture is a very complex subject. As Martin has noted (1977), movement itself has been considered by neurologists such as Holmes (1922) to be nothing more than a series of postures. There is evidence, however, that this is not so, mainly from patients who have disturbances in posture without necessarily having a loss or disturbance of voluntary movement (see Martin, 1977).

---

[5]Another similar definition describes synergistic muscles as those that eliminate undesirable movement when the main muscle involved passes over two or more joints (see Wilson, 1925).

Posture is often considered in two different ways. In the first, posture is considered to be the relationship of the parts of the body to each other and of the body as a whole to the environment; this is a *static* conception of posture. In the second, posture is thought to be the neuromuscular maintenance of balance and support of the body in the face of physical forces, especially gravity; this is a *dynamic* conception of posture. In a static view of posture mention is often made of the phenomenon of postural fixation, whereby the range of motion around a joint is limited in one or more directions, usually by the co-contraction of agonist and antagonist muscles. From a dynamic viewpoint posture is considered to be an activity rather than simply the relationship of the parts of the body to each other and is often conceived of as being maintained by a set of postural reflexes. Here, postural fixation is considered to be a postural reflex concerned with the balance and maintenance of body structures appropriate to a given moment. Other postural reflexes include (1) the righting reflex, which allows the body to regain its normal upright position; (2) the staggering reflex, which enables the body to prevent itself from falling when suddenly displaced from the side; (3) tilting reflexes, which allow the body to remain upright when the base of support is changing; (4) locomotory reflexes, which enable the body to remain upright during locomotion; and (5) certain falling reflexes concerned with protecting the body during a fall. Martin (1967) believes these main postural reflexes to be part of the function of the basal ganglia. He has differentiated them from antigravity mechanisms related to the maintenance of upright posture, which are controlled by centers in the brainstem and mediated by local spinal cord reflexes.

General Principles of Movement from a Neuropsychiatric Perspective

In terms of interface between neurology and psychiatry, the two most important motor systems are the pyramidal and extrapyramidal systems. These systems have strong connections with cortical association areas and with the limbic system, both of which are psychiatrically important. Generally, the volitional control of movement is dependent on a variety of psychological factors that, when disturbed, can manifest as disturbances in movement. Therefore psychological factors operate on a level higher than what we have termed the putative motor planning functions of the basal ganglia, because the former factors determine what action is to be carried out, and not merely how it is to be carried out. Equally as important, however, are the effects of a disturbance of movement back on psychological factors. Paralysis and tics, myoclonus and cataplexy are bound to influence the psychic state of their sufferers. Finally, pathological conditions that affect the higher levels of brain organization may influence both the psychic state of an individual and motor function at the same time. For example, whatever underlies illnesses such as catatonia may simultaneously affect areas of the brain subserving psychiatric and neurological motor functions.

Any attempt to disentangle the complex ways that psychological and motor problems interact in a given individual often proves exceedingly difficult, if not impossible. Yet we firmly believe that it is a worthwhile undertaking to attempt to do so, and may often lead to better understanding, not only of patients' clinical presentations, but of the patients themselves. We shall return to this issue at the conclusion of this book, in Chapter 27.

SIGNS AND SYMPTOMS OF DISORDERED MOVEMENT
A. Increased Movement

CHAPTER THREE

Chorea, Athetosis, and Ballismus

INTRODUCTION

The disorders discussed in this chapter refer to nonrepetitive muscular contractions, usually of the extremities and face. Although they may be generalized, this is not usual except for more severe cases.

Chorea was the first of the three disorders to be described. Although it is likely that choreiform disorders have existed throughout history, there is little evidence that they were clearly described prior to the Middle Ages. It is not clear exactly when the term "chorea" was first used, but it appears to have become popular in descriptions of the outbreaks of "dancing mania" that began in 1374 A.D., approximately 25 years after the beginning of the plague (Bruyn, 1968). (The word "chorea" itself derives from the Greek term for dance.) It is probable that many different hyperkinetic disorders were subsumed under the term "St. Vitus's dance" for many years until Sydenham clearly separated postinfectious chorea minor from the rest of the group in 1686. Later, in 1872, George Huntington delivered his famous lecture on chronic progressive hereditary chorea. Much of what he said was drawn from the observations of his father and grandfather, both of whom were also physicians.

The word "athetosis" was introduced into the medical literature in 1871 by W. A. Hammond, one of the first great American neurologists. The term, Greek in origin, means "without fixed position," and was used to describe a slow, fluid type of hyperkinesis that usually occurs in brain-damaged children.

Ballismus, a term first used in 1885 by Kussmaul and Fischer (Meyers, 1968) and derived from the Greek word meaning "to throw," was so named because the muscular contractions observed are so severe that the limbs appear to be flung about by the body. It is almost always seen in a unilateral presentation called *hemiballismus* or *hemiballism*. This condition is sometimes also called hemichorea, and many neurologists use the terms interchangeably. However, because of certain pathophysiological and clinical considerations to be discussed later, it is probably better to consider ballismus or hemiballismus to be a special type of choreiform movement, deserving its own name. The disorder is rare and generally seen in the elderly.

DESCRIPTIONS

Chorea

Chorea is characterized by a random pattern of irregular, involuntary, rapid contractions of a group of muscles. The contractions may involve any part of the body, but usually the face and extremities are most severely affected. Electrophysiologically, the movements may resemble normal contractions (Lance & McLeod, 1981), but there is wide variation in the electromyographic picture, with muscle activity ranging from myoclonus-like to dystonia-like, often within a single muscle over time (Marsden et al., 1983a). When the legs are affected, the gait is often described as "dancing" or "clownish," and consists of irregular trajectory and awkward placement of the legs when stepping. The movements almost always attenuate during sleep, and, during the waking state, are usually less severe with rest. Emotional stress and attempted voluntary movement frequently exacerbate the hyperkinesis.

Athetosis

Athetosis consists of slow, sinuous, irregular movements most obvious in the distal extremities. They are usually more rhythmic than choreiform movements and are always much slower. In the hands the athetotic movements are often superimposed on a characteristic hand posture with pronated forearm, flexed wrist, and hyperextended fingers. When the face is involved the patient presents with slowly fluctuating grimaces. Athetosis and chorea frequently coexist, or a form intermediate between them may be seen. This is called *choreoathetosis*. Athetotic movements are usually worse with anxiety and with attempted voluntary movement, and they attenuate during sleep.

Ballismus

Ballismus consists of wild flinging movements of the limbs. Usually, only unilateral limb involvement, called hemiballismus, is observed. The movements resemble choreiform movements, but are more severe and more stereotyped. They often do not involve the face or trunk. Hemiballismus is one of the rare involuntary movement disorders that may not attenuate during sleep—in fact, some patients are awakened by being struck by their own limbs.

DIFFERENTIAL DIAGNOSIS

As already discussed, it can be very difficult to distinguish between chorea, athetosis, and ballismus. For example, chorea and athetosis frequently occur together and in intermediate forms, and hemichorea and hemiballismus have often been considered to be different names for the same disorder. Nevertheless, there are some distinguishing features.

Chorea and hemiballismus tend to appear in proximal muscles as much as (or more than) in distal ones, whereas the opposite is true of athetosis. Ballismus, in contrast to the other two conditions, is almost always unilateral, has an abrupt onset, and often does not disappear with sleep. Choreiform disorders—in particular, Huntington's disease (excepting the rigid variant) and Sydenham's chorea are often accompanied by hypotonia, whereas athetosis is frequently accompanied by hypertonia (such as rigidity in Wilson's disease and spasticity in cerebral palsy). Chorea and ballismus are less frequently accompanied by the postural abnormalities that are found along with athetosis.

Distinguishing between hemiballismus and hemichorea is often so difficult that many neurologists have advocated considering them to be on a continuum (Koller *et al.*, 1979). However, Meyers (1968) has proposed some differentiating features, including the following: (1) the hyperkinetic activity in chorea is more intermittent than in ballismus; (2) proximal muscles are more involved in ballismus; and (3) the limb movements in ballismus are more complex and combined than choreiform movements. Ballismic and choreiform movements may coexist, but in such cases the ballistic movements improve first (Koller *et al.*, 1979).

There are other clinical conditions that at times can resemble these three. Myoclonus and tics can resemble chorea, but myoclonic movements are generally quicker and tics more stereotyped and more subject to voluntary control. Tics also often occur in much more complex patterns than do these other hyperkinesias. Dystonic movements may resemble athetosis, but the tone is usually more severely increased in dystonia and the movements are much slower, involving proximal and trunk musculature. It should be noted that athetosis and dystonia frequently coexist, however. There is also a condition, known as "pseudoathetosis," that is a result of a loss of proprioception. In contrast with true athetosis, pseudoathetosis is usually not associated with disturbances in tone and is often worse when the eyes are closed. Finally, certain types of repetitive movements, such as stereotypies and bruxism, may be confused with athetosis in particular, but these can often be distinguished by accompanying clinical phenomena. This issue is addressed further in the chapters on repetitive movements (Chapters 5–8).

PATHOPHYSIOLOGY

The pathophysiology of these conditions is unknown, but in each case damage to the basal ganglia and their connections is thought to play a role.

Chorea

Most of what is known about chorea in humans is the result of studies on patients with Huntington's disease. There is some evidence that the cells of the striatum can be divided cytologically into three populations—small, medium-sized, and large—that may be differentially affected in different variants of Huntington's disease (Klawans, 1973). In the usual variant of Huntington's disease where chorea is one of the primary manifestations, the small and medium-sized cells may be pathologically affected to a much greater extent than the large cells. In the rigid akinetic variant, however, the different types of cells may be more equally affected (Dom *et al.*, 1973; Lange *et al.*, 1976). Because the chorea responds to dopamine blocking agents (such as neuroleptic drugs) and is made worse by L-dopa, and the akinesia appears to be somewhat responsive to L-dopa, it has been suggested that the smaller cells are dopamine facilitated and mediate the chorea, whereas the large cells are dopamine inhibited and mediate the akinesia and rigidity (Klawans, 1973). However, there is evidence that large cells may actually be spared in the rigid variant, which goes against this hypothesis (see Bugiani *et al.*, 1984).

Part of the difficulty with these studies based on cytological characteristics of the striatum in Huntington's diseases lies in the fact that such studies do not take into account the full complexity of the fine structure of the basal ganglia. In contrast to the three types of striatal cells described above, Golgi and electron-microscopic studies have revealed that there may be many different types of striatal cells, along with many different types of striatal neurotransmitters (see Pasik *et al.*, 1979). These different cells have been divided into two major groups, spiny and aspiny, based on the presence or absence of dendritic spines. The spiny cells appear to form the major striatal efferents, with spiny type I (SI) cells utilizing γ-aminobutyric acid (GABA) and enkephalin as transmitters, and spiny type II (SII) cells utilizing substance P (SP). The aspiny cells appear to be primarily interneurons and to utilize acetylcholine (ACh), GABA, and possibly somatostatin (SS). The output of SI cells is thus largely inhibitory, and these cells form the bulk of the efferent tracts, whereas the output of SII cells is mainly excitatory. The size ranges of the cells vary considerably, but basically the SI cells appear to be medium-sized, whereas the SII cells are large. The aspiny cells utilizing ACh are also large, whereas the aspiny cells utilizing GABA and SS are medium to small (Aronin *et al.*, 1983; Groves, 1983, Carpenter, 1984). It can be seen that simple descriptions of large- or small-sized cell loss in different variants of Huntington's disease can be very difficult to interpret. The finding that, in Huntington's disease, GABA, SP, ACh, and enkephalins are decreased, whereas SS and possibly DA are increased implies that certain cells are differentially affected in the disease. There is further evidence that SS increases dopaminergic transmission in the striatum (Aronin *et al.*, 1983), which implicates SS in the genesis of chorea. Whatever the exact neurochemical mechanism, it appears that chorea is related to an altered excessive response of the striatum to dopamine.

How disordered dopaminergic responsivity in the striatum might relate to the production of hyperkinetic movements is unknown. Given the fact that dopamine appears to be released into the striatum in accordance with the general motoric demands of a given situation, the effect of dopamine on the striatum could be to allow for the performance of "more discrete algorithms necessary for controlled movements" (Schultz *et al.*, 1983, p. 178). Since damaged striatal neurons may show an altered response to dopamine (Klawans, 1973), and considering the evidence implicating the basal ganglia in the control of motor programs (Cools *et al.*, 1984), it is possible that choreiform movements represent the haphazard triggering or release of fragments of motor programs as a result of altered dopaminergic responsivity in striatal neurons. This could also explain why choreiform movements often become worse with attempted voluntary movement.

Another way of looking at choreiform movements involves considering the abnormalities in long-latency reflexes, including the tonic stretch reflex and some postural reflexes, that have been shown to be present (Martin, 1967; Lance & McLeod, 1981). In essence, there may be an inappropriate release of tonic reflexes rather than of motor programs. A similar phenomenon may occur in athetosis, hemiballismus, and, possibly, dystonia, as will be discussed later.

Athetosis

As in chorea, there is evidence for impairment of tonic stretch reflexes in athetosis (Lance & McLeod, 1981). Although these reflexes are occasionally normal or diminished in athetosis, as the underlying pathological condition progresses the tone often increases until a final dystonic posture with flexed arms and extended legs is reached (the "striatal position").

It is not clear whether the abnormal athetotic movements are themselves directly related to disordered tone, although this has long been assumed.

Electromyographically, two types of clinically apparent involuntary movements have been described: (1) an irregular, slow (<2 cycles per second) fluctuation in posture, and (2) an accompanying tremor, usually 2–3 cycles per second, resembling a rubral tremor. Neither of these is clearly directly related to disordered tone (Lance & McLeod, 1981). There may nonetheless be an indirect relationship of athetosis to the impairment in tone, as both may result from impaired function of the basal ganglia. As mentioned in the previous chapter, although the basal ganglia may have a direct effect on muscle tone, they appear to affect tone indirectly, probably through cortical connections. This effect on tone may be related to the postural functions of the basal ganglia, as the basal ganglionic control of posture and tone may both be cortically mediated. Athetosis is frequently described as a disorder of posture (Denny-Brown, 1968) and appears to involve impaired postural fixation of the distal extremities. Therefore, athetosis (as a disorder of posture) and impaired tonic reflexes may both result from underlying basal ganglia disease. Related to this idea is Denny-Brown's (1968) suggestion that striatal damage can lead to an irregular release of frontal cortex "grasping and groping" reactions and parietal cortex "withdrawal" reactions. These could manifest as the continual change in posture observed in athetosis. How this idea relates to a possible irregular release of stored motor programs, as previously discussed in chorea, is unclear.

Hemiballismus

Hemiballismus, like chorea and athetosis, has been hypothesized to represent a release phenomenon. Because most cases have involved damage to the subthalamic nucleus it has been postulated that this nucleus exerts negative feedback control on impulses from the globus pallidus. Martin (1967) has offered evidence indicating that the globus pallidus is important in the production of postural reflexes, and that the wild flinging movements of hemiballismus represent exaggerated responses to body instability, the result of unrestricted output from the globus pallidus. In keeping with this idea, there is evidence that a functioning globus pallidus is necessary for ballismus to occur (Koller *et al.*, 1979). Lance and McLeod (1981) regard hemiballismus as a disorder of postural fixation of the proximal limbs, and note that some patients are able, by making compensatory trunk movements, to fix the distal portion of the arm long enough to pick up a glass and drink from it. Thus, in a sense, hemiballismus may represent a disorder of proximal muscle postural fixation, just as athetosis may be a disorder of distal muscle postural fixation. Because dopamine blocking agents are sometimes effective in controlling hemiballismus, it is possible that dopaminergic mechanisms are involved. However, it is also possible that dopamine blockade limits the dyskinesia merely by inducing parkinsonian hypokinesia and rigidity.

SYNDROMES IN WHICH CHOREA, ATHETOSIS, AND BALLISMUS MAY OCCUR

Table 3-1 offers a listing of the important syndromes in which chorea, athetosis, and ballismus may occur. In the remaining part of this section of the chapter, we shall briefly review some of the more common neurological

Table 3-1. Important Causes of Chorea, Athetosis, and Ballismus

Chorea	
Huntington's disease	Lupus erythematosus
Sydenham's chorea	Polycythemia rubra vera
Chorea gravidarum	Basal ganglia tumor
Wilson's disease	Dentate nucleus lesion
Paroxysmal choreoathetosis	Tardive dyskinesia
Senile chorea	Other drug-induced dyskinesias (including
Prechtl's choreiform syndrome	L-dopa, anticonvulsants, stimulants,
Congenital choreoathetosis	neuroleptics, lithium, etc.)
Birth-control pills	Hysteria
Thyrotoxicosis	Schizophrenia (?)

Athetosis
Congenital choreoathetosis
Wilson's disease
Hallervorden–Spatz disease
Huntington's disease (especially Westphal variant)
Ataxia telangiectasia
Alpers's disease
Tardive dyskinesia
Other drug-induced dyskinesias (as above)
Schizophrenia (?)

Ballismus (almost always hemiballismus)[a]
Vascular disease of subthalamus
Hyperglycemia
Multiple sclerosis
Encephalitis
Arteriovenous malformation
Metastatic carcinoma
Head trauma

[a]See Koller *et al.* (1979).

and psychiatric disorders that may present with these hyperkinetic movements.

Neurological Disorders

Huntington's Disease and Sydenham's Chorea

The two best-known neurological disorders in which chorea is the primary feature are Huntington's disease and Sydenham's chorea. In the early stages of both these conditions the patient often begins looking "fidgety" and restless. Emotional lability may also be present in both, leading to diagnostic confusion. For example, both disorders may be misdiagnosed as hysteria, and Sydenham's in particular may be confused with Tourette's disorder or other tic disorders because it sometimes begins with facial grimaces and body twitches in children. The presence of emotional lability and occasional psychotic symptoms in the early stages of Huntington's disease sometimes leads to the misdiagnosis of schizophrenia or depression (VanPutten & Menkes, 1973; McHugh & Folstein, 1975; Caine & Shoulson, 1983). Sydenham's chorea may also be associated with psychosis. A recent study (Nausieda et al., 1983) has indicated that there may be residual chronic dopaminergic sensitivity in patients who previously suffered from Sydenham's, and that this may manifest itself not only as residual choreiform movements or as susceptibility to adverse reactions to stimulants and other drugs, but also as a predisposition to thought disorder, including psychosis. Finally, personality disturbances and neurosis have also been reported to be associated with Huntington's disease (McHugh & Folstein, 1975) and with Sydenham's chorea (Krauss, 1946; Freeman et al., 1965).

The choreiform movements themselves of Huntington's and Sydenham's often appear to be very similar, and the wide range of individual variation within each disorder may make it difficult to identify the underlying condition acutely. In general, however, Sydenham's tends to be more unilateral than Huntington's and to have a much more acute onset, with greater severity at first. Huntington's disease and Sydenham's chorea are discussed further in Chapter 22.

Chorea Gravidarum

Chorea gravidarum is a disorder that occurs during pregnancy and consists initially of increasing agitation and "fidgetiness" and usually progresses to choreiform movements of the limbs, usually unilateral. The disorder in many ways resembles Sydenham's chorea and, indeed, has been hypothesized to represent a reemergence of Sydenham's during pregnancy (Donaldson, 1978).

In many cases a previous history of Sydenham's chorea or rheumatic fever can be elicited. As with Sydenham's, the women afffected with this disorder are often thought to be suffering from hysteria. The involuntary movements may involve the face, mouth, and tongue, as well as the limbs. This condition, although rare, is virtually identical with choreiform movements that result from the use of estrogens (Nausieda et al., 1979). It has been proposed, therefore, that changes in sex hormones might alter either neurotransmitter levels or receptor sensitivity to neurotransmitters, especially dopamine (Nausieda et al., 1979; Ichikawa et al., 1980). These conditions usually resolve spontaneously and do not require treatment. Both have declined in incidence over the past 20 or 30 years for unknown reason.

Wilson's Disease

Wilson's disease may be associated with choreiform as well as athetoid movements. This disorder, too, often presents initially with emotional lability and personality changes and may be confused with schizophrenia. Wilson's disease is discussed further in Chapter 22.

Paroxysmal Choreoathetosis

Paroxysmal choreoathetosis is one of the most interesting choreoathetotic disorders and is characterized by episodes of jerking and writhing of the limbs and trunk. There appear to be two forms: (1) a rare familial form, known as paroxysmal dystonic choreoathetosis of Mount and Reback, which has an autosomal dominant pattern of inheritance, is precipitated by exertion, excitement, or ingestion of caffeine or alcohol, and lasts anywhere from several minutes to several hours (Richards & Barnett, 1968; Lance, 1977; Lance & McLeod, 1981); and (2) paroxysmal kinesigenic choreoathetosis, which is not familial and involves choreoathetotic attacks lasting up to 30 seconds that are usually precipitated by movement (Kertesz, 1967; Lance & McLeod, 1981) but that may occur as a reaction to startle (McHugh & Folstein, 1975). The kinesigenic form may occur by itself or be associated with other disorders, such as multiple sclerosis. Both disorders may resemble a form of epilepsy called "extrapyramidal" or "striatal" epilepsy, where the seizures involve flexion of the arm and extension of the leg on one side lasting at most a few minutes (Lance & McLeod, 1975). These dystonic seizures may occur in patients with multiple sclerosis, cortical scarring, or basal ganglia pathology. Also to be differentiated from the above disorders are paroxysmal choreoathetotic movements due to thyrotoxicosis (which is reversible) and hyperekplexia, which will be discussed in Chapter 10. It is important to note that all of the paroxysmal disorders above are frequently confused with hysterical reactions, especially those disorders that are precipitated by stress.

Paroxysmal choreoathetotic disorders are all responsive to anticonvulsants, although electroencephalographic abnormalities are usually not present during the attacks.

Senile Chorea

Rarely, geriatric patients with no previous history of medications or illnesses that are associated with movement disorders develop jerky movements of the extremities and sometimes of the mouth, tongue, and trunk. Although some cases may be Huntington's disease with very late onset, this probably does not explain the majority of cases. In many of these patients there is often associated anxiety or depression. Usually no abnormalities are found on routine laboratory tests, electroencephalography (EEG), or radiological investigation. The disorder may progress over weeks to months, and many patients respond to small doses of neuroleptics. Whether this disorder simply reflects age-related degenerative changes in the brain or some other pathological process is unknown. It is important to determine in these patients any history of estrogen use or prior use of other drugs (such as neuroleptics) that could cause tardive dyskinesia manifesting later in life. Many elderly people have been treated with antipsychotic medications such as thioridazine or trifluoperazine for sleeping difficulties and anxiety. Yet, many patients might not mention these medications when asked about previous drugs, thinking them merely to be "sleeping pills," or they may not remember ever taking them. Another possibility to be kept in mind is that there is evidence that depression may aggravate dyskinesias (Cutler & Post, 1982; Casey, 1984). Therefore, it is important to evaluate the patient with senile chorea carefully for evidence of depression and to bear in mind the possibility that treatment of the depression alone may result in improvement of the chorea.

Prechtl's Choreiform Syndrome

Prechtl's choreiform syndrome is a disorder that occurs in childhood and that can be mistaken for Sydenham's chorea, for Huntington's disease, and also for minimal brain dysfunction. Some of the children affected apparently go on to develop tics and possibly even Tourette's syndrome, but in most cases the disorder is self-limited (see Denckla & Heilman, 1979).

Congenital Choreoathetosis

Congenital choreoathetosis is one of the disorders commonly subsumed under the general category of cerebral palsy. There is a transition from the spastic forms of cerebral palsy to the choreoathetotic forms, with all patterns of combination of the two being seen. Certain patients with congenital choreoathetosis are considered to have "double athetosis," a condition marked by bilateral athetoid movements and pathologically associated with aberrant myelination of the basal ganglia, resulting in a marbled appearance of the tissue; the so-called *status marmoratus* or *état marbré*. There are no definite consistent psychiatric abnormalities associated with these conditions except mental retardation, which may be present in varying degrees. It should be noted that some of these affected patients, because of the presence of dysarthria, are often incorrectly assumed to be retarded, whereas they may actually have above-average intellectual abilities.

Psychiatric Disorders

Today, primary (not drug-induced) choreoathetoid or ballismic movements in patients with primary psychiatric disorder are not commonly seen, but this was perhaps not always the case. Although none of these movement disorders have ever been reported to occur commonly in affective disorders, they have been reported in schizophrenia and hysteria. For example, Kraepelin (1919/ 1971), among others, noted the presence of choreoathetotic movements in schizophrenia, and many observers reported the presence of such movements in hysteria (Ziehen, 1910). The reasons why these hyperkinetic movements are rarely seen in primary psychiatric disorders today is unclear, but is perhaps related to a change in the nature of the psychopathological process, or to masking effects of the drugs used to treat the psychiatric problem, as will be discussed in the remaining part of this section.

Schizophrenia

Schizophrenia may be accompanied by hyperkinetic movements (see also Chapter 22). Kraepelin (1919, 1971) called the choreoathetoid movements "athetoid ataxia," and later investigators, such as Wernicke (Jaspers, 1973) and Kleist (1960), called similar conditions "parakinesias." Today, it is not clear how common dyskinesias are in the schizophrenic population. The difficulty lies in the confusion caused by neuroleptics. These drugs may mask any underlying choreiform disorder, as well as cause a choreoathetotic disorder of their own—tardive dyskinesia. Therefore, one must look at studies that examined schizophrenic patients never treated with neuroleptics. Jones and Hunter (1969) found four out of 45 never-treated schizophrenic patients to have choreoathetoid movements. Brandon (1971) reported that 12% of 162 male and 29% of 123 female schizophrenic patients, all previously untreated, had evidence of facial dyskinesias. A recent study found a high incidence of dyskinesias, especially of the face, in never-treated schizophrenic patients (Owens et al., 1982). Another recent study (Crow et al., 1982), which looked at dopamine receptor changes in neuroleptic-treated rats and postmortem striatal tissue from schizophrenic patients, concluded that dyskinesias in schizophrenia may be a part of the disease process itself. These findings challenge the belief that true choreoathetotic movements, and especially facial dyskinesias, are rare in schizophrenia and, when present, are related to neuroleptics or to associated neurological disease (see Marsden *et al.*, 1975).

A study by Yarden and Discipio (1971) not only supports the idea that choreoathetoid movements may occur in schizophrenia, but also indicates that such movements may be associated with more severe schizophrenic illness. These authors studied 18 schizophrenic patients who exhibited choreoathetoid movements and who had received either no neuroleptic medication or "mild or moderate doses" (exact amounts unspecified) for short periods (Yarden & Discipio, 1971, p. 321) and at a control group of 36 schizophrenic controls who had no evidence of abnormal movements. The movement-disorder group was found to have a much earlier age of onset, a steadily progressive course, a poorer response to medication, and more severe thought disorder than did the control group. However, it should be noted that some of the patients with movement disorders, having been previously treated with neuroleptics, might have developed tardive dyskinesia. Also, it is not clear how much neuroleptic medication, which might have suppressed any abnormal movements in the control group, was given to that group, both before and during the study.

Affective Disorders

Hyperkinetic movement disorders appear to be rare in affective disorders (Marsden *et al.*, 1975). It is true that agitated depressives may repeatedly wring their hands, rub their fingerpads together, or touch their faces, and that manics may exhibit wild flailing of the limbs, but these are usually easily distinguished from athetosis and ballismus, respectively. However, there is some evidence that patients with a subclinical choreoathetoid disorder, such as tardive dyskinesia, may manifest the disorder during depression and not during mania (see Casey, 1984). It should also be noted that there is some evidence for a greater prevalence of tardive dyskinesia in patients with bipolar affective disorder than in patients with schizophrenia (Yassa *et al.*, 1983; Kane *et al.*, 1984).

Hysteria

Choreoathetoid and ballismic movements are relatively rare in hysteria today compared with other motor conditions such as hysterical tremor, but in the early part of this century appear to have been much more common (Ziehen, 1910; Weintraub, 1983). It is difficult to say whether or not many of these early cases of hysterical chorea were really postinfectious in nature, but, considering evidence for a great prevalence of hysterical conversion disorders throughout most of history until recently, it is quite likely that hyperkinetic

movements were relatively common. Ziehen (1910) commented that hysterical chorea tends to resemble chorea minor (Sydenham's chorea), but is
generally more unilateral and rhythmic. Also, the presence of other hysterical
phenomena, as well as evidence for imitative development of the movements,
speaks for a hysterical basis (see also Chapter 21).

Medication-Induced Disorders

From a neuropsychiatric point of view, one of the most important, controversial, and least understood medication-induced hyperkinetic disorders is tardive dyskinesia. This disorder will be more fully discussed in Chapter 26.
There are, in addition, a number of other choreoathetoid disorders, addressed below, that are currently believed to be induced by medications that
are used primarily for psychiatric and neurological disorders.

L-Dopa

One of the commonest and most disturbing side effects of L-dopa in the
treatment of Parkinson's disease is the development of dyskinesias. Although
the dyskinesias are usually choreoathetoid in nature, there is a large diversity
in the types of movements that may be observed, including myoclonus and
blepharospasm (Klawans, 1973). Most often, the movements involve the face
and tongue in a manner similar to tardive dyskinesias, but it appears that L-
dopa-induced hyperkinesias more frequently involve the lower extremities
than does tardive dyskinesia (Karson et al., 1983). The prevalence of L-dopa-
induced dyskinesias is related both to the length of treatment and to the
duration of the disease. In patients with Parkinson's disease of 4 years or less
duration, the prevalence may be as high as 50%, and this increases to as high
as 80% with a duration of 15 years or more (Klawans, 1973). There is no clear
relationship of the prevalence of the dyskinesia to the amount of L-dopa
received.

There is some evidence that L-dopa-induced dyskinesias can be broadly
separated into two groups: those dyskinesias that occur during the period of
maximal clinical improvement with the drug (interdose dyskinesias), and
those that occur at the beginning and the end of the period of clinical
response (onset- and end-of-dose dyskinesias). The former are very commonly observed and clinically appear to be more choreoathetoid in nature,
whereas the latter are less common and appear to be more dystonic or
ballismic (Agid et al., 1979). The latter type of dyskinesia is also associated
with younger and more severely akinetic and rigid patients with Parkinson's
disease.

The pathophysiological mechanism of L-dopa-induced dyskinesias is
unknown, but it has been proposed that the movements result from the effect

of dopamine on neurons that have undergone denervation hypersensitivity. Another possibility is that there is more than one type of dopamine receptor in the striatum, one of which mediates the chorea while another mediates the akinesia (Klawans, 1973). The effect of dopamine on these receptors would be manifest in a patient with Parkinson's as either an improvement in the akinesia, an appearance of dyskinesias, or both, depending on the pathological state of the different dopamine receptors. This could explain why akinesia and dyskinesia can occur separately or together in different patients.

Several therapeutic strategies are available to combat the dyskinesias. The simplest and most effective is merely to reduce the dose of L-dopa, which procedure often reverses the condition. However, this is usually at the expense of worsening parkinsonian symptoms and signs. Also, this strategy of reducing and possibly fractionating the dose does not seem to be of much benefit for the onset- and end-of-dose dyskinesias. Increasing reliance on anticholinergics and amantadine may be of benefit, but usually the benefit is small. Neuroleptic medications, such as haloperidol, may be used, but these too may exacerbate the parkinsonism.

Anticonvulsants

Both phenytoin and carbamazepine have been reported to cause choreoathetoid and dystonic movements (Kooiker & Sumi, 1974; Shuttleworth et al., 1974; Chadwick et al., 1976; Joyce & Gunderson, 1980). The choreoathetoid disorders caused by these drugs occur as a toxic manifestation of the drugs, and they are almost always reversible when the dosage is decreased or the medication stopped. The dyskinesias can occur in the absence of other toxic signs and in the presence of an apparent "therapeutic" plasma level. The movements themselves resemble those of tardive dyskinesia and other neuroleptic-withdrawal dyskinesias. The mechanism by which these drugs cause dyskinesias is unknown, but it has been suggested that the dopamine–acetylcholine balance in the striatum may be affected by toxic levels of these medications. Appropriate treatment consists of reduction or discontinuation of the medication. The movements usually abate within 4 weeks after terminating the drug.

Stimulants

It has long been known that stimulants can produce a variety of abnormal movements, including those of choreoathetoid nature. A number of stimulants have been reported to cause dyskinesias. These stimulants include amphetamine (Lundh & Tunving, 1981), methylphenidate (Weiner et al., 1978), and pemoline (Nausieda et al., 1981). The movements usually involve the face, but the limbs and trunk may also be involved. It appears that this disorder can occur not only in stimulant abusers, but also in children treated for attention-deficit disorders. The movements can rarely last for months or years after the stimulants have been discontinued. Here, as in the previously mentioned causes of dyskinesia, altered striatal dopaminergic sensitivity has been proposed as the pathophysiological mechanism.

Lithium

Choreoathetosis can occur as a sign of lithium toxicity. It usually occurs in association with other signs of lithium neurotoxicity (Apte & Langston, 1983; Zorumski & Bakris, 1983). It has been suggested that if symptoms and signs of lithium neurotoxicity are present and the lithium level is clearly in the toxic range, then immediate hemodialysis should be seriously considered.

Transient Neuroleptic Withdrawal Dyskinesia

This represents a syndrome that clinically is very similar to tardive dyskinesia, but that has an onset within several days of neuroleptic discontinuation and abates within 6 months (Gardos et al., 1978). Within the 6-month period, there is, as yet, no good way to differentiate this syndrome from persistent tardive dyskinesia, and the underlying mechanism is thought to be similar.

CHAPTER FOUR

Hyperactivity, Akathisia, and Related Conditions

INTRODUCTION

In this chapter we shall discuss conditions that involve a generalized increase in movement, including such disorders as hyperactivity, akathisia, and certain syndromes of motor restlessness.

Hyperactivity, agitation, restlessness, fidgetiness, and other words are often used interchangeably to describe states of increased activity. Unlike clinical states marked by focal or multifocal increases in movement, conditions marked by a generalized increase in activity are much less well defined, and many different terms exist that appear to describe similar conditions. In fact, the existing criteria for discriminating between different clinical states marked by hyperactivity are dependent more on the accompanying features of each of the conditions than on the differences in the clinical appearance of the hyperactive states themselves. This has resulted in considerable diagnostic confusion, especially as regards disorders in which hyperactivity is the primary feature. Questions are still raised, for example, as to the diagnostic validity of such disorders as minimal brain dysfunction or attention-deficit disorder with hyperactivity.

Hyperactivity is a word that has come to be primarily associated with disorders of excessive activity in children, and for many years was thought to relate to some type of brain damage. Early in this century, investigators described children with varying degrees of brain damage who demonstrated hyperactive behavior (Still, 1902; Tredgold, 1908). The work of later investigators, such as Strauss and Lehtinen (1947) and Ounsted (1955), further contributed to the idea that hyperkinesis in children is associated with brain damage. Such terms as "hyperkinetic syndrome" and "minimal brain damage" arose, and were often used indiscriminately. Other investigators, such as Childers (1935), Bax and McKeith (1963), and Rutter *et al.* (1970), noted that there was little evidence for brain damage in many of these hyperactive children, and these and other researchers contributed to a shift in emphasis from a biological view of these disorders, to behavioral and psychoanalytic views. The term "minimal brain damage" was changed to "minimal brain dysfunction" (MBD). More recently, another change in focus has occurred, as it has been noted that many children have difficulties with attention and learning just as hyperactive children do, but without the hyperactivity. Thus, the current recommendations for the nosology of these disorders involve considering them primarily as disorders of attention, with or without hyperactivity (American Psychiatric Association, 1980).

Although it was once thought by many researchers that hyperkinetic children improved over the course of early life and that hyperkinesis did not persist into adulthood (Laufer & Denhoff, 1957), there is now a large body of evidence indicating that this is not so (Weiss *et al.*, 1979; Amado & Lustman, 1982). Findings such as these have stimulated some interesting questions regarding the nature of the hyperkinetic syndrome and its relationship to other disorders, both in children and adults. In children, the relationship of hyperkinetic disorders to affective disorders is unclear. Many hyperkinetic children are depressed and many depressed children are agitated and overactive, often making the distinction between the two difficult. In addition, both disorders may respond to antidepressant medication, leading to further confusion. Some children with Tourette's syndrome or learning disabilities also demonstrate difficulties maintaining attentional focus and may be hyperactive at times. In adults, hyperactivity can be observed in mania or hypomania as well as in schizophrenia and other disorders. It is likely that many adults with attention-deficit disorders that persist into adulthood are misdiagnosed as having other psychiatric or neurological conditions.

Akathisia is another syndrome of excessive activity which can occur both in adults and children. The word was originally applied to hysterical patients, and was coined in 1902 by Haskovec from the Greek terms meaning "not sitting still." Bing (1923, 1939), Wilson, and others (see Freyhan, 1958) associated it with parkinsonism, both of the idiopathic and postencephalitic varieties. It was considered to be a rare manifestation of these disorders. Within the past 20 to 30 years it has become very common, however, because it is one of the most frequently observed side effects of neuroleptic drugs. Another syndrome that is sometimes confused with akathisia is restless-legs syndrome, or Ekbom's syndrome. Although the syndrome has been observed for decades, attention was first drawn to it in 1944 by Ekbom. It has since proven to be a distinct clinical entity, and is probably quite common.

DESCRIPTIONS

Hyperactivity

Hyperactivity, as mentioned earlier, can describe many different states of excessive movement, and therefore it is difficult to give to the term a single definition that encompasses all the states. Most investigators use the term to describe a state in which the patient demonstrates an inability to sit still, impulsive running, jumping, and other behaviors, and excessive speech, fidgetiness, and restlessness. These are often accompanied by attentional difficulty, irritability, and emotional lability. The term "hyperactivity" was used for many years as a name for a single disorder seen in children, but the more recent trend is to regard the term as a name for a sign that may be seen in the syndrome of attention-deficit disorder, and not as a name for the disorder itself.

The focus in the past on hyperactivity as a syndrome has resulted in few investigators' venturing a definition for hyperactivity as a sign. For example, Denckla and Heilman's (1979) definition of hyperactivity as a sign of "excessive restlessness or inappropriate non-goal-directed movement" (p. 574) is representative of many definitions, in that it does not exclude many types of hyperkinetic movement disorders, such as chorea, tremor, or myoclonus. Such definitions basically equate hyperactivity with hyperkinesis, but most authors do not really intend these terms to be equivalent. In this book we shall use the term hyperactivity in a more restricted sense, to indicate a state of prolonged (longer than several minutes) generalized increased activity that is largely involuntary but may be subject to some voluntary control. It is not highly stereotyped but, rather, manifests as continuous changes in total body posture or in excessive performance of some simple activity such as pacing under inappropriate circumstances. Unlike conditions such as dystonia musculorum deformans, which can also manifest as a continuous change in posture, hyperactivity involves movements that resemble normal changes in position but occur more rapidly and to an excessive degree.

Akathisia

Akathisia may be considered to be a special type of hyperactivity. In its mildest form, however, it may exist only as a subjective feeling of desiring or needing to move, rather than as clinically apparent hyperactivity. The uncomfortable subjective feeling is the most consistent indicator of akathisia, although some patients with communication difficulties might not be able to verbalize this feeling clearly. The feeling is rarely painful and is often exceedingly difficult for the patient to describe. Though usually more localized to the legs, it may involve the entire body. On rare occasions it may be asymmetrical or unilateral. The patients sometimes experience partial relief of the sensation when they move about, but it usually promptly returns with cessation of activity. Commonly, patients are observed to stand and shift their weight from one leg to the other, or to repeatedly cross and uncross their legs while sitting. When it is more severe the patients may pace up and down the halls or continuously shuffle their feet while sitting. At its most severe, patients exhibit constant frenzied motion: running, jumping, or tearing at their throats or other parts of their bodies in agony. In this latter state, patients are at risk for suicide (Shear *et al.*, 1983). Although akathisia is sometimes considered to be associated with parkinsonism, it can occur in the absence of any other parkinsonian symptoms or signs.

DIFFERENTIAL DIAGNOSIS

There are a number of conditions that can resemble hyperactivity as described above. Choreoathetoid movements, especially in the early stages, can appear to be similar to hyperactivity, but, in general, choreoathetoid movements are, at any one point in time, focal or multifocal movements in isolated muscular groups, and can usually be differentiated from generalized excessive activity. Still, some children with Sydenham's chorea are occasionally misdiagnosed initially as being hyperactive, but the diagnosis usually becomes clear as the disorder progresses and if, as is usually the case, there is no history of past hyperactive behavior. Because the movements of hyperactivity appear as excessively performed normal movements, disorders such as dystonia musculorum deformans or other dystonias can usually be easily differentiated. Tremors, tics, and stereotypies can also usually be ruled out because these signs are highly repetitive in nature, although some complex tics such as occur in Tourette's syndrome may be variable enough and subject to enough voluntary control to make a diagnosis difficult.

Akathisia, as a specific type of hyperactivity, must be differentiated from other conditions that accompany parkinsonism or result from neuroleptic medications. In patients with Parkinson's disease, akathisia must be differentiated from anxiety. Similarly, many patients with anxiety disorders or with anxiety accompanying another primary psychiatric disorder (such as schizophrenia or depression) are often treated with neuroleptic medications, and the resulting symptoms of akathisia must be carefully differentiated from the underlying anxiety. The desire to move is the cardinal feature of akathisia, and separates it from anxiety. Also, akathisia is not usually accompanied by the pulse and blood-pressure elevations that often occur in anxious states.

Akathisia must also be differentiated from tardive dyskinesia. Munetz and Cornes (1983) offer the following suggestions to help distinguish between these two: (1) subjective distress is present in akathisia and usually not in tardive dyskinesia; (2) akathitic movements are voluntary responses to subjective distress,[1] whereas tardive dyskinetic movements, although susceptible to small amounts of voluntary control, are mainly involuntary in nature; (3) akathisia is usually of much earlier onset (less than 3 days for oral drugs, 1 to 4 days for intramuscular depot drugs); (4) the movements of akathisia are usually more centered in the lower extremities, although they can be generalized, whereas the movements of tardive dyskinesia usually involve the face, jaw, and tongue; (5) other extrapyramidal signs, such as akinesia and tremor, much more frequently accompany akathisia than they do tardive dyskinesia; (6) the responses of the two to pharmacologic intervention are different, with akathisia occasionally responding to anticholinergic agents (tardive dyskinesia usually does not) and usually improving with a reduction in neuroleptic dosage and worsening with an increase in it (tardive dyskinesia frequently improves with an increase and worsens with a reduction).

PATHOPHYSIOLOGY

Hyperactivity

One of the major problems involved in trying to uncover the pathophysiological mechanisms for hyperactive disorders is that it is not clear whether hyperactivity is the primary manifestation of some underlying brain dysfunction or merely represents a secondary response of the patient to a more basic problem. For example, in the syndrome of attention-deficit disorder, some investigators, such as Satterfield (1973), have postulated that the observed excessive motor activity represents an attempt to increase sensory input. Similarly, the motor restlessness observed in akathisia is thought by many to be the response of the patient to subjective unease, and not a primary phenomenon.

Nevertheless, a number of theories have been advanced for a neurological cause of hyperactivity in children. Some have held that the problem lies in the frontal lobes, because frontal-lobe lesions in animals and man can result in excessive activity (Denckla & Heilman, 1979; Laufer & Shetty, 1980). In keeping with this hypothesis, it has been argued that there may be a maturational lag in the development and myelinization of the frontal (especially prefrontal) cortex. Other theorists have focused on disturbances of the reticular activating system as the cause of the hyperactive behavior and possibly of the attentional problems as well (see Laufer & Shetty, 1980). Because of the response of many of the affected children to stimulants, some researchers were led to propose catecholamine theories of hyperactivity. Most of these

[1]It should be noted that many patients with akathisia appear to have no control over their hyperactive state.

have concentrated on abnormalities of either dopamine (DA) receptors or their turnover (Arnold *et al.*, 1973; Shetty & Chase, 1976), although abnormalities in norepinephrine have also been postulated (Shekim *et al.*, 1978). At present, the evidence in support of any of these hypotheses is unconvincing.

Experiments on animals are, of course, difficult to interpret when dealing with analogues of so complex a disorder as human hyperactivity. Still, many animal studies have also implicated dopaminergic mechanisms as being involved in hyperactivity or hypermotility. Some studies have shown that, in particular, the nucleus accumbens may be involved, in that hypermotility can result from injections of DA agonists into this region (Pijnenburg & Van Rossum, 1973; Jackson *et al.*, 1975). More recently, it has been proposed that the globus pallidus (GP) is involved in the production of hyperactive states, because the injection of γ-aminobutyric acid (GABA) into the GP causes a decrease in hypermotility resulting from dopaminergic stimulation of the nucleus accumbens, and that DA-induced hypermotility is associated with elevated rates of neuronal firing in the GP (see Everett *et al.*, 1984). Everett *et al.* (1984) have also proposed that hypermotility in animals is seen after low doses of DA agonists and is mediated by the GP, whereas stereotypies and posturing are seen after high doses and are mediated by the substantia nigra pars reticulata.

Akathisia

Akathisia has also been postulated to involve abnormalities of dopaminergic transmission in the brain. Marsden and Jenner (1980) have hypothesized that akathisia may result from dopaminergic blockade in mesocortical dopaminergic pathways. They noted that destruction or blockade of these pathways may produce excessive motor activity, just the reverse of what occurs when nigrostriatal or mesolimbic dopaminergic pathways are blockaded. This would mean that akathisia may be pathophysiologically different from other neuroleptic-induced extrapyramidal signs, an idea for which there is some clinical support (see Chapter 23). For example, all of the other acute neuroleptic-induced extrapyramidal signs usually respond quickly and well to anticholinergic medications, whereas akathisia often proves to be unresponsive to such agents. Recent reports of the efficacy of propranolol in akathisia (Adler *et al.*, 1985) indicate that, at least in some cases, noradrenergic mechanisms may be important as well.

The underlying basis for other disorders marked by hyperactivity is even less well known than the above. Restless-legs syndrome, because it is often accompanied by myoclonus (Boghen & Peyronnard, 1976), has been thought to result from dysfunction in the central nervous system, but the exact site is unknown. Other disorders marked by hyperactivity, such as stimulant-induced states and mania, have been related to excessive norepinephrine activity in the brain, but, again, the exact mechanism of action is unknown.

SYNDROMES IN WHICH HYPERACTIVITY OCCURS

Attention-Deficit Disorder with Hyperactivity

Attention-deficit disorder with hyperactivity is the syndrome that usually comes to mind when the word "hyperactivity" is mentioned. Estimates on the incidence of this syndrome have varied considerably, ranging from 1 in 1,000 to 1 in 5 school-aged children. The true incidence may lie in the range of a few percent of school-aged children, with differences in the reports being due to the variable inclusion of other disorders (such as learning disorders), and the amount of reliance placed on anecdotal information. Boys seem to predominate, with the boy-to-girl ratio being somewhere between 3 to 1 and 10 to 1.

The syndrome may become apparent within the first few days of life, and is almost always evident before second or third grade. Problems are often first noticed when the child begins school and is forced to sit and pay attention for more prolonged periods of time. The syndrome usually does not begin to show signs of remission until the beginning of adolescence. The rate and amount of remission is highly variable, with some children showing complete remission in their early teenage years, whereas other children suffer significantly from various components of the syndrome and complications, especially distractability, beyond the age of 20.

Besides hyperactivity there are a number of other signs and symptoms that may be present. Attentional problems and excessive distractability are, by definition, always present. In addition, impulsivity, emotional lability, poor self-esteem, and antisocial behavior may occur in varying degrees of severity.

The hyperactivity, although usually present in some form, need not always be clinically obvious. Frequently, these children are able, on examination, to suppress the hyperactivity, necessitating heavy reliance on parental and school reports of hyperactive behavior. Sometimes the hyperactivity becomes apparent only at certain times, such as when sitting in church or at the dinner table, with no evidence of it at all when the child is watching television or playing games. The hyperactivity can also be present during sleep, and these children are frequently reported to exhibit motor restlessness at night, sometimes with difficulty falling asleep.

There may be accompanying neurological abnormalities, including EEG abnormalities and the presence of various soft signs (Stevens *et al.*, 1968; Haller & Axelrod, 1975), but it is not clear exactly how these related to the symptoms and signs of the disorder, especially since there are many children in whom no neurological abnormalities can be found.

When the disorder persists into adult life it is usually called *residual attention-deficit disorder* or *adult attention-deficit disorder*. Often, there is no evidence of hyperactivity per se in the adult form. Residual attention-deficit disorder should be kept in mind in the differential diagnosis of adult patients with hyperactivity as some of these patients are diagnosed as having only bipolar affective disorder, schizophrenia, or alcoholism (Plotkin *et al.*, 1982; Amado & Lustman, 1982) and thus may be deprived of appropriate treatment with stimulant medications (see Wood *et al.*, 1976; Wender *et al.*, 1981).

A variety of different treatments have proven effective for patients with attention-deficit disorders and hyperactivity, and in some ways the different response of individuals to various treatments may indicate the presence of subcategories of the disorder. At the present time probably the most effective and certainly the most controversial treatment involves medication. Among these, stimulants are the most widely used, including dextroamphetamine, methylphenidate, and pemoline. Somewhere between two-thirds and three-quarters of hyperactive children respond to these medications, which leaves a significant number who do not. In addition, these medications have troublesome side effects, including weight loss, insomnia, and anorexia, along with gastrointestinal upset, headache, dyskinetic movements, seizures, and possible growth suppression. Other medications, including imipramine and lithium, have been used and may be effective in some children, but these, too, have significant side effects. Because of the problems involved in medicating young children, both in terms of side effects and in terms of psychosocial consequences, many physicians try to limit the amount of medication and use other therapeutic strategies (such as behavioral therapy or other psychotherapies) as much as possible. Other strategies include giving medications only when they are most needed, such as during school, and eliminating or significantly reducing the dosage on weekends and during school vacations.

Akathisia and Other Disorders Involving Hyperactivity

Apart from attention deficit disorder with hyperactivity, there are other disorders presenting in childhood that may include hyperactivity as a major sign. These include Prechtl's choreiform syndrome (discussed in Chapter 3), Tourette's disorder (discussed in Chapter 19), lead poisoning, and depression and mania in children. Hyperactivity may also possibly be caused by perinatal hypoxia, food additives, food and other allergies, and medications that have stimulant properties, such as certain antihistamines.

Akathisia is a sign that may occur in children and adults treated with antipsychotic medications. It appears to be somewhat more common following treatment with higher-potency antipsychotics, such as haloperidol and fluphenazine (Ayd, 1961), but may occur with any antipsychotic, including reserpine (Haase, 1955). Akathisia can occur at any time during treatment, and may appear after the first dose of neuroleptic or after years of neuroleptics (Braude & Barnes, 1983). Estimates on prevalence have varied from 15% to 45%, and probably much of the difference in these estimates is due to the different neuroleptic drugs used (Munetz & Cornes, 1983). Akathisia usually remits following discontinuation of the neuroleptic medication, but this may not always be so, as there are reports of akathisia persisting many months following drug discontinuation; this condition is known as *tardive akathisia* (see Chapter 23).

Many of the patients who take antipsychotic medications are schizophrenic, psychotically depressed, or mentally retarded, and, as a part of the illness, have difficulty describing uncomfortable feelings in a way that is readily understandable. Many of these patients, when distressed, behave in a way suggesting a worsening of the underlying condition, and neuroleptic medications are often increased, which often leads to further clinical decline. It is important to note that any deterioration in the clinical state of patients on neuroleptic medications may be due to the presence of akathisia, regardless of whether the patient is adequately able to voice the uncomfortable feelings (see VanPutten, 1975).

It has been proposed that there may be two forms of akathisia: one that is related to severe parkinsonian signs (and responds to anticholinergic medications), and one that is not (Braude *et al.*, 1983). This hypothesis remains to be verified by other studies, but, if correct, would support the idea of different pathophysiological mechanisms being involved in the production of akathisia. These investigators (Barnes & Braude, 1985) have recently suggested that there may be as many as seven subtypes of akathisia, but this is less clear (Stahl, 1985).

Akathisia may also occur in idiopathic and postencephalitic parkinsonism. Although akathisia was apparently not uncommon in postencephalitic parkinsonism, it is not usually seen in the idiopathic variety. Nevertheless, its occasional appearance is worth keeping in mind, especially in parkinsonian patients who complain of excessive feelings of restlessness and anxiety. It has also been proposed that akathisia occurs in schizophrenia without neuroleptic treatment (Demars, 1966).

The most common treatment for akathisia in this country is the use of anticholinergic agents, some of which are used prophylactically in order to avoid drug-induced extrapyramidal signs and problems with patient compliance. We, however, advocate a trial of dosage reduction of the antipsychotic agent whenever possible. Anticholinergic agents, although effective, are not as effective for akathisia as for other drug-induced extrapyramidal signs and symptoms, and it is not worth subjecting patients to the distressing side effects of anticholinergic agents when frequently a simple dosage reduction of neuroleptic will suffice. In many cases, however, anticholinergic agents must be used. Other agents that have been reported to be effective include benzodiazepines (Donlon, 1973), Greenblatt *et al.*, 1977), and propranolol (Lipinski *et al.*, 1984; Adler *et al.*, 1985).

Restless-Legs Syndrome

Restless-legs syndrome, or Ekbom's syndrome, is frequently confused with akathisia. Like akathisia, the syndrome is characterized by inner discomfort resulting in the patient's wishing to move. The exact relationship of these two disorders is unclear, but there are a number of differences. Restless-legs syndrome occurs without previous exposure to antipsychotics and may occur in the absence of accompanying disorders. It is usually more highly localized to the legs than akathisia, and the uncomfortable feelings are more peripheral in nature, with patients reporting creeping sensations or difficult-to-describe itching feelings deep within their legs. Unlike akathisia, the uncomfortable feelings usually completely disappear with movement, although they, too, are worse with rest. Upon retiring, the patients may note that the sensations gradually appear over the course of 5 to 30 minutes, then gradually cease in a matter of minutes to hours. There are no associated neurological abnormalities. The disorder may begin at any age and may last for years, with periodic exacerbations and remissions. Ekbom (1960) reported an incidence of 5% among 500 healthy normal subjects. In Ekbom's series, the ratio of men to women was approximately 3 to 4.

The disorder may be accompanied by myoclonus, and appears to be exacerbated by anemia. Some have reported restless legs to be extremely common in patients with uremia, with as many as 15% to 20% of the patients who receive dialysis being reported to suffer from the condition (Read *et al.*, 1981).

It is important to differentiate this syndrome from peripheral neuropathies, such as are caused by diabetes or meralgia paraesthetica. Paresthesias secondary to hyperventilation should also be distinguished. More difficult to diagnose is an unusual condition that is marked by delusions of insect infestation (sometimes known as *formication*) and that is one of a group of disorders called *monosymptomatic hypochondriacal delusions*. In this condition, patients experience the delusion that ants or other small creatures are crawling around beneath their skin (see Munro, 1980). Here, it is important to note any other symptoms of psychosis or delirium that may be present, as is seen in cases of severe alcohol withdrawal.

Most treatment methods for restless legs syndrome have met with limited success. Vasodilator drugs have been tried, with some improvement, as well as iron therapy in patients with anemia (Ekbom, 1960). More recently, clonazepam has proven to be quite helpful, especially in cases occurring in patients with uremia (Boghen, 1980; Read *et al.*, 1981).

Wandering

It is a common observation that elderly patients with disorientation, confusion, or dementia may move about in an apparently aimless manner, a phenomenon known as wandering. Because such patients have been observed to be more active than their nonwandering counterparts (Snyder *et al.*, 1978), wandering must be considered in the differential diagnosis of hyperactivity in the elderly. Wandering has been shown to occur more frequently in persons who, premorbidly, were more active in leisure activities and whose behavioral style and coping mechanisms involved motoric activities such as pacing (Monsour & Robb, 1982). Wandering is an important contributing factor to falls and hip fractures in the aged, and as such should be monitored carefully. Since a number of demented patients are treated with neuroleptics, it is important to differentiate wandering from akathisia, and a reduction in the dosage of neuroleptic or addition of an anticholinergic drug may be helpful in this regard. Wandering should also be differentiated from somnambulism (see Chapter 24). The treatment of wandering may prove difficult, but structuring the environment and using behavior-modification techniques may be useful (Monsour & Robb, 1982; Hussian, 1982).

Apart from the above conditions, hyperactivity may be seen in cases of anxiety, hypomania, mania, schizophrenia (especially catatonic excitement), and hysteria, as well as in cases of hypoglycemia and hyperthyroidism.

CHAPTER FIVE

Tremor

INTRODUCTION

Tremor has been recognized clinically for almost 2,000 years, clearly being noted by Galen (McHenry, 1969) and undoubtedly observed long before his time. There is, however, little evidence that different types of tremor were carefully distinguished until the famous physician Sylvius made the following observations over 300 years ago:

. . . The Animal Spirits are mov'd Unequally, Inordinatly and beside, or against the Will through the Nervs to the moveable Parts in a Convulsive Motion, and force Trembling, or Shaking of the Lims. For this troublesom Trembling, though the Body rest and lie down, is to be distinguisht from the Trembling Motion . . . which ceases when the Body is at rest, and returns again the same being mov'd. . . . The Convulsive Motion whether Universal, or Particular, procedes from the encreas'd but alternat Motion of the Animals Spirits against the opposite Muscles. (Le Boë [Sylvius], 1675, pp. 385–386)

This remarkable passage not only represents the first clinical separation of resting from postural or intention tremor, but is also one of the first clear attempts to divide a particular disorder of movement into different forms.

DESCRIPTION

"Tremor" refers to a simple involuntary movement consisting of rhythmical oscillations of a part of the body about a fixed point. It can occur in any part of the body subserved by striated muscle. Most types of tremor attenuate or disappear during sleep (except physiological tremor-at-rest) and almost all are made worse with stress and anxiety.

Investigators differ as to how to subdivide tremors. Tremors have been classified according to their appearance, the conditions under which they occur, and their putative underlying anatomical substrates and physiological mechanisms. These different classification schemes have resulted in great confusion. Practically every type of tremor has been confused with every other type. For example, what one person has called an action tremor, another has called postural, essential, or intention tremor. Postural tremor has been confused with resting tremor. Parkinsonian tremor has been called a resting tremor, and yet many investigators do not believe this tremor occurs with true rest.

Part of the problem lies in the fact that the dividing lines between different types of tremors are not as clear as often believed. For example, the resting tremor of Parkinson's disease often persists during activity, and the intention tremor of cerebellar disease does not always cease with rest. Another example concerns the widely held belief that parkinsonian tremor consists of alternating contraction of antagonistic muscles, whereas essential tremor consists of coactivation of antagonists. There is evidence that coactivation can occur in the tremor of Parkinson's disease and that alternation can occur in essential tremor (Stein & Lee, 1981).

From the point of view of clinical description, it is most helpful to subtype the various tremors according to their gross appearance and the circumstances under which they appear. Such a subdivision is presented in Table 5-1. Possible mechanisms of different tremors will be discussed in the later sections of this chapter.

PATHOPHYSIOLOGY

Before we discuss the putative mechanisms of individual tremors it may be helpful to review briefly some theoretical issues regarding the properties of oscillating systems, discussed in the Appendix. Basically, oscillatory movements can take place either as a result of (1) the mechanical characteristics of the system, (2) the oscillatory tendencies of short-loop reflexes, (3) the oscillatory tendencies of long-loop reflexes, or (4) the oscillatory tendencies of higher-level closed-loop feedback control systems. Before we proceed, it should be mentioned that this fourth type of oscillation—central oscillation—is so poorly understood that there may be other mechanisms accounting for some forms of it. Because not all central oscillations may be dependent on either inter- or intraneuronal closed-loop feedback mechanisms (for example, some central oscillations are probably linked to external rhythms such as day–night or seasonal cycles), we shall refer to central oscillations as those that do not appear to depend on peripheral feedback mechanisms.

With this theoretical introduction we may now look at the different types of tremors to see what mechanisms may apply in each. We shall discuss these issues in the section following differential diagnosis.

Table 5-1. Types of Tremors, Divided According to Clinical Characteristics

Tremor type	Other names	Frequency (cycles per second)		Muscle pattern	Putative mechanism
		Common range	Total range		
Physiological tremors					
Physiological resting tremor		11-13	5-15	—	Cardioballistic impulse and passive resonances of limbs
Physiological postural tremor		8-12	1-25	Mainly coactivation	Unknown
Abnormal tremors					
Tremor-in-repose	Resting Parkinsonian Static Striatal Postural	4-7	3-9	Mainly alternation	Oscillations in long-latency reflexes?/thalamic generator?
Postural tremor	Action Kinetic	8-10	3-12	Mainly coactivation	Unknown/oscillations in spinal reflexes?
Intention tremor	Cerebellar Action Endpoint	3-5	1-7	Mainly alternation	Oscillations in long-latency reflexes?
Axial tremor	Truncal Postural	3	1-3	Mainly alternation	Oscillations in long-latency reflexes?
Tremor-like phenomena					
Clonus		5-8		Mainly alternation	Oscillations in spinal reflexes
Rhythmic myoclonus (palatal)		2		—	Unknown

DIFFERENTIAL DIAGNOSIS

Tremor must be carefully differentiated from other types of hyperkinesia. In general, the irregularity of hyperkinetic states such as chorea, ballismus, and athetosis, and the complexity of stereotypies clearly separate these signs from tremor. However, it should be noted that athetosis may have a tremorous component. Rhythmic myoclonus may be difficult to differentiate from tremor, but the pattern of tremor is usually more sinusoidal and regular than myoclonus. Palatal myoclonus may be especially difficult to differentiate from tremor, as it is usually very regular and often involves extraocular and shoulder muscles. In fact, some researchers have advocated considering palatal myoclonus to be a type of tremor. (See Chapter 1.)

Akathisia may occasionally resemble tremor, but can usually be distinguished by the subjective discomfort that accompanies it, although tremor may be associated with states of anxiety. Also, akathitic movements often appear to involve more complex activities, such as leg-shifting or hand-rubbing, than does tremor. (See Chapters 3 and 23.)

Asterixis is a condition marked by repeated, brief losses of tone in antigravity muscles. Occasionally, asterixis may resemble tremor, especially postural or intention tremors. Electromyographically, asterixis can be easily differentiated from tremor by the silent periods on EMG that usually last approximately 0.1 second. Asterixis usually accompanies hepatic or renal encephalopathy, although it can also be seen in pulmonary failure, malabsorption syndromes, and anticonvulsant therapy, and can occur as a result of lesions in the brainstem and thalamus (Leavitt & Tyler, 1964).

Simple repetitive tics may resemble tremors, but the tics usually have a more complex appearance, are slower, and are usually more complex. (See Chapter 7.)

Finally, tremor should be differentiated from shivering and shuddering, which are normal physiological responses to cold and severe stress and are more generalized than most tremors. However, there is evidence that shuddering attacks in some children may be a precursor of essential tremor, especially when associated with posturing (Vanasse et al., 1976).

TYPES OF TREMOR

Physiological Tremor

The clinical entity that has variously been called normal or physiological tremor has undergone many recent conceptual changes. It is now clear that one must distinguish between physiological tremor-at-rest and tremor-with-action (or postural physiological tremor), and that the frequency range of physiological tremor is much greater than was previously believed. Many investigators in the past considered the range of physiological tremor to be around 8 to 12 cycles per second, whereas it is now believed that the range may be as great as 1 to 25 cycles per second.

Thus, physiological tremor is much more complex than was previously thought. If we focus first on the normal physiological tremor-at-rest, it appears that this tremor is a product of mechanical effects arising from the beating of the heart (Brumlick & Yap, 1970). The mechanical effects of the heart, which are reflected in the ballistocardiogram (BCG), induce passive resonances in the limbs, most powerfully in the 8-to-12-cycle-per-second range. This passive tremor is influenced by sympathomimetic drugs, alcohol, and physiological states that affect cardiac rate and output. It may also be the only tremor (with the possible exception of palatal myoclonus, which some neurologists consider to be a tremor) that does not abate during sleep.

Physiological action or postural tremor, although also containing a BCG component, largely arises as the result of other, more poorly understood, mechanisms. Any underlying BCG component probably does not account for more than 10% of normal postural tremor (Marsden et al., 1969a). The exact mechanisms of this tremor are still debated. It is likely that many factors are involved, and that, in various disease states, different factors may be pathologically exaggerated. For example, there is evidence that segmental spinal reflexes play a role (see Hagbarth & Young, 1979). Yet, physiological tremor does not seem to be totally dependent on the synchronizing tendencies of the stretch reflex, for it can persist after deafferentation (Marsden et al., 1967b), and the tendency toward synchronization of discharges itself does not appear to be very strong (Allum et al., 1978).

The fact that physiological tremor can be enhanced with β-adrenergic stimulation, such as occurs with hyperthyroidism, anxiety, or isoproterenol infusion, has led to proposals that the β-adrenergic system plays a role (Marsden et al., 1967a, 1969b). Although it is clear that catecholamines are involved in accentuated physiological tremor, their exact role in normal physiological tremor remains undefined.

In conclusion, it is likely that a number of mechanisms are involved in the production of physiological tremor, including (1) synchronizing tendencies of segmental spinal reflexes and (2) mechanical resonant properties of the body. In addition, there may also be contributions from (3) interactions among the firing patterns of motor units involved in maintaining muscular contraction and (4) some as yet unspecified central oscillatory component (see Stein & Lee, 1981).

Tremor-in-Repose, or Resting Tremor

This tremor, which, in man, has been studied almost exclusively in Parkinson's disease, consists of a clear alternation in contraction between agonists and antagonists. There is substantial evidence for a predominantly central origin of resting tremor. Lesions surgically placed in dentatorubrothalamic or corticopallidothalamic pathways frequently alleviate resting tremor, whereas transection of dorsal roots does not obliterate it (see Young & Shahani, 1979). Further, unlike physiological tremor, clear bursts in the 4-to-7-cycle-per-second range are evident on EMG. Central-nervous-system mechanisms are thus important in the generation of resting tremor. This is further supported by the fact that it is difficult to reset the phase of parkinsonian tremor by external mechanical means (Lee & Stein, 1981). The ease of resetting the phase of a particular tremor is thought to be related to the involvement of spinal reflex mechanisms in the tremor. It should be noted, however, that the phase of resting tremor can be reset to a mild degree (Teravainen et al., 1979), which indicates that there may be some peripheral contribution.

Exactly where in the central nervous system tremor-in-repose originates is not clear. The fact that a number of patients with Parkinson's disease improve with L-dopa has led to studies attempting to substantiate the role of the nigrostriatal tract in resting tremor. Unfortunately, tremor-in-repose is one of the least responsive signs of Parkinson's disease to L-dopa and is, in fact, more responsive to anticholinergic drugs. It is therefore not surprising that most animal studies have shown that lesions of the substantia nigra alone do not give rise to tremor. It appears that damage to other areas around the substantia nigra, especially to the ventral tegmental area, is necessary (Ohye et al., 1979). The tremor of Parkinson's disease is nonetheless partially responsive to L-dopa and is present in perhaps greater than 95% of patients with Parkinson's disease (Dupont, 1980), which indicates some connection with the nigrostriatal dopamine tract.

Thus, any theory of the pathophysiology of resting tremor must take into account several lines of evidence:

1. The tremor is not completely dependent on intact dorsal roots (Pollock & Davis, 1930).
2. The tremor can be influenced to some extent by peripheral manipulations (e.g., the phase of the tremor can be reset by limb displacements) (Teravainen et al., 1979; Rack & Ross, 1986).
3. The nigrostriatal dopamine system is probably involved in the tremor, but to an unknown degree.
4. Lesions of the ventrolateral thalamus can consistently abolish resting tremor on the contralateral side (Cooper, 1969).

Although tremor-in-repose could possibly be explained in terms of a central tremor generator alone, the above evidence indicates that both peripheral and central factors may play a role (Rack & Ross, 1986). Recently, it has been proposed that long-latency reflexes might be involved in the production of resting tremor, and that this could explain the involvement of both central and peripheral factors (Teravainen *et al.*, 1979). The long-latency loop may extend as follows: (1) motor cortex down to lower motor centers, (2) up to cerebellum, (3) then to ventrolateral thalamus, and (4) back to motor cortex. Because the globus pallidus also outputs into the ventrolateral thalamus, abnormal globus pallidus output could theoretically change the gain or loop time of the long-loop reflex, sending it into oscillation. This model would also explain substantia nigra involvement in tremor, for lesions in the nigrostriatal pathway alter globus pallidus output (Filion, 1979). This model is similar to one proposed by Cooper (1969), where either aberrant globus pallidus or cerebellar input into the ventrolateral thalamus could cause tremor, with aberrant globus pallidus output causing more of a resting tremor with rigidity, and aberrant cerbellar input causing more of an intention tremor and hypotonia. Cooper focused more on the possibility of a thalamic pacemaker for tremor than on considering the thalamus as part of a large feedback loop. These theories, though interesting, await further experimental verification.

Postural or Action Tremor

Most of the research on postural tremors has been performed on essential tremor, the most common abnormal tremor. Unlike tremor-in-repose, postural tremor develops when a part of the body is involved in maintaining a position requiring a constant input of energy. Although there may occasionally be a small alternating component, postural tremors usually involve a coactivation of antagonistic muscles rather than a clear alternation. Postural tremors of the limbs often appear to be more flexor–extensor in nature as opposed to the pronator–supinator muscle involvement seen in tremor-in-repose.

The mechanism of postural tremor is unclear. There appears to be more peripheral component than is observed in tremor-in-repose, as evidenced by the higher resetting index of essential tremor (Lee & Stein, 1981). Some have proposed that the peripheral component involves β-adrenergic mechanisms, because propranolol can effectively abolish the tremor in many patients. However, the β-adrenergic contribution to the tremor probably occurs within the central rather than peripheral nervous system. Peripheral β-adrenergic receptors function normally in patients with essential tremor, and intravenous propranolol does not acutely diminish essential tremor, whereas long-term propranolol therapy does (Young *et al.*, 1975).

The anatomical basis of postural tremor is unknown, but it has been proposed that a circuit including the cerebellum, red nucleus, and inferior olive is involved (Lee & Stein, 1981). In general, it appears that there are both central and peripheral contributions to postural tremor similar to those in physiological tremor, but the exact mechanisms are unknown.

Intention Tremor

"Intention tremor" refers to a tremor that occurs during a voluntary movement whereby oscillations are noted around the desired trajectory of movement during its execution. Usually, the tremor is most severe at the endpoint of the movement.

Intention tremor is characteristically produced with disease or injury to the cerebellum; therefore, most of the proposed mechanisms for intention tremor have involved this structure. Most investigators have proposed that there is dysfunction of cerebellar outflow tracts, at the level of either the deep cerebellar nuclei (especially the dentate nucleus), the superior cerebellar peduncle, or the red nucleus. There are occasional references to a specific tremor, the so-called *rubral tremor*, thought to be due to lesions of the red nucleus, but some investigators doubt the existence of this tremor as an entity separate from intention tremor, although it does appear to contain a postural component (Stein & Lee, 1981).

Of all tremors, intention tremor most closely resembles the pattern of an underdamped feedback control system described in the Appendix. In keeping with this, Mauritz *et al.* (1981) discovered that long-latency reflexes are delayed in late cerebellar atrophy, and they postulated this to be part of the mechanism for cerebellar axial tremor. These investigators further noted that the dominant frequency of this axial tremor (usually around 3 cycles per second) decreases with an increase in long-loop latency as cerebellar atrophy becomes more severe.

There is no well-accepted treatment of intention tremor. No pharmacologic agents are beneficial (Koller, 1984). However, adding weights to a tremorous limb may reduce the amplitude of the tremor. There is evidence that stimulation of deep brain structures in the contralateral midbrain and basal ganglia may suppress the tremor (Brice & McLellan, 1980).

It should be noted that cerebellar damage not only produces intention tremor, but in some cases postural and possibly a resting tremor, as well (Young & Shahani, 1979; Jankovic & Fahn, 1980).

SYNDROMES IN WHICH TREMOR OCCURS

Table 5-2 offers a listing of important causes of tremor, divided according to type of tremor. In the remainder of this section we shall discuss some specific disorders in which tremor occurs.

Parkinsonism

The two most common conditions in which tremor-in-repose is observed are idiopathic Parkinson's disease and neuroleptic-induced parkinsonism. In

Table 5-2. Disorders in Which Tremor Occurs, Divided According to Type of Tremor

---

Accentuated physiological postural tremor

Metabolic: including hypoglycemia, thyrotoxicosis, pheochromocytosis

β-Agonist drug-induced: including caffeine, theophylline, theobromine, isoproterenol, isoetharine, metaproterenol, terbutaline, dextroamphetamine, methylphenidate, pemoline

Other drug-induced: including lithium, tricyclic antidepressants, monoamine oxidase inhibitors, neuroleptics, L-dopa, sodium valproate, corticosteroids

Neuropathic: including diabetic polyneuropathy, uremic polyneuropathy, paretic neurosyphilis, Guillain–Barré (Said *et al.*, 1982)

Alcohol and opiate withdrawal

Anxiety and fatigue

Abnormal postural tremor

Essential tremor (autosomal dominant and sporadic)

Senile tremor

Parkinsonism

Wilson's disease

Charcot–Marie–Tooth disease

Torsion dystonia, such as torticollis

Tremor-in-repose (resting tremor)

Parkinson's disease

Parkinsonism due to other causes: including neuroleptic-induced, postencephalitic, disease and damage to the basal ganglia

Wilson's disease

Striatonigral degeneration

Olivopontocerebellar atrophy

Progressive supranuclear palsy

Shy–Drager disease

Normal pressure hydrocephalus

Poisons: including mercury (hatter's shakes), arsenic, manganese, phosphorus, carbon monoxide

---

Intention tremor

Cerebellar degenerations

Cerebellar damage

Damage or disease of cerebellar connections

Severe Parkinson's disease

Severe essential tremor

Wilson's disease

Multiple sclerosis

Drug-induced: including phenytoin, carbamazepine, barbiturates, alcohol, mercury spite of many similarities, there are differences between the tremors observed in these two disorders. Tremor in idiopathic Parkinson's disease is usually one of the first symptoms to occur, whereas in drug-induced parkinsonism, it is one of the later extrapyramidal side effects to appear. Ayd (1961) reported tremor to be a presenting sign of neuroleptic extrapyramidal effects in only about a third of patients and to eventually develop in only 60%. This is in contrast with idiopathic Parkinson's disease, where over half the patients have tremor as an early presenting sign, and most patients usually develop it at some time during the course of their illness. There are also some differences in appearance between the two tremors, with neuroleptic-induced tremor being usually (though by no means always) more symmetrical than is idiopathic tremor.

The tremor-in-repose of both idiopathic and neuroleptic-induced parkinsonism often begins with a subjective sensation of tremor before the actual tremor is clinically apparent. Sometimes the tremor can be uncovered at this stage by having the patient perform finger-tapping with each hand, whereby the patient can sometimes be seen to accelerate gradually the speed of tapping until the 4-to-7-cycle-per-second range is reached.

Tremor-in-repose usually begins distally in an upper limb and, as the condition progresses, spreads along one side of the body and begins to involve the other side. The head, neck, and face may become involved, but this is unusual. In fact, if head tremor appears in the absence of distal tremor and other signs of parkinsonism, a diagnosis of essential tremor is likely.

Tremor-in-repose may vary in frequency and amplitude between different parts of the body over time. It can persist into the performance of an action, but attenuates with sleep and true rest (although it may transiently appear during rapid-eye-movement sleep).

There are at least two types of tremor in Parkinson's disease, and probably in drug-induced parkinsonism as well: (1) the classic tremor-in-repose and (2) a higher-frequency postural tremor. It is important to note that the cogwheel phenomenon, wherein a ratchet-like rigidity is perceived with passive flexion and extension about a joint, is related to the postural tremor of parkinsonism, and not to the tremor-in-repose (Lance et al., 1963; Findley et al., 1981). Other types of tremor that have been described in Parkinson's disease include accentuated physiological tremor, myoclonic tremor, and a distinctive writing tremor (see Young & Shahani, 1979).

Essential Tremor

Essential tremor has long been known to be quite common, and a recent study reports a prevalence of approximately 4% in persons over 40 years of age (Haerer et al., 1982). Other studies have found a prevalence in the 1% to 7% range (Dupont, 1980). There is no clear consensus as to the male/female prevalence ratio, but in general the prevalence appears to be approximately equal across genders.

Essential tremor usually involves the upper limbs, neck, and head, and occasionally may be seen in the lower limbs. The vocal cords and pharyngeal musculature may be involved, but trunk involvement is uncommon (Critchley, 1972). The tremor is worse with anxiety, writing, and β-adrenergic stimulation, and is improved with β-adrenergic blockade and alcohol. The frequent head involvement and exacerbation with writing are two helpful signs in differentiating this tremor from tremor-in-repose, which rarely involves the head and often improves with writing. Other parkinsonian signs are almost always absent in essential tremor. Later in life, the tremor may take on the characteristics of an intention tremor. There may also be some loss of facial expressiveness and mild gait instability.

Some cases of essential tremor are believed to have a genetic component. Critchley (1972) found evidence for a possible autosomal dominant mode of transmission in 12 out of 42 patients he studied. Some forms of essential tremor may be genetically linked to Charcot–Marie–Tooth diseae (Salisach, 1976).

There appears to be a connection between essential tremor and dystonia. A study of patients with torticollis revealed 25 out of 30 patients to have essential tremor (Couch, 1976). Another study found that patients with long-standing essential head tremor were at increased risk for developing dystonia, especially torticollis (Baxter & Lal, 1979). This increased incidence of dystonia, especially in the later stages of essential tremor, can make for difficulty in differentiating essential tremor from the tremor of Parkinson's disease.

The treatment of choice for essential tremor is oral propranolol, as other β-blockers may not be as efficacious (Young & Shahani, 1979). Alcohol, however, does appear to be more effective than does β-blockade (Koller & Biary, 1984). Although it has been reported that some patients may develop alcoholism secondary to this treatment for essential tremor (Nasrallah et al., 1982b) this must not be very common, for the prevalence of alcoholism in essential tremor does not seem to differ significantly from its prevalence in other chronic neurological disorders (Koller, 1983a). The mechanism by which alcohol exerts its antitremor effects is unknown, but the effect cannot be completely explained by the sedative effects of alcohol (Young & Shahani, 1979). Alcohol certainly works faster than does propranolol, usually relieving tremor within several minutes, as opposed to the hours or longer required for oral propranolol.

Hysterical Tremor

Hysterical tremor, though rare today, was apparently much more common in the last century and before. One of the hallmarks of hysterical tremor, like most hysterical phenomena, is its inconsistency, both between individuals and within the same individual. It can mimic tremor-in-repose, postural or intention tremor, or may be some combination of the three. Usually, a single arm or, on occasion, both arms may be involved. Rarely, the legs alone are involved (Ziehen, 1910). The frequency and amplitude may vary considerably over time, with changes in both frequency and excursion being seen on a second-to-second basis in some cases. The movements are rarely very slow, very fast, or of very small amplitude. If the tremor involves more than one part of the body, the tremor frequency may be different in each part. Diversions such as counting backward from 100 by 7's may result in a significant decrease in hysterical tremor, whereas tremor-in-repose usually increases in such cases, if it changes at all. Sometimes, remarkable phenomena, such as the coexistence of tremor and paralysis in the same limb, may be observed.

Psychological factors are, of course, very important in the manifestation and form of the tremor. Primary and secondary gain are usually evident. Nevertheless, hysterical tremors often require multiple observations for correct diagnosis.

Tremor in Chronic Alcoholism

Koller *et al.* (1985) noted that almost one-half of 100 chronic alcoholic patients had a postural hand tremor after 3 to 4 weeks of abstinence. In contrast with essential tremor, the tremor of alcoholism involved only the hands, and not the head or voice. Only 1% of the alcoholic patients, as compared with 46% of the 50 patients with essential tremor, had a family history of tremor. Propranolol therapy was more effective in the alcoholic group, although it did improve essential tremor as well.

CHAPTER SIX

Bruxism

INTRODUCTION

Bruxism is one of those clinical conditions that are so common that one cannot easily say whether they represent disorders or are simply normal characteristics of human beings. Estimates of the prevalence of bruxism have been as high as 20%. Nevertheless, it is clear that bruxism can damage teeth and gums, as well as cause considerable pain. Bruxism has probably existed as long as civilization, perhaps longer. Even the term itself is very old, being derived from the Greek *brucho*, which means "to grind teeth."

DESCRIPTION

Bruxism consists of regular, repetitive, usually lateral movements of the jaw in which the upper and lower teeth are brought into contact with each other. It can occur during wakefulness or during any stage of sleep (nocturnal bruxism) (Reding *et al.*, 1968). The movements usually cause abnormal tooth wear, as well as periodontal inflammation, masticatory muscle hypertrophy and shortening, temporomandibular joint damage, and a number of different types of facial pains and headache. The movements can almost always be controlled voluntarily during the waking state for a variable period of time, depending on the level of consciousness and understanding of the patient.

DIFFERENTIAL DIAGNOSIS

Bruxism must be carefully differentiated from a variety of other orofacial dyskinesias. The repetitive rhythmic nature of the movements and the fact that they often occur during sleep separates them from most choreoathetoid, dystonic, and ticlike movements. Also, the movements of bruxism are more subject to voluntary control than are most of the other disorders. They are, unlike many other dyskinesias, strictly limited to the orofacial muscles.

Daytime bruxism may appear to be compulsive in nature, as it is often associated with anxiety. Nocturnal bruxism, however, is clearly not a compulsion, for no compulsions occur during sleep.

Finally, bruxism may be differentiated from orofacial dystonias, such as trismus or Meige's syndrome, by the usually rhythmic movements of bruxism, as well as the lack of involvement of nonmasticatory muscles.

PATHOPHYSIOLOGY

Glaros and Rao (1977) have reviewed proposed etiologies of bruxism, and divided them into three broad categories: (1) local/mechanical theories, (2) psychological theories, and (3) systemic/neurophysiological theories.

In the local/mechanical etiological scheme, certain cases of bruxism are thought to arise from dental abnormalities, especially malocclusion. A common argument has been that, with malocclusion, a positive feedback loop may arise between mandibular proprioceptors and the brain. Occlusal problems may cause a lowering of what has been termed the "irritability threshold," and may result in bruxism. The bruxism itself may then reduce the irritability threshold further, causing more bruxism. This theory does not explain a large number of bruxists with good occlusion, however (see Glaros & Rao, 1977).

As for the psychological theories, Glaros and Rao (1977) note that while a number of studies have linked bruxism to anxiety, stress, aggression, and other psychological variables, other studies have reported no such connections. Part of the reason for these discrepancies may be found in the work of Olkinuora (1972a, 1972b, 1972c), which suggests that there are two different types of bruxists. Those of the first type are called strain bruxists. Their characteristics include clenching more than grinding, and more daytime bruxism, more emotional disturbances, and more aggressiveness than is characteristic of those of the second type, who are called nonstrain bruxists. The latter grind more than clench, are less aggressive, have fewer emotional problems, and appear to have a familial predisposition to bruxism.

Finally, Glaros and Rao (1977) discuss a number of neurophysiological theories of bruxism. Some investigators have proposed a relationship with nutritional deficiencies or gastrointestinal disturbances,[1] and others have noted an increased frequency of bruxism in cerebral palsy and mental retardation syndromes, especially Down's syndrome. Animal experiments have shown that bruxism can be induced by stimulating the anteromedial cortex or the limbic system, including the lateral hypothalamus. In human beings,

---

[1]It has been claimed that bruxism in childhood may be related to intestinal worms.

the frequent occurrence of bruxism during sleep has stimulated a number of investigators to study the relationship of bruxism to sleep and arousal. It appears that bruxism can occur during all stages of sleep, with the exception of REM sleep, which is characterized by bursts of eye movement. Satoh and Harada (1973), on the basis of polysomnographic studies of bruxists, have proposed that bruxism is a reaction to arousal, because (1) it usually occurs in the transitional period from a heavier to a lighter stage of sleep; (2) it is accompanied by other arousal phenomena, such as vasoconstriction, tachycardia, and skin potential changes; and (3) it can be provoked by arousing stimuli such as tones, white noise, or flashing lights. These investigators further postulated that bruxism may be released when arousal mechanisms (which may be dopaminergic) are not immediately followed by the organization of cortical motor function centers (presumably norepinephrine-mediated) that accompanies wakefulness. Thus, bruxism may be the result of a dissociation of regulatory sleep centers in the brain.

SYNDROMES IN WHICH BRUXISM OCCURS

Idiopathic bruxism has been estimated to affect somewhere between 5% and 20% of the population, with no significant difference between sexes or between children and adults (Glaros & Rao, 1977). Though often considered to be a single disorder, it has been postulated to occur in more than one form. For example, the idea that there are strain versus nonstrain bruxists has already been mentioned.

Bruxism can accompany other conditions, such as cerebral palsy, infantile autism, and Down's syndrome. It is often seen in children with mental retardation, especially those with a variety of storage diseases. It has also been noted to occur with L-dopa treatment for Parkinson's disease (Magee, 1970). Reports of bruxism accompanying tardive dyskinesia (e.g., Kamen, 1975) must be considered with care, for although tardive dyskinesia can cause irregular tooth wear and other types of dental and jaw problems, tardive dyskinesia, unlike bruxism, is under less voluntary control, often affects areas besides the face and jaw, and always attenuates with sleep. Amphetamines have also been reported to cause bruxism (Ashcroft et al., 1965; Brandon, 1969; Lewis et al., 1971).

The treatment of bruxism has included occlusal adjustment, tension reduction, aversive conditioning, biofeedback, massed practice (where patients deliberately clench their teeth repeatedly for short periods of time during the day), hypnosis, and psychotherapy. All of these have met with variable or uncertain success (see Glaros & Rao, 1977).

CHAPTER SEVEN

Tics and Related Conditions

INTRODUCTION

It is to the French that we owe the beginning of our understanding of tics. Perhaps it was the fact that the word "tic" was already in use as a lay term in France that facilitated its early adoption by French physicians and its greater recognition in that country. *Tic* (*tique* or *ticq*) was apparently first used in France to describe repetitive habits in animals, particularly horses, in the mid-17th century (Meige & Feindel, 1907). By the next century the term was in use by physicians to describe a variety of spasmodic conditions. One condition, however, received greater attention than did the others, and served not only to further the use of the word "tic" medically, but also to cause confusion regarding the nature of tics. This was *tic douloureux*, which, being one of the most painful conditions to which mankind is heir, overshadowed the painless disorders. In fact, many investigators were forced to adopt the term *tic non douloureux* for painless tic conditions—a curious development considering that *tic douloureux* was later considered to not be a true tic disorder at all.

The first clear modern description of tics was in 1873, with Trousseau's clinical definition:

Non-dolorous tic consists of abrupt momentary muscular contractions more or less limited as a general rule, involving preferably the face, but affecting also neck, trunk, and limbs. Their exhibition is a matter of every day experience. In one case it may be a blinking of the eyelids, a spasmodic twitch of cheek, nose, or lip; in another, it is a toss of the head, a sudden, transient, yet ever-recurring contortion of the neck; in a third, it is a shrug of the shoulder, a convulsive movement of diaphragm or abdominal muscles,—in fine, the term embodies an infinite variety of bizarre actions that defy analysis.

These tics are not infrequently associated with a highly characteristic cry or ejaculation—a sort of laryngeal or diaphragmatic chorea—which constitute the condition; or there may be a more elaborate symptom in the form of a curious impulse to repeat the same word or the same exclamation. Sometimes the patient is driven to utter aloud what he would fain conceal. (as translated and quoted in Meige & Feindel, 1907, p. 27)

Following Trousseau, a number of investigators, including Charcot, Gilles de la Tourette (1885), Brissaud, Pitre, Crasset, Cruchet, Meige, and Feindel, became interested in tics. Of special importance are Charcot, who first clearly hypothesized a psychological component to tic, and Tourette, who described in detail the disorder of complex tics that now bear his name (although he did not differentiate this disorder from *latah*, *myriachit*, jumping, and others; see Chapter 10). Also of critical importance is the 1902 book of Meige and Feindel, *Les tics et leur traitement*, which, in the revised and translated version by S. A. K. Wilson in 1907, spread knowledge and recognition of tics to English-speaking physicians, and remains perhaps the finest clinical account of tics written to this day.

During the middle of this century psychoanalytic theories predominated, with most tics considered to be neurotic in nature.[1] Following the advances in the chemotherapy of tics of the early 1960s, the last two decades have witnessed an increasingly biological approach to tics and Tourette's disorder.

DESCRIPTION

The manifestations of tic are protean. According to Fahn (1982) tics exhibit variability in time, location, frequency, amplitude, duration, distribution, and complexity. With this vast range of clinical form, a definition or description of the basic phenomenon is very difficult to formulate, if tics truly represent a unitary disorder.

Nevertheless, many investigators believe that most tics are fundamentally related. In this regard we offer the definition of tic of Shapiro and Shapiro (1980):

Tics are involuntary movements or utterances involving contractions of functionally related groups of skeletal muscles in one or more parts of the body. These symptoms are brief, frequent, rapid, sudden, unexpected, repetitive, purposeless, inappropriate, stereotypic, sometimes irresistible, and of variable intensity. They occur at irregular intervals, and usually involve a number of muscles in their normal synergistic relationships. Symptoms may be stable over time, decrease during non-anxious distraction or concentration, disappear during sleep, and increase with tension. Tics can be voluntarily suppressed for a variable period of time, but the effort causes an increase in tension which usually results in subsequent symptomatic discharge. (p. 4)

[1]It should be noted that Freud later in his career apparently felt tic to be a neurological condition (Weingarten, 1968).

Tics usually involve the face and, less commonly, the head, neck and upper extremities. The trunk, lower extremities, and pharyngeal and diaphragmatic musculature may be involved as well. Tics are usually named and characterized according to either the part of the body involved or the action the tics resemble. In Table 7-1 we present a list of tics divided in these two ways.

It is important to remember that tics are very frequently associated with a state of psychic tension, in a manner similar to compulsions. Also, many patients with tics can attribute the tic to a definite time or experience. Some patients, for example, will recall having developed a tic during a time of extreme anxiety. Others relate the onset to some abnormality that developed in their body, such as a cracking noise in their neck or a sore on their tongue. Still others ascribe a tic's origin to an imitation of someone else's habits or tics. The presence of a tendency toward imitation or mimicry is found in many tic patients, even those with simple tics.

Table 7-1. Common Tics, Divided According to Distribution and Action Resembled

According to distribution	
Auditory (stapedius muscle contraction)	Jaw
Chin	Labial
Diaphragmatic	Neck
Ear (external ear contraction)	Nose
Extremity	Palpebral
Eyelid	Shoulder
Facial	Tongue
	Trunk

According to action resembled or type of action	
Aboiement (grunts and noises)	Mastication
Affirmation (head nodding)	Negation (head shaking)
Biting	Scratching
Blinking	Sniffing
Blowing	Snoring
Coughing	Sobbing
Eructation	Striking
Expectoration	Sucking
Hiccup	Swallowing
Leaping	Tossing
Licking	Vomiting
	Whistling

DIFFERENTIAL DIAGNOSIS

Because of their repetitive and often highly coordinated nature, tics can usually be distinguished from chorea and athetosis without much difficulty. Tics are also relatively easy to differentiate from signs of generalized hyperactivity, although in some disorders, such as Tourette's syndrome, tics and hyperactivity may coexist.

Simple highly repetitive tics may resemble coarse tremors, but tics are more variable in appearance and lack the smooth sinusoidal appearance of tremors. Also, tics more commonly involve the face, head, and neck, whereas tremors are most often seen in the extremities.

Myoclonus may be very difficult to distinguish from rapid tics, and, in cases of very simple tics that last less than 100 milliseconds, the distinction may be impossible. Complex tics do not usually present problems in differentiation from myoclonus.

Although spasms are often clinically confused with tics, they represent a different pathological process. Spasms are the result of irritation in local spinal or brainstem reflex circuits or in muscles, whereas tics are the result of some higher central pathology (which is clearly evident in the more complex tics). One type of spasm that is easily confused with tic is *hemifacial spasm*. Hemifacial spasm is due to abnormal activity in the facial nerve and is often accompanied by weakness and synkinesis.[2] Usually, both the upper and lower facial muscles are affected on one side, although, rarely, both sides of the face may become involved. The frequency of spasms ranges from rare to nearly incessant, and the spasms themselves often wax and wane in intensity. Occasionally, there are remissions, but these are usually only temporary. Although there have been a few reported cases following Bell's palsy or caused by tumors, arteriovenous malformations, aneurysms, and other pathological structures impinging on the facial nerve as it exits the brainstem, in most instances no cause can be found. Sometimes, decompression of the facial nerve may provide relief, but at the present time no generally adequate treatment exists. There is, however, a recent case report on the efficacy of baclofen in this condition (Sandyk, 1984). The synkinesis and facial weakness, along with the anatomical pattern of facial-nerve involvement, distinguish this disorder from facial tics.

Here we should briefly mention a condition that has been called "habit spasm." Habit spasms are considered to be benign twitches of primarily facial muscles in which there is no known pathological basis. The movements are highly stereotyped and persist over a lifetime. There is, in our experience, little reason to separate this entity from a simple tic condition, as the two

---

[2]Used in this sense to refer to an inappropriate spread of nerve activity to structures not usually innervated by the facial nerve, causing, for example, eye closing while smiling.

appear to be clinically identical and both become worse with anxiety and disappear during sleep.

Myokymia is a fine repetitive twitching of muscle bundles, usually around the eyes or lips. It may involve other parts of the face and head (including the stapedius muscle and platysma) as well as other parts of the body. It is almost always a benign and transient condition and occurs in just about everyone at some time during his or her lifetime. Severe myokymia may infrequently be seen accompanying multiple sclerosis, posterior fossa tumors, and Guillain–Barré syndrome (VanZandycke et al., 1982).

As mentioned earlier, certain tics may be associated with echo phenomena (discussed in Chapter 9), but, unlike echo phenomena, tics persist beyond the initial mimicry. Some patients with tics show exaggerated startle responses, but the full syndrome of hyperekplexia (Chapter 10) is not present. There are similarities between Tourette's disorder and certain culture-bound syndromes, such as *latah* and *myriachit*, which are described later, in Chapter 10. Tourette himself in 1885 first drew attention to the possible relatedness of these disorders. Tics, however, are not an important part of the culture-bound syndromes, and exaggerated startle reactions only occasionally accompany tics.

Finally, the most difficult signs to distinguish from tics are stereotypies and compulsions. Differentiating stereotypies and compulsions from simple tics is usually fairly straightforward, but in the case of complex tics such a task may be impossible. There may be a senseless repetition of bizarre motor acts or the development of ritualistic tension-reducing behaviors that strongly resemble stereotypies and compulsions, respectively. In fact, the resemblance may be so strong that it is difficult to determine which term best applies to a given action. At times, it may be more helpful to view these signs as being on a spectrum, as follows:

	Stereotypies	*Complex tics*	*Compulsions*
Conscious awareness . . .	lesser ←	→	greater
Conscious control . . .	lesser ←	→	greater
Repetitiveness . . .	lesser ←	→	greater
Relationship of act to anxiety . . .	lesser ←	→	greater

Table 8-3, in the next chapter, also addresses differential diagnostic aspects of tics, stereotypies, and compulsions.

It is a tribute to the enormous clinical variability of tics that they may be nearly impossible to distinguish from the simplest of all movement disorders, such as myoclonus, and also from the most complex, such as compulsions.

PATHOPHYSIOLOGY

Through much of this century, theories regarding the etiology of tics have been dominated by psychoanalytic thought. Recently, it has become clear that, at least in the case of Tourette's syndrome, tics may be primarily a biological disorder, although psychological factors are undoubtedly impor-

Table 7-2. Syndromes in Which Tics Occur

Idiopathic tic disorders		
Disorder	Location of tics[a]	Comments
Transient simple tic disorder	Tics in <3 muscle groups	Occurs in 12% of children, begins in early childhood, lasts >1 month, <1 year
Transient multiple tic disorder	Tics in >3 muscle groups	Begins in early childhood, lasts >1 month, <1 year
Subacute simple tic disorder	Tics in <3 muscle groups	Begins in childhood, lasts >1 year, ends before end of adolescence
Subacute multiple tic disorder	Tics in >3 muscle groups	Same as above
Chronic simple tic disorder	Tics in <3 muscle groups	Begins either before adolescence or after age 30, lasts >1 year, may last throughout life
Tourette's disorder	Tics in >3 muscle groups, often with vocal tics	Usually (>90%) begins before end of adolescence, lasts >1 year, often from 10 to 80 years

Secondary tic disorders	
Postencephalitic states (especially encephalitis lethargica)	Multiple sclerosis
Huntington's disease	Neurosyphilis
Sydenham's chorea	Thyrotoxicosis
Wilson's disease	Porphyria
Hallervorden–Spatz disease	Tardive Tourette's (postneuroleptic)
Autism	Stimulant-induced: including pemoline, dextroamphetamine, methylphenidate
Mental retardation	Tricyclic antidepressant-induced
Down's syndrome	Anticholinergic medication-induced
Schizophrenia (?)	PCP-induced
Poststroke	Acute neuroleptic-induced (?)

[a]Shapiro and Shapiro (1980).

tant in the form and appearance of the individual tics (Cohen *et al.*, 1982). We shall discuss the pathophysiology of tics in more detail in the chapter on Tourette's disorder (Chapter 19).

SYNDROMES IN WHICH TICS OCCUR

In Table 7-2 we present a listing of important syndromes in which tics may be a feature. The idiopathic tic disorders, including Tourette's disorder, are discussed in greater detail in Chapter 19.

CHAPTER EIGHT

Complex Repetitive Movements

INTRODUCTION

The clinical signs discussed in this chapter are different forms of complex movements, most of which are repetitive to some degree. That is, they involve repeated performances of fragments of actions, complete actions, or behaviors. They range from being completely automatic (as seen in temporal-lobe automatisms) to being partially responsive to the dictates of the conscious mind.

The term "automatism" was introduced by Hughlings Jackson in the late 19th century to describe a state of activity accompanying seizures. Later, the term was used to describe many different complex behaviors seemingly devoid of willful control, including a number of strange and bizarre movements seen in schizophrenia. We will discuss some of the ambiguity and confusion surrounding this and other similar terms throughout this chapter.

DESCRIPTIONS

Automatisms

An automatism is, strictly speaking, any nonreflex motor act that occurs outside of willful control in the face of a depressed level of consciousness. In actuality, distinguishing between what is and what is not outside consciousness can be most difficult. For example, although many patients performing automatisms appear to have no conscious control over what they are doing and later have no memory of what they have done, other patients relate a vague, ill-defined sense of awareness of activity. Still others speak about being passive observers during the actions.

The action itself is often moderately complex, such as buttoning or unbuttoning a shirt, but may range from fairly simple activities, such as opening and closing a hand, to very complex ones, such as driving a car. For this reason, the action may or may not appear to be goal-directed. Automatisms, with the exception of some of the most complex ones, are often repetitive.

Stereotypies

A stereotypy is a repetitive nonreflex non-goal-directed motor activity that is carried out in exactly the same way during each repetition. Stereotypies often appear to be fragments of a normal action that are continually repeated without purpose, but some may simply be reiterated bizarre purposeless acts. Although the level of consciousness is unimpaired, conscious control seems to be lacking. The movements are usually uniform, but at times incomplete forms of a given stereotypy may be observed. For example, instead of rocking back and forth, a patient may merely nod his or her head. One stereotypy can metamorphose into another over time, or stereotypies can be combined. Although patients usually have little control over stereotypies, the movements often decrease when the patients engage in drawing, counting, or other activities (Jones, 1965). Some more common stereotypies are listed in Table 8-1.

Complex Tics

Complex tics have been discussed in Chapter 7. It is, however, worth comparing Table 7-1 to Tables 8-1 and 8-2, to note the considerable degree of overlap among stereotypies, compulsions, and complex tics.

Table 8-1. Common Stereotypies

Rocking
Biting
Touching self with tongue
Grimacing
Smiling
Frowning
Walking in circles or back and forth
Touching or stroking parts of the body with hands and fingers
Fragments of common actions (such as smoking, combing hair)

Table 8-2. Compulsions and Phobias

Compulsions	Phobias (fears)
Ablutomania: (compulsive) body-washing	Aelurophobia: (fear of) cats
Agromania: (compulsion) to be away from everyone	Aichmophobia: painted objects
	Agoraphobia: groups of people
Arithmomania: counting or numbering	Algophobia: pain
Cheilophagia: lip-biting	Amathophobia: dust
Contrectation: to touch members of the opposite sex	Amaxophobia: being in a vehicle
	Apeirophobia: infinity
Dromomania: to run away	Arachnophobia: spiders
Ecdysiasm: to disrobe in public	Astraphobia: storms
Folie du pourquoi: incessant questioning	Basophobia: standing up
Haphemania: touching	Bathophobia: depths
Klazomania: shouting	Brontophobia: thunder
Kleptomania: stealing	Carcinophobia: cancer
Lavomania: washing (especially hands)	Catagelphobia: being ridiculed
Letheomania: drug-taking	Cenophobia: large halls
Mythomania: lying	Claustrophobia: small enclosed places
Oniomania: buying	Entomophobia: insects
Onychophagia: nail-biting	Geriophobia: age or aging
Pyromania: fire-setting	Gynephobia: women
Thanatomania: to attend funerals, read obituaries	Kainophobia: change
	Kakorraphiophobia: failure
Theomania: to join many religious or other cults	Keraunophobia: lightning
	Laliophobia: speaking
Trichotillomania: hair-pulling	Mysophobia: dirt
Compulsive eating	Nyctophobia: darkness
Compulsive (pathological) gambling	Ochlophobia: crowds
	Ophidiophobia: snakes
	Pathophobia: disease
	Taphephobia: being buried alive
	Thanatophobia: death
	Triakaidekophobia: the number 13
	Uranophobia: heaven (or punishment after death)
	Xenophobia: strangers

Compulsions

A compulsion is a more or less repetitive goal-directed behavior that is usually, though not invariably, aimed at reducing anxiety. Consciousness is unimpaired, and there is a variable amount of conscious control over the activity. Compulsions can be simple repetitive behaviors, such as continual handwashing (lavomania) or hair pulling (trichotillomania), but, usually, these are an attempt to reduce tension, or else anxiety will occur if the action is prevented. We also consider complex behaviors such as kleptomania, compulsive eating, pyromania, and pathological gambling to be compulsive in nature, although they can be considered to be compulsive in a slightly different sense. These compulsions may briefly bring pleasure to the patient at times, whereas the compulsions of obsessive–compulsive disorder, in contrast, are almost always associated with distress (ego-dystonic).

Anxiety, although usually a part of the compulsive picture, is not always present. Some patients do not report that their compulsive behaviors are an attempt to lessen anxiety, nor that anxiety results if the action is not performed. Rather, these patients relate a sense of being "forced" to perform an action over which they have little or no control. This quality of feeling compelled distinguishes compulsions from most other behaviors, with the exception of certain tics. A listing of some common (and not so common) compulsions, along with a listing of phobias (which are frequently seen to accompany compulsions), is offered in Table 8-2.

Perseveration

Perseveration is the uniform repetition of a goal-directed motor act or fragments thereof beyond the point of completion of the goal. There is usually very little conscious control, and it may occasionally cause anxiety in the patient.

Mannerisms

Mannerisms are odd or bizarre ways of performing normal activities. They are repetitive insofar as the normal underlying activities, such as eating or walking, are repetitive. The term "mannerism" is frequently used to refer to the minor idiosyncrasies we all manifest when performing certain activities. In this book, however, the term refers to obvious unusual or grotesque behaviors that would be recognized in any given culture or community as departing from normal.

There remain, apart from the above disorders, certain bizarre behaviors that are not highly repetitive and also that are not simply a strange way of performing what would otherwise be a normal activity. There is no widely accepted name for such actions. Frequently, they are called mannerisms but, given the way in which we and others have defined "mannerisms," it may be helpful if they are given a different name. Some investigators have used the term "parakinesia" for some of these movements (see Leonhard, 1979); others have used such names as "bizarreries" or "grotesqueries" (see Fish, 1974). Because "parakinesia" has been used to refer to a variety of different hyperkinesias, including choreoathetoid movements, we advocate the use of the term *bizarrerie* to describe unusual behaviors that are not highly repetitive and seem to serve no purpose.

DIFFERENTIAL DIAGNOSIS

Table 8-3 presents a listing of different complex repetitive movements, along with some distinguishing characteristics of each. Caution must be exercised, however, because the signs discussed in this section present a number of problems in differential diagnosis. One major problem is that many of the different terms can describe very similar clinical phenomena, a result of the fact that a number of the terms were initially invented to serve in different contexts. For example, "automatism" usually refers to behavior seen in neurological patients, "mannerism" refers to that seen in psychiatric patients, and "tic" refers to that seen in both. Another problem concerns the way that terms such as "stereotypy" are used in the animal literature to describe conditions that may (but probably do not) have any exact counterparts in man. A third problem revolves around the use of such terms as "stereotypical" and "manneristic" to describe not only movements or behaviors, but also postures.

Automatisms may be differentiated from the other disorders because of their association with a depressed level of consciousness. There are times, though, when difficulties arise in determining when consciousness truly is depressed. In patients with partial complex seizures, depression of consciousness is usually clearly present, but in patients with pseudoseizures it is often hard to say. It is frequently difficult to judge whether or not a patient with catatonia or psychotic depression has a depressed level of consciousness, and whether stereotypies should actually be called automatisms in such cases. Most of the time, however, these distinctions are clear.

Another point of confusion surrounds the differentiation of stereotypies from mannerisms. Manneristic behaviors can occasionally be somewhat repetitive, but the distinguishing feature is that every repetitive action serves a purpose. If a patient brushes his or her teeth in a strange or bizarre way,

Table 8-3. Repetitive Complex Movements and Their Differential Diagnosis

	Automatism	Stereotypy	Complex tic	Mannerism	Perseveration	Compulsion	Bizarrerie
Level of consciousness	Usually depressed	Usually normal	Normal	Normal	Usually normal	Normal	Normal
Degree of repetitiveness	Low to high	High	High	Low	High	Low to high	Low
Frequency of repetitions	Low to high	High	Low to high	Low	High	Low to high	Low
Control over motor act	Little or none	Very little	Usually present	Usually little	Little	Variable	Little
Appearance of motor act itself (disregarding context)	Usually normal	Normal or bizarre	Normal or bizarre	Bizarre	Usually normal	Usually normal	Bizarre
Time span of each motor act[a]	Usually short	Short	Short (up to many per minute)	Short to long	Short	Short to long	Short to long
Relationship of motor act to anxiety	Little or none	Little or none	Act relieves anxiety	Usually little	Act may cause anxiety	Act relieves anxiety	Usually little
Purposefulness or goal-directedness of motor act	Usually absent (but may appear to be present)	Absent	Absent	Present	Absent	Present	Absent
Frequent accompanying symptoms or diseases	Epilepsy (especially partial complex seizures)	Schizophrenia, autism, mental retardation, dementia	Simple tics, anxiety, echolalia, coprolalia	Schizophrenia, mania	Frontal lobe dysfunction, schizophrenia, dementia	Obsessions, anxiety, depression	Schizophrenia

[a]"Short" means "on the order of seconds or less."

making repeated grimaces and odd hand movements with each stroke, that is manneristic, not stereotypic, behavior. Similarly, if a patient walks with an unusual gait consisting of a combination of hopping on one foot, limping, and rhythmic arm flinging, that is manneristic walking and not a stereotypic gait. Each step serves a purpose, regardless of how bizarre the step is. On the other hand, if a patient walks around in circles, or back and forth across the room repeatedly and to no purpose, that is a stereotypy. Similarly, if a patient is observed to repeatedly raise his hand and tap the top of his head three times with only his index and fourth finger in exactly the same way every time, even if this action occurs only several times a day, it is probably a stereotypy.

Perseverative activities can resemble stereotypies, but may be differentiated because they begin as goal-directed actions. Once begun, they are either entirely or partially repeated many times. Patients are, in essence, unable to stop what they have started. Stereotypies do not depend upon the initiation of a goal-directed motor act, and, unlike perseverative actions, are frequently very bizarre in appearance.

The distinction between stereotypies and tardive dyskinesia can be most difficult in patients with schizophrenia or mental retardation who are treated with neuroleptic medications. In many cases it is almost impossible to tell the two kinds of conditions apart (which causes one to wonder whether on some level they are dependent on similar brain mechanisms). There are, however, certain characteristics by which stereotypies and the movements of tardive dyskinesia may be differentiated. These are listed in Table 8-4.

Table 8-4. Features Useful in Distinguishing Stereotypies from Tardive Dyskinesia[a]

Stereotypies	Tardive dyskinesia
1. Highly repetitive	Less repetitive
2. Often, complex movements involving muscles in normal synergistic relationships	Usually, simple movements
3. Often, fragments of actions or pseudo-purposeful behavior	Purposeless movements
4. Often, contact between widely separate body parts (such as hand-to-face, hand-to-leg), or translation of the body as a whole through space (such as rocking, walking in circles)	Movements limited to localized parts of the body, usually face, jaw, and distal extremities
5. Tend to be asymmetrical	Tends to be more symmetrical

[a]See also Chapter 23.

Complex tics are very difficult to differentiate from stereotypies, and, in fact, there may be little difference between the two. Usually, the distinction is made on the basis of accompanying features, such as the presence of simple tics. Patients who experience tics also often relate an uncomfortable feeling of tension that occurs should they try to suppress the movements, a feeling that is usually absent in patients suffering from stereotypies. Complex tics may be equally difficult to distinguish from certain simple compulsive behaviors, and patients with such complex tic disorders as Tourette's often develop many compulsive ritualistic behaviors in addition to their tics. In the previous chapter we discussed some of these issues, along with the idea that stereotypies, complex tics, and simple compulsions may possibly be considered to be on a continuum, and may all ultimately relate to similar underlying brain mechanisms.

PATHOPHYSIOLOGY

All complex behavioral abnormalities are poorly understood, and what little is known about the repetitive forms has largely been the result of general theories regarding repetitive activity in the nervous system. A theoretical discussion of oscillations is presented in the Appendix, and many of the principles discussed there may apply to complex movements as well. Peripheral factors in the genesis of complex repetitive movements are undoubtedly less important than they are in that of simple movements, and, if feedback cycles are important in complex iterations, it is likely that they take place on a central level.

A neural feedback control model for highly repetitive complex actions is theoretically possible, and is certainly reasonable for such phenomena as automatisms and perseveration, where one can easily envision some reverberative brain process leading to the repetitive actions. For those actions that are less repetitive, however, such a model becomes less attractive, and alternative theories must be entertained. There are theories ranging from the notion that certain motor programs are episodically released from storage by some pathological process (much as was described for chorea in Chapter 3) to the idea that the actions themselves are created and repeated in response to behavioral conditioning. Although there is supportive evidence for both of these models (especially the behavioral model) our knowledge of the brain is too limited to allow us to specify the biological mechanisms through which they might operate.

So, leaving the realm of general theory, we move to what is known about the pathophysiology of complex repetitive actions. Our focus is on neurobehavioral mechanisms, but other theories will be introduced where appropriate.

Automatisms

Automatisms have mainly been described in epilepsy, although they have been considered by some to occur in other conditions, such as schizophrenia (Bleuler, 1911/1950) and locked-in syndrome (a condition characterized by lower bulbar palsy and quadriparesis usually secondary to bilateral infarction of the ventral pons) (Bauer et al., 1982). Although many neurologists have focused on automatisms as a sign of seizures that involve the temporal lobes, it is clear that they can occur in other seizure conditions as well, such as petit mal epilepsy (Penry & Dreifuss, 1969), seizures involving the supplementary motor area (Green et al., 1980) and seizures involving the anterior frontal area (Penfield, 1952). Feindel and Penfield (1954) demonstrated that, at least in the case of temporal-lobe automatisms, the deep mesial structures of the temporal lobe (including the uncus, amygdala, ventral claustrum and deep anterior temporoinsular cortex) are responsible for initiating automatisms. Jasper (1962) discovered that spread of discharge to hippocampus and alterations in lateral temporal-lobe electrical activity are concomitants of automatisms, and are possibly necessary for automatisms to occur.

More recently, it has been shown that automatisms may differ in different types of complex partial seizures. It has been observed that patients whose seizures respond to temporal lobectomy (and thus presumably have pathology more localized to one temporal lobe) usually have seizures consisting of an initial motionless stare followed by stereotyped automatisms and reactive quasipurposeful automatisms. These have been called Type I complex partial seizures. They have been differentiated from Type II seizures, in which the ictus begins with quasipurposeful automatisms, such as running, walking, and boxing, and which are unresponsive to temporal lobectomy (Walsh & Delgado-Escueta, 1984). Studies such as these may in the future help to further the understanding of the mechanisms of automatisms.

Stereotypies

Studies on the origin of stereotypies in man have predominately involved developmental and behavioral approaches. This is because most of the studies have centered upon stereotypies in mentally defective children, especially those with infantile autism. Although the individual theories differ in details, all of these theories have attempted to address the following questions: (1) How do stereotypies arise? (2) What governs their form? and (3) What maintains their existence?

As for the first question, it is clear that in childhood many stereotyped behaviors can be normal phenomena. According to Berkson (1967), "at least some stereotyped behaviors may be closely identified with neonatal motor patterns which normally function to maintain close contact with the mother" (p. 88). These include, for example, sucking and clasping behaviors. It is the added factor of isolation, however, that may turn these normal behaviors into autistic stereotypies such as thumb-sucking and self-clasping. These observations in children have been confirmed for primates and other animals that are isolated in development.

Thus, some stereotypies can occur either normally or as a result of isolation, but there are others for which the cause is obscure. For example, the rocking and head-banging that occur in mentally retarded children may possibly be related to a tendency for these children to be isolated or for them to be effectively isolated by their mental handicap, but this is far from certain. Alternatively, it has been proposed that stereotypies in these children may be the result of an attempt to decrease what is, to them, an overstimulating environment (Hutt et al., 1965). On the other hand, it has been proposed that stereotypies are an attempt to increase self-stimulation to a predetermined level (Baumeister & Forehand, 1973).

The second question, regarding the form of stereotypies, has been approached in two ways. One has involved the normal developmental process of children, whereby the stereotypic form is thought to be determined by the abilities of a child at a certain developmental level. Thus, sucking can occur very early in development, but body-swaying must await the formation of appropriate neuromuscular mechanisms that do not occur until years later (see Berkson, 1967). The second approach has been a behavioral one, whereby certain stereotypies are thought to arise from essentially normal behaviors that are further shaped by a process of operant conditioning (Baumeister & Forehand, 1973). These hypotheses are certainly not mutually exclusive and, in fact, may be components of a general process giving rise to certain stereotypical forms. A stereotypy such as rocking could initially develop as the expression of a certain stage in the development of the neuromotor system, which could be further modified by contingent stimuli. Other theories have been proposed to account for certain stereotypies—for example, rocking being a manner of genital masturbation and head-banging being an attempt to simulate the mother's heartbeat—but there is very little experimental support for these conjectures (Berkson, 1967). Few neuropathological theories concerning the form of stereotypies have been proposed.

Finally, regarding the question of the maintenance of stereotypical behaviors in certain conditions, heavy reliance has again been made on behavioral theories. In this context, through operant conditioning, a stereotypy is thought to take on a certain form and to be maintained in that form.

It is well known that a number of stereotypical behaviors can be induced in animals by catecholaminergic drugs, including stimulants and dopaminergic agonists. Unfortunately, such animal stereotypies as repetitive biting, turning, and circling are not clearly related to similar behaviors in man.[1] However, because stereotypies are observed in autism, mental retardation, and schizophrenia, and because neuroleptics have a beneficial effect on all three, it is possible that dopaminergic mechanisms are involved in human as well as animal stereotypies. Further supportive evidence is provided by the finding that stereotypies can occur in amphetamine psychosis (Ellinwood, 1967).

Theories on the involvement of the mesolimbic dopamine system in schizophrenia might lead one to speculate that this system is important in the production of stereotypies in man. In animals, however, there is evidence that it is the nigrostriatal dopamine system that is involved (see DeLong & Georgopoulos, 1981). Caution is warranted, though, because stereotypies are different in different species, and the word "stereotypy" is often used in the animal literature to describe activities that are not clearly stereotyped (Randrup & Munkvad, 1967).

Even in animals, the importance of dopaminergic mechanisms in the production of stereotypies is not clear. Antelman and Caggiula (1977) proposed that norepinephrine as well as dopamine may be involved in the production of stereotypies in animals. These authors suggested that norepinephrine may modulate dopaminergic activity in the brain. For example, they noted that amphetamine-induced stereotypies can be greatly attenuated by preferentially depleting dopamine in the brain, leaving norepinephrine content relatively unchanged, whereas depleting both dopamine and norepinephrine does not appear to affect stereotypies significantly.

If we allow that dopaminergic and possibly noradrenergic mechanisms are important in the production of stereotypies, it still remains to be determined which brain structures are involved. Luria (1973) proposed that pathology of the frontal cortex—especially the prefrontal cortex—is important in the etiology of a number of abnormal complex behaviors. These include stereotypies, perseveration, echo phenomena, and what we would describe as automatic obedience. Luria has further suggested that if the frontal-lobe pathology is limited to prefrontal areas, then the patient suffers the involuntary actions but recognizes them as abnormal or incorrect. With massive frontal damage, however, the patient does not even recognize that anything is wrong. Although the patient may perfectly well remember the required task, the task cannot be carried out, and the patient remains unaware of this. The exact mechanisms by which these behaviors arise with pathological conditions of the frontal lobes is unknown.

---

[1]In fact, it is interesting that, in man, the putative signs of dopaminergic excess and deficiency (i.e., chorea and hypokinesia) appear to correspond to stereotypies and catalepsy in rodents. In man, stereotypies and catalepsy are often considered higher psychomotor disturbances, and are difficult to produce with drugs. It is curious that disorders so readily produced in rodents should be considered higher-level dysfunctions in man, but such are the ways of mice and men. It should be noted, though, that human and animal stereotypies are somewhat different phenomenologically.

The cingulate cortex cortex may also be involved in the production of stereotypies. This area has already been implicated in the genesis of tics and of compulsions. Stimulation of area 24 (anterior cingulate gyrus) produces complex repetitive involuntary movements such as licking, rubbing, and pointing (Talairach *et al.*, 1973).

At present, it is impossible to extract from all of this information a unified conception of the etiology of stereotypies, but there may be some underlying connections between the cingulum, frontal cortex, and certain aspects of dopaminergic transmission in the brain. The anterior cingulum is an area that receives heavy dopaminergic input (Moore *et al.*, 1982), and it has recently been determined in rats that frontal-lobe damage may possibly increase both dopamine content and transmission subcortically, especially in the basal ganglia (Pycock *et al.*, 1980). Thus, it is possible that stereotypies (and perhaps also tics and certain compulsions) may result from excessive dopaminergic flow to the anterior cingulate gyrus. This remains speculative, however. The cingulum is discussed elsewhere in this volume in relation to tics (Chapter 19) and compulsions (next section).

Compulsions

Before moving to a neurophysiological discussion of compulsions, it is worth devoting some attention to the psychiatric approaches to these phenomena that have dominated during this century. Although compulsions have been a part of man's behavior for centuries, it was Freud who first separated them from other psychiatric disorders and propounded the first comprehensive theory to explain them. In Freud's earlier writings there is no clear separation between obsessive–compulsive and phobic neuroses, and, in fact, these two syndromes are closely allied. They both relate to repetitive, orderly behaviors that have been grouped under the more inclusive term *anancasms*. Anancasms refer to habits or thoughts that are difficult to stop or control, and begin to take on, so to speak, a life of their own. Because of the close relationship of compulsions to phobias, we include a listing of both in Table 8-2.

Freud eventually distinguished obsessions from phobias, and further elaborated on the relationship of obsessive–compulsive neurosis to hysterical neurosis (Nemiah, 1980a). Basically, both types of neuroses represent the outcomes of unconscious defenses against painful or unacceptable ideas. The differences lie in the following: hysteria (or, more specifically, hysterical conversion disorder) represents a somatic expression of affect that occurs instead of a verbal expression (the latter having been repressed); obsessive–compulsive symptoms represent a displacement of "affect" from a less acceptable to a more acceptable idea. Thus, the defense of the hysteric against an impulse involves "binding" the energy of the impulse by expressing it in a nonverbal form, whereas the defense of the obsessive–compulsive involves "binding" the energy of the impulse by displacing the energy onto another idea. Although a certain equilibrium may be reached in the case of either of these two neurotic mechanisms, conversion is by far the more powerful and more stable. Patients with conversion symptoms rarely experience anxiety associated with the underlying unconscious conflict, whereas patients with obsessive–compulsive symptoms are frequently very anxious, and often give the impression that the underlying conflict is under such tenuous control that it may emerge at any minute (Nemiah, 1980b).

In psychoanalytic theory, three main defense mechanisms have been proposed to account for obsessive–compulsive symptoms. These are: (1) *isolation*, in which a certain thought is deprived of both its affect and other associated thoughts; (2) *undoing*, in which an act is performed that is designed to correct or undo the consequences that the patient anticipates will result from an unbridled impulse or thought; and (3) *reaction formation*, where thoughts, attitudes or behaviors that are directly the opposite of the underlying unconscious impulse are manifested. The latter two defense mechanisms are important in the appearance of compulsive behavior, which frequently occurs when the mechanism of isolation fails.

Psychoanalytic theory further proposes that obsessive–compulsive behavior is related to disturbance or arrest in the *second psychosexual developmental* stage, the so-called "anal–sadistic" phase. This is used to explain the preoccupation with dirt and aggression so often observed in patients with obsessive–compulsive disorder.

Apart from psychoanalytic theory, the other major psychological approach to compulsive behavior has involved *behavioral* or *learning theory*. Here, an obsession is considered to be formed when an originally neutral thought is paired with an unconditioned stimulus that causes anxiety, and compulsions secondarily arise when a patient discovers that performance of a certain act reduces the anxiety associated with the obsessional thought.

For many years the major approaches to obsessive–compulsive disorders have been either psychodynamic or behavioral. There have been, however, a variety of observations and conjectures throughout this century concerning the neurological basis of compulsions.

There are numerous early reports of obsessions and compulsions in patients with postencephalitic states (see Schilder, 1938), and these led a number of investigators to propose an organic etiology for compulsive behavior. In many of these cases, true compulsions appear to have been observed. Interestingly, in many instances the obsessive–compulsive phenomena accompanied oculogyric crises, sometimes preceded by the crises, sometimes co-occurent with them (Brickner *et al.*, 1940). Such findings tend to implicate the extrapyramidal motor system in the genesis of compulsive behavior, but this is highly speculative.

More recently, there has been renewed interest in the neurological basis of compulsions. In 1964, Grimshaw reported that the incidence of previous neurological disease in obsessive–compulsive patients approaches 20%, as compared to under 8% in a matched control group. Most common among the neurological illnesses were Sydenham's chorea, infantile seizures, and diphtheria. Even more recently there has been a report of four patients who developed compulsions within 24 hours of head trauma (the site of damage appears to have been more posterior, but this is not completely clear), and in three out of four of these patients there was no evidence of premorbid obsessionality (McKeon *et al.*, 1984).

Jenike (1984) has proposed that the cingulum and, possibly, the orbital frontal cortex are sites of pathology in obsessive–compulsive disorder. This idea is based predominantly on reports of the efficacy of cingulotomy and of surgery on the orbital frontal lobe in cases of severe obsessive–compulsive disorder. Jenike proposed that clinical states such as obsessive–compulsive disorder might reflect iterative neuronal activity in the limbic system. Another study that compared patients with obsessive–compulsive disorder to normals on their performance on a battery of neuropsychological tests (as well as their power-spectrum electroencephalographic [EEG] characteristics) reported left frontal dysfunction in the group with obsessive–compulsive disorder, further implicating frontal-lobe pathology (Flor-Henry *et al.*, 1979).

Apart from the above studies, there is very little other evidence for neurological dysfunction in obsessive–compulsive disorder. Although Behar *et al.* (1984) reported ventricular enlargement on CT scan in obsessive–compulsive patients, other investigators have not found evidence of either CT scan or EEG abnormalities (Insel *et al.*, 1983a). Although this latter study reported some neuropsychological deficits in the obsessive–compulsive group, the finding of left-frontal-lobe dysfunction reported by Flor-Henry *et al.* (1979) could not be replicated. Furthermore, there is little evidence for a strong genetic component for obsessive–compulsive disorder (Hoover & Insel, 1984). There is, however, a case report of concordant, independently developed obsessive–compulsive disorder in two identical-twin pairs (McGuffin & Mawson, 1980), which may indicate a genetic component in at least some cases of obsessive–compulsive disorder.

As far as the other disorders (including mannerisms and bizarreries) discussed in this section are concerned, very little is known about their pathophysiological basis. A recent study by King and coworkers (1985), however, implicates disordered serotonergic function in schizophrenic or schizoaffective patients with mannerisms and posturing, as measured on the Brief Psychiatric Rating Scale. These researchers reported a positive correlation of mannerisms and posturing with increased levels of 5-hydroxyindoleacetic acid (5-HIAA, the major metabolite of serotonin) in cerebrospinal fluid and with increased levels of serotonin in platelets. The authors further hypothesized that a hyperserotonergic state may possibly be associated with decreased frontal metabolic activity in schizophrenics and with a stereotyped behavioral syndrome seen in animals (Jacobs & Klemfuss, 1975).

SYNDROMES IN WHICH COMPLEX REPETITIVE MOVEMENTS OCCUR

Table 8-5 offers a listing of some of the more important conditions in which complex repetitive movements may be a feature. In the remaining part of this chapter we shall discuss several of these conditions in more detail.

Table 8-5. Syndromes in Which Complex Repetitive Movements Occur

Automatisms	Perseveration
Psychomotor epilepsy	Frontal-lobe damage (including trauma, tumor, stroke)
Petit mal epilepsy	
Psychogenic fugue states	Dementia
Alcoholic blackouts	Schizophrenia
Twilight states of unknown etiology	Postencephalitic states
Catatonic stupor (severe)	
Frontal-lobe damage	
Dementia (severe)	

Stereotypies	Compulsions
Catatonia	Obsessive–compulsive disorder
Autism	Major depression
Pervasive developmental disorder of children	Tourette's disorder
Congenital deafness	Postencephalitic states
Congenital blindness (blindisms)	Schizophrenia
Mental retardation (moderate to severe)	
Agitated depression (severe)	
Postencephalitic states	
Asperger's syndrome (Wing, 1981)	

Mannerisms	Bizarreries
Catatonia (especially accompanying schizophrenia)	Catatonia (especially accompanying schizophrenia)
Autism	Autism
Pervasive developmental disorder of children	

Complex Partial Seizures

In most cases of complex partial seizures, pathology of the temporal lobes has been implicated, although, as mentioned earlier, this is not invariably the case. The term "temporal-lobe epilepsy," frequently considered to be synonymous with "complex partial seizures," can therefore be a misleading term.

Complex partial seizures are seen in approximately one-fourth of all epileptic patients. With the possible exception of posttraumatic epilepsy, there appears to be very little familial contribution to the etiology of these seizures, as most cases arise without familial precedent. Seizures usually first appear in early adolescence, although in many cases the first seizures to appear are generalized fits. Complex partial fits often do not appear until months or years later.

The psychiatric symptomatology that accompanies complex partial seizures is still highly debated. It appears to be true that a wide range of psychopathology can be seen, ranging from personality disturbances to affective disorders and psychosis. These conditions may closely resemble disorders such as schizoid or schizotypal personality disorder, paranoid personality disorder, depression, and schizophrenia. What is not yet clear is whether the psychopathology that accompanies complex partial seizures is distinctive in some way from the psychiatric disorders just mentioned, and whether such psychopathology is seen only in connection with complex partial types of seizures or may accompany other types of seizures as well (Stevens, 1983).

The mainstay of treatment is anticonvulsant medication—in particular, phenytoin and carbamazepine. When psychosis is also present, these agents may be somewhat effective in controlling it. There are many cases, however, in which the degree of seizure control appears to be inversely related to the amount of psychosis (Blumer, 1975). In these cases, neuroleptic medication is often effective in controlling the psychotic symptoms.

Autism and Related Conditions

Autism is a rare childhood condition (prevalence less than 0.04% in children), with a male to female ratio of approximately three to one. There appears to be a familial predisposition to the disorder. It usually begins before 2½ years of age and manifests initially with infrequent crying, indifference to being held, irritability, and flaccidity. With time, the indifference grows. There is a lack of interest in toys and human contact by the age of 6 months. At age 2 to 3, gross impairments in speech and language become evident. There may be total absence of speech or peculiar speech patterns, such as echolalia, pronoun reversal, or highly idiosyncratic use of words. Fantasy and imagination are usually severely impaired, and there is a profound resistance to any type of environmental change. Frequently, there is a pathological preoccupation with moving (especially spinning) objects. There is intensive and sometimes bizarre self-stimulating behavior, such as bruxism, repetitive scratching and touching, head-banging, and rocking. In spite of the many severe deficits, there may be functional areas that are unimpaired or even exceptional. For example, some children may be able to recall phrases or songs years after hearing them, reproduce piano pieces after a single hearing, or perform prodigious feats of numerical calculation. Probably, many individuals who have been called "idiot savants" have been autistic.

Most children with autism are also mentally retarded, with approximately 40% having an IQ below 50 (Schopler & Dalldorf, 1980). Children in the below-50-IQ range usually develop seizures as well, but seizures are rare in the relatively few children with a normal IQ.

The prognosis is poor, and generally related to the child's IQ. Even in the group with an IQ greater than 70 (about 30% of autistic children) only half show reasonable social adjustment.

The neurological basis of autism is unknown. A variety of brain structures, including the brainstem (and especially the vestibular system), the temporal lobe, the mesolimbic cortex, and neostriatum have been proposed to be involved (see Damasio & Maurer, 1978; Piggott, 1979; Hetzler & Griffin, 1981; Ornitz, 1983). A number of neurochemical abnormalities have been postulated as well. Hyperserotonemia has been reported in a variety of studies (Young et al., 1982). There have also been findings implicating the dopaminergic system. Interestingly, those more severely impaired children (including those found to have more severe stereotypies) have been noted to have higher homovanillic acid levels in their cerebrospinal fluid (Cohen et al., 1974, 1977).

Treatment approaches have been disappointing in their results. Behavioral therapy has been used with some success, especially in modifying more dangerous self-destructive behaviors. Antipsychotic medications have also been used, and appear to have some effect in decreasing apathy and increasing the child's ability to learn, but they have very little effect on the long-term outcome of the disorder.

There are other disorders in children that may also cause stereotypical behavior and that must be differentiated from autism. These include *childhood onset pervasive developmental disorder* (which is similar to autism but occurs after 2½ years of age and does not present with the complete clinical picture of autism), congenital deafness and blindness, childhood schizophrenia, and mental retardation. It should also be noted that children with phenylketonuria and prenatal rubella or cytomegalovirus infections may develop an autistic syndrome.

Sakuma (1975) studied 400 children with autism, deafness, blindness, and/or mental retardation, and noted some important differences regarding the nature of the stereotypies in these groups. His findings include the following:

1. Stereotypies are much more bizarre and highly repetitive in autistic children than in those in the other groups.
2. The stereotypies of visually disturbed children (blindism) strongly resemble those of autism.
3. The stereotypies of deaf children are accompanied by noises, whereas those of blind children are not.
4. The degree of mental retardation present is strongly associated with the severity of stereotypical behavior. In particular, mildly mentally retarded children show no stereotypies, whereas severely retarded children show many.

Obsessive-Compulsive Disorder

Obsessive-compulsive disorder is a rare condition that appears to affect men and women equally. It usually begins in adolescence or young adulthood, but may begin in childhood. It is usually seen in the face of an obsessive-compulsive behavior style or a compulsive personality disorder. In contrast with compulsions seen in other disorders (such as compulsive eating or pathological gambling), the compulsions of obsessive-compulsive individuals are ego-dystonic and never bring pleasure. They are also usually recognized by the patient as being senseless or fruitless. The most common compulsions characteristic of obsessive-compulsive disorder are lavomania (washing), arithmomania (counting), haphemania (touching), and repetitive checking (e.g., returning home repeatedly to see whether the door is locked or repeatedly assessing oneself in the mirror).

The most effective treatment is behavioral. Recently, clomipramine hydrochloride has been found to be effective in some patients with obsessive-compulsive disorder (Insel et al., 1983b). Clonidine has been especially effective in treating certain forms of ritualistic compulsive behavior accompanying Tourette's disorder (Cohen et al., 1980), but its efficacy against obsessive-compulsive disorder is unknown.

CHAPTER NINE

"Positivism": Echo Phenomena, Automatic Obedience, and Other Conditions of Complex Excessive Reactivity

INTRODUCTION

The signs discussed in this chapter represent excessive reactions to certain stimuli. In contrast to the signs discussed in Chapter 10, these reactions are not sudden or explosive, but, rather, appear to be deliberate and sometimes even methodical, and yet still occur outside of conscious control. And unlike negativism (Chapter 14), the reactions in this chapter appear to be in agreement with the stimuli: there is an unconscious acquiescence with, or mimicry of, what is seen or heard. As such, these signs could perhaps be grouped under the general title of "positivism," although this word, to our knowledge, has never been used for this purpose.

DESCRIPTIONS

Echo Phenomena

Echo phenomena have in common imitation or mimicry of some stimulus in the environment. The stimulus usually involves the expression or language of other people, but it can derive from a variety of different sights or sounds, such as animal noises or moving objects. In general, the pathological echo occurs very soon after the stimulus—at times even before the stimulus has completely ended (this is often true for negativistic phenomena as well)—and it appears to occur without the interposition of volition. The most common types are *echolalia*, in which words, phrases, or sounds are mimicked, *echo-*

praxia, in which complex and coordinated movements are imitated, and *echomimia*, in which facial expressions are repeated. Sometimes *echokinesia* is used as a general term for echo phenomena.

Automatic Obedience and Heterokinesis

"Automatic obedience" refers to the immediate, unhesitating compliance with a command or request, apparently without conscious control. A patient with this disorder, when asked to shake hands or stick out his tongue will do so, even when his tongue is pricked with a pin. Occasionally a patient will respond to a request with an action other than that desired, but not necessarily the opposite of what is requested. This condition is called *heterokinesis*, and is probably related to both automatic obedience and negativism. For example, a patient, when asked to shake hands, may raise his leg or hop up and down, and do this whenever a handshake is requested.

Forced Grasping

Forced grasping, or the *instinctive grasp reaction*, is a condition in which the patient grasps any object that touches his hand. Unlike the grasp reflex, forced grasping is a coordinated grasping reaction, rather than simply a flexion of the fingers (Seyffarth & Denny-Brown, 1948). When the condition is severe, patients continually grab and hold onto anything that touches them. While lying in bed they may clutch sheets, pillows, or parts of their own bodies. The force of the grasp is often stronger than one would imagine, considering the debilitated state of many of the patients who exhibit it, and more than one patient has left bruises on an examiner or pulled out securely attached central lines.

Mitgehen and *Mitmachen*

Finally, there are the related phenomena of *Mitgehen* and *Mitmachen*. *Mitgehen*, from the German "to go with," describes a state in which the patient passively moves in response to the lightest touch of the examiner. For example, such a patient, while standing, can be turned around and around simply by applying gentle pressure to his or her hand. *Mitmachen* is from the German "to make with," and refers to a state in which the patient's body can be easily molded into a new posture, but promptly returns to its resting position after contact with the examiner. This state is very similar to catalepsy, except that, in the case of *Mitmachen*, the new position is not maintained for any length of time. Note should be made of the so-called *magnet reaction* of Kleist (Hamilton, 1984), which is an exaggerated form of *Mitgehen*. Here, contact does not even have to be made with the patient; intent is all that is necessary. The classic example occurs with handshaking: when the examiner's hand is presented, the patient presents his, and, should the examiner move his hand around, the patient will do likewise, like a piece of iron being attracted to a magnet. The magnet reaction, as it is similar to *Mitgehen*, echopraxia and forced grasping, serves to emphasize the essential relatedness of some of the conditions in this chapter. Some patients with forced grasping also manifest a magnet reaction.

DIFFERENTIAL DIAGNOSIS

The conditions discussed in this chapter are so distinctive that they can, without much difficulty, usually be distinguished from other disorders. Random or highly repetitive movements can be clearly differentiated in most cases. Some investigators, however, have proposed that certain complex repetitive movements such as stereotypies may in fact be echo phenomena in which the initiating stimulus is provided by the patient. The term "autoechophenomena" has been proposed for such conditions. We do not advocate the use of this somewhat cumbersome theoretical term, because the notion of self-induced echokinesis, although interesting, remains to be convincingly demonstrated.

The disorders of paroxysmal excessive reactivity, such as cataplexy and hyperekplexia, discussed in the next chapter, can be differentiated from automatic obedience, echo phenomena, and the others by their suddenness and their simplicity. The paroxysmal conditions do not involve the complex synergistic changes in muscle tone and activity that accompany these disorders.

It is common for children to mimic actions, and this is in no way pathological. Instead, it probably represents a fundamental aspect of the learning process of children. Imitative behavior may persist into adulthood, occasionally as a component of dependent, histrionic, or borderline personality disorder. Mimicry or imitation, however, should be distinguished from the signs discussed here, where the response occurs almost immediately after the observed action or environmental change, and cannot be influenced voluntarily.

PATHOPHYSIOLOGY

In general, the more complex an action is, the more difficult it is to understand, and this is certainly true of these disorders. The pathophysiology is unknown. These rapid, almost-reflex responses to environmental change that appear without conscious intervention seem to result from what is perhaps a "short circuit" in the brain. A stimulus is perceived and acted upon through some localized brain pathway without the influence of any pertinent complex associative areas.

In the case of echo phenomena there exists a possible neurological model for just such a loss of associative input in certain of the *transcortical aphasias*. These aphasias are usually the result of vascular compromise in the border-zone areas between the middle cerebral and anterior or posterior cerebral arteries. In particular, transcortical sensory aphasia and mixed transcortical aphasia result in marked echolalia. Echolalia is such a distinctive part of these syndromes that it was the major focus of early discussions (Benson, 1979). (Even today, the presence of echolalia in transcortical aphasias results in some individuals' being misdiagnosed as having schizophrenia.) The loss of associative cortex that accompanies vascular compromise in borderzone areas implies a sort of short-circuiting in which the processing of language involves only the primary receptive and expressive speech areas (Wernicke's and Broca's areas, respectively) and the connections between them.

Luria's (1973) ideas on the involvement of the frontal lobes in echo phenomena were mentioned in the last chapter. His descriptions of clinical states following frontal-lobe damage also include a number of behaviors that we would regard as examples of automatic obedience. Interestingly, forced grasping and grasp reflexes are also thought to be due to frontal-lobe dysfunction, particularly involving the supplementary motor cortex (Shahani *et al.*, 1970; Brodal, 1981). Recently, grasp reflexes have been described as accompanying catatonia (Lohr, 1985). Catatonia encompasses most of the clinical features discussed in both this chapter and the last, and may, in the future, provide the link between many of the complex repetitive actions and the "positivistic" behaviors discussed here. Catatonia will be further discussed in Chapter 20.

SYNDROMES IN WHICH "POSITIVISM" OCCURS

Table 9-1 gives a listing of important conditions marked by complex excessive reactivity, broken down according to clinical sign.

There is a tendency for both neurologists and psychiatrists to consider some of these signs of "positivism," such as echo phenomena or automatic obedience, to be rare today. However, two issues should be kept in mind. First, the signs may easily be missed if they are not present in their most blatant form. They may not appear spontaneously when mild, and must therefore be actively sought out and elicited. A patient's echopraxia or automatic obedience may consist merely a shoulder twitch instead of a handshake.

Table 9-1. Syndromes in Which "Positivism" Occurs

Echo phenomena	Forced grasping (instinctive grasp reaction)
Catatonia	Frontal-lobe dysfunction (? involving supple-
Autism	mentary motor cortex)
Pervasive developmental disorder of	Dementia
children	Catatonia?
Congenital blindness	
Congenital deafness	
Mental retardation	
Tourette's disorder	
Frontal-lobe dysfunction	
Transcortical aphasias	
Myriachit, latah, jumping, and other related culture-bound syndromes	

Automatic obedience	*Mitgehen* and *Mitmachen*
Catatonia	Catatonia
Frontal-lobe dysfunction	Frontal-lobe dysfunction

Second, it should be remembered that all of these signs are features of catatonia, a condition that can occur in a variety of neurologic and psychiatric disorders. It has been estimated that as many as 10% of schizophrenics are catatonic (see Chapter 20), making catatonic schizophrenia possibly more common than Parkinson's disease and certainly more common among younger individuals. Thus, it should be remembered that the conditions discussed in this chapter may be not so much rare as unobserved or ignored.

CHAPTER TEN

Cataplexy, Excessive Startle Reaction, and Other Signs of Paroxysmal Excessive Reactivity

INTRODUCTION

The signs, symptoms, and disorders discussed in this chapter involve excessive reactions to some type of change in emotional state or sensory stimulus, usually of an abrupt nature. The exaggerated response may take different forms, such as the partial or complete loss of tone of cataplexy, the exaggerated startle response of hyperekplexia, the myoclonic jerk of reactive myoclonus, or the seizure of startle epilepsy.

Cataplexy was probably the first type of paroxysmal excessive reactivity to be described, and in the clinical literature was first noted to be a part of the narcoleptic syndrome. Although descriptions of narcolepsy in the scientific literature existed as early as 1862, the term was first introduced by Gelineau in 1880. In Gelineau's description of narcolepsy, cataplexy also appears to have been described, but the term "cataplexy" did not appear until it was coined by Henneberg in 1916 (Passouant, 1976). Many early investigators thought that cataplectic attacks were a form of chorea or seizure, and further confusion arose when a large number of cases of excessive daytime sleepiness occurred following the appearance of epidemic encephalitis in 1919 (Passouant, 1976). It was not until the 1940s to 1960s that idiopathic narcolepsy and the narcoleptic tetrad (including cataplexy, sleep paralysis, and hypnogogic hallucinations) were clearly differentiated from the excessive daytime sleepiness that occurs as a symptom of other conditions, such as postencephalitic states. Beginning in the 1960s, narcolepsy and cataplexy were more frequently recognized, and were eventually discovered to be disorders of sleep architecture.

In 1880, the same year that Gelineau published his observations on narcolepsy, Beard reported at the Sixth Annual Meeting of the American

Neurological Association an unusual syndrome (Beard, 1880). The patients, most of whom lived in the Moosehead Lake region of Maine, suffered from a previously undescribed syndrome of excessive reactivity to sounds, along with automatic obedience, and were called "jumpers" or "jumping French-men of Maine":

One of the jumpers while sitting in his chair with a knife in his hand was told to throw it, and he threw it quickly, so that it stuck in a beam opposite; at the same time he repeated the order to throw it. . . . He also threw away his pipe when filling it with tobacco when he was slapped upon the shoulder. Two jumpers standing near each other were told to strike, and they struck each other very forcibly. . . . When the commands are uttered in a quick loud voice the jumper repeats the order. When told to strike, he strikes, when told to throw it, he throws it, whatever he has in his hands. . . . They could not help repeating the word or sound that came from the person that ordered them any more than they could help striking, dropping, throwing, jumping, or starting; all of these phenomena were indeed but parts of the general condition known as jumping. It was not necessary that the sound should come from a human being: any sudden or unexpected noise, as the explosion of a gun or pistol, the falling of a window, or the slamming of a door, provided it be unexpected and loud enough, would cause these jumpers to exhibit some one or all of these phenomena. . . . It was dangerous to startle them in any way when they had an axe or knife in their hand. . . .(Beard, 1880, pp. 487–488)

Beard stated that the condition ran in families, rarely affected women, and could be seen in children as young as four or five. There was apparently no evidence of hysteria and, regarding prognosis, Beard was quoted as saying "once a jumper, always a jumper" (pp. 489–490).

Accounts of similar conditions in other parts of the world soon followed. Hammond described *myriachit* in Siberia in 1884, and *latah*, which was originally described in Malaysia, was later noted to occur in Northern Japan (where it was called *imu* among the Ainu), in the Phillipines (where it was called *mali-mali* or *silok*), in Burma (where it was called *yaun*), in Lapland (where it was called *Lapp panic*), and in the Sahara desert, as well as in North Africa and Yemen (Yap, 1951; Simons, 1980). All these conditions probably involved automatic obedience, echolalia, coprolalia, and excessive startle reactions to some degree. The growing number of reports of these conditions at the end of the last century eventually led Gilles de la Tourette to organize them into a cluster that he apparently considered to be the same as the syndrome which now bears his name (Stevens, 1965).

During this century, "jumpers" have either disappeared from the Western world or been ignored, although some relatively recent cases of the disorder may have been observed (Stevens, 1965; Kunkle, 1967). There have, however, been a growing number of reports of a hereditary condition marked by exaggerated startle responses without the additional features of automatic obedience and echolalia (Suhren *et al.*, 1966; Gastaut & Villeneuve, 1967; Andermann *et al.*, 1980; Kurczynski, 1983; Saenz-Lope *et al.*, 1984). Hyperekplexia (or, less correctly, hyperexplexia) from the Greek "to startle" is the name that has been given to this disorder, and it may be more common than is currently appreciated.

DESCRIPTIONS

Cataplexy

Cataplexy consists of sudden partial or complete loss of muscle tone (although the extraocular and respiratory muscles are usually uninvolved) with clear consciousness. It is considered to be a component of the narcoleptic syndrome, which consists of narcolepsy (sleep attacks), cataplexy, sleep paralysis (in which the patient is paralyzed for short periods of time in the transitional states between waking and sleeping), and hypnogogic (falling asleep) and hypnopompic (waking up) hallucinations. Cataplexy frequently occurs in response to a sudden change in the patient's emotional state, such as laughter or anger. It may also occur as a response to being startled, just as in hyperekplexia or startle epilepsy. Most of the time, the paralysis is partial, and in some cases the only manifestation of an attack may be the feeling of a slight relaxation in the arms or some other part of the body. Most patients are able to speak during the attacks, although the speech may be slurred and difficult to comprehend. There may be a relationship between the strength of the emotional stimulus and the severity of the cataplectic attack (Levin, 1932). There is a great variation in the frequency of attacks between patients—anywhere from one or two per year to almost (but not quite) continual attacks during the day, the latter constituting a very rare clinical state known as *status cataplecticus*. Consciousness is unimpaired during the attacks, which usually end in either an immediate resumption of the former position or a lapse into narcolepsy. The attacks usually last anywhere from 30 to 90 seconds, but may last as long as 30 minutes. Most patients report an inability to resist these episodes, although some profess a small amount of voluntary control over them (Kales *et al.,* 1982a), and some are able to bring on the attacks by an effort of will. Many patients report the attacks to be worse with tension, fatigue, or anxiety. During the time of the episode the patients are hypotonic in the affected portions of the body, and exhibit depression of deep tendon and H reflexes in those same areas (Guilleminault, 1976).

Excessive Startle Reaction

Excessive startle reaction represents an exaggeration of the normal startle reaction in terms of the frequency of the reactions, the severity of the reactions, or both. The startle reaction is a normal response to an unexpected stimulus, and consists of facial grimacing, blinking, and abduction and pronation of the arms, along with contraction of the abdominal musculature and bending of the knees (Landis & Hunt, 1939). Some patients, however, have been found to exhibit startle responses to an excessive degree, and their lives are plagued by continual falls provoked by a variety of unexpected sensory events, especially loud noises. Consciousness is unimpaired during these episodes. In contrast to patients with cataplexy, patients with exaggerated startle reaction usually exhibit hypertonia during the attack, rather than hypotonia. Severely affected individuals may show a clumsy broad-based gait that is reminiscent of cerebellar ataxia and is adopted because of the patient's fear of falling (Saenz-Lope et al., 1984). Indeed many of these patients injure themselves because they are unable to use their arms to break falls; the arms are instead flung out of the way during the episode. Between attacks, the muscle tone may be slightly increased (but normalizes during sleep), and the reflexes may, on occasion, be hyperactive.

Startle epilepsy, reactive myoclonus, and paroxysmal choreoathetosis are described in Chapters 3 and 11.

DIFFERENTIAL DIAGNOSIS

Cataplexy does not usually present many problems in diagnosis. The paroxysmal loss of muscular control and tone with unimpaired consciousness and the frequent accompanying features of narcolepsy, sleep paralysis, and hypnogogic hallucinations usually make the diagnosis clear. Occasionally, these patients may be confused with patients with startle epilepsy, paroxysmal choreoathetosis, or reflex myoclonus, but the absence of seizures, choreoathetosis, and myoclonus, the unimpaired state of consciousness, and the absence of electroencephalographic (EEG) and electromyographic (EMG) evidence of these other conditions should distinguish among them.

Hyperekplexia, in contrast to cataplexy, consists of an increase, rather than a decrease, in muscle tone. Also, patients with cataplexy usually remain prostrate for several seconds, whereas patients with hyperekplexia spring to their feet immediately after falling (Saenz-Lope et al., 1984). Sudden emotional changes tend to precipitate cataplexy but not hyperekplexia. Hyperekplexia may also be distinguished from the other conditions of excessive reactivity mentioned above by means similar to that in which cataplexy is differentiated. It is worth noting, however, that some patients with hyperekplexia have EEG abnormalities and that a large number of them have seizure disorders. Also, a significant number of hyperekplectics exhibit nocturnal myoclonus, which may further cloud the diagnosis.

Approximately 20% of patients with Tourette's syndrome can have excessive startle reactions, but the presence of tics and other typical features will usually make the diagnosis clear. It should be noted that there are a number of disorders, such as *latah*, that involve echolalia and coprolalia, just as does Tourette's. The distinction between these so-called "culture-bound" disorders and Tourette's is far from having been elucidated, although these latter conditions do not appear to involve tics.

Some patients with hysteria have "falling spells" and pseudoseizures that may on occasion resemble some of the above-mentioned conditions. It will usually be noted, though, that hysterics, in contrast to other patients, rarely injure themselves severely, managing to break their falls deftly with their arms or a nearby object. They do not always manage to do so, however, and special attention and care should be given to patients with presumed hysterical features who have borderline personality disorders in which patients frequently do themselves harm.

Patients with certain anxiety and panic disorders may have exaggerated startle reactions, but posture and tone are not severely affected as in hyperekplexia. (Patients with hyperekplexia often manifest significant anxiety associated with fear of falling, though, and some patients with generalized anxiety disorders may also have a generalized increase in tone, occasionally accompanied by cogwheeling.)

Other conditions in which falls may occur, such as hypoglycemia and ischemic drop attacks, are easily distinguished from the above disorders by the impairment in consciousness, as well as by other features mentioned above.

PATHOPHYSIOLOGY

Cataplexy

Most of the evidence available today points to an association of cataplexy with rapid-eye-movement (REM) sleep mechanisms. In this scheme, cataplexy is thought to be due to the activation of atonic REM sleep mechanisms during the waking state. Thus, cataplexy represents the intrusion of only one component of sleep—motor inhibition—into wakefulness.

The exact mechanism of either REM sleep or cataplectic atonia is not known. It has been proposed that the final pathway in the production of cataplexy includes the medullary reticular inhibitory region, which has been considered to be important in the production and maintenance of posture and tone (see Chapter 2). Activation or release of this region could produce the flexor and extensor atonia observed in cataplexy. The exact mechanism of this release is unclear, but it has been proposed that "executive" cells in the upper pons (which are cholinergic) could activate the medullary inhibitory region at the beginning of REM sleep (Hobson *et al.*, 1975; Foutz *et al.*, 1981). These executive cells may be under two main types of feedback control: (1) positive feedback control from their own cholinergic collaterals, and (2) negative feedback control from noradrenergic cells in the locus ceruleus. Thus, a balance of cholinergic and aminergic inputs into the pontine executive center may play a role in the production of both REM and cataplectic atonia. There is pharmacological evidence supporting this conjecture in dog experiments, in which it has been found that norepinephrine reuptake inhibitors and anticholinergic agents suppress canine cataplexy (Foutz et al., 1981) (see also Chapter 24).

From a neuropsychiatric viewpoint, the relationship between cataplectic attacks and sudden emotional changes is of interest. Vizioli (1964) has proposed involvement of the limbic system in cataplexy, where activity in the limbic system of cataplectics may cause activation of the reticular inhibitory system (perhaps by overcoming the systems involved in inhibiting the reticular inhibitory region). As Guilleminault points out (1976), even in normal people strong emotional stimuli, such as extreme fear or laughter, can cause a sensation of leg weakness or "knee-buckling," and in cataplectics this response is exaggerated.

Exaggerated Startle Response

Landis and Hunt (1939) divided the normal startle response into two parts, the eye-blink, which remains throughout life, and the facial–bodily response, which is often attenuated with repeated startles. These investigators discovered that the startle response replaced the Moro response in infants at the age of approximately 4 months. In most later studies it is this normal startle response that is thought to be pathologically exaggerated in hyperstartlers.

The pathophysiology of exaggerated startle response is unknown. Most investigators believe that there is increased neuronal excitability in some part of the brain, but it is unclear whether this is primary hyperexcitability or whether it is secondary to reduced inhibition from some other part of the brain. The exact brain structure involved is also unknown; hypotheses range from those implicating brainstem to those implicating cortex as the principal structure involved. Experiments on animals have shown that startle responses can be attenuated by removal of the superior colliculi, and further experiments involving destruction of areas of the brainstem, especially including the nucleus gigantocellularis in the medullary reticular formation, have implicated brainstem pathology or loss of higher inhibitory control of brainstem structures in the pathogenesis of abnormal startle (Halliday, 1975; Saenz-Lope et al., 1984).

Other investigators have reported excessive long-loop reflexes in patients with hyperekplexia; assuming that these reflexes involve cortical pathways (and this is not completely clear) this implies excessive cortical excitability to be the cause of exaggerated startle responses (Markland et al., 1984). It has also been proposed that serotonergic mechanisms are involved, because of the response of patients with hyperekplexia and other startle disorders (such as startle epilepsy) to clonazepam (Andermann *et al.*, 1980; Saenz-Lope *et al.*, 1984). As can be seen, the pathophysiology of exaggerated startle is far from being clearly understood.

SYNDROMES IN WHICH PAROXYSMAL EXCESSIVE REACTIVITY OCCURS

Cataplexy

Although there have been reports of cataplexy occurring with upper brainstem tumors, multiple sclerosis, and systemic lupus erythematosis (Stahl *et al.*, 1980) these are very rare; cataplexy may, for practical purposes, be considered to occur almost exclusively as part of the syndrome of narcolepsy. This syndrome affects approximately 0.05% of the population, and appears to be equally common in men and women. The classical tetrad consists of sleep attacks, cataplexy, hypnogogic (or hypnopompic) hallucinations and sleep paralysis, but sleep attacks and cataplexy are far more common than the other components. Although the excessive daytime sleepiness that accompanies the narcoleptic syndrome may begin in the first decade of life, cataplexy does not usually occur until later. In rare patients cataplexy may occur alone at first, but it is usually later accompanied by other symptoms and signs from the tetrad (Kales *et al.*, 1982a).

A variety of cognitive and behavioral abnormalities may occur in individuals with narcolepsy. Hynogogic hallucinations are, of course, an integral part of the syndrome, and these almost invariably consist of visual hallucinations, occasionally accompanied by auditory hallucinations as well. Hallucinations of taste, touch, and smell are rarely observed (Ribstein, 1976). The hallucinations usually occur upon falling asleep, although they may, rarely, occur on waking or during the day, such as when driving. Unlike the hallucinations of schizophrenics, which are often bizarre or fantastic, these hallucinations are often mundane and simple, being scenes from life, simple patterns, or ordinary objects. The accompanying emotional state may range from bland indifference to anxiety or panic. Often the hallucinations are so terrifying that patients loathe going to sleep, for fear of what they may see.

Kales *et al.* (1982b) have also reported an increased incidence of depression and personality disorders in narcoleptics, but most of these findings are thought to be consequences of narcolepsy rather than primary phenomena. Half of the narcoleptics in the Kales *et al.* (1982b) study were otherwise psychiatrically normal, but the other half were thought to have developed additional psychiatric problems as the result of psychosocial pressure during development, as well as problems resulting from attempts made by the patients to control not only their environment but their emotional state as well.

The treatment of cataplexy and narcolepsy usually consists of stimulants for the sleep attacks and tricyclic antidepressants for the cataplectic episodes.

Hyperekplexia

Hyperekplexia as a disorder is sometimes confused with excessive startle response as a sign, but in actuality the exaggerated startle response is only one component of the syndrome of hyperekplexia. In addition, there is also generalized muscular rigidity in infancy, nocturnal myoclonus, and a high incidence of umbilical and inguinal hernias (Suhren et al., 1966; Kurczynski, 1983). The disorder runs in families and is different from the disorders described earlier in this section, such as jumping, latah, or myriachit, in that there are no echo phenomena present. Responses to a variety of different treatments including clonazepam, sodium valproate, 5-hydroxytryptophan, and piracetam, have been reported (Gastaut & Villeneuve, 1967; Saenz-Lope et al., 1984).

Latah

This disorder is very similar to "jumping" which was described earlier in the chapter. It is a culture-bound condition found in Malaysia and Indonesia; however, similar syndromes probably exist around the world In addition to exaggerated startle response, its sufferers also manifest coprolalia, echolalia, echopraxia, and automatic obedience. Often, latah reactions are deliberately provoked in those with the disorder, for the amusement of others at various festivities (Simons, 1980). The condition appears to be more common in women, as it may be considered less acceptable to provoke the reaction in men, who might retaliate more effectively.

There has been considerable debate on both the nature of the disorder and its cultural dependence and significance. Simons (1980) has proposed that the basis for the disorder is excessive startling, which is molded into a distinctly geographical phenomenon by specific cultural factors. Others, such as Kenny (1983), believe that the human startle response is inconsequential to the development of latah, and that the condition should be viewed as solely a cultural phenomenon. Still others, such as Murphy (1983), advocate a psychoanalytic approach to understanding the clinical picture of latah. Much of the debate stems from differences in the relative importance relegated to physiological as opposed to psychological and cultural factors, and the issue is certainly far from being resolved. What should be noted, however, is that most of the basic phenomena seen in latah—specifically, hyperstartling, coprolalia, echolalia, echopraxia, and automatic obedience—have been described in other conditions, such as hyperekplexia, Tourette's syndrome, and catatonia, all of which are currently believed to have significant neuropatho-physiological underpinnings.

Other disorders involving paroxysmal excessive reactivity include reflex myoclonus, paroxysmal choreoathetosis, startle epilepsy, and Tourette's syndrome. These disorders are discussed elsewhere in this volume.

CHAPTER ELEVEN

Myoclonus

INTRODUCTION

Myoclonus can occur as excessive random, repetitive, or reactive movement. It can be focal or generalized, and it can arise from just about anywhere in the central nervous system that has anything to do with movement. The distinguishing features of myoclonus, therefore, relate not to the pattern and location of the disorder, but, rather, to speed of the movements and to their lack of susceptibility to voluntary control.

The term was apparently first used by Friedreich (1881) in a case report of a patient with rapid multifocal muscle twitches. Freidreich named the disorder *paramyoclonus multiplex* because it could involve many different muscles on both sides of the body. The word "myoclonus" was derived from the Greek terms for muscle and turmoil. Before Friedreich, there were many case descriptions in the literature that may have represented myoclonic disorders, but these were confused with other disorders, such as chorea (a term which, for many years, was one of the very few available to describe excessive movement), epilepsy, tics, and hyperekplexia.

Following Friedreich's initial work in the area, the confusion surrounding myoclonus gradually dissipated. In the last half of the 1800s, Gilles de la Tourette (1885) and Meige and Feindel (1907) separated tic from the other movement disorders. Also during this time Unverricht (1891) and Lundborg (1903) described and characterized familial myoclonic epilepsy. After these observations, many other cases of myoclonus, occurring either alone or in association with other neurological diseases, were reported. For an excellent discussion of the history of the concept of myoclonus, see Marsden *et al.* (1981a).

DESCRIPTION

"Myoclonus" refers to an isolated rapid contraction of a muscle or group of muscles that cannot be influenced by effort of will. It can occur spontaneously or as a reaction to sensory stimulation. It may manifest in an irregular, random pattern, in a highly rhythmic, repetitive pattern, or somewhere in between. Myoclonus, in contrast to many of the other movement disorders in this book, may be a normal phenomenon. As such, it is sometimes termed physiological myoclonus, and includes hypnic or sleep jerks, stress- and exercise-induced jerks, and hiccups. Myoclonus that is considered to be pathological (either because of its frequency or severity) may occur as an isolated phenomenon (essential myoclonus) or may accompany epilepsy and other pathological conditions (symptomatic myoclonus).

DIFFERENTIAL DIAGNOSIS

It is the speed of the muscular jerks that characterizes myoclonus, and many movement disorders can be distinguished from it on the basis of this characteristic alone. Typically, the duration of the muscle jerk in most forms of myoclonus is between 10 and 50 milliseconds, and is rarely longer than 120 milliseconds. Thus myoclonus is easily differentiated from such disorders as athetosis and dystonia, which involve much slower movements (although it should be noted that myoclonus can occur in combination with torsion dystonia—a combination that can create considerable diagnostic confusion; see Obeso et al., 1983).

Rapid simple tics may resemble myoclonic jerks, but most tics are susceptible to a certain amount of voluntary control, and tics often assume complex characteristics not observed in myoclonus. Myoclonus of an irregular random pattern may resemble chorea, but the movements of myoclonus are usually more abrupt and lack the continuous flowing character of choreiform movements.

Rhythmic myoclonus may resemble tremor, but tremor motion is smooth and sinusoidal, whereas myoclonus, even when rhythmic, has more of an abrupt, square-wave appearance.

Finally, reactive myoclonus may resemble hyperekplexia, and at the present time it is difficult to say whether these disorders may actually be closely related. Nocturnal myoclonus frequently occurs in patients with hyperekplexia. When falls occur in patients with myoclonus, however, the falls are the result of widespread-action myoclonus, and such widespread myoclonus is not observed in patients with hyperekplexia (Saenz-Lope et al., 1984). Thus, there is evidence that hyperekplexia may be a different, though possibly related, disorder.

PATHOPHYSIOLOGY

The pathophysiological mechanisms involved in the production of myoclonus are still not clearly understood, in part because of the many different forms myoclonus can take and the many conditions with which it is asso-ciated. Different hypotheses have been offered, all of which have drawbacks. In this discussion we follow the scheme of Marsden *et al.,* (1981a, 1983a). Myoclonus is here divided according to the putative site of origin of the aberrant electrical activity responsible for the muscle jerk. Basically, three sites have been proposed: cortical, subcortical, and segmental or spinal, although sometimes segmental myoclonus has been grouped with the subcortical types.

Cortical Myoclonus

Cortical myoclonus has been reported to occur in several forms, including (1) a *cortical reflex form*, in which the myoclonic jerk is triggered by some peripheral sensory event or by attempted voluntary movement (this latter form is also sometimes called *action myoclonus*), (2) a *spontaneous cortical form*, which is similar to the cortical reflex variety, but in which the jerks arise without any provocative stimulus, and (3) *epilepsia partialis continua*, which consists of repetitive myoclonic jerks lasting for days to weeks. The above forms are usually focal, and can usually be demonstrated to be time-locked to some cortical electrical event on electroencephalography or electrocortico-graphy.

Subcortical Myoclonus

Subcortical myoclonus has also been reported to occur in several different varieties. The more common forms include (1) a *reticular reflex form*, which, like cortical reflex myoclonus, is triggered by peripheral sensation or by action, (2) a *spontaneous reticular form*, and (3) a *cortically triggered reticular form*, in which an electrical event in the cortex may cause a subcortical site to generate a myoclonic jerk. The subcortical types of myoclonus differ from the cortical types in that the muscle jerk in the former does not appear to be timelocked to any cortical event, and the jerks are usually generalized, as opposed to being focal.

Segmental Myoclonus

Segmental myoclonus is one of the commonest forms of myoclonus. It is occasionally also called *spinal* or *rhythmical myoclonus*, although it is not always rhythmical, nor is it always limited to the spinal cord. Neither is it true that all rhythmical myoclonias are segmental in origin. Segmental myo-clonus is thought to originate from an irritative lesion in the spinal cord or brainstem. The most common form is palatal myoclonus, which is very regular and which some investigators consider to actually be a tremor instead of a form of myoclonus (see Chapter 5). Palatal myoclonus is one of the rare movement disorders that does not disappear during sleep. It has been associated with lesions of the brainstem, particularly involving the Guillain–Mollaret triangle (rubro-dentato-olivary circuit) (Guillain & Mollaret, 1931).

Apart from the above, very little is known about the pathophysiology of myoclonus, especially of the nonrhythmic varieties. A large number of different pathological lesions have been reported (see Bonduelle, 1968; Van Woert & Hwang, 1978), but there is, as yet, no clear pattern.

Neurochemically, there is evidence that certain types of myoclonus may be related to disorders of serotonin metabolism (such as has been proposed in hyperekplexia; see Chapter 10). In particular, myoclonus has been postulated to be associated with a hyperserotonergic state (see Van Woert & Hwang, 1978). Further investigation is needed to elucidate the exact neurochemical abnormalities, however.

Table 11-1. Common Forms of Myoclonus and Conditions in Which They Occur

Physiological	
Hypnic (sleep) jerks	Occurs in first stage of sleep.
Hiccups	
Anxiety-, stress-, or exertion-induced myoclonus	
Essential	
Familial (including paramyoclonus multiplex)	Often involve face and proximal musculature.
Sporadic	
Nocturnal	Usually involves legs.
Symptomatic	
Spinocerebellar degenerations (including Friedreich's ataxia)	
Baltic myoclonus (Unverricht–Lundberg)	
Dyssynergia cerebellaris myoclonia (Ramsay–Hunt syndrome)	Many different types of myoclonus may be seen, involving spinocerebellar degeneration, occasionally accompanied by epilepsy.
Subacute sclerosing panencephalitis	Often stereotyped, 6–10 per minute, widespread.
Postencephalitic (especially following encephalitis lethargica)	Usually bilateral and symmetrical, approximately 1 per second.
Creutzfeldt–Jakob disease	Often irregular.
Leukodystrophies (including Krabbe's, Pelizeus–Merzbacher)	Often extensive or massive, occasional seizures.
Lipidoses (including Tay–Sachs, Lafora body, Batten's)	Often rhythmic and in response to stimulation.

A variety of different treatments have proved useful for various types of myoclonus, including clonazepam, valproic acid, and 5-hydroxytrytophan (Kobayashi, 1982). However, no single drug has proved to be generally effective.

SYNDROMES IN WHICH MYOCLONUS OCCURS

Table 11-1 lists the more common syndromes in which myoclonus may be a feature. We follow in part the divisions of Bonduelle (1968) and of Marsden *et al.* (1983a) in grouping the myoclonias into three main types: (1) *physiological myoclonus*, which can occur in normal people, (2) *essential myoclonus*, in which the myoclonic movements are pathological, but there are no other associated signs or symptoms, and (3) *symptomatic myoclonus*, in which myoclonus is present as a part of a more complex neurological picture, often in association with epilepsy. In addition to the disorders listed in Table 11-1, myoclonus may be seen to accompany other epileptic disorders (including infantile spasms and myoclonic astatic epilepsy) basal ganglia disorders (including Huntington's and Wilson's diseases), and toxic–metabolic encephalopathies (including hepatic and renal failure and heavy-metal poisoning), and may follow almost any other conceivable type of insult or injury to the brain (especially hypoxia).

B. Decreased Movement

CHAPTER TWELVE

Hypokinesia

INTRODUCTION

Of the different ways that motor function may be lost, including paralysis from nerve injury or weakness from myopathy, one of the least understood is hypokinesia. In the presence of preserved consciousness and unimpaired muscle and peripheral nerve function, individuals who have this condition suffer difficulty in performing voluntary movements, especially in terms of the initiation and speed of movement.

For centuries, this state was poorly described and probably not differentiated from catalepsy and various palsies. One of the earliest investigators to focus on akinesia as a distinct entity was Wernicke, who considered it to be one of the three cardinal forms of psychomotor disorder (the other two being hyperkinetic and parakinetic forms; see DeAjuriaguerra, 1975). Wernicke did not believe that akinesia was the result of disordered will, but, rather, that the will encountered obstacles in forming higher-level associative motor groupings or plans.

Over the course of this century, the concept of akinesia has been discussed both as a psychomotor condition (as possibly observed in catatonia) and as a neuromotor disorder (as in Parkinson's disease). Kleist, for example, considered akinesia to be predominantly a disorder of psychomotor initiation, whereas Martin and Denny-Brown have concentrated on the purely neurological aspects of akinesia (Martin, 1967; Denny-Brown,1968; DeAjuriaguerra, 1975)

Today, these problems are still far from being resolved. Most of the time, the terms "akinesia," "bradykinesia," and "hypokinesia" refer to aspects of the clinical picture of parkinsonism, although they are occasionally used to refer to states that occur in other neurological conditions (such as akinetic mutism) and in a variety of psychiatric disorders.

DESCRIPTIONS

Akinesia

"Akinesia," strictly speaking, means an absence of movement, but many investigators do not use the term in this sense. Akinetic mutism is an example of a disorder in which there may be true akinesia with almost no voluntary movement at all. Most commonly, however, the term is used to refer to one of the major signs of parkinsonism in which difficulty arises in the *initiation of movement*, and this occurs with unimpaired consciousness and fully functioning peripheral movement effector mechanisms (peripheral nerves, muscles, and their connections). Although it is true that, when severe, this parkinsonian akinesia may resemble a true akinetic state, it is worth remembering that the term is used in two different senses. In general, in this book we use the term to refer to difficulty in initiating movement.

Bradykinesia

"Bradykinesia" refers to a slowing of movement. As akinesia relates to problems in initiating movements (and roughly corresponds to the time it takes to react to a stimulus), bradykinesia relates to a disturbance in the time it takes to perform a movement. (Akinesia is often quantitatively approximated by what has been called the *reaction time*, whereas bradykinesia is approximated by the *movement time*.) A patient who walks very slowly but with relatively normal arm swing excursion and step length is solely bradykinetic. Similarly, if a patient, while drinking from a cup, languorously raises the cup to his lips, but otherwise does so in a normal fashion, he is bradykinetic. Bradykinesia rarely exists in isolation from other forms of reduced movement, such as akinesia or loss of associated or synkinetic movement.

Hypokinesia

"Hypokinesia" is the general term that refers to any loss of voluntary movement in the presence of preserved consciousness and unimpaired peripheral nerve and muscle function. It incorporates bradykinesia and akinesia, as well as a loss of associated movements or any other reduction in motor function, some of which may be difficult to describe. Many different signs of decreased movement tend, of necessity, to look more alike with increasing severity. This fact, along with the observation that different types of motor-function loss tend to occur together, makes hypokinesia a convenient, if not very exact, term.

DIFFERENTIAL DIAGNOSIS

The fact that hypokinesia occurs in the presence of normal peripheral motor effector mechanisms clearly separates it from many cases of paresis and paralysis, such as those caused by peripheral-nerve injury and spinal-cord trauma. Also, central causes of paresis and paralysis may be differentiated because they are almost always focal or multifocal in presentation.

Weakness, such as is seen in myopathic conditions and myasthenia gravis, may be more difficult to differentiate from hypokinesia. Although hypokinesia can occur in the presence of normal muscle strength, it is frequently accompanied by muscle weakness, which may cloud the diagnosis. Often, the only way to distinguish these two conditions is on the basis of the other characteristic signs that accompany such disorders as muscular dystrophy or myotonia congenita.

"Akinetic mutism" is a term first used by Cairns et al. (1941) to describe a clinical state of generalized sensory unresponsiveness in the presence of visual following and the appearance of being awake. It was initially reported in association with an epidermoid cyst of the third ventricle (Cairns et al., 1941) and has since been described with other third-ventricle tumors, basilar artery thrombosis, and bilateral anterior cingulate gyrus damage, as well as damage to the globus pallidus and hypothalamus (Barris & Schuman, 1953; Cravioto et al., 1960; Klee, 1961; Ross & Stewart, 1981). The cause is unknown, but a recent study has demonstrated the effectiveness of a dopamine agonist (bromocriptine) on akinetic mutism following surgical removal of an anterior hypothalamic tumor (Ross & Stewart, 1981). These authors suggest that the akinesia may be due to dopaminergic pathway damage involving the mesolimbic or mesocortical projections from area A-10 (ventral tegmental area of Tsai) to the anterior cingulate gyri. Thus, the akinesia of akinetic mutism may be related to the akinesia of Parkinson's disease.

Catalepsy or negativism may coexist with hypokinesia, but these two signs are quite distinctive and should not usually present problems in differential diagnosis.

PATHOPHYSIOLOGY

Although we have outlined various ways to distinguish between some of the subtypes of hypokinesia, such as akinesia and bradykinesia, most research performed on hypokinetic states does not adequately discriminate between them. This is especially true of animal research, where akinesia is usually the only term used for a reduction of movement, and generally refers to what we have described as hypokinesia. We shall look at possible pathophysiological mechanisms of hypokinesia in general, and discuss, where possible, proposed mechanisms of more specific signs, such as bradykinesia.

Basically, there are three main hypotheses concerning the etiology of hypokinesia, and these are by no means mutually exclusive. The first proposes that *hypokinesia may be the result of a general loss (or change) in pallidal outflow.* This is based on evidence that, after neurosurgical lesions of the globus pallidus, some patients suffer an exacerbation of their hypokinesia, and also that pallidal lesions abolish the effectiveness of dopamine agonists on hypokinesia in animals (DeLong & Georgopoulos, 1981).

This latter finding is related to the second hypothesis: that *hypokinesia may be the result of interruption of dopaminergic transmission from the substantia nigra pars compacta to the striatum.* There is an abundance of evidence from animal experiments indicating that bilateral ablation of the substantia nigra results in marked hypokinesia (see DeLong & Georgopoulos, 1981). It is also well known that patients with Parkinson's disease (where the most clearly and consistently described pathological abnormalities involve the substantia nigra pars compacta) often show marked akinesia.

These first two hypotheses are certainly not mutually exclusive, as very little is known about the effects of nigrostriatal pathway disruption on pallidal outflow. Filion (1979) has demonstrated that, in monkeys, interruption of the migrostriatal tract results in a change in the firing pattern of pallidal neurons, but without a change in the mean firing rate. He observed that, following nigrostriatal lesions, the normal characteristic high firing rates of medial pallidal neurons and the normal long pauses between firing of lateral pallidal neurons are replaced by a disorganized pattern of bursts of activity. Further, this same disorganization was found in monkeys that received dopamine antagonists, and was associated in both cases with signs of parkinsonism. These signs (and especially hypokinesia) were abolished when the monkeys were given apormorphine, and this was accompanied by a decrease (rather than an increase) in medial pallidal firing. This study indicates that in certain cases of hypokinesia, the relationship of pallidal outflow to hypokinesia may be more complicated than a mere reduction in pallidal neuron firing rate, and may instead involve changes in the pattern of pallidal firing.

The third hypothesis, and one that is most interesting from a neuropsychiatric point of view, *implicates dysfunction in neural pathways involving the nucleus accumbens septi and mesocorticolimbic pathways in the genesis of hypokinesia.* Evidence for this hypothesis derives from the findings that reserpine-induced hypokinesia in rats can be reversed by injection of dopamine agonists into the nucleus accumbens, but not into the striatum proper (Anden & Johnels, 1977), and that hyperactivity induced by L-dopa can be abolished by lesions of the accumbens (Harik & Morris, 1973). Related to this idea is the finding that dopamine agonists can reverse the hypokinesia of akinetic mutism, as was described earlier in this chapter.

One of the major difficulties with these three hypotheses involves the interpretation of hypokinesia in animals. In man, there may be several distinct types of hypokinesia—say, a parkinsonian, a huntingtonian, and a catatonic type. It is not clear what these would correspond to in animals, because they all might look the same, especially in lower mammals. Thus, it is possible that the first hypothesized mechanism of hypokinesia (related to a loss or change of globus pallidus outflow) might occur in Huntington's disease with massive destruction of the striatum. Similarly, the second proposed mechanism (related to a loss of nigrostriatal transmission) might underlie the poverty of movement in Parkinson's disease. And, finally, the third mechanism of hypokinesia (related to dysfunction involving nucleus accumbens, a structure that has been implicated in the pathophysiology of schizophrenia) might be the cause of catatonic hypokinesia. These ideas, though interesting, are highly speculative and serve to show how complex the issue of the etiology of hypokinesia really is.

So much for the possible structures involved in the production of hypokinesia. The question remains, however, as to what is happening physiologically that could account for poverty of movement. Although there are many causes of hypokinesia, here we must largely limit our discussion to parkinsonian hypokinesia, which has been more thoroughly investigated than have the other types of hypokinesia.

The hypokinesia of Parkinson's, as mentioned earlier, has been studied largely in terms of reaction time (RT) and movement time (MT) (Heilman et al., 1976). In general, both of these have been found to be prolonged over normal, but MT has usually been found to be much more disturbed than has RT (Evarts et al., 1979). This much is clear, but we are still left without the exact reasons for the slowness and delay.

Originally, during the early part of this century, many investigators thought that the rigidity of Parkinson's disease caused the loss of movement. However neurologists such as Wilson noted, as early as 1928, that there was little convincing evidence of a major direct causal relationship between rigidity and hypokinesia (although there is evidence that facial muscle rigidity may contribute to facial hypokinesia; Hunker et al., 1982). Following the advent of neurosurgical approaches to Parkinson's disease during the latter half of this century (most of which were aimed at disrupting pallidal outflow), it became clear that there were many cases in which the rigidity could be partially or completely ameliorated without much effect on the hypokinesia. As is the case with similar procedures on animals, in many cases following neurosurgery the hypokinesia actually became worse.

Since hypokinesia does not appear to be strongly related to rigidity, other factors that might correlate with the loss of movement have been sought. Recently, MHPG (3-methoxy-4-hydroxyphenylglycol) levels in the cerebrospinal fluid have been found to correlate with RT in patients with Parkinson's disease, thus implicating altered norepinephrine metabolism in the etiology of hypokinesia (Stern *et al.*, 1984). It has also recently been reported that L-dopa can improve movement speed without loss of accuracy in Parkinson's disease patients (Baroni *et al.*, 1984). Thus, it appears that altered catecholamines and catecholamine metabolism may play a role in the etiology of hypokinesia.

Other work on the physiology of hypokinesia has focused on the putative motor planning functions of the basal ganglia. Joubert and Barbeau (1969), after studying patients with Parkinson's disease hypokinesia on a variety of performance tests, concluded that

the delay in initiating a movement or in changing from one motor pattern to another in akinetic patients is the result of a defect in *discriminative* sensations (mainly proprioceptive and visual) resulting in the inability to elaborate a motor pattern or plan of action . . . in the time required for the resultant movement to be adequate. This constant delay and effort in sensory–motor integration ("central processing") leads to progressively more difficult postural adjustments and, eventually, to complete inactivation of all motor mechanisms. (pp. 374–375)

In contrast to Joubert and Barbeau, who proposed that postural difficulties may arise from defective motor planning, other investigators have hypothesized that defective postural mechanisms might contribute to hypokinesia. Stark (1968) postulated that for a person to engage in rapid open-loop or ballistic movement, postural mechanisms must be shut off, and that patients with Parkinson's disease experience difficulty in doing this. Thus, the hypokinesia of Parkinson's disease may be the result of conflicting messages being sent to the muscles.

It has become clear in recent years that open-loop fast (or ballistic) movements are abnormal in patients with Parkinson's disease (Flowers, 1975, 1976; Hallett & Khoshbin, 1980). In particular, the normal triphasic (agonist–antagonist–agonist) firing pattern of muscles is disturbed. It is not clear, though, whether this is related to faulty postural mechanisms or to a disturbance in some other function of the basal ganglia. For example, Hallett and Khoshbin (1980) have postulated that the basal ganglia, in carrying out a motor plan, are responsible for "energizing" the important muscles involved, and that disturbance in this function results in clinically apparent bradykinesia. L-Dopa has been reported to improve the disturbance in muscle firing pattern in Parkinson's disease (Baroni *et al.*, 1984).

We should add one note in passing before concluding this section, which is that RT has been found to be increased in schizophrenia. Most of the recent work in this area has revolved around hypotheses relating RT to attention and information processing, and has not focused on the fact that most of the schizophrenics reported in these studies have probably been on neuroleptic medications that can cause parkinsonism (Steffy & Galbraith, 1974, 1980). Of interest, however, are several studies that reported increased

Table 12-1. Conditions in Which Hypokinesia Occurs

Parkinson's disease

Parkinsonism secondary to other causes (e.g., postencephalitic, neuroleptic-induced, "arteriosclerotic," carbon disulfide and manganese; see Table 22-2)

Huntington's disease (especially Westphal, rigid–hypokinetic variants)

Wilson's disease

Hallervorden–Spatz disease

Progressive supranuclear palsy

Shy–Drager syndrome and other multisystem atrophies

Basal-ganglia damage or dysfunction

Catatonia (with stupor)

Hysteria

Depression (with stupor, especially bipolar depressive episodes)

Sensory neglect syndromes (often secondary to parietal lesions)

Frontal-lobe damage or dysfunction

Dementia

Cerebellar lesions or atrophy

Hypothyroidism

Systemic lupus erythematosus

Pickwickian syndrome

Akinetic mutism

Autism and mental retardation (severe)

RT in schizophrenic patients and that were carried out before the advent of
neuroleptic drugs (Wells & Kelley, 1922; Rodnick & Shakow, 1940). Also,
there are several studies demonstrating that RT in medicated schizophrenics
is at least as fast as that in nonmedicated schizophrenics (Heilizer, 1959; Held
et al., 1970; Braff, 1981). It is still not clear exactly what increased RT in
schizophrenia means, but it is certainly possible that, just as in Parkinson's
disease, it may be related to basal-ganglia dysfunction. This will be further
discussed in Chapter 22.

SYNDROMES IN WHICH HYPOKINESIA OCCURS

Table 12-1 offers a listing of important conditions marked by various types of
hypokinesia.

CHAPTER THIRTEEN

Catalepsy

INTRODUCTION

The notion of catalepsy is an ancient one. For two millenia, the term has referred to a clinical state in which patients maintain postures for very long periods of time. Some physicians in ancient times, however, used the term in an altogether different sense. "Catalepsy," coming from the Greek terms meaning "down" and "seizure," was used by Galen to refer to a form of seizure that was to be differentiated from the other types—"epilepsy" and "analepsy." He called seizures that began in the brain epileptic, those that began in the stomach analeptic, and those that began elsewhere (especially the limbs) cataleptic (Temkin, 1971).

The use of the word "catalepsy" to refer to a type of seizure gradually faded over time, whereas its other meaning survived. Here is a 17th-century description:

Of a catalepsis

The Signs of this stupendous Disease are very manifest. The Patients on a sudden are speechless, all stiff and immoveable, their Senses weak and dull, they remain in the same posture wherein they were taken; for they shut not their Eyes, if they were open before, but look stead-fastly on something. (Dolaeus, 1686, p. 94)

This description may represent seizure activity, and it is easy to see how "catalepsy" came to stand for both malleable posturing and an epileptic disorder.

Up until the 19th century, "catalepsy" was one of the few terms available to label states of decreased mobility (Berrios, 1981a, 1981b). As medicine moved from a symptom-oriented to a disease-oriented science it was inevitable that catalepsy would eventually be subsumed within a syndrome, and that syndrome was catatonia (Kahlbaum, 1874/1973). Before catatonia claimed catalepsy as a cardinal sign, other clinical entities had been associated with it, such as various ill-defined stuporous states, but it is to catatonia that catalepsy has remained firmly attached. In fact, these two terms are often confused and used interchangeably, especially in the animal literature. Almost all of the recent studies on catalepsy have involved animals, but one must be careful about extending these findings to man, as cataleptic states reported in animals may not be equivalent to those in humans.

Catalepsy has also been called *cerea flexibilitas*, or waxy flexibility, but not all physicians have agreed with the synonymous use of these terms. Bleuler (1911/1950), for example, held that "waxy flexibility" should refer to a less severe form of catalepsy, and Morrison (1973) noted that "waxy flexibility" has occasionally referred to a state of "plastic" or "lead-pipe" rigidity without the malleable posturing. In this book we shall follow the common trend to regard catalepsy and waxy flexibility as synonymous, but we nevertheless recommend that care be taken in interpreting reports that use these terms.

DESCRIPTION

"Catalepsy" refers to a clinical state in which a patient's body can be placed in awkward and uncomfortable positions by the examiner, and these are maintained for prolonged periods of time. The associated level of consciousness is variable, but usually somewhat depressed. Catalepsy can occur with varying degrees of severity. It is almost always found in association with a generalized decrease in voluntary movement, but in a mild form may be manifest only as a momentary postural pause after placement in a certain position, after which the resting position is quickly reassumed. Some investigators do not believe this latter condition represents true catalepsy and have given the separate name of *Haltungsverharren* to this mild malleability of posture (Fish, 1976). This may be a valid point, but it is probably simpler and less confusing to call all of these mild states catalepsy, and then note the severity.

Severe cataleptic episodes can also be diagnostically confusing, as the limbs may be nearly frozen in position and may require considerable effort to be moved. Nevertheless, to qualify as catalepsy, the limbs should retain their new position, even if they are difficult to move. This helps differentiate catalepsy from other conditions in which there may be marked resistance to passive movement, such as in various states of rigidity (see Chapter 16).

Cataleptic states may be variable in several other ways as well. The degree of muscular resistance varies, as has just been mentioned, but most commonly the resistance is of a steady, even nature, with possible cogwheeling, and is not marked by changes in resistance with the force of the examiner's motion (as in *Gegenhalten*) or changes over the course of the motion (as in spasticity). Some patients are actually hypotonic.

The length of time the posture is maintained may vary from a few minutes to many months, although the severely protracted courses do not appear to be as common as they once were. The reflexes are usually depressed and there is frequently an accompanying state of decreased sensibility (Jastrow, 1940) that may occasionally be confused with stuporous states. The episode may occur suddenly, or may develop slowly over many weeks, and it appears that the more sudden the onset is, the more abrupt and rapid is the recovery.

Kraepelin (1919/1971) believed catalepsy to be a form of automatic obedience or command automatism, and this viewpoint has also been taken by Marsden *et al.*, (1975). However, because catalepsy often occurs in the absence of more typical forms of automatic obedience, it is probably better to regard these as separate clinical states that can occur together (see Chapter 20, on catatonia).

It should be mentioned that there are two other senses in which the term "catalepsy" has been used. One is "cerebellar catalepsy," which refers to the observation that some patients with cerebellar disease, after a moment of dysmetria and asynergia, are able to hold their limbs and trunk in a fixed position much steadier than can normal persons (Wechsler, 1963). This is not related to the cataleptic state described here, however. The second sense is as one of the stages of a hypnotic trance (Bramwell, 1921), in which the relationship to the phenomenon at hand is unclear. Both hypnosis and barbiturates have been reported to relieve conversion disorders, and the fact that some cataleptic states are also relieved by these techniques implies an interesting connection between certain conversion disorders and catalepsy (see Chapters 20 and 21).

DIFFERENTIAL DIAGNOSIS

Catalepsy is such a distinctive phenomenon that its diagnosis is not usually difficult. None of the other hypokinetic states involves the moldability and maintenance of postures for prolonged time periods that catalepsy does. *Mitmachen* is a similar and probably related phenomenon, but the positional changes are not maintained by the patient. Also, in *Mitmachen*, the patient's posture may be easily changed by the examiner, whereas in catalepsy the posture may be rigidly held and difficult to change, but once altered is maintained by the patient.

Occasionally, patients in complex partial status epilepticus or petit mal status epilepticus may appear to be having cataleptic episodes (Drake & Coffey, 1983). Because some patients with catalepsy may be partially or completely unresponsive to stimulation, and some patients in complex partial status may be able to respond to questions in a simple, rudimentary fashion, differentiating between these two states on clinical examination may at times be difficult. In our experience, the occurrence of true postural malleability in patients with seizures is exceedingly rare, but when it is present, we see no reason why it should not be called catalepsy. All patients with cataleptic signs should, if possible, have an electroencephalogram (EEG), and, if the signs of catalepsy are only episodically present, an EEG should be performed during the episode, as electrical abnormalities may not be detectable between episodes.

PATHOPHYSIOLOGY

The pathophysiology of catalepsy is unknown. There have been claims that it is related to disorders of the basal ganglia because of its occurrence in parkinsonian and neuroleptic-drug-induced states. In animals, bilateral lesions of the striatum and especially the caudate nucleus have produced cataleptic states (Mettler, 1945; Gybels et al., 1967), but this was not observed to be a specific effect of bilateral basal-ganglia damage. Although catalepsy is routinely produced by most neuroleptics in animals, this is very rare in man. Nevertheless, this finding is evidence for dopaminergic blockade being involved in the production of catalepsy. Bulbocapnine, a drug that appears to be a dopamine antagonist and is structurally related to apomorphine, has been shown to produce catalepsy in animals and possibly in man as well (DeJong, 1956; Loizzo et al., 1971; Costall & Naylor, 1973). Roberts (1965) has postulated that catalepsy and catatonia may be related to dysfunction in the anterior thalamic nuclei and anterior limbic areas. From these conjectures it appears possible that catalepsy may result from dopaminergic blockade involving the anterior limbic areas, but this is highly speculative. These issues will be discussed further in the chapter on catatonia (Chapter 20).

Some investigators have held that catalepsy is purely a "functional" disorder, being a disturbance of willed movement related to higher functions of the brain. The concept of "disturbance of will" is common to many signs and symptoms of the catatonic syndrome, and is more fully discussed in Chapter 20.

SYNDROMES IN WHICH CATALEPSY OCCURS

Catatonia is of course the most common syndrome in which cataleptic states have been described. It has been estimated that catalepsy occurs in approximately 30% of patients with catatonic schizophrenia (Plum & Posner, 1980). It is not known how common cataleptic phenomena are in catatonia that accompanies other disorders, such as postencephalitic parkinsonism (Jelliffe, 1927), or "arteriosclerotic parkinsonism" (Critchley, 1929). Mild cataleptic states may rarely be seen in true Parkinson's disease, and this is probably

Table 13-1. Syndromes in Which Catalepsy
Occurs

Catatonia
Hysteria (conversion reaction)
Postencephalitic parkinsonism
Multi-infarct dementia
Parkinson's disease (severe)
Encephalitis
Epilepsy (especially complex status)
Arterial malformations
Subdural hematomas
Systemic lupus erythematosus
Hepatic dysfunction with cirrhosis
Bulbocapnine-induced catalepsy (De Jong, 1956)
Neuroleptic-induced catalepsy
Disulfiram-induced catalepsy (Weddington *et al.*, 1980)

related to the difficulty in initiating changes in posture that is found in the more severe cases. Other conditions in which catalepsy has been reported to occur are listed in Table 13-1.

There are several strategies that may be employed to help determine the underlying condition responsible for the cataleptic episode. After a thorough history and physical examination and appropriate laboratory tests to rule out more obvious causes, there may still be questions regarding a "structural" versus a "functional" etiology, and the use of barbiturates or benzodiazepines may help to differentiate between these two. It appears that a large percentage of patients with structural brain disease do not respond to these agents, whereas many patients with more typical psychiatric pathology do (Frumkin *et al.*, 1981). Care should be taken in employing this method as a diagnostic tool, however, because many patients with underlying psychiatric disease do not respond, whereas some patients with neurological or medical illnesses do.

Clues to the underlying clinical syndrome may be apparent after the cataleptic episode has subsided. Afterward, memory of the episode is often poor, although some patients recount command hallucinations, grandiose fantasies, and other mental experiences that may aid in the differential diagnosis. Jelliffe (1927) has drawn attention to the importance of the way the patient responds to an episode, and has pointed out the fact that while cataleptic states may appear identical in, say, schizophrenia and postencephalitic parkinsonism, the parkinsonian patients usually display more insight into the phenomenon and often attempt to rationalize it, whereas the schizophrenic patients often attribute the attack to external forces, such as "the influence of electricity, or the watchful eye of the Freemasons" (Jelliffe, 1927, p. 430).

CHAPTER FOURTEEN

Negativism

INTRODUCTION

Negativism is one of the least understood of all motor phenomena. The term has been applied by different investigators to behaviors occurring in a variety of neurological and psychiatric disorders, including catatonia, passive–aggressive personality, and dementia. It has even been applied to behaviors arising in the course of normal personality development. It is not clear how these different forms of "negativism" are related, if indeed they are related at all. Negative phenomena have not been as carefully described as "positivistic" phenomena (see Chapter 9), perhaps because negativistic behaviors are less obvious to the examiner. Nevertheless, negativistic behaviors do exist, sometimes in flagrant and sometimes in subtle forms.

Negativistic behavior has been observed for centuries. Berrios (1981b), in a discussion of the conceptual history of stupor, noted four main stages in the development of the concept, and these may apply to negativism as well. In the first stage, lasting from Greek and Roman times up until the 1830s, stupor was conceived of as a behavioral nonresponsiveness caused by a "'numbness' of the senses." The second stage, lasting until the 1890s, was marked by greater clinical insight into the phenomenon, with importance placed on the subjective experience of the patients. In this period there were attempts to distinguish between different forms of stupor, some of which included negativistic behavior. In the third stage, extending from the 1890s through the turn of the century, stupor was conceptualized as a behavioral interaction between the patient and others, especially as regards conditions such as negativism and echo phenomena. Finally, in the fourth stage, extending through today, psychopharmacological and neurobehavioral approaches have been applied to stupor.

Although many different behaviors have been called negativism, in this book we consider negativism to consist of an unconscious drawing away from or disobedience over which the patient has little or no control. As such it is conceptualized as the reverse of "positivistic" conditions, such as automatic obedience, grasp reactions, and echo phenomena discussed in Chapter 9.

DESCRIPTION

Negativism is a propensity to do the opposite of what is expected or required in a certain situation. It may also consist of simply doing nothing when some action is required. It occurs in the presence of normally functioning peripheral nerves and muscles, and it appears to be beyond clear conscious control.

In a short monograph entitled *The Theory of Schizophrenic Negativism*, Bleuler (1912) proposed that negativism could be subdivided in different ways. One division he proposed consisted of a dichotomy between *passive negativism*, in which "the patient, by outside influences, by command, will not do precisely, what under normal conditions would be.expected" and *active negativism*, in which the patient does exactly the opposite of what would be expected (Bleuler, 1912, p. 3).

Bleuler provided a number of examples of active negativism, including the following:

They stretch the arm out in order to proffer the hand but flex the forearm and hand so that the hand can not be taken. . . . On the request to show the tongue they put it out but turn away the head. . . . Sometimes [patients destroy what they have made] as if in anger, sometimes as if from a free resolution, sometimes compulsively, resenting it in the doing. (pp. 4, 5)

Active and passive forms of negativism are still observed today, although the forms not infrequently occur in the same patient at different times. There is often a highly fluctuating character to negativistic behaviors, as they may be present one second and absent the next, sometimes to be replaced by automatic obedience, echopraxia, or some other behavior.

Bleuler also divided negativism in another way, into what he termed *external negativism*, consisting of negation of external influences, such as commands or responsibilities, and *inner negativism*, characterized by thoughts and motivating feelings that are contrary to the will.

To these two different ways of dividing negativism, we would add a third—*simple* versus *complex* negativism. Simple negativism consists either of a lack of activity when action is required (as in passive negativism) or of elementary active negativistic movements (e.g., *Gegenhalten*). Complex negativism consists of coordinated activity that appears to be contrary to either the patient's own wishes or to those of others.

Since in this book we are concerned primarily with the motor aspects of negativism, the distinction between external and inner negativism is of lesser importance. And because passive negativism is always simple in nature, we are left with three forms of negativism—*passive, simple active*, and *complex active negativism*.

DIFFERENTIAL DIAGNOSIS

Passive Negativism

Passive negativism is difficult to diagnose without the accompanying features of active negativism. When a patient with normally functioning peripheral nerves and muscles and an unimpaired level of consciousness is unresponsive to commands, it is difficult to say whether the patient's lack of activity is due to negativism or to some other process, such as an extreme poverty of thoughts and movement. Although the distinction is important, it is often impossible to make.

Simple Active Negativism

Simple active negativism can also be very difficult to diagnose. Patients who pull away from the observer when approached, often saying something such as "no" or "don't," may be mistaken for paranoid patients, even though there may be no state of fear accompanying their actions. *Gegenhalten* (or *paratonia*) must be differentiated from other states of increased muscular tone, such as rigidity and spasticity. This can sometimes be accomplished by noting that in *Gegenhalten* the muscular tone is directly proportional to the applied muscular effort of the clinician, whereas this is not true in most cases of rigidity and spasticity (although in the rigidity of Parkinson's disease there may be a relationship of the tone to the speed of flexion or extension of a limb, and in cases of constantly changing muscular tone, such as in certain cases of dystonia, the investigator may be misled into thinking that there is a relationship between the examiner's force and the muscle tone).

Complex Active Negativism

Complex active negativism is usually much easier to identify, because it often resembles goal-directed behavior, except that the goal is contrary to what would be expected. Sometimes this behavior has the character of mannerisms—that is, it appears strange or bizarre as well as negativistic. Other times, the behavior is oppositional, but normal in appearance. Negativistic behavior may resemble compulsive behavior, and, indeed, at times there may be a compulsive component, but usually negativistic behavior is more highly situation dependent than is compulsive behavior, which occurs regardless of the particular environment of the patient. Compulsions are marked by their sameness across different situations and their lack of susceptibility to influence by others, whereas negativisms are often the result of requests or expectations of others.

PATHOPHYSIOLOGY

The pathophysiology of negativistic phenomena, especially of complex phenomena, is unknown. For simple negativistic behaviors, such as *Gegenhalten* or simple pulling away when approached, Denny-Brown has proposed that parietal-lobe damage may be involved. He noted that the frontal lobes and the parietal lobes were almost opposites in this regard. Frontal-lobe damage often resulted in "positivistic" phenomena, such as forced grasping or appearing to be stuck to the floor, and parietal-lobe damage resulted in such "negativistic" actions as pulling away, avoiding, or withdrawing.

As summarized by Langworthy (1970):

The behavioral organization represented by the central nervous system is arranged to serve two general types of reaction to the environment: the one, a series of positive tropisms; the other a series of negative tropisms. This is one of the most fascinating theories of Denny-Brown. The first reaches out into the environment; the second pulls away, or avoids. In the normal individual they are in equilibrium, but cortical lesions may release one or the other. At the cortical level, they are under tactile and visual control. Both types of activity employ subcortical mechanisms. . . . Avoiding reactions being chiefly of the nature of flexion and adduction, are more simply organized than grasping responses.

The instinctive tactile grasp reflex is controlled by the parietal lobe. . . . It is released by removal of the anterior portion of the cingulate gyrus and adjacent portions of areas 6 and 8 in the frontal lobe. The response is a complex series of orienting movements of the hand so as to bring the palm of the hand into contact with the contacting stimulus. This is the basis for exploring space.

Removal of the parietal lobe controlling the instinctive contactual reflex releases the tactile instinctive avoiding reflex. Then contact to the dorsal surface of the hand induces extension of fingers and wrist, flexion of the elbow and pronation. (pp. 6–7)

For more complex types of negativistic behavior, such as are observed in catatonia, it was proposed by some investigators that contrasting or conflicting ideas occurring simultaneously lay at the root of the behavior. Gadelius (1933) commented, for example:

In negativism the patient's will is impeded by *contrasting ideas*. He is continually forced to act contrary to the intentions which would be suggested to a mentally sound person in the same situation. Indeed, the patient perhaps often experiences a fragment of the right intention, but it has hardly time to arise before it changes into its own contrast. . . . What the antagonism between our flexors and extensors is to our movements, antithesis—i.e. ideas and contrasting ideas—is to our ideational life. (pp. 345–346)

Bleuler (1912) quoted an intelligent catatonic patient as saying, "If one utters a thought, one sees always the opposite thought. That reinforces itself and extends so quickly that one does not know which was the first." (This subjective state is also often described by patients with dyslexia.) Kraepelin (1919/1971) considered negativism to fall under a more general type of dysfunction, called *parabulia*, which he considered to include disorders of volition, in which "side impulses" that may arise in the performance of any normal movement gain in power, to become "cross impulses" that may interfere with the movement. Actions become deflected, and metamorphose into different actions or their negation, or are stopped completely. Kraepelin considered negativism to be the most important form of parabulia, as it is marked by contrary impulses interfering with movements. In Kraepelin's experience, many patients attributed their negativistic actions to influences (often external influences) on their will, over which they could exert little control. In some cases, patients mentioned that delusions or hallucinations caused their behavior.

Thus, it appears, at least in some patients with negativism, that there is a parallel subjective state of conflicting ideas underlying the motor dysfunction. However, this does not necessarily mean, as often interpreted, that the ideational state is causative. It could be that the ideational state and the negativistic behavior are both the result of some other process. There are many negativistic patients who deny any cognitive conflicts or are unable to express what is happening to them. Even Kraepelin noted that only "here and there" do patients attribute their behavior to specific mental symptoms.

In normal personality development, it is well known that children at approximately age two pass through a stage marked by negativistic behavior, sometimes called the "terrible twos." It is unclear whether this negativistic behavior is in any way related to negativism seen in disease states later in life. Psychoanalytic theory provides a coherent link between the two, however (Freeman, 1976). Although the psychoanalytic approach to psychosis is not a unified theory, in most cases different analysts agree that psychosis represents regression to or fixation at a very early stage of personality development, although the reasons for the fixation or regression are not clear. Most commonly, the critical stage of development of psychotic symptoms is considered to be pre-oedipal or "autoerotic," generally occurring before age three. This stage is thought to be predominated by "primary process thinking," in which conflicting ideas may be held simultaneously without the cognitive dissonance seen in the more advanced "secondary process thinking." (For a review of psychoanalytic theories of schizophrenia and psychosis, see Pao, 1979.) Negativism fits well into this scheme, for it is often thought to represent a state of poorly controlled volitional conflict. Thus, in normal developmental negativism, the integrative functions of the ego are in a stage of formation, whereas in schizophrenic negativism, the integrative capacity of the ego is impaired. The fact that the ego is not functioning in a normal adult way suggests a link between childhood and schizophrenic negativism. As attractive as this theory is, it lacks experimental verification, although it certainly highlights the possibility that some basic integrative or synthetic capacity of the brain is improperly functioning in the production of different forms of negativism.

SYNDROMES IN WHICH NEGATIVISM OCCURS

The classic syndrome in which negativism occurs is, of course, catatonia, which may accompany schizophrenia and mania and may possibly occur independently. However, even observers in the 18th century noted that negativistic behavior occurred in melancholic or depressive states, and this appears to be true today as well. Other conditions in which negativism may occur include hysteria, mental retardation and autism, frontal-lobe disease, parietal-lobe disease, dementias (including Alzheimer's disease and multi-infarct dementia), and postencephalitic states.

C. Disordered Muscle Tone

CHAPTER FIFTEEN

Dystonia

INTRODUCTION

The first reports of dystonia were made during the early part of this century. Schwalbe's 1908 description of a Jewish family with slowly progressive involuntary movements was followed by three reports of a similar condition, all of which were published in 1911 (Flatau & Sterling, 1911; Oppenheim, 1911; Ziehen, 1911). The report of Oppenheim was the first to use the term "dystonia" to describe the characteristics of the involuntary movement, and to draw attention to the hypotonicity as well as hypertonicity that occurred in some patients. Since then, dystonia has had a confusing history, for some investigators have concentrated on dystonia as a separate clinical entity, whereas other have stated that is is only a nonspecific neurological syndrome. Still others have claimed that dystonia has no neurological basis at all, but is a psychological disorder (see Zeman, 1976). These different viewpoints have led to considerable nosological confusion surrounding the concept of dystonia, and even today not all researchers agree as to exactly what constitutes dystonia.

DESCRIPTION

As Fahn and Eldridge (1976) point out, the term "dystonia," unlike other terms, such as "chorea," "tremor," "tic," or "myoclonus," has been used to describe not only a clinical sign, but also a neurological syndrome. In addition, the term "dystonia" has been used to refer to abnormal movements as well as to abnormal postures. "Dystonia" literally refers to an abnormality in tone, but generalized abnormalities in tone are usually called rigidity, not dystonia. Dystonic movements are thought to arise as a result of some changing abnormality in tone, and yet, as we have discussed in Chapter 3, the mechanisms of muscular tone are not clearly understood, and abnormalities in tonus have also been proposed to underlie the development of other disorders, such as athetosis. According to Fahn and Eldridge (1976):

Dystonic movements are sustained, involuntary twisting movements, which may affect muscle groups of varying size in the limbs, trunk, neck or face. The movements are generally slow, but may be rapid, in which case the term dystonic spasm is apt. Dystonic spasms may be repetitive, jerky, or even tic-like; they do not have the flowing or fluid character of chorea. Dystonic movements may be generalized (affecting the entire body), segmental (affecting just one or two limbs or the neck and one limb), or focal (affecting localized muscle groups such as those of the forearm—writer's cramp, or of the jaw—oromandibular dystonia). . . . The movements are generally not present during sleep. (p. 1)

It can be seen that "dystonia" may describe a quick jerky movement, a slow writhing movement, a sustained muscular contraction, or an abnormal posture, as well as other clinical conditions, which clouds the distinction between dystonia and many other clinical signs, such as chorea, tic, athetosis, and rigidity.

One major problem is the fact that dystonia as a sign is usually considered to be a condition marked by very slow contractions (lasting on the order of seconds or more) of a muscle or group of muscles, whereas dystonia as a disorder may consist of many different types of abnormal movements, including very rapid ones. We prefer to use the term "dystonia" to refer only to the clinical sign of slow muscular contraction lasting seconds to hours. This clearly differentiates dystonic movements from choreiform movements (lasting only 100 milliseconds or more) and myoclonus (lasting less than 100 milliseconds). By this definition, slow athetoid movements may resemble fast dystonic movements, and it is possible that athetosis and dystonia may be on a continuum. We believe that the rapid movements seen in dystonic syndromes should be called *dystonic spasms*, and that the clinical syndromes in which dystonic movements occur should be referred to by the term "syndrome," to clearly differentiate dystonic syndromes from dystonic signs and from other motor signs.

In some patients, the dystonic movements are spontaneous, whereas, in others, activity brings them out. These latter conditions are sometimes called action dystonias. Included in this form are certain cases of ormandibular dystonia, brought on by chewing; palatal dystonia, triggered by swallowing; writers', typists', violinists', and pianists' cramps; and others. Other characteristics of dystonic movements include disappearance with sleep and lack of susceptibility to voluntary control.

DIFFERENTIAL DIAGNOSIS

The very slow writhing movements or posturing characteristic of dystonia usually do not present problems in differential diagnosis. Differentiating dystonia from disorders such as chorea, athetosis, myoclonus, and rigidity may be difficult, often because these different conditions frequently coexist.

However, in both focal and generalized torsion dystonias, rapid movements may predominate, especially during the early stages of the conditions. These rapid movements may resemble tics, tremors, and choreoathetoid movements, and may be superimposed upon the slowly contorting movements more characteristic of dystonic conditions. As mentioned earlier, we prefer to call these rapid movements dystonic spasms. Fahn (1984) has pointed out that these rapid, jerky movements may not resemble those of other rapid hyperkinetic conditions, in that they often have a continual twisting, repetitive nature. In many cases, these rapid movements may represent the patient's attempt to fight the dystonic contortion by contracting antagonist muscles and thus intermittently breaking the dystonic posture. The twisting character of these dystonic spasms serves to distinguish them from chorea, ballismus, and myoclonus, and the repetitive character serves to distinguish them from chorea, ballismus, and most forms of myoclonus. Simple tics may be very difficult to differentiate from dystonic spasms, but simple tics often accompany more complex-patterned tics. Also, tics are usually abrupt and episodic, whereas rapid dystonic movements are usually continual. Tics, unlike dystonic movements, are often associated with a compulsive urge and may be suppressed voluntarily for short periods of time. Highly repetitive dystonic spasms may resemble tremors, but usually lack the smooth sinusoidal character of tremors. Also, the alternating pattern seen in tremorlike dystonic spasms is often due to the patient's voluntarily contracting muscles antagonist to those that are dystonic. Asking the patient to stop fighting the movements may allow the sustained dystonic contraction to emerge.

Dystonia may be differentiated from rigidity in that dystonia usually presents at some point with abnormal movements (or changing postures), whereas rigidity is directly evident only when one examines for passive resistance of muscles, and it does not cause the slow changes in muscular contraction evident as abnormal movement.

Dystonic movements frequently coexist with tremor, myoclonus, and parkinsonism. A high incidence of essential tremor is seen in patients with torsion dystonia (Couch, 1976). Subgroups of patients with dystonia have myoclonic jerks superimposed on the more sustained dystonic movements, and this complex of signs has sometimes been called "myoclonic dystonia" (Obeso et al., 1983). Finally, there have been descriptions of "dystonia–parkinsonism" conditions sometimes seen in children (Allen & Knopp, 1976; Sunohara et al., 1985).

PATHOPHYSIOLOGY

The pathophysiology of idiopathic dystonias is completely unknown. No consistent pathological abnormalities have been reported, for either generalized or focal forms. Basal-ganglia dysfunction has been proposed, but this is mainly because many of the secondary conditions in which dystonia is observed (such as Huntington's disease, Hallervorden–Spatz disease, Wilson's disease, and manganese poisoning) are clearly associated with basal-ganglia pathology. The lack of a clear pathological substrate for dystonic syndromes led to their being considered psychologically based disorders for many years (Zeman, 1976), especially the focal forms, such as writer's cramp and torticollis. There is, however, little evidence for psychological dysfunction's being instrumental in any of the primary dystonic conditions.

In many of the secondary causes of dystonia, lesions are described in the basal ganglia. Burton *et al.* (1984) and Perlmutter and Raichle (1984) described contralateral basal-ganglia abnormalities on CT scan and PET scan, respectively, in patients with poststroke and posttraumatic hemidystonia. There is further evidence that the putamen in particular may be involved, as there are a number of reports of focal dystonias with damage to this structure and its outflow tracts (Foerster, 1933; Dooling & Adams, 1975; Burton *et al.*, 1984; Narbona *et al.*, 1984; Larsen *et al.*, 1985; Stoessl *et al.*, 1986; Marsden *et al.*, 1986).

A variety of neurochemical abnormalities have been suggested in dystonic conditions. It is clear that autosomal dominant torsion dystonia is associated with increased activity of dopamine β-hydroxylase (DBH) (Wooten *et al.*, 1973; Ebstein *et al.*, 1974), the enzyme that catalyzes the conversion of dopamine to norepinephrine. This implies that noradrenergic mechanisms may be important in at least some cases of torsion dystonia (this has also been proposed for tardive dyskinesia; see Chapter 23). However, not all patients with dystonia have elevated DBH activity. Abnormalities in the dopamine–acetylcholine balance have also been proposed, as cholinergic antagonists (Stahl & Berger, 1982) and dopaminergic agonists (Lang, 1985) cause improvement in many patients, whereas cholinergic agonists and dopaminergic antagonists often exacerbate the dystonia (Fahn, 1983). Finally, Korein *et al.* (1981) and Ziegler (1981) have reported that γ-aminobutyric acid (GABA) agonist drugs also improve dystonia in some patients, possibly indicating GABA-ergic deficiency in some cases.

The physiological mechanism of dystonia is not clear, although Rothwell *et al.* (1983a) have noted that there may be problems in the reciprocal inhibition of muscles in dystonic disorders. There is often co-contraction of antagonist muscles in dystonic conditions, and this may possibly be due to abnormalities in reciprocal inhibition. The classic short-duration reciprocal antagonist inhibition that occurs when an agonist fires appears to be normal in patients with forearm dystonia, but there are delayed phases of inhibition that occur after the classic disynaptic phase. These latter delayed inhibitory phases (lasting from 10 to 60 milliseconds) are reduced compared to normal, and this reduced inhibition may account, in part, for the observed co-contraction of muscles in dystonia. However, more research is necessary to elucidate the mechanism involved, and to determine if it holds true for other dystonic conditions, such as torticollis.

SYNDROMES IN WHICH DYSTONIA OCCURS

Syndromes in which dystonia may occur are listed in Table 15-1. In the remainder of this section we shall discuss specific dystonic syndromes in more detail.

Dystonia Musculorum Deformans (DMD)

DMD comprises a group of disorders that have also been called hereditary torsion dystonias, and has been divided according to hereditary pattern and clinical symptomatology. Autosomal dominant, autosomal recessive, and X-linked recessive forms have been described (Zeman & Dyken, 1967; Eldridge, 1970; Lee et al., 1976), as well as forms associated with parkinsonism (Allen

Table 15-1. Conditions in Which Dystonia Occurs[a]

I. Primary conditions
    A. Generalized dystonia
        1. Hereditary (dystonia musculorum deformans, idiopathic torsion dystonia)
        2. Idiopathic torsion dystonia
    B. Segmental dystonia (focal dystonias appearing in two or more contiguous body areas)
    C. Focal dystonia
        1. Torticollis, retrocollis, tortipelvis
        2. Writers' cramp and other so-called "occupational neuroses"
        3. Meige's syndrome (blepharospasm–oromandibular dystonia)
II. Secondary causes
    A. Associated with other neurological illnesses
        1. Wilson's disease
        2. Huntington's disease
        3. Hallervorden–Spatz disease
        4. Juvenile neuronal ceroid-lipofuscinoses
        5. Dystonia with neural deafness
        6. Amyotrophic dystonic paraplegia
        7. Dystonia with subcapsular cataracts
        8. Myoclonic dystonia with nasal malformation
        9. Familial paroxysmal choreoathetosis
      10. Hereditary nonprogressive chorea of early onset
      11. Familial benign chorea with intention tremor
    B. Due to other causes
        1. Pre- or perinatal brain injury
        2. Encephalitic or postencephalitic
        3. Brain trauma, tumor, or stroke
        4. Neuroleptic-induced (acute, tardive)
        5. Toxin-induced (manganese, carbon monoxide, carbon disulfide)
        6. Hysterical?

[a]Based in part on Fahn and Eldridge (1976).

& Knopp, 1976) and forms with marked diurnal variation (Segawa *et al.*, 1976).

Eldridge (1970) distinguished two different hereditary forms: an autosomal dominant and an autosomal recessive form. The autosomal dominant form usually begins in late childhood or adolescence and is slowly progressive, whereas the recessive form begins earlier in childhood and is progressive over a few years. The recessive form is also often associated with Ashkenazic Jews of high intelligence. A nonhereditary form of the disorder has also been described.

In general, the condition begins in preadolescence, often with gait difficulty due to dystonic foot movements, and, possibly, mild clumsiness of the hand due to hand posturing. Frequently, the initial movements are quite rapid, and may be considered tics. As the illness progresses, the entire limb becomes involved, with constant slow twisting movements. At its most severe, continual irregular slow contorting movements of the limbs and axial musculature give way to frozen contorted postures, and the speech become dysarthric.

As mentioned earlier, no consistent pathological findings have been reported. In the autosomal dominant form of the disorder, however, elevated dopamine β-hydroxylase activity and elevated norepinephrine levels have been noted.

Although some physicians throughout this century have believed that torsion dystonia represents some sort of psychological conflict, it appears that the main psychological problems of afflicted individuals relate to having to cope with a severe illness—that is, psychological problems are secondary, not primary. There is very little evidence of hysteria in these patients (Cooper *et al.*, 1976).

There is no specific generally effective medical treatment. Anticholinergic agents, haloperidol, L-dopa, carbamazepine, and calcitonin have been used with success in some cases, but the results are inconsistent. The most impressive results have been obtained with surgery, in which lesions are made predominantly in the ventrolateral thalamus (Cooper, 1976).

Torticollis

Torticollis (also called wryneck) is a focal dystonia in which the neck is pulled to one side by overactivity of the sternocleidomastoid (SCM) muscle on the opposite side. The involved SCM muscle is often larger and firmer than the uninvolved muscle. Related conditions include retrocollis (in which the head is pulled back, due to contraction of the posterior cervical muscles) and anterocollis (also called antecollis or procollis, in which the head is pulled forward, due to bilateral SCM contraction). The condition has been recognized for centuries, and was probably known to the Hippocratic school and to Celsus, among others (Wilson, 1955). Although tics and trigeminal neuralgia may cause repetitive jerking of the head to one side, the jerking movements of torticollis represent the patient's attempt to break the continual hypertonus of the SCM muscle. Torticollis may occur as an independent condition, or may accompany other dystonias. Often, there is a history of previous trauma to the neck or head or a history of viral encephalitis, but, in other cases, no precipitating factors can be found. Torticollis often begins in adolescence, but may begin at any time during life. Familial and congenital forms have been described. Torticollis may also occur as an acute or tardive dystonic reaction to neuroleptic medications (see Chapter 23). Remissions have been reported in from 10% to 38% of cases (Meares, 1971; Jayne et al., 1984).

Treatment is often difficult. Some patients respond to anticholinergic agents, benzodiazepines, amantadine, L-dopa, haloperidol, and carbamazepine, but there are no clear features predictive of response to one or more of these agents. Biofeedback has been reported to be helpful in some cases, and thalamotomy may ameliorate the dystonia in severe cases (see Eldridge & Fahn, 1976).

Occupational Dystonias

Earlier in this century, occupational dystonias were called occupational or craft neuroses, because they were believed to be due to degenerative diseases of the nervous system, although no lesions could be found. They have also been termed professional, occupational, or craft spasms or cramps. The best known example is writers' cramp, which serves as a model for the others. In general, the onset is gradual, almost imperceptible at times. Patients begin by feeling fatigued after writing for short periods of time, and next experience difficulties controlling the pen. The pen may be held too tightly, and occasional spasms and jerks may occur. Over time, writing degenerates as the patient may become almost unable to hold the pen or pencil, and may frequently drop it or drive its point into the paper. Wilson (1955) has noted that there may be several different forms of writers' cramp, with the most common form being the "spastic" form just discussed. Other types may include a "tremorous" or "tremulous" form, and a "paralytic" form, wherein the patient feels weak and unable to hold the pen shortly after beginning to write. The exact incidence and prevalence of the syndrome is not known, but it is probably fairly common (a similar syndrome, telegraphists' cramp, was noted to have a prevalence of 4% among telegraphists in the early part of this century) (Wilson, 1955). Usually, the condition begins between the ages of 20 and 50, and is probably about equally distributed between men and women who write frequently. Sheehy and Marsden (1982) have considered writers' cramp to be a form of focal dystonia because of the frequent accompanying features of basal-ganglia dysfunction, especially other dystonias. These investigators noted no higher incidence of psychiatric disturbance in these patients than in the normal population, indicating that the condition is not hysterical in nature, at least in the majority of cases.

Other forms of occupational dystonia include typists' cramp, pianists' cramp, and violinists' cramp, among many others. The condition can occur in any profession in which continual manual action and dexterity are required. Treatment response is similar to that in patients with torticollis.

Meige's Syndrome, or Blepharospasm–Oromandibular Dystonia Syndrome

The syndrome of blepharospasm and oromandibular dystonia was first described in 1910 by Meige, who called the syndrome *spasme facial median* and noted that patients might have dystonic movements of other axial muscle groups as well. After Meige's initial description, the condition was virtually ignored until reports began to appear in the early 1970s (Altrocchi, 1972; Paulson, 1972). Marsden (1976) described a large series of patients, and noted that the syndrome usually begins late in life, after the sixth decade, and may present with either blepharospasm or oromandibular dystonia. Some patients go on to develop dystonia in other parts of the body as well, such as in the neck and upper extremities. Jankovic and Ford (1983) reported results on 100 patients with Meige's syndrome. In their series, the mean age at onset was 51.7 years, with a female-to-male ratio of 3 to 2. The majority of patients presented between the ages of 40 and 70, and blepharospasm was the initial manifestation in 58 patients, with 61 patients eventually developing the full syndrome, and 60 patients having torticollis or generalized dystonia in addition to the blepharospasm and orofacial dystonia.

Meige's syndrome can be quite disabling. The blepharospasm may render patients functionally blind, and the orofacial dystonia may severely impair eating and speaking. Some patients also develop spasmodic dysphonia, essential tremor, tics, choreiform movements, rigidity, and other signs of basal-ganglia disease (Tolosa, 1981). Depression is a frequent concomitant of the condition, occurring in approximately one-third of patients (Marsden, 1976; Tolosa, 1981).

Marsden has considered Meige's syndrome, along with other focal dystonias, such as torticollis, to be manifestations of idiopathic torsion dystonia in adults. Tolosa (1981) has questioned this idea, on the basis that the clinical features are different (e.g., prolonged blepharospasm with exposure to light or when reading is observed in Meige's syndrome but not in torsion dystonia; Meige's syndrome is not seen in torsion dystonia; and in Meige's syndrome there is a frequent history of depression). Tolosa has proposed that Meige's syndrome may thus be a distinct entity from torsion dystonia. The question of the relationship of Meige's syndrome and torsion dystonia will probably remain unresolved until the pathophysiological basis of these two conditions is better understood.

The pathophysiology of Meige's disease is unknown. Recently, Berardelli et al. (1985) determined that there was an abnormality of both the early and late components of the blink reflex, suggesting abnormal supranuclear control of this reflex, which results in hyperexcitability of the reflex arc. The increased excitability of the reflex may be due to increased drive from the basal ganglia, although this is not completely clear. Also, the nature of the possible basal-ganglia pathology is unknown. Although a neuropathological study of Garcia-Albea et al. (1981) did not report any basal-ganglia abnormalities, Altrocchi and Forno (1983) noted a mosaic pattern of neuronal cell loss and gliosis in the dorsal halves of the caudate and putamen in a case of Meige's syndrome. Further neuropathological studies are required before any conclusions can be drawn.

A syndrome similar in appearance to Meige's syndrome has been described following long-term therapy with L-dopa in Parkinson's disease (Weiner & Nausieda, 1982) and following neuroleptic treatment (Weiner et al., 1981; Glazer et al., 1983). In the cases following neuroleptic treatment, it appears that the Meige's-like syndrome was a form of tardive dystonia (see Chapter 23). Meige's syndrome is important in the differential diagnosis of tardive dyskinesia and tardive dystonia.

Treatment is often unsatisfactory, but some patients respond to tetrabenazine, lithium, trihexyphenidyl, or clonazepam (Fahn, 1983; Jankovic & Ford, 1983).

Neuroleptic-Induced Dystonic Reactions[1]

Dystonic reactions to neuroleptic drugs were noted shortly after their introduction in the early 1950s. It appears that approximately 10% of patients treated with high-potency neuroleptics (such as haloperidol and fluphenazine) develop dystonic reactions. A smaller percentage of patients develop dystonic reactions to lower-potency neuroleptics, such as chlorpromazine. The most common dystonic reactions are torticollis, "swollen" tongue, trismus, and oculogyric crises (Swett, 1975), although some patients develop a Meige's-like syndrome and some severe dystonias, such as opisthotonos. Jaw and pharyngeal dystonias are of particular concern because they can functionally cut off the airway.

The mechanism of neuroleptic-induced dystonias is not clear. Kolbe et al. (1981) have proposed the following mechanism: (1) Acute administration of a neuroleptic causes acute dopamine receptor blockade; (2) this receptor

[1]See also Chapter 23.

blockade results in a short-lived increase in postsynaptic receptor sensitivity, as well as an increase in dopamine release; (3) after approximately 24 hours, the dopamine receptor blockade disappears, resulting in increased dopamine release on supersensitive receptors, which causes the dystonia. This is an attractive model, for it explains the common occurrence of dystonic reactions approximately 24 hours after the introduction or dose increase of neuroleptics. Nevertheless, further work is needed to determine the validity of this model.

Acute dystonic reactions usually respond rapidly to anticholinergic agents, and even when untreated usually disappear within a day or two. However, there have been a number of reports of neuroleptic-induced dystonias that do not abate with discontinuation of the drug, and that also may not respond to anticholinergic drugs. These have been called *tardive dystonias*, a term chosen to show the possible relationship of these reactions to tardive dyskinesia. Tardive dystonia is discussed further in Chapter 23.

CHAPTER SIXTEEN

Rigidity and Hypotonia

INTRODUCTION

This chapter discusses disturbances of muscular tone that occur as a result of pathology in the central nervous system. The abnormalities of tone are generalized, although there may be regional differences between upper and lower extremities, limbs and trunk, or proximal and distal musculature. Rigidity has been subdivided in a number of ways (e.g., into parkinsonian, spastic, catatonic, decerebrate, and decorticate forms). However, the distinctions between these forms is not always clear. Hypotonia has been investigated less thoroughly than has rigidity, and little is known of mechanisms or possible subtypes.

DESCRIPTIONS

Rigidity

Muscular tone is determined by the underlying contractile state of muscles when they are at rest, and is operationally defined as the amount of resistance the muscle affords to passive movement. The term *rigidity* has been used in two different ways: as a general term for hypertonia, and as a more specific term to refer to the state of increased muscular tone seen in parkinsonism. *Plastic* or *lead-pipe rigidity* refers to increased muscular tone that is relatively independent of the degree of force used in passive movement, and that does not vary throughout the excursion of the passive movement. Sometimes this rigidity is referred to as *parkinsonian*. *Cogwheel rigidity*, in which the muscles are felt to ratchet or catch periodically during passive movement, is often superimposed upon lead-pipe rigidity, especially in parkinsonism.

Gegenhalten

Gegenhalten, or paratonia, is a form of increased muscular tone character-ized by resistance to passive movement that varies in direct proportion with the force applied by the examiner. It is observed in catatonia, dementia, mental retardation, and other conditions, especially those marked by dys-function of the frontal lobes. Catatonia and dementia may also be accompa-nied by lead-pipe rigidity, and sometimes both lead-pipe rigidity and *Gegen-halten* coexist.

Spasticity

Spasticity is a form of increased tone that has been defined as "a motor disorder characterized by a velocity-dependent increase in tonic stretch re-flexes ('muscle tone') with exaggerated tendon jerks, resulting from hyper-excitability of the stretch reflex, as one component of the upper motor neuron syndrome" (Lance, 1980, p. 485). It is considered to be a form of rigidity only when the term "rigidity" is used broadly to refer to increased muscular resistance. In the lower limbs, spasticity may resemble a "clasp knife," as there is increasing resistance with passive movement up to a point when the resistance suddenly gives way, which resembles the resistance offered by knives with a spring-catch when an attempt is made to open or close them. Frequently, spasticity is accompanied by clonus, spread (or irradiation) of reflexes to other parts of the body, a Babinski sign, and flexor spasms. There is also an accompanying loss of dexterity in addition to these other signs and symptoms. The terms "spasticity" and "upper motor neuron syndrome" are often used synonymously. Spasticity is related to decerebrate and decorticate rigidity, which were discussed in Chapter 2.

Hypotonia

"Hypotonia" is the term used to describe states in which muscular tone is decreased. It is clear that hypotonia can result from dysfunction in many different regions of the motor system, including pathology of muscles, neuro-muscular junctions, peripheral nerves, anterior horn cells, the pyramidal tract, and the cerebellum. Depending on the underlying pathology involved, hypotonia may be accompanied by weakness, paralysis, and a loss of deep tendon reflexes (such as with peripheral-nerve or anterior-horn-cell damage), or by normal or even slightly exaggerated tendon reflexes and only minimal weakness (such as with cerebellar dysfunction). The reduction in tone often manifests as hyperflexibility of joints and pendular knee jerks.

DIFFERENTIAL DIAGNOSIS

Distinguishing the different forms of hypertonicity can prove difficult, and many patients with spasticity, *Gegenhalten*, or parkinsonism are confused with one another by physicians. The muscular resistance of parkinsonism is steady and even, and is usually accompanied by cogwheeling, whereas in spasticity the muscular resistance varies according to the degree of contraction, and often exhibits the clasp-knife phenomenon. In *Gegenhalten* the resistance varies in direct proportion with the force exerted by the examiner. Different types of rigidity may occur in the same patient, such as is seen in patients with dementia and upper-motor-neuron damage or in catatonic patients (for a further discussion of rigidity in catatonia, see Chapter 20).

Generalized hypertonicity should be differentiated from more focal or multifocal abnormalities in tone (which were discussed in the previous chapter on dystonias). When multifocal dystonic disorders are severe the clinical state may resemble severe generalized rigidity. Dystonia, however, may also be accompanied by hypotonia, which is not observed in rigidity. Also, in dystonia there is usually a history of slow writhing movements at some point during the progress of the condition. In rigidity, such abnormal movements do not occur as a part of the hypertonic condition.

The cause of increased or decreased muscular tone may be difficult to determine. In order to make an accurate diagnosis, a number of variables should be taken into account, including coexisting hyper- or hyporeflexia or other neurological abnormalities, as well as possible associated metabolic, endocrine, infectious, neoplastic, or other conditions. Causes of both hypertonicity and hypotonicity are listed in Tables 16-1 and 16-2.

PATHOPHYSIOLOGY

Hypertonicity

Increased muscular tone can result from pathology of peripheral nerves and muscles as well as of structures in the central nervous system. Any pathological process that causes generalized increased muscular contractility at rest may produce rigidity or spasticity, and a number of these causes are listed in Table 16-1.

Parkinsonian Rigidity

The underlying pathophysiological basis of parkinsonian rigidity is poorly understood. It has been proposed that the brain can influence the muscular

Table 16-1. Conditions in Which Rigidity Occurs

Muscular abnormalities
  Myotonia congenita and other myotonias (muscular tone is usually normal at rest, however)
  Tetany (due to abnormalities in calcium and phosphorus metabolism)
  Tetanus (clostridium tetani may also act on motor nerve endings and anterior horn cells)
  McArdle's disease
Neuropsychiatric disorders
  Catatonia
  Dementia (*Gegenhalten*, paratonia)
  Conversion disorders
Decerebrate or decorticate rigidity
Stiffman syndrome
Parkinsonism (see Table 22-2)
Spasticity, secondary to:
  Stroke
  Tumors of the central nervous system
  Multiple sclerosis
  Trauma to brain, brainstem, and spinal cord
  Encephalitis
  Cerebral palsy
  Leukodystrophies
  Amyotrophic lateral sclerosis
  Familial spastic paraplegia
  Striatonigral degeneration
  Creutzfeldt–Jakob disease
  Tuberous sclerosis
  Central pontine myelinolysis

tone in two ways: through direct α-stimulation or through indirect γ-stimulation (Granit, 1955). These two systems were described in Chapter 2. Granit and others believed that rigidity was probably the result of excessive muscular stimulation from one or the other of these two systems, and the terms "α-rigidity" and "γ-rigidity" were used to describe these two conditions. The γ-system, however, is very difficult to assess in man, and conflicting data arose regarding the importance of γ-rigidity in parkinsonism. Some reports (e.g., Rushworth, 1960) have supported the concept of γ-rigidity, whereas other reports (e.g., Angel *et al.*, 1966) have indicated that the γ-system is normal in Parkinson's disease. More recent studies have indicated that the segmental spinal reflexes of patients with Parkinson's disease resemble those of normal patients who are not fully relaxed (Burke *et al.*, 1977; Burke, 1983).

Currently, it is believed that abnormalities in long-latency stretch reflexes (see Chapter 2) are important for the production of rigidity. Tatton and Lee (1975) reported abnormally large M_2 and M_3 responses in rigid parkinsonian patients when compared with normals, but not in nonrigid parkinsonian patients. These investigators further noted that the amplitude of the long-latency reflexes decreased in direct proportion with the decrease in rigidity observed after treatment with L-dopa (Lee & Tatton, 1978). Other investigators have largely confirmed the finding of enhanced long-latency components of the stretch reflex in Parkinson's disease (Mortimer & Webster, 1979; Berardelli *et al.*, 1983; Rothwell *et al.*, 1983b; Tatton *et al.*, 1979, 1984; Cody

Table 16-2. Conditions in Which Hypotonia Occurs

Muscular abnormalities
    Muscular dystrophies (including Duchenne's, fascioscapulohumeral, limb-girdle)
    Myositides (including idiopathic polymyositis and dermatomyositis, viral polymyositis)
    Myopathies (including carcinomatous, steroid-induced, thyrotoxic, alcoholic)
    Hypo- or hyperkalemic periodic paralyses
Neuromuscular junction dysfunction
    Myasthenia gravis
    Eaton–Lambert syndrome
Peripheral nerve dysfunction
    Trauma
    Polyneuritidies (including Guillain–Barré syndrome, infectious-mononucleosis-associated, hepatitis-associated)
    Polyneuropathies (including diphtheritic, porphyric, paraneoplastic, alcoholic, vitamin B_{12} deficiency, heavy-metal-induced, toxic, diabetic, uremic)
Disorders of anterior horn cells and spinal cord
    Poliomyelitis
    Syringomyelia
    Werdnig–Hoffmann disease
    Trauma
    Tumors
Cerebellar disorders
    Developmental anomalies (including cerebellar agenesis, platybasia, Arnold–Chiari malformation)
    Degenerative cerebellar disorders (including spino-cerebellar degenerations)
    Trauma
    Tumors
    Hypoxia
    Encephalitis
    Drug- and toxin-induced (including cytosine arabinoside, anticonvulsants, barbiturates, alcohol, lead)
    Paraneoplastic syndrome
Other causes
    Cataplexy
    Sleep paralysis
    Delta sleep
    Certain choreiform disorders (such as Huntington's disease)
    Akinetic epilepsy
    Leigh's disease
    Hysteria

et al., 1986). What is not clear is the significance of long-latency stretch reflexes in terms of underlying pathophysiology. For instance, there is still debate over whether the longer latency reflects involvement of long-loop reflexes (such as transcortical reflexes) as opposed to short-loop (intraspinal) reflexes containing group II muscle afferents (Cody *et al.*, 1986). Also, exactly how long-latency reflexes might be produced following basal-ganglia dysfunction is unclear. Tatton and Lee (1975) proposed that one function of the basal ganglia might be to modulate the responsiveness of motor neurons in the cerebral cortex to proprioceptive input from the periphery. In the event of basal-ganglia dysfunction secondary to a loss of dopaminergic input, basal-ganglia output through the globus pallidus may not be able adequately to modulate the cortical response to proprioceptive input, resulting in increased M_2 responses to proprioceptive stimulation. Cody *et al.* (1986) proposed that there may be a central interference with some counteracting inhibitory mechanism that normally suppresses stretch-induced excitation of motor neurons. Both these ideas remain to be validated.

One complicating factor in studies of parkinsonian rigidity concerns the probable existence of different forms of parkinsonian rigidity. For example, parkinsonian rigidity has been described in a form in which there is steady, even resistance (lead-pipe) and in another form, in which there is a ratchetlike quality (cogwheel). It appears that cogwheel rigidity is simply lead-pipe rigidity with an overlying tremorous component that rhythmically interrupts the hypertonicity. The tremorous component of cogwheel rigidity derives from the 7–12-cycle-per-second essential tremor of parkinsonism rather than the better-known 4–7-cycle-per-second tremor-in-repose (Lance *et al.*, 1963). In a different subtyping scheme, Webster and Mortimer (1977) have separated the rigidity of Parkinson's disease into two forms, *resting* and *activated*. Resting rigidity is measured when the patient is relaxed, and is believed to be responsive to medications and to correlate with the amount of clinical improvement. In contrast, activated rigidity is measured during voluntary movement (of the opposite extremity), is not relieved by medications, and does not correlate with clinical improvement. Interestingly, these investigators noted that a patient with Wilson's disease who also had both activated and resting rigidity had dramatic improvement in both following treatment with penicillamine.

Spasticity

Spasticity is the result of a loss of supraspinal control on segmental spinal reflexes. The two segmental reflex systems usually released from control are the myotatic, or simple stretch, reflex and the flexor reflex afferents (see Chapter 2 and Figure 2-1). The myotatic reflex is usually released because of damage to the lateral corticospinal tract, whereas the flexor reflex afferents are released after damage to the dorsal reticulospinal tract. These two tracts are topographically located in the same area of the spinal cord, accounting for their common involvement in many pathological processes. The release of the stretch reflex accounts for the hypertonicity, increase in deep tendon reflexes, spread of reflexes, and clonus. The release of the flexor reflex afferents accounts for the clasp-knife phenomenon in the quadriceps, the Babinski response, and flexor spasms, particularly after severe spinal-cord injury. The increased tone of spasticity appears to result from overactivation of α-motoneurons directly, for there is little direct evidence of increased fusimotor drive (Burke, 1983). For an in-depth discussion of the mechanisms of spasticity, see Lance and McLeod (1981).

Hypotonia

Dysfunction of the contractile properties of muscles or disturbances of the innervation of muscle can cause hypotonia. In many cases, the pathophysiological mechanism is obvious, for muscles depend on intact protein contractile systems and appropriate nervous stimulation in order to maintain any state of tonic contraction. A variety of conditions marked by abnormalities in peripheral neuromuscular mechanisms in which hypotonia may occur are listed in Table 16-2.

Pure pyramidal-tract damage causes hypotonia, but this is rare in man. The mechanism is not completely known, but it appears that destruction of the pyramidal tract may result in a decrease in fusimotor tone (Gilman, 1973).

Cerebellar dysfunction has been studied the most extensively as a central cause of hypotonia. Just as in Parkinson's disease, the phasic or segmental spinal reflex mechanisms are intact in cerebellar disease (McLeod, 1969), and it is the long-latency or functional stretch reflexes that are abnormal. In contrast with parkinsonian rigidity, the long-latency components of the stretch reflex are diminished or delayed in cerebellar disease (Marsden et al., 1977). This may account for both the loss of tone observed in cerebellar disease, and also, at least in part, the ataxia and intention tremor. Patients with Huntington's disease, a condition that commonly involves hypotonicity, have decreased long-latency reflexes as well (Noth et al., 1984). This may be due to cerebellar involvement in Huntington's disease (Jeste et al., 1984a; Lohr et al., 1985).

SYNDROMES IN WHICH RIGIDITY OR HYPOTONIA OCCUR

Different conditions that are associated with generalized hyper- or hypotonicity are listed in Tables 16-1 and 16-2.

D. Disordered Complex Motor Performance

CHAPTER SEVENTEEN

Disorders of Expression

INTRODUCTION

This chapter is concerned with motor aspects of communication or expression. As the field of expressive disorders is very large, and is beyond the scope of this volume, we consider, specifically, disorders of facial expression and apraxias.

DISORDERS OF FACIAL EXPRESSION

There are two main organs of nonverbal expression in the human body—the face and the hands, and, of these, the face is probably the more important. Through different constellations of facial muscle contraction, a wide variety of emotions can be expressed almost instantaneously, and often involuntarily.

One of the first scientists to study expression was the noted English neurosurgeon Sir Charles Bell, for whom Bell's palsy is named. Bell was interested in art as well as medicine, and he made many anatomical drawings throughout his life. His *Essays on the Anatomy of the Expression in Painting* was first published in 1806 and greatly influenced a number of later scientists—in particular, Charles Darwin.

The greatest milestone in the history of the study of expression is undoubtedly Darwin's *The Expression of the Emotions in Man and Animals*, first published in 1872. In this book, Darwin put forward the idea that behavior patterns evolve just as anatomical structures do. According to Lorenz (1872/1965), from the preface of the book: "Darwin shows in the most convincing manner that analogous processes have taken place in the evolution of motor patterns, as for instance, in the case of 'snarling,' in which an expression movement with a purely communicative function has developed out of the motor pattern of actual biting which, as a means of aggression, has practically disappeared in the human species" (p. xii).

Expression clearly displays the deep connections between emotion and movement. In this section we look at some of the ways facial expression may become disturbed in different neuropsychiatric disorders.

The Face in Psychiatric Disorders

Affective Disorders

Over the years it has become clear that Darwin was probably correct in proposing the existence of universal facial expressions of emotion (Ekman & Friesen, 1975). Most often, these expressions are fleeting, lasting only a few seconds or so. When they are longer lasting, they are more reflective of the mood of an individual.

Whatmore and Ellis (1959) studied residual motor activity of different areas of the body in depressed patients. They noted that, when compared with controls, there is an abnormally high level of residual facial muscle activity in both agitated and psychomotorically retarded depressed patients.

Schwartz et al. (1976) reported differences in facial muscle activity between depressed patients and controls in four different facial muscle regions—namely, the frontalis, corrugator, masseter, and depressor regions. These investigators also asked their subjects to imagine past situations that made them feel happy, sad, or angry. There were a number of significant differences between the groups, but, in particular, depressed patients tended to maintain greater corrugator muscle contraction during the "typical day" (or average emotional) condition and when imagining happy situations. Depressed patients also had greater frontalis muscle contraction during sadness and the "typical day" condition than did controls. Greden et al. (1986) recently confirmed these findings, and showed further that corrugator muscle contraction could be used to differentiate endogenous, but not nonendogenous, depressives from normals.

These findings of increased muscle activity in the forehead and especially in the corrugator-muscle region may explain a frequently observed characteristic of depressed facies—the so-called omega sign or Omega Melancholium. The omega sign receives its name from the pattern of wrinkles that form on the forehead when the eyebrows are drawn together and inner portions raised, creating a pattern resembling the Greek letter omega, Ω. Darwin (1872/1965) noted this sign to occasionally accompany states of depression or bereavement, and dubbed the muscles in the corrugator region "grief muscles." Greden et al. (1985) have recently related the omega sign to states of psychomotor agitation accompanying depression. These investigators also reported a frequent co-occurrence of the omega sign with Veraguth's folds, a facial sign of depression that was named for the neurologist Otto Veraguth. The Veraguth's fold is a wrinkle of skin on the lateral two-thirds of the upper eyelid, slanting down toward the nose.

The significance of these abnormalities of facial expression in affective disorders is not clear. It is commonly believed that characteristic patterns of facial muscle contraction are secondary to specific affective states. However, a recent study by Ekman *et al.* (1983) challenges this view. These investigators reported clear differences in the pattern of autonomic activity (as measured by heart rate, hand temperature, skin resistance, and forearm flexor-muscle tension) between the different facial expressions of disgust, anger, fear, sadness, surprise, and happiness, thus indicating emotion-specific patterns of autonomic activity. The emotional expressions were elicited in two ways: either by having the subject relive an emotional experience, or by having the subject simply contract the muscles appropriate to a given expression. An interesting finding was that the autonomic activity patterns produced by having the subjects assume certain expressions were more clear-cut than those produced when the subjects relived the emotional experience. This suggests that the facial expression itself may be responsible for some aspects of the emotive process, and not the other way around, as is commonly assumed. If this idea is confirmed, it may have important implications for the understanding and treatment of affective disorders.

Schizophrenia

In contrast with depression, where most interest in facial expression has concentrated on the forehead, in schizophrenia the "eyes have it." In the chapter on catatonia, Chapter 20, we discuss some of the unusual facial motor characteristics of schizophrenic patients, including grimacing and *Schnauzkrampf.* In the remainder of this section, we shall concentrate on the eyes of schizophrenics.

The most extensively studied aspect of oculomotor functioning in schizophrenia concerns abnormalities in smooth-pursuit eye movements (Lipton *et al.*, 1983; Holzman, 1983). Basically, when the eyes of some patients track an object, the normal smooth tracking is interrupted by saccadic movement, especially during low-velocity target tracking (Stark, 1983).

Although abnormalities of smooth-pursuit movements appear to be common in schizophrenia (50% to 80% may be affected) the significance of this finding is unclear. These abnormalities may be associated with the underlying biological basis of psychosis and may be genetically linked to schizophrenia, although they are by no means pathognomonic of schizophrenia, for they occur in other psychiatric and neurological disorders as well. Because the saccadic intrusions are of normal latency and trajectory, it is likely that the brainstem sites for the generation of eye movements are functioning normally, and the location of pathology is probably in the higher motor integrating centers of the brain (Stark, 1983). Dysfunction in the cerebral cortex has been proposed (Levin, 1983), but more work is needed to confirm this conjecture.

In contrast to the above difficulties with smooth pursuit (which are usually difficult to detect clinically), many schizophrenic patients exhibit grossly abnormal lateral eye movements. Stevens (1973) has divided these into three types: (1) fast irregular lateral movements, which appear as though the patient is searching for the source of hallucinations, (2) rhythmic lateral saccades, and (3) singular sustained lateral movements, sometimes called *lateral glances*. These movements tend to occur in more severely ill patients, especially those with very intense hallucinations or delusions. It is not known, however, whether the movements are responses to hallucinatory experiences or represent a more basic underlying oculomotor dysfunction in schizophrenia.

Spontaneous blinking has been noted to be abnormal in schizophrenia (Stevens, 1978; Karson *et al.*, 1981). A wide range of blink-rate abnormalities has been reported, from states of catatonic staring, in which patients may blink only two to three times a minute, to states in which their eyelids may flutter two to three times a second. In general, schizophrenics as a group blink faster than is normal, which may be related to a hyperdopaminergic state (Karson *et al.*, 1981, 1982). In contrast, patients with Parkinson's disease blink more slowly than is normal, which may be reflective of a hypodopaminergic state (Karson *et al.*, 1984). A recent report of blink rates in mentally retarded persons noted an inverse relationship between blink rate and percent of time the patient was engaged in stereotypic behavior (MacLean *et al.*, 1985). This suggests that stereotypic behavior may be associated with a hypodopaminergic state, rather than a hyperdopaminergic state, as is commonly assumed. This finding may relate to the possibility of a hypodopaminergic state in catatonia, which is discussed in Chapter 20.

Facial Hypomimesis in Neurological Disease

The best-known example of a neurological disease causing a loss of facial expressiveness is Parkinson's disease. The face is often described as being "masked" or "masklike," with a "serpentine stare." In some patients with Parkinson's disease there may be a subtle loss of facial expression years before clear-cut signs of the illness develop. The facial expression in Parkinson's disease does not accurately reflect the subjective emotional experience of the patient, as the face is hypokinetic. The exact reasons are unknown, although it may in part relate to increased rigidity of the facial musculature (Hunker *et al.*, 1982). Occasionally, patients with Parkinson's disease show a breakthrough of facial expression, much like "paradoxical kinesis," which could be called "paradoxical mimesis." Disorders related to Parkinson's disease also present with hypomimesis, such as Shy–Drager syndrome, progressive supranuclear palsy, drug-induced parkinsonism, parkinson–dementia complex of Guam, and others. Other disorders of the basal ganglia, such as Wilson's disease, Huntington's disease, or basal-ganglia tumors, may present with hypomimesis as well.

In recent years it has become clear that patients who suffer strokes of the right hemisphere of the brain may develop *emotional* language deficits corresponding to the aphasias that follow left-hemisphere damage. *Aprosodias*, or *aprosodies*, as these emotional language deficits are called, may be receptive (sensory) or expressive (motor), just as is the case for aphasias (Ross, 1981). Expressive aprosodias are of interest here because they render the patient unable to express emotion in speech and facial expression, and are usually seen after lesions localized to the nondominant frontoparietal operculum (Ross, 1981; Ross *et al.*, 1981; Weintraub *et al.*, 1981). This hypomimesis is also of clinical importance in stroke patients who develop endogenous depression, as there may be few expressive signs of the depressive illness, although the full complement of "neurovegetative" signs, such as sleep and appetite disturbances, may be present (Ross & Rush, 1981).

An unusual neurological cause of hypomimesis is *Möbius's syndrome*, in which masklike facies are accompanied by poor social functioning and unilateral or bilateral median positioning of the pupils. The disorder appears to involve pathology in the cranial-nerve nuclei, peripheral nerves, and/or muscles. It has been proposed that the underdeveloped social skills of these patients are secondary to an inability to transmit social cues (Giannini *et al.*, 1984).

Facial Hypermimesis in Neurological Disorders

Excessive expressionality of the face can occur in a variety of neurological conditions. Most commonly, it manifests as either pathological laughter or crying. Disorders that have been associated with pathological hypermimesis include cerebrovascular disease (especially multi-infarct dementia), brain tumors, brain trauma, multiple sclerosis, and epilepsy. The hypermimetic episodes may occur during wakefulness or sleep. The expressions are pathological because they occur outside of conscious control, are unrelated to the context of the situation in which they occur, and are often unaccompanied by the usual underlying affective state, such as joy or sadness.

The most common cause of pathological expression is probably pseudobulbar palsy resulting from widespread but diffuse cerebral damage, such as from numerous lacunar infarcts or multiple sclerosis. Patients are sometimes described as having "emotional incontinence," in which there is a veritable flood of emotional expression out of proportion to the stimulus.

Epilepsy is another cause of inappropriate expressionality. Pathological laughing (*gelastic*) or crying (*dacrystic*) fits have been described by many researchers (Daly & Mulder, 1957; Gascon & Lambroso, 1971; Loiseau *et al.*, 1971). Gascon and Lambroso (1971) proposed that laughter associated with seizures originating in the temporal lobes was accompanied by a congruous affective state, whereas no such state accompanied seizures originating in the diencephalon.

Black (1982) proposed that pathological laughter results from neuronal disinhibition occurring at higher brainstem levels. Black's suggestion was based on the ideas of Wilson (1924), who postulated the existence of a coordinating center in the brainstem for the motor aspects of laughter and crying, involving the brainstem nuclei subserving facial and respiratory musculature. This brainstem center was thought to be under the control of a higher "synkinetic" center, probably in the region of the hypothalamus. The synkinetic center was believed to integrate the bulbar and cortical components of the expression of emotions. Disinhibition of these hypothalamic and brainstem regions could then result in pathological laughter.

Sackeim *et al.* (1982) studied 119 cases of pathological laughter and crying associated with localized brain damage, and noted a highly significant relationship between pathological crying and left-hemisphere lesions, and between pathological laughter and right-hemisphere lesions. These investigators proposed that "destructive lesions result in disinhibition of contralateral regions regulating emotional experience" (p. 216).

It has recently been shown that pathological laughter and crying may be related to a hypodopaminergic state. Udaka *et al.* (1984) reported excellent results of L-dopa or amantadine treatment in 10 of 25 cases of pathological emotionality. Most of these cases were associated with cerebrovascular disease. The patient groups with pathological laughter and crying had a significantly lower level of homovanillic acid (a major metabolite of dopamine) in their cerebrospinal fluid than did neurological control groups with and without cerebrovascular disease.

Although it is difficult to reconcile these different findings, it is possible that a "synkinetic" brain center, as proposed by Wilson (1924), may regulate some specific aspect of dopamine transmission that is associated with emotional expressiveness. A reduction in dopamine transmission would then result in hypermimesis, and the occurrence of pathological laughter or crying would depend on which hemisphere was most affected by the hypodopaminergic state. Because dopaminergic neurons predominantly innervate frontal and temporal lobes (Brown *et al.*, 1979; Bjorklund *et al.*, 1978), it is possible that direct damage to these cortical areas could also cause hypermimesis. All this is highly speculative, and the exact relationship of the dopaminergic system and emotional expression is not known, but is an interesting area for future research. One problem with the idea of hypodopaminergia in emotional incontinence is the fact that patients with Parkinson's disease have decreased, rather than increased, facial expressiveness. Although it is possible that the hypomimesis of Parkinson's disease is due to more peripheral factors (such as facial-muscle rigidity), and that facial-muscle rigidity might prevent the expression of what may actually be increased emotionality in these patients, there is little evidence for such a notion. Thus, it is likely that more is involved in hypermimesis than simple dopaminergic dysfunction. Nevertheless, it would not be too surprising that dopamine, a neurotransmitter so important for motor and psychiatric function, plays a role in the expression of emotions.

APRAXIAS

Apraxia consists of the inability of a patient to perform purposeful or skilled motor acts in the absence of paralysis, sensory loss, abnormal posture or tone, abnormal involuntary movements, incoordination, poor comprehension, or inattention. The existence of apraxia is usually tested for by having the patient perform some motor act either on command or by imitation. The first accounts of patients with apraxia appear to have been made by Hughlings Jackson (see Taylor, 1932), although it was the German neurologist Hugo Liepmann (1900, 1905, 1908) who first studied the disorder in detail. Liepmann described a number of different forms of apraxia, including: (1) ideational, in which the basic conception of the execution of particular movements is lost, (2) ideomotor, in which the motor plan is intact but dissociated from kinesthetic memories of the movement, and (3) limb-kinetic, in which motor execution is disturbed, although there is an intact motor plan and kinesthetic memories can be accessed. The first two forms resulted in apraxias that were bilateral, whereas the third resulted in unilateral apraxia. Liepmann (1920) and VonMonakow (1914) both proposed that motor engrams (or memory traces) for skilled or complex motor acts are located in the parietal lobe.

Over the ensuing years, a number of investigators have addressed the concept of apraxia, and, in general, Liepmann's ideas have proven to be largely correct. Geschwind (1965, 1967) has provided the basis for our current conception of apraxia. Auditory information is believed to reach Heschl's gyrus in the temporal lobe, and, after preliminary analysis, is transferred to Wernicke's area in the posterior segment of the superior temporal gyrus. An important arcuate fasciculus connects Wernicke's area with the motor association cortex in the frontal lobe, and the right and left motor association cortices are connected to each other through the corpus callosum. Finally the right and left motor association cortices are connected with the respective primary motor cortices in the precentral gyri. Geschwind suggested that apraxias result from disconnections of some of these areas. Heilman et al. (1982) have further proposed that visuokinesthetic motor engrams may be stored in the dominant parietal lobe, and that these engrams may be disconnected from cortical areas decoding language. Taken together, these hypotheses suggest the following (for further discussion, see Heilman, 1979):

1. Patients with lesions of Heschl's gyrus and Wernicke's area may suffer apraxia because of impaired comprehension. (This has been considered to be a form of ideomotor apraxia.)

2. Patients with lesions of the arcuate fasciculus suffer a disconnection of the posterior comprehension centers from the motor association cortices, and thus cannot perform motor acts on command or by imitation with either hand. (This has been considered to be a form of ideomotor apraxia.)

3. Patients with callosal lesions who have kinesthetic motor memories stored in the dominant parietal lobe have a left-hand apraxia both on command and by imitation, but normal right-hand praxis. (This has been considered to be a form of unilateral ideomotor apraxia, sometimes called a callosal apraxia.)

4. Patients with callosal lesions who have kinesthetic motor memories stored in both parietal lobes (probably more common in left-handers) have a left-hand apraxia only on command (imitation is normal) and normal right-hand praxis. (This has also been considered to be a form of unilateral ideomotor apraxia sometimes called a callosal apraxia.)

5. Patients with damage to the dominant parietal lobe marked by lesions disconnecting language decoding centers from kinesthetic engrams may suffer inability to respond to any motor commands, but may be able to imitate movements well. (This has been considered to be a form of ideational apraxia.)

6. Patients with damage to one frontal lobe, especially the precentral gyrus (Brodmann's area 4), may suffer excessive clumsiness in performing skilled movements with the opposite hand. (This has been considered to be a form of limb-kinetic apraxia, sometimes called a motor apraxia.)

Other forms of apraxia have also been described. These include constructional apraxia, in which patients are unable to assemble whole structures from the components, and dressing apraxia, in which patients are unable to clothe themselves properly, often leaving the left half of the body unclad. Both of these types of apraxia are thought to be secondary to parietal-lobe lesions, more often of the nondominant parietal lobe (see Walsh, 1978). Orofacial apraxias have also been described, in which patients are unable to imitate movements such as sticking out their tongue or sucking on a straw or are unable to speak articulately. These orofacial apraxias are usually secondary to dominant frontal-lobe damage, and are often accompanied by nonfluent aphasia. Finally, gait apraxias, ocular apraxias, and writing apraxias have been described. Geschwind (1975), however, has argued against calling these other types of deficits apraxias, as they may not necessarily share the same pathophysiological basis as the conditions described above.

Apraxia is most often caused by strokes, tumors, and dementiform conditions, and is usually accompanied by other neurological signs, such as

Table 17-1. Common Causes of Apraxias

Callosal apraxia
  Multiple sclerosis
  Callosal and pericallosal tumors
  Marchiafava–Bignami disease
  Postsurgical section of the corpus callosum
Limb-kinetic or motor apraxia
  Frontal-lobe strokes and tumors, especially involving the precentral gyrus
Ideomotor or ideational apraxia
  Strokes (especially of the middle cerebral artery)
  Parietal-lobe tumors
  Parietal-lobe arteriovenous malformations
  Trauma
  Alzheimer's disease
  Pick's disease

paresis, aphasia, and agraphia. Common causes of different apraxias are listed in Table 17-1. The frequent accompanying neurological signs usually differentiate apraxia from psychiatric conditions such as hysteria and malingering. The course of apraxia is variable, with some patients recovering completely in weeks or less, and others manifesting a lifelong deficit. Left-handers appear to become apraxic less frequently than do right-handers, and to recover more quickly and more completely (perhaps because of a lesser degree of lateralization of functions across hemispheres in left-handers). Therapy, such as teaching patients alternative ways of performing certain activities, has been advocated, although there is as yet no conclusive proof that it alters the course of the condition (Heilman, 1979).

CHAPTER EIGHTEEN

Disorders of Posture and Gait

INTRODUCTION

The human bipedal stance is the result of an exceedingly complex set of skeletomuscular interactions. Unlike the quadrupedal stance, which offers a firm antigravitational foundation, the bipedal stance is inherently unstable, and requires continuous muscular activity for its maintenance. Bipedal gait is an even more complex phenomenon, requiring a sophisticated balancing apparatus that maintains an unstable structure in the upright position while in continuous motion. Given these problems, it is remarkable that human beings are able to stand and walk at all, let alone run and jump.

In this chapter we briefly discuss some of the neurophysiological mechanisms involved in stance and gait, many of which were addressed in Chapter 2. We then offer a discussion of posture and gait abnormalities in a variety of neuropsychiatric disorders.

NEUROPHYSIOLOGY OF STANCE AND GAIT

The stability of posture is governed by feedback mechanisms operating through a set of postural reflexes. These reflexes have been described in Chapter 2. The stability of posture is related to information derived from peripheral senses, most notably the eyes, the vestibular apparatus, and somatosensory organs. The contributions of each of these three to posture, and how they are integrated in the brain, are poorly understood. Visual and vestibular information is probably analyzed in the cerebellum. Somatosensory input may be used to correct instabilities in posture at different brain levels through long-latency postural reflexes discussed in Chapter 2. Nashner (1981) has provided an excellent recent review of the complex subject of stance and posture.

Gait is even more complicated than stance, for it requires balance during locomotion. Most of the research on gait has been performed on animals, in which localized spinal pattern generators have been discovered that appear to govern the alternating pattern of muscle activation necessary for stepping to occur (Orlovsky & Shik, 1965; Grillner, 1975; Shik & Orlovsky, 1976). Unlike most nonprimate mammals, man does not appear to possess spinal generators for walking, and higher brain areas are probably involved. The bipedal stance is an unusual one in the animal kingdom, and the transition from four-legged to two-legged walking was undoubtedly accompanied by profound alterations in nervous-system control. Therefore, many of the findings on gait mechanisms reported in lower mammals may not apply to humans, or even to advanced primates. For example, it has been determined that supraspinal control centers are probably much more important in monkeys than in cats (Eidelberg et al., 1981). Nevertheless, there probably is some type of pattern generator in the human central nervous system for gait. For example, feedback from the vestibular and visual systems does not appear to be a critical factor in the maintenance of gait, although such influences are important when adapting gait to changes in the walking environment. Where the human pattern generator is located is not known, but most likely several different brain regions are involved.

Berger et al. (1984), using electrophysiological techniques, have studied the development of normal gait in children. They noted that gait development begins at approximately 6 to 7 months of age, culminating in what finally resembles a normal adult gait at age 5 to 6. During the early stages of development, when children are just learning to stand, these investigators observed coactivation of antagonistic leg muscles that gradually gave way to a more reciprocal pattern as children began to walk. The coactivation of muscles in early stance development appears to be more related to vestibular function than to visual or sensorimotor function. In addition, Berger et al. noted pronounced segmental spinal reflex activity in the gastrocnemius muscles of children up to the age of 4 that appeared to arise independently from the development of the centrally generated alternating muscle activation pattern. They proposed that this reflex activity was gradually integrated into the central pattern, allowing for a more stable gait over irregular or uneven surfaces.

IMPAIRMENT OF STANCE AND GAIT IN NEUROPSYCHIATRIC DISORDERS

Posture and gait have been studied most extensively in neurological disorders, and have received little attention in psychiatric illnesses. In this section we present a brief review of the problems of standing and walking in different neuropsychiatric disorders.

Parkinsonism

Abnormalities of posture and gait are often the initial manifestations of Parkinson's disease. In some patients postural dysfunction remains the only observable characteristic of the disorder for a number of years. The patient with parkinsonism suffers impaired postural reflexes (Martin, 1967; see Chapter 2), and this fact contributes to the characteristically stooped hyperflexed posture, as well as the narrow-based, short-stepped gait, often described as a *festinating gait*. When turning, instead of the smooth one-stepped operation seen in most persons, patients with Parkinson's disease take a number of small steps, facing in the direction of their feet at each step without the normal head rotation preceding the turnaround. In attempting to walk, the patients often appear to be glued to the floor, and have great difficulty taking a first step. Sometimes, having the patients deliberately step over an object placed on the floor will enable them to start ambulating. Some patients have difficulty controlling their gait after they begin walking, and their unstable flexed posture often carries them forward so that they take many rapid steps before either falling or stopping themselves against a wall or other object. This is called a *propulsive gait*. Such gait characteristics are also seen in a backward or side-to-side direction, which are then called *retropulsive* or *lateropulsive gaits*, respectively. The parkinsonian gait has been considered to represent a regression to a more childlike walking pattern (Forssberg et al., 1984).

The degree of armswing is often a good indicator of any laterality difference in the disease, as there is usually a greater reduction in armswing on the more affected side. Armswing is a very subtle indicator of impairment, and laterality differences may be observable even when tremor and rigidity appear to be equal on both sides. This is an important issue, as a difference in the swing between the two arms may be the first observable sign of Parkinson's disease. Grossly asymmetrical Parkinson's disease may present with a patient who appears to be limping.

The gait and stance of patients with other parkinson-like disorders (including postencephalitic parkinsonism, progressive supranuclear palsy, the rigid (Westphal) variant of Huntington's disease, and drug-induced parkinsonism) is similar to that described above. Drug-induced parkinsonism can also be asymmetric in distribution, with effects on gait similar to those described above for idiopathic Parkinson's disease.

Some patients with frontal-lobe damage or with dementia may develop a hyperflexed stance and a festinating gait similar to those of patients with parkinsonism. These patients also appear to be "stuck to the floor," a phenomenon that may be related to grasp reactions. The step-length and turnaround characteristics of these patients may be more normal than in patients with Parkinson's disease, however.

Huntington's Disease

The gait of Huntington's disease may take many forms. In the rigid variant it is often quite similar to a parkinsonian gait. In the typical choreoathetoid form there is often a hopping, jumping, or dancing quality. The gait may be ataxic (Koller & Trimble, 1985), but whether this reflects the influence of choreiform movements on gait or is the result of inherent cerebellar dysfunction in Huntington's disease is unknown. We believe that underlying cerebellar damage is probably one of the important factors in the ataxic character of the gait (Jeste *et al.*, 1984a; Lohr *et al.*, 1985).

Cerebellar Disease

Dysfunction of the cerebellum (especially of the anterior vermis) and its outflow tracts often causes an ataxic gait. The stance is wide-based, with the feet spread apart and often turned outward or inward for greater stability. The severity of the disorder ranges from difficulty standing on one foot without falling to falling over even while seated. The gait is often described as staggering, with patients cautiously lifting and quickly setting down a foot during each step, to prevent falling. The risk of falling is exacerbated by the associated hypotonia seen in most cerebellar disorders.

Cerebellar degenerative disorders, as well as cerebellar tumors or strokes, may produce this gait on a permanent basis. Some drugs, such as cytosine arabinoside or alcohol consumed chronically, may also produce permanent ataxia. Other drugs, such as phenytoin in acutely high doses, may produce transient ataxia, but their ability to produce permanent cerebellar damage is not clear. Diseases of the inner ear affecting the labyrinth may also produce an ataxic gait, but usually only on a temporary basis, as the disease remits or other mechanisms of the central nervous system compensate.

Upper and Lower Motor Neuron Damage

Upper motor neuron damage, most often caused by cerebral strokes or tumors, often results in weakness and spasticity that frequently affect gait. Usually the arm opposite the affected cerebral hemisphere is weak, and flexed at the elbow, with wrist-drop. The leg is not bent adequately at the knee, the hip is overly circumabducted, and the foot drops. The impaired leg is swung around the body rather than being appropriately lifted and placed. The foot may drag along the ground, and in general there is a tendency to fall toward the affected side.

In cases of mild hemiparesis the patient may complain of hip and leg pain, due to the development of traumatic arthritis, before noticing gait difficulties. In such patients foot drag may be apparent only with fatigue. In more severe cases, usually due to stroke or multiple sclerosis, the leg spasticity may be so great that constant adduction causes the legs to touch each other throughout much of the stepping cycle. The resulting step appears similar to the opening and closing of the two blades of a pair of scissors, and is thus sometimes called a "scissors" gait.

Lower motor neuron damage affecting leg muscles may also cause characteristic gait patterns. One of these is the "steppage gait," seen with foot drop or impaired position sense. Here, the patient raises the leg higher than normal, either because the foot drop necessitates greater lift for ground clearance, or because impaired position sense causes the patient to lift higher than is necessary. In the past, this pattern was frequently seen in tabes dorsalis and poliomyelitis, but now is more common in peripheral neuropathies resulting from diabetes mellitus, vitamin B_{12} deficiency and spinal-cord injury.

Catatonia

The bizarre catatonic gaits seen predominantly in schizophrenia and manic–depressive illness are often difficult to describe or classify (see Stoddart, 1909). These gaits may be stereotypic, with repetitive walking back and forth, or manneristic, where the gait itself appears odd or unusual, or some combination of the two. It is important in these cases to distinguish between the catatonic gait itself and the contribution of drug-induced parkinsonism or tardive dyskinesia. The catatonic gait is often bizarre, with a peculiar twist of ankle, an unusual flexion of hip or knee, or a strange armswing or head movement that repeats (although usually not exactly) through each step cycle. Other stereotypies, mannerisms, or bizarreries (such as nose-touching, shoulder-shrugging, or head-patting) are often superimposed on the gait. "Withdrawn" or "stuporous" catatonic patients may stand or sit in bizarre postures for minutes to days at a time. In spite of the strange appearance, the patients usually show no proclivity to fall, and, in fact, when tested for balance are usually quite stable. These gaits may or may not be responsive to neuroleptic medications or lithium, and in some cases (particularly with schizophrenia) the gaits may remain quite bizarre even when psychiatric symptoms have apparently improved. Rarely, patients may give a psychotic explanation for their way of walking, but usually they cannot explain their gait. Also, a psychotic explanation should not be taken as conclusive evidence of a psychiatric etiology for their gait, as many patients give psychotic explanations for drug-induced parkinsonism and tardive dyskinesia as well.

Hysteria

The classic hysterical gait pattern has been called *astasia–abasia*, and is uncommonly encountered today in the United States. "Astasia–abasia" means inability to stand and walk, although the disorder usually presents as a fear of standing or walking, prompting physicians such as DeJong (1979) to suggest the term *stasibasiphobia*.

The stance of some patients displays a marked kyphosis, but with upturned head, sometimes called *camptocormia* (Monrad-Krohn, 1964). The gait itself is often more awkward than truly unbalanced. When patients start to fall, a bed, table, or wall is often conveniently located nearby, and sometimes they will lurch around the room from one support to another. Patients with irregular-appearing gaits often show remarkably regular wear on the soles and heels of their shoes. Although most patients do not appear to injure themselves as much as one would expect with such an impairment, it is important to remember that patients with hysterical conversion disorders may possess borderline personality characteristics and hurt themselves to attract attention.

Monrad-Krohn (1964) has distinguished two different types of astasia–abasia: a paralytic form, in which the patient simply sinks to the ground, and an ataxic form, which is marked by numerous unnecessary movements that cause the patient to come close to falling. The absence of hypertonicity is often a characteristic distinguishing the latter form from a spastic or hemiplegic gait. In addition, the patient with hemiparesis can often walk sideways toward the unaffected side without too much difficulty, but walking toward the affected side results in foot-dragging and imbalance. In contrast, the hysterical patient walks equally poorly toward both sides (Monrad-Krohn, 1964).

As in many hysterical conversion disorders, imitation is often an important factor in determining the characteristics of the gait, and frequently the patients will give a past history of gait disorder or relate such a problem in a close family member or friend.

Affective Disorders

The depressed patient is often stooped, and moves with slow plodding steps, especially when there is significant psychomotor retardation. The gait of the retarded depressive patient often resembles the pseudo-parkinsonian gait described later, in the section on senile gaits. In contrast, the agitated melancholic may pace, but with a minimum of hip movement, and most movement is in the ankles and knees (Stoddart, 1909).

The manic patient is often very erect, springs up from the bed or chair abruptly, and walks briskly, sometimes running or skipping. "The trunk sways freely as the patient walks, and when he runs, there is exaggerated movement at the hips" (Stoddart, 1909, p. 197). Manic patients sometimes manifest catatonic gait characteristics as well.

Autism

Vilensky et al. (1981), in a quantitative analysis of 21 autistic children, noted similarities between the gait of these children and the gait of patients with Parkinson's disease. When compared to normal children, the autistic children had a shorter stride length and reduced hip angle at toe-off, but maintained a relatively normal cycle duration. These results imply abnormalities in the motor system of autistic children that may be related to dysfunction in the basal ganglia or long-latency reflexes.

Tardive Dyskinesia

Simpson and Shrivastava (1978) reported some of their observations on the gait of patients with tardive dyskinesia. They noted that, out of 42 patients, 18 (43%) had "peculiar" gaits and 9 (22%) were frankly abnormal. The primary abnormalities consisted of a broad-based, unsteady gait with wide armswing (9 patients) and a spastic-appearing gait with foot-drag (2 patients). The other 9 patients had abnormal but atypical gaits. It is not clear what caused the underlying gait abnormality. Our own observations in 20 patients with tardive dyskinesia (Lohr & Jeste, unpublished observations) suggest that cerebellar dysfunction, including gait ataxia, either does not occur or is extremely rare in tardive dyskinesia, suggesting that the abnormal gaits of such patients may be due more to the influence of truncal choreoathetoid and dystonic movements on gait.

Senile Gait

The so-called "senile gait" is not a single diagnostic entity, but rather a group of different gait patterns that may occur in normal senescence. A large array of physiological changes, some of which are discussed in Chapter 26, occur in normal aging, and many of these probably contribute to different gait characteristics of the elderly. The "senile" gait often has a parkinsonian quality, with a broad-based, flexed posture, small steps, slowed turnaround time, a tendency to fall, difficulty initiating walking, and diminished armswing. In a sample of 50 patients over the age of 60, Weiner et al. (1984) noted severe impairment of postural reflexes in 44% and moderate impairment in an additional 24%, so that postural instability may account for a large percentage of the abnormalities seen in the "pseudo-parkinsonian" senile gait. One study has reported that gait abnormalities do not seem to be related to the presence of dementia (Koller *et al.*, 1983), although another study reported more severe gait disturbance in Alzheimer's disease (Visser, 1983). Apart from the "pseudo-parkinsonian" gait (which actually may be related to true parkinsonism) another type of senile gait, which appears similar to the astasia–abasia described above, has been described, and has been called *fear of further falling* (3 F's), *insecure gait*, or *post-fall syndrome* (Critchley, 1956, 1965; Murphy & Isaacs, 1981; Nutt, 1984). Some physicians have wondered whether this type of gait represents a form of senile hysteria or a form of gait apraxia (*Gangapraxie*) (see Critchley, 1965). (See Chapter 26 for a further discussion of senile gait and falling.)

SPECIAL TOPICS IN NEUROPSYCHIATRIC MOVEMENT DISORDERS

CHAPTER NINETEEN

Tourette's Syndrome and Related Conditions

INTRODUCTION

Throughout history, there have been reports of strange behaviors that may have represented what we now call Gilles de la Tourette's syndrome. One of the earliest accounts occurs in the infamous Renaissance manual on witch-hunting, the *Malleus Maleficarum*, written by two Dominican monks, Heinrich Kramer and Jakob Sprenger (1489/1948). An exorcism priest who appears to have suffered from multiple complex motor and vocal tics was described:

. . . in all his behaviour he remained a sober priest without any eccentricity, except during the process of any exorcisms; and when these were finished, and the stole was taken from his neck, he showed no sign of madness or any immoderate action. But when he passed any church, and genuflected in honour of the Glorious Virgin, the devil made him thrust his tongue far out of his mouth; and when he was asked whether he could not restrain himself from doing this, he answered: "I cannot help myself at all, for so he uses all my limbs and organs, my neck, my tongue, and my lungs, whenever he pleases, causing me to speak or to cry out; and I hear the words as if they were spoken by myself, but I am altogether unable to restrain them; and when I try to engage in prayer he attacks me more violently, thrusting out my tongue." (pp. 131-132)

Nineteenth-century physicians before Gilles de la Tourette appear to have been aware of tic disorders. For example, the French physician Itard described a case in 1825 which very well may have been a case of Tourette's syndrome.[1] Nevertheless, Gilles de la Tourette, on the basis of his two classic

[1]The case was that of the Marquise de Dampierre, who developed tics at the age of seven, and later manifested coprolalia and vocal tics. She felt forced to withdraw from society for the last 70 years of her life. According to Enoch and Trethowan (1979), "She died at over 90 years of age, still cursing."

191

papers on the subject (1884, 1885), is generally acknowledged to be the first to attempt to define clearly the clinical characteristics and evolution of complex tic disorders, although he himself did not clearly differentiate the disorder that now bears his name from conditions such as *latah* and *myriachit* (see Chapter 10). He called the disorder *maladie des tics compulsifs*, and other titles, such as *maladie des tics convulsifs, maladie des tics impulsifs, maladie des tics dégénérés, mimischer Krampfneurose*, and *myospasia impulsiva*, have been used (Enoch & Trethowan, 1979). The eponym "Gilles de la Tourette" was affixed to the condition by Charcot in 1885, in honor of his student's initial descriptions of the disorder.

Following Tourette and Charcot, many investigators continued to report patients with these unusual motor signs. A variety of etiological theories were proposed, ranging from psychological dysfunction (Guinon, 1886) to inflammatory disease (Wilder & Silbermann, 1927). Psychoanalytic theories were popular from the 1920s to the 1950s. Even these differed greatly in detail, including Ferenczi's (1921) view that the disorder was a form of narcissistic onanism, Abraham's (1960a) belief that it was an expression of anal sadism, and Mahler's (Mahler *et al.*, 1945) theory that it represented inhibited aggression.

In the late 1950s and early 1960s, increased understanding of the genetically based vulnerability to the syndrome (Eisenberg *et al.*, 1959), along with the discovery of neuroleptics as effective treatment (Kelman, 1965), helped establish the biological approach that frames our current conception.

In the remainder of this chapter we shall review selected aspects of the literature concerning Tourette's syndrome. The chapter is divided into parts that deal with the following topics: demographic data, clinical symptomatology, neurological and neuropsychological studies, treatment issues, and related tic disorders. The reader is also referred to Chapter 7, where tics were discussed in a more general way.

DESCRIPTION

The third edition of the *Diagnostic and Statistical Manual of Mental Disorders* (American Psychiatric Association, 1980) offers the following diagnostic criteria for Tourette's syndrome:

1. Age of onset between 2 and 15 years.
2. Presence of recurrent, involuntary, repetitive, rapid, purposeless motor movements affecting multiple muscle groups.
3. Multiple vocal tics.
4. Ability to suppress movements voluntarily for minutes to hours.
5. Variations in the intensity of the symptoms over weeks or months.
6. Duration of more than 1 year.

These criteria, though useful for diagnosis, do not fully convey the prodigious symptomatology that may be seen in Tourette's syndrome. Table 19-1 lists a few of the different symptoms and signs that may be observed in patients with Tourette's syndrome.

Patients with Tourette's syndrome often manifest both simple and complex motor tics. Motor tics are usually simple at first, progressing to more complex forms throughout life. Many patients exhibit a rostrocaudal progression of tics, with eye, face, head, and neck tics occurring early in life, later to be either supplanted or supplemented by truncal and peripheral tics. Tics can occur at variable times, from a few tics per hour to over 90 tics a minute. The average age of onset of motor tics is 7 years, whereas phonic tics usually begin several years later, with an average age of onset of 11 years. Attentional problems, along with impulsivity and hyperactivity, may precede the development of tics, and as much as 50% of patients with Tourette's syndrome meet criteria for attention-deficit disorder (Cohen *et al.*, 1984). Compulsive and ritualistic behaviors often appear during the course of the illness, and may actually predominate in later life.

In addition to motor phenomena, a variety of sensory symptoms have been reported in Tourette's syndrome. Many patients relate the onset of their tics to strange sensations, such as "itches" or "urges," in parts of their bodies that may be relieved when a tic occurs. Reports, such as the self-description from a lifetime sufferer of Tourette's syndrome (Bliss, 1980), indicate that sensory experiences probably play a very important role in the disorder. In

Table 19-1. Signs and Symptoms of Tourette's Syndrome

Simple motor tics (face > head and neck > limbs > trunk)

Phonic tics (such as barking, grunting, snorting, sniffing, squealing, screaming, coughing, smacking lips, clicking tongue, and clearing throat)

Complex tics (such as jumping, skipping, running, hitting, dancing, and kicking)

Haphemania (especially, touching face, people, and nearby objects with hands or lips)

Coprolalia

Echolalia and echopraxia

Excessive startle reactions

Compulsive behavior

Avoidance behavior

Attention-deficit disorders

Impulsivity

Paroxysmal aggressiveness

Stuttering and stammering

Paroxysmal sensory phenomena

later stages of the illness it is often difficult to separate these uncomfortable feelings relieved by complex tics from compulsive phenomena. In fact, there may be little difference between the two.

Coprolalia, or compulsive swearing, is often one of the most embarrassing and disturbing facets of this disorder. Patients have little control over this symptom, which often progresses from simple one-syllable words such as "shit" or "fuck" to complete sentences, often of an insulting or denigrating nature, usually spoken very rapidly and often accompanied by other tics.

A small percentage of patients suffer from other problems, such as learning disabilities, excessive startle reaction, echolalia and echopraxia, haphemania (compulsive touching), and self-abusive or self-mutilating behavior.

DEMOGRAPHIC DATA

Tourette's syndrome occurs in men and women of all social classes and racial groups. Men appear to be more commonly affected than are women, with the male:female ratio reported to be somewhere between 3 to 1 and 9 to 1 (Shapiro et al., 1978). Also, persons of Jewish or Italian extraction may be more commonly affected than are others (Eldridge et al., 1975). There is no clear relationship of the syndrome to birth weight, birth order, parental age at the time of birth, medical history of patients or their families, psychiatric history, or social class (Shapiro & Shapiro, 1982a). The estimated incidence of the disorder by the Tourette's Syndrome Association is 0.046%, or about 100,000 individuals in the United States. The average age of onset computed by Shapiro et al. (1973) was approximately 7 years, with a range of 2 to 16 years.

Although females are less commonly affected than are males, it has been noted that they have a higher proportion of affected relatives (Kidd et al., 1980). This observation led to the suggestion that there may be an X-linked pattern of inheritance for the disorder. A more recent study suggests that there may be an autosomal pattern of inheritance in some families (Kurlan et al., 1986). Whatever the exact mode of inheritance, familial factors appear to be important in many instances. Clear cases of Tourette's syndrome have been described in mother and son, in uncle and nephew (Hajal & Leach, 1981), in identical twins (Jenkins & Ashby, 1983), and in sisters (Friel, 1973). Larger studies have revealed that approximately 30% of patients with Tourette's syndrome have a family history of the disorder (Wilson et al., 1978), and that an additional 32% have a family history of tics (Nee et al., 1980). A recent twin study (Price et al., 1985) reported a concordance rate of 53% in 30 monozygotic twin pairs with Tourette's syndrome, and 8% in 13 dizygotic pairs. Thus, there certainly appears to be a genetic component to the illness, although other factors are undoubtedly important as well.

NEUROCHEMICAL STUDIES

The three main neurochemical networks currently thought to be involved in the pathogenesis of Tourette's syndrome are the dopaminergic, adrenergic, and cholinergic systems. Most of the experimental support for the involvement of these different systems in Tourette's syndrome derives from studies of medication response.

Of the three systems, the largest amount of work has been done on the theory of dopaminergic involvement, as dopamine receptor blocking drugs (such as neuroleptics) suppress the tics, whereas dopamine agonists exacerbate them (Feinberg & Carroll, 1979). Although such findings tend to implicate a hyperdopaminergic state in Tourette's syndrome, *reduced* levels of homovanillic acid (HVA), the principal metabolite of central-nervous-system dopamine, have been reported (Butler *et al.*, 1979; Cohen *et al.*, 1979). This observation led Friedhoff (1982) to suggest that there may be "supersensitive" presynaptic dopaminergic receptors in Tourette's syndrome that could result in a decrease in HVA in the cerebrospinal fluid, but a clinical response to neuroleptics. Of course, the above findings would also be consistent with postsynaptic dopaminergic supersensitivity secondary to a loss of dopaminergic cells (Devinsky, 1983). As apomorphine, a dopaminergic agonist, has been reported to relieve signs and symptoms of Tourette's syndrome (Feinberg & Carroll, 1979) it appears that supersensitive presynaptic receptors are more likely to be involved, for it is known that apomorphine, in low doses, has greater affinity for presynaptic receptors. However, the issue is far from resolved.

The evidence for adrenergic system involvement in Tourette's syndrome stems largely from clinical studies demonstrating the benefit of adrenergic agonists on tics. The most extensively investigated agent is clonidine, which is believed to act primarily by stimulating presynaptic α_2 adrenergic receptors, thereby reducing synaptic release of norepinephrine (NE) (Cohen *et al.*, 1980, 1984). Clonidine has been shown to lower the level of plasma free 3-methoxy-4-hydroxyphenylglycol (MHPG), the principal metabolite of NE in the brain (Leckman *et al.*, 1980). Other investigators have proposed that the clinical efficacy of clonidine is not dependent on its α_2-activity, for clonidine is clearly effective when α_2-receptors may be reduced or absent (such as in neonatal narcotic abstinence syndrome; Hoder *et al.*, 1981).

Interrelationships between the noradrenergic and dopaminergic systems have been demonstrated in animal studies by Antelman and Caggiula (1977) and in clinical studies by Borison *et al.* (1982). In the latter studies it was reported that a positive response to haloperidol predicted a positive response to clonidine. Thus, both noradrenergic and dopaminergic mechanisms, or some interaction of the two, may be critical factors in the etiology of Tourette's syndrome.

Cholinergic mechanisms have also been thought to play a role in Tourette's syndrome. Some studies have reported the clinical efficacy of cholinergic agonists such as lecithin and physostigmine (Stahl & Berger, 1980; Barbeau, 1980), although other studies have not confirmed these findings (Polinsky *et al.*, 1980; Tanner *et al.*, 1982). Apart from these drug-response studies, there have been a small number of investigations that looked at other measures of cholinergic function. Hanin *et al.* (1979) reported increased red-blood-cell choline content in patients with Tourette's syndrome, and Rickland *et al.* (1980) noted a reduced uptake of choline into fibroblasts in Tourette's syndrome patients. More recent studies on acetylcholinesterase activity in cerebrospinal fluid have failed to find differences between untreated and haloperidol-treated patients with Tourette's syndrome and controls (Singer *et al.*, 1984). It is possible that cholinergic abnormalities may be important in only a subgroup of patients with Tourette's syndrome. Merikangas *et al.* (1985) recently demonstrated that a subgroup of patients with Tourette's syndrome and with an elevated red-blood-cell/plasma-choline ratio responded better to clonazepam than to haloperidol. So the exact relationship of cholinergic mechanisms to the etiology of Tourette's syndrome is still in question.

In the past, serotonergic mechanisms were thought to possibly be important in Tourette's syndrome (Cohen *et al.*, 1979), but there exists little recent evidence in support of the idea. The manipulation of serotonergic activity with medications has produced no consistent results in Tourette's syndrome (Cohen *et al.*, 1984).

NEUROPHYSIOLOGICAL AND NEUROANATOMICAL STUDIES

Physioanatomical investigations of Tourette's syndrome may be divided into the following categories:

1. Electroencephalographic (EEG) studies, including studies of pre-movement EEG potentials.
2. Electromyographic (EMG) studies.
3. Evoked-response studies.
4. CT-scan studies.

EEG Studies

Although some investigators have reported that EEG abnormalities exist in a high proportion of patients with Tourette's syndrome (as much as 75% of patients have been reported to have abnormal EEGs by Shapiro *et al.*, 1978), other scientists have reported no difference in the incidence of abnormal

EEGs in Tourette's syndrome when compared with normals (Krumholz *et al.*, 1983). Even when abnormalities are found, they are usually nonspecific and not synchronized with the tics. The most commonly reported features have been nonlocalized sharp wave or slow-wave activity that does not exhibit clear clinical or prognostic significance. Furthermore, epileptiform activity appears to be uncommon (Bergen *et al.*, 1982). It should also be noted that a large proportion of the patients reported in EEG studies have been on haloperidol, which is known to produce EEG abnormalities (Bergen *et al.*, 1982).

Apart from these studies of general EEG characteristics of Tourette's syndrome, some investigators have looked at premovement EEG potentials, or the changes in EEG immediately preceding voluntary movements (Kornhuber & Deecke, 1965). It has been proposed that the tics of Tourette's syndrome are not generated through normal voluntary motor pathways, because the normally observed slowly rising negative potential that precedes willed movements (the so-called *Bereitschaftspotential*) is not seen prior to tic activity (Obeso *et al.*, 1982).

EMG Studies

The EMG changes observed in Tourette's syndrome have been found to depend on the muscle group involved, as well as on the complexity of the tic (Obeso *et al.*, 1982). An individual may exhibit different EMG patterns at different times. Complex tics are often quite difficult to analyze, but simple tics have been noted to be associated with a burst of muscle activity lasting up to 200 milliseconds and occurring in both agonist and antagonist muscles.

Evoked-Response Studies

Although the study of Domino *et al.* (1982) demonstrated wave IV abnormalities in visually evoked potentials of patients with Tourette's syndrome, the study of Krumholz *et al.* (1983) failed to find significant differences in visual, auditory, or somatosensory evoked responses between 17 patients with Tourette's syndrome and age- and sex-matched control subjects.

CT-Scan Studies

There are discrepancies in the reports of CT scan abnormalities of patients with Tourette's syndrome, from the study of Pakkenberg *et al.* (1982) reporting no abnormalities in 12 medicated patients, to the report of Caparulo *et al.* (1981), which stated that 37% of 16 patients with Tourette's syndrome showed abnormalities, most commonly ventricular dilatation. In this latter study, four out of the six patients with CT-scan abnormalities also had an abnormal EEG, whereas only one out of 10 with normal CT scans had any EEG abnormality.

In summary, although a variety of different physioanatomical abnormalities have been observed in patients with Tourette's syndrome, in many cases the results of studies are inconsistent and the exact significance of the findings is not clear. The reader is referred to Chapter 7 for further discussion of the pathophysiology of tics.

TREATMENT

Many different medications have been tried in the treatment of Tourette's syndrome, including neuroleptics (such as haloperidol and fluphenazine), clonidine, pimozide, and lecithin. The most popular medication today is haloperidol, although there is evidence that this may not be the best medication for all cases of Tourette's syndrome. We shall briefly discuss some of the currently available medical treatments of Tourette's syndrome, but we wish the reader to bear in mind that fact that the treatment of Tourette's syndrome is still controversial.

The use of haloperidol in Tourette's syndrome dates back to 1961, when investigators in France (Seignot, 1961) and Italy (Caprini & Melotti, 1962) began to explore the potential of neuroleptic medications in nonpsychotic disorders. Since then, it has become the most widely used medication in Tourette's syndrome. In current medication regimens low-dosage treatment is emphasized, as many patients experience improvement with as little as 0.5 milligram orally a day (Shapiro & Shapiro, 1982b), with the usual maximum dose being in the region of 5 milligrams a day. Above this dose, even if the medication controls the symptoms and signs, its overall effect may be detrimental. The typical neuroleptic side effects of lethargy, cognitive dulling, dystonic reactions, weight gain, parkinsonism, and others appear to be especially prominent and disabling in Tourette's syndrome. Additionally, over the past several years, there have been a number of case reports of tardive dyskinesia occurring in patients with Tourette's syndrome (Caine et al., 1978; Caine & Polinsky, 1981), as well as reports of school avoidance and social phobia thought to be induced by haloperidol (Mikkelsen et al., 1981). This latter social phobia-like syndrome appears to occur in both sexes and all age groups, usually appearing early in treatment (average length of treatment, 8.1 ± 7.8 weeks), and the symptoms may disappear completely with reduction or discontinuation of haloperidol.

Although haloperidol has been considered by many to be the mainstay of treatment, recent evidence suggests that another neuroleptic—fluphenazine—may be more effective in some patients. Goetz *et al.* (1984), in a 5-year study of 21 patients with Tourette's syndrome who had been given haloperidol in the past with poor results, reported that fluphenazine was equally as effective as, if not superior to, haloperidol in the majority of patients.

Clonidine hydrochloride, an imidazole derivative, is thought to stimulate presynaptic α-adrenergic autoreceptors on some neurons, especially those regulating the activity of the locus ceruleus (Svensson *et al.*, 1975). The improvement rate with clonidine is similar to that seen with haloperidol—70% reported by Cohen *et al.* (1980) in a study of 25 patients with Tourette's syndrome. Some investigators believe that the drug may be particularly effective for the treatment of compulsive symptoms, aggressive behaviors, and attentional problems (see also Chapter 9, on compulsive movements). The usual dose of clonidine varies from 0.15 milligram to 0.6 milligram a day.

Pimozide, a diphenylbutylpiperidine drug, has also been used in the treatment of Tourette's syndrome. This medication is a dopamine receptor blocker that may be more selective for dopamine receptors than is haloperidol (Seeman & Lee, 1975). Some studies of pimozide have reported it to be more effective than haloperidol (Shapiro *et al.*, 1983). Dosages range from 5 milligrams to 30 milligrams a day.

Tetrabenazine has also been reported to show some promise as a treatment of Tourette's syndrome (Jankovic *et al.*, 1984), but more studies are required for an accurate assessment of its clinical efficacy and side effects.

OTHER TIC DISORDERS

Although TS represents the most severe form of tic disorder, the spectrum of tic disorders is quite broad, as is evident from Table 7-2. Many tic disorders are transient. For example, acute simple tics (also called "habit spasms") last anywhere from 1 week to 1 year and occur in as many as 12% of children (Shapiro *et al.*, 1978). If simple tics persist for longer than 1 year, the disorder is sometimes called chronic simple tic disorder. Simple tics often develop before age 15, although there are many case reports of simple tics beginning in middle age (Shapiro *et al.*, 1978).

Subacute tic disorders have a duration of greater than 1 year but usually remit by the end of adolescence. Subacute tic disorders may occur in either simple or multiple form, although the term is usually reserved for multiple tic disorders. If the tics persist beyond adolescence, the possibility of Tourette's syndrome should be strongly considered.

In addition to the above idiopathic tic disorders are tics that result from known medical conditions. Minor brain damage, some forms of epilepsy, and toxic reactions to medications (e.g., methylphenidate and pemoline) may precipitate tics. Neuroleptic medications have been implicated in what has been referred to as "tardive Tourette's" or "tardive tic" syndrome, in which patients show classical Tourette's syndrome after a period on neuroleptics that remits following discontinuation of neuroleptic medication (see Chapter 23). Encephalitis lethargica (von Economo's encephalitis) has also been described as producing a generalized tic syndrome, but postencephalitic tic disorders are rarely reported today. Other medical and neurological causes of tics are listed in Table 7-2.

CHAPTER TWENTY

Catatonia

INTRODUCTION

Anyone walking through the grounds of large mental institutions around the world would undoubtedly be struck by the large number of patients exhibiting a vast array of unusual movements, gaits, and postures. Many of these patients carry the diagnosis of schizophrenia—in many cases, catatonic schizophrenia. These patients are sequestered from the practice and experience of the majority of investigators interested in movement disorders, yet they represent a truly enormous number of patients about whom very little is known. And most of the motor signs these patients manifest have been called catatonia.

Few phenomena in psychiatry or neurology are as enigmatic as catatonia. This is a fact in large part due to the many contradictions surrounding the concept. Catatonia has been described as a disease but also as a syndrome. It has been considered to be a subtype of schizophrenia, and yet has been claimed to be more common in affective disorders. It has been reported to be both caused and ameliorated by neuroleptic drugs. It has been reported to represent a state of stupor so profound that its sufferers die from medical complications, and has also been reported to represent a state of excitement so marked that physical restraints are necessary.

In this chapter we present a review of some important aspects of catatonia that have appeared since its first description over 100 years ago. We begin with a discussion of the history of the subject, highlighting points in the past at which we feel some of the current confusion originated. After this, we address some basic questions about the phenomenon, later moving on to more complex questions. We hope to present this series of questions in what we believe is a natural progression, with each question supported by and predicated upon answers to the preceding questions. Not all of the questions can be satisfactorily addressed, however, with the result that the discussion of more complex issues will of necessity be less complete. Nevertheless, we hope to draw attention to some areas that we feel are in need of further investigation.

THE HISTORY OF CATATONIA

Some understanding of the confusion surrounding catatonia may be gained by a brief survey of its history. The word itself was coined by the great German psychiatrist Karl Kahlbaum in the late 1860s and was popularized with the publication of his book *Die Katatonie, oder das Spannungsirresein* (1973), which was first published in 1874 and which freely translates as *Catatonia, or the Insanity of Tension.* The word "catatonia" is Greek in origin and means "negative tension" or "cast down." According to Kahlbaum (1874/1973), catatonia was a disease that progressed through a series of stages marked by "symptom-complexes":

Catatonia is a brain disease with a cyclic, alternating course, in which the mental symptoms are, consecutively melancholy, mania, stupor, confusion, and eventually dementia. One or more of these symptoms may be absent from the complete series of psychic "symptom-complexes." In addition to the mental symptoms, locomotor neural processes with the general character of convulsions occur as typical symptoms. (p. 83)

Kahlbaum based his concept of catatonia in large part on the model that had earlier been created for general paresis of the insane (GPI). Through careful clinical observation with special attention devoted to the course and associated complaints of patients with GPI, French neurologists and psychiatrists in the mid-1800s linked GPI with tabes dorsalis, and eventually unraveled the three-stage presentation of syphilis. Kahlbaum felt that this careful attention to the clinical course was the key to understanding psychiatric illnesses. "Only a comprehensive and intensive application of the clinical method can enable psychiatry to progress and to increase the understanding of psychopathological processes" (Kahlbaum, 1874/1973, p. 3). Most of Kahlbaum's book is a series of case presentations, and, from a careful reading of these cases, it is clear that no single modern clinical diagnosis applies to them all. Some of the cases appear to represent patients with schizophrenia, others represent affective disorder, and still others do not seem to correspond to any clearly defined psychiatric entity today (Mahendra, 1981). What appears to have linked the cases together were the unusual motor signs.

The next major step in the scientific conception of catatonia occurred with Emil Kraepelin's analysis and description of dementia praecox. In the

Kraepelinian scheme, catatonia was lowered from an independent disease to a subtype of dementia praecox. Kraepelin was aware, however, that many catatonic signs can occur in other illnesses; he noted signs such as automatic obedience and stereotypical behaviors to also occur in a variety of other brain diseases. But he did not believe that the presence of catatonic signs and symptoms alone made for the diagnosis of catatonia, by which term he meant the catatonic form of dementia praecox:

As undeniable as it is, that all these disorders [catatonic signs and symptoms] in no other disease come under observation in such extent and multiplicity as in dementia praecox, just as little, however, may the appearance of one, or even of several, of these disorders be regarded as infallible proof of the presence of that malady. (Kraepelin, 1919/1971, p. 257)

Eugen Bleuler extended the concept of dementia praecox to include cases with better prognosis, and renamed the entire group "the schizophrenias" (Bleuler, 1911/1950). Like Kraepelin, Bleuler considered catatonia to be a subtype of the schizophrenias, but was less clear about restricting the use of the term to apply only to schizophrenia. "As a rule catatonic symptoms mix with the manic and the melancholic conditions in some instances, to such a degree that the catatonic symptoms dominate the clinical picture and one can speak of a manic or melancholic catatonia" (Bleuler, 1911/1950, p. 211). At times, Bleuler's discussion of catatonia is reminiscent of Kahlbaum's, where a strong affective component was frequently described. Bleuler was also influenced by Freud, and, in his attempt to apply Freud's theories to dementia praecox, he helped advance the psychoanalytic approach to understanding schizophrenia.

After Kraepelin and Bleuler, other investigators, such as Kleist (1960), Fish (1974), Hamilton (1984), Leonhard (1979), and Astrup (1979), continued to define catatonia as a subtype of schizophrenia, and even went so far as to subdivide the catatonic subtype as well. In addition, Gjessing (1974, 1979), who spent many years studying periodic catatonia, felt he was dealing with a subtype of schizophrenia.

By the middle of the 1900s, many psychiatrists conceptualized catatonia as the subtype of schizophrenia characterized by abnormalities of movement. However, paralleling the work on the subtype nature of catatonia were an increasing number of reports of catatonia occurring in conditions other than schizophrenia. As early as the late 1800s, stuporous conditions in many different psychiatric patients were often called "catatonia" (Zilboorg, 1941), and during the first few decades of the 20th century such conditions as postencephalitic and "arteriosclerotic" parkinsonism were frequently reported to have catatonic features (Jelliffe, 1927; Critchley, 1929). Even today, the few surviving patients with postencephalitic parkinsonism resulting from the epidemic of von Economo's encephalitis manifest signs and symptoms usually considered catatonic in nature (Sacks, 1983).

The experiments of DeJong (1945, 1956) and others (Henry, 1931; Ferraro & Barrera, 1932) on bulbocapnine-induced catatonic signs in animals and man were another major addition to the literature on catatonia. These studies stimulated further interest in animal models of catatonia (and schizophrenia in general) and led to a large body of literature on catatonia and catalepsy in animals. Many investigators have reported findings indicating that these drug-induced states in animals may not be the equivalent of catatonia in man, however (Ferraro & Barrera, 1932; Cervantes et al., 1977; Davis & Dysken, 1978; Abrams et al., 1978). Nevertheless, many researchers have prematurely concluded that animals can serve as a model for catatonia.

Over the course of this century, the concept of catatonia has become confused and no longer refers to a single discrete clinical entity. Some of the literature refers to catatonia as a subtype of schizophrenia, whereas other literature reports catatonia to be a syndrome that can occur not only in various neurological and psychiatric diseases but also as an effect of drugs. Kraepelin's belief that catatonic signs and symptoms do not by themselves allow for the diagnosis of catatonia but must be accompanied by other schizophrenic symptoms is far from universally accepted.

In retrospect, it appears that there were two important points of confusion in the conceptual history of catatonia. The first point arose when Kraepelin adapted Kahlbaum's term "catatonia" to refer only to schizophrenia. This adaptation amounted to a redefinition of the disorder, for it excluded many patients with catatonic motor signs and predominantly affective symptoms. However, the redefinition of catatonia as a subtype of schizophrenia was only partially adhered to, and this resulted in the second point of confusion. Those who conceptualized catatonia as the subtype of schizophrenia characterized by motor abnormalities did not describe the discrete cluster of signs and symptoms essential for the diagnosis of catatonia. For these investigators the crucial diagnosis was schizophrenia, and any one of a whole host of motor abnormalities could qualify the patient for a diagnosis of catatonia. Other investigators, however, applied the term to conditions other than schizophrenia, assuming that the various catatonic signs in some way made up a coherent, well-defined syndrome—an assumption that led many scientists to study catatonia without ever defining exactly what it was. This would be similar to calling patients with ketoacidosis "diabetic" irrespective of the etiology of the ketoacidosis, and without clearly defining what constitutes "diabetic."

In the past 20 years, it has become increasingly popular to view catatonia as a nonspecific syndrome. Nevertheless, as Abrams and Taylor (1977) have pointed out, "the presence of a single catatonic feature does not define catatonia, and the present state of psychiatric diagnosis does not provide for 'pathognomonic' illness features" (p. 463).

WHAT CHARACTERISTIC SIGNS AND SYMPTOMS HAVE BEEN DESCRIBED IN CATATONIA?

Over 40 different signs and symptoms have been considered at one time or another to belong to the catatonic syndrome. The most important of these (and the ones most consistently reported) are listed in Table 20-1. Most of these signs have been discussed in detail elsewhere in this volume. In the remainder of this section, we shall further comment on some of these previously discussed signs, as well as introduce others that are important in understanding catatonia.

Stupor

In both psychiatry and neurology, stupor represents a state of unresponsiveness to the environment. The neurological concept usually includes, in addition, depression of the level of consciousness, whereas this is not necessarily true from the psychiatric perspective. Bleuler (1911/1950) appears to have made this distinction, having stated that stupor "in [the] precise sense . . . [occurs] almost only in the clouded [catatonic] states, obviously as a consequence of generally reduced psychic activity, or of total 'blocking'" (p. 184). Berrios (1981a) and Plum and Posner (1980) have also commented on the

Table 20-1. Some Important Signs and Symptoms Thought at Some Time to Belong to the Catatonic Syndrome

Catalepsy	Palilalia
Negativism	Echokinesis
Automatic obedience	(including echolalia and echopraxia)
Mutism	Perseveration
Staring	Verbigeration
Grimacing	Impulsivity
Posturing	Combativeness
Excessive muscular tension	Denudativeness
(including *Schnauzkrampf* and catatonic	Prankishness
rigidity)	Forced grasping and grasp reflexes
Mitgehen	Signs of autonomic instability
Mitmachen	(including cyanosis, tachycardia, tachyp-
Gegenhalten	nea, hyperpyrexia, pupillary abnormali-
Stupor	ties)
Stereotypies	Choreoathetoid movements
Mannerisms	Tics
Bizarreries	

difficulty in distinguishing between neurological and psychiatric stupors. Stupor is a phenomenon that is not clearly understood at the present time.

Negativism

Although we have discussed negativism in detail elsewhere (Chapter 14), we should mention here that Kahlbaum (1874/1973), Kraepelin (1919/1971), and Bleuler (1911/1950) considered negativism to occur in almost every case of catatonia at some time during the course of the condition.

Muscular Tension

Aberrant muscular tension is the clinical phenomenon for which catatonia was named. Various abnormalities of muscular tone have been reported in catatonia, but the most common is that of *excessive* muscular tension, which has been discussed earlier, in the chapter on rigidity (Chapter 16). Catalepsy has occasionally been considered to be a type of rigidity, but excessive muscular tone is not necessary for waxy flexibility to occur (Gadelius, 1933). Grimacing and, in particular, *Schnauzkrampf* (snout spasm)—in which the patient's face assumes a frozen attitude, with the lips pursed and the eyes usually tightly shut (blepharospasm)—have also been related to excessive muscular tension (Kraepelin, 1919/1971).

Impulsivity

Here, patients engage in sudden acts of an often senseless nature. They jump up and down, run down the halls, tear off their clothes, and scream, all apparently without any forethought or purpose (Gadelius, 1933). Sometimes the acts are of a prankish or malicious nature, sometimes violent, but they usually do not appear to be associated with any particular affective state (Rosanoff, 1927).

Combativeness

The combativeness described in catatonia does not appear to be so much a willed resistance as a form of negativism, usually with impulsive features.

In addition to these main categories of catatonic signs and symptoms, numerous others have been described. Rarely, other motor signs, such as choreoathetoid movements, tremors, and tics, have been noted (Kraepelin,

1919/1971; Strecker & Ebaugh, 1935; Leonhard, 1979). Some investigators have reported that certain catatonic patients seem to lack sensitivity to pain (Stoddart, 1909). A number of signs of autonomic instability, including tachycardia, fever, tachypnea, and cyanosis, have also been reported. Although these signs of autonomic dysfunction are most consistently noted in lethal catatonia, they have been observed in the nonlethal types as well.

DO THE VARIOUS SIGNS AND SYMPTOMS OF CATATONIA REPRESENT A DISTINCT CLINICAL ENTITY?

During the earlier part of this century, most psychiatrists believed that the signs and symptoms that we have discussed in the previous section were but parts of a single clinical phenomenon, although, of course, they realized that not all the signs might be present in a single patient or at a given time. A number of case reports and other studies that support this belief have appeared (Rosanoff, 1927; Strecker & Ebaugh, 1935; Olkon, 1945; Hearst et al., 1971; Abrams & Taylor, 1976; Raichman et al., 1981). There have, however, been few studies in which an attempt was made to determine how the different catatonic signs and symptoms actually cluster together. Abrams et al. (1979) performed a factor analysis on 55 psychiatric patients who showed one or more of eight catatonic features. They found two factors that accounted for 32% of the variance. Factor 1, which included the signs of mutism, negativism, and stupor, was noted to be unrelated to diagnosis, sex, age at onset, family history, and treatment response. Factor 2, which included the signs of mutism, stereotypy, catalepsy, and automatic obedience, was found to be possibly associated with the diagnosis of mania. The authors stated that factor 2 appeared to correspond more closely to the classical concept of catatonia. Although we have reservations about whether one or the other of these factors more closely corresponds to "classical" catatonia, or whether they are an accurate reflection of catatonic subtypes, this study does serve to show that a number of different features frequently considered to be "catatonic" tend to occur together.

In spite of the paucity of objective clinical studies on the nature of the catatonic syndrome, many researchers have assumed, predominantly on the basis of numerous case reports and personal observations of reputable psychiatrists, that catatonia does indeed represent a distinct entity. Some have even gone so far as to subdivide it. Most commonly, catatonia has been divided into two forms—*stuporous* (also called retarded or withdrawn) catatonia, and *excited* catatonia. Kleist and his school (Leonhard, 1979; Astrup, 1979) have additionally separated catatonia into *systematic* and *periodic* forms, both of which may include stuporous or excited signs. These are listed in Table 20-2. Finally, *lethal* catatonia has been described as a subtype, but it is not clear how it relates to the other groups just mentioned. In the remain-

Table 20-2. The Kleist and Leonhard Diagnostic Classification Scheme for
Catatonia[a]

1. Periodic catatonia: Remissions and exacerbations are present throughout the course of the
   illness. Patients may be stuporous or excited at different times, and may appear normal
   between episodes or may exhibit schizophrenic defects.
2. Systematic catatonias:
   a. Parakinetic catatonia: Dominated by bizarre, often jerky involuntary movements, some-
      times resembling choreiform movements. There is frequent grimacing.
   b. Speech-prompt catatonia: Stiffness of movement and loss of facial expressiveness is
      common. Patients exhibit *Vorbeireden*, or talking beside the point, especially when
      questions are highly affect-laden.
   c. Proskinetic catatonia: Patients exhibit automatic obedience, *Mitmachen, Mitgehen,* and
      other signs of what we have termed "positivism."
   d. Speech-inactive catatonia: Patients appear to be constantly hallucinating and speaking to
      themselves, but give very few if any answers to the questions of others.
   e. Manneristic catatonia: Frequent mannerisms and stereotypies accompany a general
      stiffness of posture and movement. *Gegenhalten* may occur.
   f. Negativistic catatonia: Often appears to be the opposite of proskinetic catatonia, with a
      refusal to be touched or to carry out requests.

[a]See Astrup (1979).

der of this section we present a brief discussion of these different subtypes of
catatonia, but we wish the reader to keep in mind the fact that since catatonia
has not been fully defined, any studies concerning catatonic subtypes must be
carefully appraised.

Stuporous and Excited Catatonia

The hallmark of stuporous catatonia is a generalized decrease in motor
activity. Catalepsy is commonly reported to be present, along with mutism,
negativism, and different manifestations of muscular tension. Also, automatic obedience, stereotypies, and even combativeness have been reported to
occur. In contrast, the distinguishing feature of excited catatonia is excessive
movement. Most of the signs described in stuporous catatonia have also been
described in the excited form—in particular, negativism, mutism, automatic
obedience, stereotypies, mannerisms, and rigidity, although impulsivity and
combativeness are usually thought to be more common in the excited form.
Early in this century, many psychiatrists believed that these two different
forms of catatonia were but different manifestations of a single underlying
disturbance in mental functioning, principally because it was observed that

many individuals would fluctuate between the two states (Kraepelin, 1919/
1971; Straus & Griffith, 1955; Gjessing, 1979). It was often observed that a
patient would have bursts of excessive activity that would be like islands in a
sea of stupor.

Morrison (1973), in a retrospective chart survey of catatonic schizophrenics, reported that, out of 250 catatonic patients, 110 were predominantly retarded or stuporous, 67 were predominantly excited, and 73 were
mixed, although the exact criteria by which subtyping was made were not
clear. Morrison advocated regarding the retarded and the excited catatonics
separately because of evidence indicating that excited patients were more
likely to develop the illness suddenly and to recover.

Systematic and Periodic Catatonia

Periodic catatonia has been extensively studied by Gjessing (1974, 1979). This
form of catatonia has been contrasted with what have been called systematic
forms by Kleist, Leonhard, Fish, Astrup, and others. Astrup (1979) described
periodic catatonia as resembling other types of motility psychoses that remit.
He stated that it is often very severe at first and frequently results in a loss of
natural grace of movement and a tendency to mannerisms and stiffness in
facial expression. The defect usually remains slight, however, and there is a
good response to phenothiazines. Astrup also reports that patients with the
periodic form tend to be more paranoid than are their systematic counterparts.

Periodic catatonia has been extensively studied by Gjessing and coworkers (Gjessing, 1964, 1965, 1967, 1974, 1979; Gjessing et al., 1967) in
terms of associated metabolic abnormalities. In particular, abnormalities
have been found in nitrogen metabolism and in the state of cholinergic/
adrenergic balance. In those patients in whom the psychotic phase was
marked by stupor (A-type), nitrogen retention was noted in the interval
phase, whereas in those cases in which the psychotic phase was excited (C-
type), there was nitrogen retention during the psychotic phase. Intermediate
cases (B-type) showed nitrogen retention during both phases. In all types, the
interval phase was marked by a state of relative cholinergic hyperactivity with
reduced heart rate, reduced basal metabolic rate, and low fasting blood
sugar, along with leucopenia and lymphocytosis. In contrast, the psychotic
phase was marked by relative hyperactivity in the adrenergic system, with
elevated pulse, blood pressure, basal metabolic rate, and fasting glucose, as
well as a leukocytosis and a severe sleep disturbance characterized by prolonged rapid-eye-movement (REM) latency and decreased total REM time.
Both lithium and thyroid hormone have been shown to be effective in
periodic catatonia.

Lethal Catatonia

This appears to be the rarest subtype of catatonia. In addition to the other signs of catatonia described in the previous section, hyperpyrexia, tachycardia, tachypnea, dehydration, and cyanosis are also present in many cases (Powers *et al.*, 1976). Bleuler (1911/1950) believed that most of these cases occurred in the presence of schizophrenic illness, and Laskowska *et al.* (1965) found that more than 80% of the patients who survived an episode of lethal catatonia were either schizophrenic to begin with, or developed schizophrenia later. Lethal catatonia appears to be very similar to another clinical syndrome, known as neuroleptic malignant syndrome (NMS), which is reported to occur as a response to neuroleptic medications (Weinberger & Kelly, 1977; Smego & Durack, 1982; Levenson, 1985; Greenberg & Gujavarty, 1985), but there is some question as to whether or not these two states are really different (Peele & Von Loetzen, 1973). The cause of death in lethal catatonia is often not clear (Penn *et al.*, 1972). The relationship of lethal catatonia to neuroleptic malignant syndrome will be discussed in greater detail later in this chapter.

In summary, there is evidence that catatonia represents a distinct clinical syndrome, but more studies are necessary to fully define and characterize it. The status of the various catatonic subtypes as independent clinical states is not clear. At the end of this chapter we offer tentative diagnostic criteria for diagnosing catatonia on the basis of existing descriptions of the phenomenon and our own personal experience.

DOES CATATONIA REPRESENT A DISEASE, A SUBTYPE OF SCHIZOPHRENIA, OR A NONSPECIFIC SYNDROME?

Catatonia as a Disease

Kahlbaum initially defined catatonia as a disease that progressed through a series of stages (1874/1973). Since his initial description, however, the notion of catatonia as an independent disease entity has virtually disappeared. There are a large number of reports of catatonic signs occurring in schizophrenia, manic–depressive illness, and various neurological disorders, and as an effect of drugs (Gelenberg, 1976b), so that the existence of catatonia as a separate disease appears unlikely. Nevertheless, every once in a while a patient presents with only catatonic signs and no evidence of hallucinations, delusions, affective problems, or other neurological or medical illnesses. We have seen several of these patients (Lohr & Wisniewski, unpublished observations), and it is not clear how they should be classified. At present, we believe that these patients, because of their concomitant poverty of thought and affect, suffer from a condition that is probably related to schizophrenia marked by a severe defect state (what has been called Type II schizophrenia by Crow, 1980, 1981, 1985).

Catatonia as a Subtype of Schizophrenia

Although there is little question that catatonic signs occur in schizophrenia, it is still not clear whether catatonia can be considered a subtype of schizophrenia. Catatonic signs can dominate the clinical picture in a given patient at one time, and yet be only marginally present or even absent at another (Hearst *et al.*, 1971; Guggenhcim & Babigian, 1974). In his long-term follow-up studies of schizophrenic patients, Astrup (1979) noted that catatonic signs may appear in a variety of schizophrenic subtypes, especially during the first 10 years of illness. However, Astrup indicates that in a small percentage of the schizophrenic population, catatonic signs always dominate the clinical picture; these patients are called catatonic schizophrenics. In the report on schizophrenic subtypes of Carpenter *et al.* (1976) from the International Pilot Study of Schizophrenia (IPSS), it was noted that the catatonic subtype is a modest exception to the general finding that the different schizophrenic subtypes have similar patterns of signs and symptoms. In fact, in their cluster analysis of schizophrenic patients, cluster 2, which is characterized by "aberrant, agitated, or bizarre behavior, incomprehensibility, unkempt appearance, incongruent or restricted affect, and absence of anxiety or depression," in many ways resembles catatonic schizophrenia. Cluster 2 contained a small percentage of the total number of schizophrenic patients (approximately 5%).

In summary, it is not clear whether catatonia represents a subtype of schizophrenia, but, if it does, its diagnosis probably requires a number of years of clinical observation so as to eliminate those patients who have only transient catatonic signs.

Catatonia as a Nonspecific Syndrome

It has become popular to view catatonia as a nonspecific syndrome that can occur in a variety of medical, neurological, and psychiatric illnesses (Gelenberg, 1976b; Abrams & Taylor, 1976; Raichman *et al.*, 1981; Sripada, 1982). Because catatonia at the present time is not well-defined as a clinical syndrome, it is questionable whether all the different clinical descriptions in the many case reports of catatonia represent the same clinical state. For example, many patients have been called catatonic on the basis of mutism and rigidity, and in many cases it is not clear what the authors considered to be catatonic (as opposed to, say, parkinsonian) signs. Table 20-3 offers a list of various neurological and medical disorders in which catatonia has been reported.

Table 20-3. Neurological and Medical Conditions That Have Been Associated with Catatonia

Neurological conditions

Encephalitis (including epidemic, bacterial, herpes, and other viral causes)

Postencephalitic states (including postencephalitic parkinsonism)

Epilepsy (including temporal-lobe epilepsy, complex partial status, petit mal status)

Brain neoplasms (including frontal-lobe and limbic tumors, periventricular pinealoma, arteriovenous malformations, tuberous sclerosis)

Vascular causes (including anterior cerebral and anterior communicating artery aneurysms, subarachnoid hemorrhage, subdural hematomas, hemorrhage into the third ventricle, biparietal infarctions, cortical venous thrombosis)

Akinetic mutism

General paresis of the insane

"Arteriosclerotic" parkinsonism

Bilateral globus-pallidus lesions

Primary pallido-nigro-subthalamic atrophy

Other medical conditions	
Hyperparathyroidism	Homocystinuria
Systemic lupus erythematosus	Pellagra
Acute intermittent porphyria	Mononucleosis
Thrombotic thrombocytopenic purpura	Uremia
Membranous glomerulonephritis	Hepatic dysfunction
Typhoid	Langerhans carcinoma
Diabetic ketoacidosis	

In the neurological literature, few case descriptions of "catatonia" include descriptions of negativism or automatic obedience, which Kahlbaum, Kraepelin, and Bleuler considered to be crucial signs in the catatonic presentation. There are, however, three disorders other than schizophrenia in which many catatonic signs have been reported to occur. These are: (1) postencephalitic parkinsonism, (2) affective disorders, and (3) neuroleptic-induced catatonic states.

Postencephalitic Parkinsonism

Many observers have commented on the appearance of catatonic signs in this condition (Ramsay Hunt, 1921; Farran-Ridge, 1926; Jelliffe, 1927; Sacks, 1983). Marsden (1982b) has pointed out that many patients with postencephalitic parkinsonism were probably thought to have suffered from schizophrenia, and Jelliffe (1927) noted that catatonic schizophrenia and postencephalitic parkinsonism may be very similar in appearance. Marsden *et al.* (1975) have drawn attention to the possibility that many choreoathetotic signs described in schizophrenia before the advent of neuroleptic drugs may have actually been secondary to organic neurological disease in individuals mistakenly identified as schizophrenic. This might be true for other catatonic signs as well.

Affective Disorders

In carefully reviewing some of Kahlbaum's initial cases, it appears that a number of them more clearly represent affective disorders than schizophrenic conditions. Kirby (1913) reported catatonic signs in manic–depressive illness, as did a number of other investigators, but the association between catatonic signs and affective disorders has been largely ignored until recently. It is not clear, however, whether the "catatonia" of affective disorders is the same as the "catatonia" of schizophrenia. A study by Bonner and Kent in 1936 showed a considerable amount of overlap between catatonic excitement and manic excitement, and these authors apparently took great care to ensure that the patients they were studying were definitely either schizophrenic or manic. Still, their data reveal that certain signs, such as waxy flexibility, stereotyped speech, mutism, and negativism, were much more common in the schizophrenic patients than in the manic patients, as shown in Table 20-4.

Abrams and Taylor (1976) studied 55 patients with one or more catatonic features and noted that in two-thirds of the cases the patients were diagnosed as manic and in only four cases were the patients schizophrenic. Further, they noted that no concentration of a single catatonic sign could be used to discriminate among the groups. Later, these same investigators (Taylor & Abrams, 1977) studied 123 patients with acute onset bipolar affective disorder and noted two or more catatonic signs in 28% of the patients. It should be noted that 21% of the bipolar patients with catatonic features also possessed first-rank Schneiderian symptoms, whereas only 6% of the other bipolars had first-rank symptoms. This latter finding raises the question of a diagnosis of schizophrenia in at least some of the catatonic bipolar patients. A consideration of the Taylor and Abrams research diagnostic criteria lends further support to the idea that probably many more schizophrenics and many fewer manics had catatonic signs than the researchers' report indicates. Their diagnostic criteria for mania are very easy to meet, compared with those for schizophrenia. Cases that, in other classification schemes, might be called "schizoaffective," in their scheme would be called manic or depressive (Endicott *et al.*, 1982).

In a recent study by Kendler and Hays (1983) of 147 schizophrenics separated into groups according to whether they had first-degree relatives with unipolar affective disorder ($n = 18$), with bipolar affective disorder ($n = 10$), or without affective disorder ($n = 98$), the authors noted a signifi-

Table 20-4. A Selection of Signs and Symptoms Recorded from 100 Cases Each of Catatonic Excitement and Manic Excitement[a]

Sign or symptom	Dementia praecox (n)	Manic–depressive (n)
Marked cyanosis	8	1
Cerea flexibilitas	15	2
Tube feeding required	27	8
Hallucinations	87	43
Paranoid ideas	66	43
Depression	42	49
Overtalkative	62	96
Flight of ideas	33	91
Stereotyped speech	29	7
Retardation	28	16
Blocking	29	2
Mutism	48	8
Seclusive	63	17
Playful	17	48
Denudative	38	38
Negativistic	52	8
Mannerisms	47	34
Attitudes	24	9

[a]Data from Bonner and Kent (1936).

cantly greater incidence of catatonic signs in the group with bipolar relatives. These patients were also much more likely to have depression in the prodromal period. The authors nevertheless believed these patients to be truly schizophrenic at the time, even though some of the patients later went on to develop symptoms of affective disorder.

In summary, it does appear that certain patients who have primarily disorders of affect can develop catatonic signs. What is still open to question is whether these patients have variants of more typical affective disorder presentations, or whether they manifest some unusual blend of schizophrenic and affective signs and symptoms. Perhaps related to this latter idea is Gjessing's (1974) observation that patients with periodic catatonia, thought to be a form of schizophrenia, can show euphoria after a stuporous episode, and also that some periodic catatonic patients respond to lithium. Other researchers have reported lithium to be effective in periodic catatonia as well (Petursson, 1976; Wald & Lerner, 1978).

Neuroleptic-Induced Catatonic States

There have been a number of reports of catatonic signs occurring after the use of antipsychotic drugs, and these are presented in Table 20-5. Most of the reports are of schizophrenic patients (May, 1959; Gelenberg & Mandel, 1977; Nakra & Hwu, 1982), and there are three reports of catatonic signs' being exacerbated by neuroleptic drugs in patients who previously appeared to be catatonic schizophrenics (De, 1973; Brenner & Rheuban, 1978; Kelwala & Ban, 1981). In addition to schizophrenia, neuroleptic-induced catatonic states have been reported in mania (Williams, 1972), in obsessive–compulsive disorder and borderline personality disorder (Gelenberg & Mandel, 1977), and

Table 20-5. Case Reports of Neuroleptic-Induced Catatonia (Excluding Malignant Forms)

Reference	Age	Sex	Associated neuroleptic drug	Diagnosis (before catatonia)
Kinross-Wright (1955)	24	M	Chlorpromazine	Schizophrenia (history of catatonic episodes in past)
May (1959)	34	F	Promazine	Probable schizophrenia
	35	F	Prochlorperazine	Probable schizophrenia
Williams (1972)	40	F	Chlorpromazine	Mania
De (1973)	46	M	Fluphenazine	Catatonic schizophrenia (neuroleptic-exacerbated)
Riley et al. (1976)	34	F	Prochlorperazine	Acute myelogenous leukemia
Gelenberg and Mandel (1977)	19	M	Fluphenazine	Schizophrenia
	55	F	Fluphenazine	Schizophrenia
	15	F	Haloperidol	Schizophrenia
	23	F	Thioridazine and Haloperidol	Schizophrenia
	44	F	Haloperidol	Obsessive–compulsive disorders
	23	M	Haloperidol	Schizophrenia
	20	F	Fluphenazine decanoate	Schizophrenia
	20	F	Haloperidol	Borderline personality
Brenner and Rheuban (1978)	19	M	Haloperidol	Catatonic schizophrenia (neuroleptic-exacerbated)
Kelwala and Ban (1981)	14	M	Haloperidol	Catatonic schizophrenia (neuroleptic-exacerbated)
Nakra and Hwu (1982)	72	F	Haloperidol	Schizophrenia
Johnson and Manning (1983)	18	M	Loxapine	Schizophrenia

in acute myelogenous leukemia after chemotherapy (Riley *et al.*, 1976). Neuroleptic-induced catatonia is further discussed later in this chapter.

It appears that, if catatonia is considered to be a clearly definable clinical entity, it is a state that can occur in a variety of psychiatric and neurological conditions. Also, there is some evidence that a small percentage of schizophrenic patients have catatonic signs thus dominate the course of the illness throughout their lives, and thus could justifiably the patients' being called catatonic schizophrenics. However, because such patients are rare, we believe that catatonia should be diagnosed separately from the accompanying mental or neurological disorder. The current *Diagnostic and Statistical Manual of Mental Disorders* (American Psychiatric Association, 1980) has no provision for catatonia existing apart from schizophrenia, and there is no way to note the presence of catatonic signs, even in schizophrenia, unless they "dominate" the clinical picture.

In stating that the evidence indicates that catatonia can occur in a variety of illnesses, it should be noted that an assumption has been made, which is that catatonia is definable by observable behavior alone, independent of delusions, hallucinations, or any other subjective symptoms. This assumption would make catatonia different from many other psychiatric disorders, in which the diagnosis of the disorder relies heavily on subjective symptoms. If catatonia is defined by the presence of bizarre behavior alone, then it does appear to be nonspecific. However, if subjective state is thought to be important in the diagnosis, then the matter is more complicated. In the next section, we review some of the psychological theories of catatonia, as well as the evidence for a neurological basis for the syndrome.

WHAT IS THE EVIDENCE FOR A PSYCHOLOGICAL VERSUS A NEUROLOGICAL ETIOLOGY OF CATATONIA?

In this section we consider briefly the evidence for psychological and neurological factors in the etiology of catatonia.

Psychological Theories

Although there have been a number of psychological theories of catatonia, most of these have been based on psychoanalytic ideas and few seem to have taken into direct account the inner subjective experience of the patients. Catatonia has been conceptualized as the result of internal conflict over opposing forces (Fenichel, 1945) or as a disintegration of the ego, marked by regression to a stage where all attention is directed inward and periods of catatonic excitement can be compared to birth anxiety (Nunberg, 1948). Such theoretical generalizations do not do justice to the complex and varied inner experience many catatonic patients report.

There are very few reports of the subjective experience of catatonics in the literature, and almost all of them appear to be of catatonic schizophrenics. Although investigators since Kraepelin have reported that delusions and hallucinations occur in catatonia, many have noted that these are often not prominent parts of the clinical picture, and, when they are present, they appear to be irrelevant to the motor features (Gadelius, 1933; Rosanoff, 1927). Jones (1965), in a study of schizophrenic stereotypies, noted that in only one out of 13 cases were the delusions relevant to the form of the stereotypy.

There appears to be an impoverishment of thought and emotionality in many catatonic schizophrenic patients (Rosanoff, 1927). In keeping with this are the findings of Andreasen and Olsen (1982) of a significant association between the so-called "negative" symptoms of schizophrenia (such as anhedonia and abulia) and catatonic features. Patients "awakening" from an episode of catatonic stupor frequently cannot give more than a vague description of the subjective experience accompanying the catatonic state. This has led some psychiatrists to postulate that the underlying disorder in catatonia is not one of "movement" but rather of "action," the latter being dependent on the intactness of the will (Straus & Griffith, 1955; Arieti, 1972). Straus and Griffith (1955) have reported that patients in catatonic stupor can often have short periods in which their motor behavior may be completely normal, and these authors have taken this to indicate that the basic problem is not in the motor system, but rather in the schizophrenic process itself. Gadelius (1933) has stated that catatonics often retrospectively reveal that the catatonic signs were involuntary.

The above discussion applies exclusively to patients considered to have the stuporous form of catatonic schizophrenia. Very little is known about the subjective experience of catatonics in periods of excitement, or about the psychological states accompanying catatonia in other conditions. Manic patients with catatonic features occasionally appear euphoric or grandiose, and Jelliffe (1927) noted, in a comparison of the mental pictures of schizophrenics and postencephalitics, that the explanation of akinetic and hyperkinetic states is often quite different for the two. "The explanation in the encephalitic tends more to rationalization—that of the schizophrenic towards a distorted symbolism" (Jelliffe, 1927, p. 461).

It seems that the subjective experience can vary dramatically. We have personally observed a very large range, from states of near psychic immobility, in which thoughts are blighted and time stands still, to states in which patients report powerful urges accompanied by irresistible voices telling them to behave a certain way, to states of euphoria accompanied by grandiose ideas, to states of bewilderment in which patients behave in a manner over which they have no control or for which they have no explanation (Lohr & Wisniewski, unpublished observations). Yet, in spite of these differences, the outward appearance of many of these patients is the same. We believe that, at the present time, it is more helpful to define catatonia on the basis of objective signs, and to classify the accompanying subjective state on the basis of already existing psychiatric diagnostic schemes. Because the psychological state of catatonic patients is so variable, purely psychological theories are not adequate to explain the behavior.

Evidence for a Neurological Etiology

Most of the theories concerning a neurological etiology of catatonia have been based on analogies with other conditions in which similar signs have been noted. Kleist (1960) proposed frontal-lobe dysfunction to be involved, and one of us has reported grasp reflexes to be present during catatonic episodes (grasp reflexes are thought to be related to frontal-lobe dysfunction; see Lohr, 1985). Dysfunction in the anterior limbic system has also been postulated to be involved (Roberts, 1965). The most common theory, however, has implicated pathology of the basal ganglia. Mettler (1955) pointed out that there are a number of catatonics who, in going into and out of catatonic rigidity, pass through a state that is virtually indistinguishable from parkinsonism. Gelenberg and Mandel (1977), in their report of patients who developed catatonia as a consequence of neuroleptic treatment, noted that the patients also developed signs of parkinsonism, and that the catatonic features and parkinsonian signs tended both to appear and to disappear together.

Hopf (1952) performed neuropathological studies on the brains of schizophrenics and reported cell loss in the globus pallidus of catatonic schizophrenics, but not in other types. Kleist (1960) stated that he confirmed this finding. Stevens (1982) reported more neuronal loss in various regions of the brains of catatonics compared to other schizophrenic patients—in particular, in the globus pallidus, substantia innominata, and nucleus accumbens. Jellinger (1985) reviewed a large number of neuropathological studies of patients with acute catatonia and noted that there have been no consistently reported abnormalities.

Almost all of the neuropathological studies so far performed have been prone to errors of subjectivity. The brain is easily duped when it studies itself. Yet there have been few objective quantitative neuropathological studies of schizophrenia, and even fewer of catatonia. Using quantitative methods, Dom (1976) noted a reduction in microneuron density in the posterior thalamus and a decrease in microneuron size in the striatum of catatonic schizophrenics, but these results require confirmation.

In conclusion, there is some evidence for basal ganglia involvement in catatonic schizophrenia, perhaps to a greater extent than in other schizophrenic subtypes, but quantitative and objective neuropathological studies are needed to confirm these findings. Also, it is unclear whether these findings apply to catatonia noted in conditions other than schizophrenia, or whether the catatonic signs are directly related to the basal-ganglia pathology.

IS CATATONIA DECLINING IN PREVALENCE?

This question can be answered only for catatonic schizophrenia, for almost all the studies on the prevalence of catatonia have expressed it as a percentage of the total schizophrenic prevalence at any given time.

Most studies that have been concerned with the prevalence of catatonic schizophrenia in the early part of this century have been retrospective, with relatively few studies on prevalence performed before 1940. May (1922) reported the percentage of schizophrenics who were diagnosed as catatonic from a number of mental institutions in different areas of the country in the few years before 1920. His findings were (p. 457):

Area	Total number of patients with dementia praecox	Number diagnosed catatonic	Percentage diagnosed catatonic
New York	6,135	468	7.6%
Massachusetts	2,921	678	23.2%
19 other institutions	3,184	438	10.6%
Total	12,240	1,584	12.1%

Achte (1961) investigated the case records of 100 schizophrenic patients in Finland admitted in the 1930s and 100 patients admitted in the 1950s. He noted a decrease in the frequency of diagnosis of catatonic schizophrenia from 37% to 11% over this time. Most of this decline occurred in the group of patients with catatonic stupor, of whom there were 14 in the 1930s but only 2 in the 1950s. Achte states that the occurrences of milder catatonic states were not essentially different over this time. However, it is worth noting that, although there was a decline in frequency of catatonic schizophrenia, there was a 2-fold increase in the number of schizophrenics in Finland during this period, apparently paralleled by a decreasing severity of schizophrenic illness. Thus, as Achte points out, it is possible that in the 1950s individuals with milder cases of schizophrenia sought admission to the mental hospitals (perhaps because of a decreasing fear of such institutions), accounting for the increase in frequency of schizophreniform and paranoid psychoses, as well as for the apparent decrease in frequency of catatonia. The total number of catatonic schizophrenics may not have changed, however.

Hogarty and Gross (1966), in a retrospective study of patients in Maryland state hospital, noted a decline, from 38% in 1953 to 25% in 1960, in the percentage of schizophrenics diagnosed as catatonic.

Morrison (1974) looked at the percentage of schizophrenic patients diagnosed as catatonic in the records of the Iowa State Psychopathic Hospital from 1920 to 1966. From 1920 to 1944, 137 out of 965 (14.2%) schizophrenics carried the diagnosis of catatonia, whereas, from 1945 to 1966, only 105 out of 1,243 (8.5%) carried the diagnosis.

Templer and Veleber (1981), in a similar study, gathered data on schizophrenic patients from the Missouri Department of Mental Health for the years 1900 to 1979. Although a general decline with time was noted in the percentage of schizophrenics diagnosed as catatonic, it was not a constant decline. The proportion fell from approximately 8.5% in 1900–1920 to approximately 5% in 1930, then rose back up to 6% in 1935, only to fall to 3% in 1960. In the 1960s the proportion again rose, to approximately 6.5%, eventually to fall to approximately 2% by 1979.

In addition to the above studies, there have been a small number that have reported on the prevalence of catatonic schizophrenia at a given point in time. Duval (1948) reported that 43% of 1,000 consecutive patients from the United States Navy were diagnosed as having catatonic schizophrenia. Thomas and Wilson (1949) reported that 12 out of 70 (17%) patients with dementia praecox were of the catatonic subtype. More recently, Guggenheim and Babigian (1974) looked at the proportion of schizophrenics diagnosed as catatonic in the early 1960s in the Rochester, New York, area. Out of approximately 625,000 inhabitants, 39,475 were seen for reasons of mental problems, of whom 8,094 were diagnosed as schizophrenic. And of these 8,094 patients, 798 (9.9%) had at some time received the diagnosis of catatonia. This would make the prevalence of catatonia in the community 1.3 per 1,000 individuals. Of the 798 catatonics, 147 (1.8% of schizophrenics) were given a diagnosis of catatonia on every admission, 122 (1.5%) received this diagnosis most of the time, 105 (1.3%) occasionally received it, and 199 (2.5%) received it only once. The other catatonic patients were either chronic inpatients (137, or 1.7%) or had been seen only once (88, or 1.1%). The authors further observed that although 13% of schizophrenics were diagnosed as catatonic at the state hospital in the area, only about 3% were so diagnosed at the university hospital.

In the Carpenter et al. (1976) report from the International Pilot Study of Schizophrenia, the proportion of schizophrenics diagnosed as catatonic varied greatly from region to region around the world. The following is a summary of these results (excluding Moscow and Prague, for which no catatonics were listed):

Area	Number of schizophrenics	Number (%) of catatonics
Denmark	53	2 (3.8%)
India	101	22 (21.8%)
Colombia	101	13 (12.9%)
Nigeria	120	10 (8.3%)
London	100	3 (3.0%)
Taiwan	86	3 (3.5%)
Washington, D.C.	97	1 (1.0%)
Total	658	54 (8.2%)

From these data, Templer and Veleber (1981) calculated that the three countries with the highest proportion of catatonics (India, Colombia, and Nigeria) are also the ones with the lowest per capita income, and that this is statistically significant.

Using the Kleist and Leonhard diagnostic classification scheme for schizophrenia, Leonhard (1979) in Germany noted that out of 833 schizophrenics, 87 (10.4%) suffered from periodic catatonia and 209 (25.1%) from the systematic form. The percentage of all catatonics was 35.4%. Astrup (1979) in Norway, using the same diagnostic classification scheme, reported periodic catatonia in 98 out 990 schizophrenics (9.9%), and systematic catatonia in 71 out of 990 (7.2%), with a total percentage of 17.1%.

There are a number of methodological problems in many of the studies mentioned above. Most importantly, diagnostic criteria for catatonia are only rarely specified. Most studies relied on retrospective chart diagnoses of catatonia, and, undoubtedly, different criteria were employed by different physicians, especially in those studies spanning a number of decades. Thus, although it is conceivable that a decline in catatonic schizophrenia has occurred over the century, what is a more striking finding from the above studies is that the percentage of catatonics varies enormously at any given time according to region, diagnostic scheme, setting (e.g., state hospital versus university hospital), and probably many other factors as well. For example, from 1900 to 1979, Templer and Veleber noted a 3.75-fold drop in the proportion of schizophrenics labeled catatonic, and, from 1920 to 1966, Morrison found a 1.7-fold drop. Compare these differences to those found between New York and Massachusetts by May (1922) around 1918 (3-fold), or to the difference found between state hospital and university hospital by Guggenheim and Babigian (1974) in the early 1960s (4.3-fold), or to the difference between India and Washington, D.C., reported for the 1970s by the IPSS (21.8-fold), or even to the difference between Germany and Norway

(Leonhard, 1979; Astrup, 1979), using the same classification scheme (2.1-fold). If we add the fact that many schizophrenic patients exhibit catatonic signs without ever receiving the diagnosis of catatonia, and the possibility that schizophrenia is becoming more common with the passage of time (Torrey, 1980), then there is little compelling reason to believe that catatonic signs and symptoms are any rarer in the world today than they ever were. They may, in fact, be more common.

THE RELATIONSHIP OF NEUROLEPTIC MALIGNANT SYNDROME TO NEUROLEPTIC-INDUCED CATATONIA AND LETHAL CATATONIA

This is a controversial area for a number of reasons, including the following:

1. Neuroleptic malignant syndrome is usually described as consisting of signs such as mutism, rigidity, and akinesia, and is not commonly reported to have more distinctive catatonic signs, such as catalepsy or automatic obedience. Nevertheless, there are a few case reports in which the typical neuroleptic malignant syndrome (hyperpyrexia, rigidity, and changes in mentation) is accompanied by more distinctive catatonic features (Weinberger & Kelly, 1977; Fricchione et al., 1983).

2. There are a large number of case reports of neuroleptic-induced catatonia without hyperpyrexia or other autonomic changes. In many of these cases the signs described appear to be a combination of catatonic and parkinsonian signs (Gelenberg & Mandel, 1977), but in some cases only catatonic signs are reported (May, 1959; Williams, 1972).

3. Patients with catatonia can die from urinary retention, aspiration pneumonia, thrombophlebitis, and other causes not related to primary autonomic changes such as are seen in lethal catatonia (Regestein et al., 1971; Sukov, 1972; Bort, 1976; Regestein et al., 1977a). Nevertheless, the fact that these patients do die can blur the distinction between lethal catatonia and death secondary to complications resulting from extreme catatonic retardation.

4. In a number of cases of neuroleptic-induced catatonia, a history of previous catatonic signs is present (De, 1973; Brenner & Rheuban, 1978). In other cases, no history of previous catatonia or even of previous schizophrenic illness can be found (Gelenberg & Mandel, 1977).

5. Lethal catatonia may or may not be accompanied by signs of parkinsonism (Feinberg, 1968; Powers et al., 1976), and in some cases lethal catatonia is reported without any truly distinctive features of catatonia at all, but merely because the patient had a history of schizophrenia (McAllister, 1978).

When the different case reports of lethal catatonia, neuroleptic-induced catatonia, and neuroleptic malignant syndrome are broken down into catatonic signs, parkinsonian signs, autonomic dysfunction (including hyperpyrexia), and association with neuroleptic drugs, the relationships depicted in Figure 20-1 may be seen. This Venn diagram shows the considerable overlap in the signs of these disorders (although the size of the overlapping areas does not reflect the relative frequency of their observation, which is not known). What is interesting is that, although there are 10 overlapping areas, there are by and large only four terms in the literature to describe them, these being neuroleptic-induced parkinsonism, neuroleptic-induced catatonia, lethal catatonia, and neuroleptic malignant syndrome. Thus, cases characterized by neuroleptic-induced catatonia and parkinsonism are sometimes just called cases of neuroleptic-induced catatonia, lethal catatonia can have parkinson-

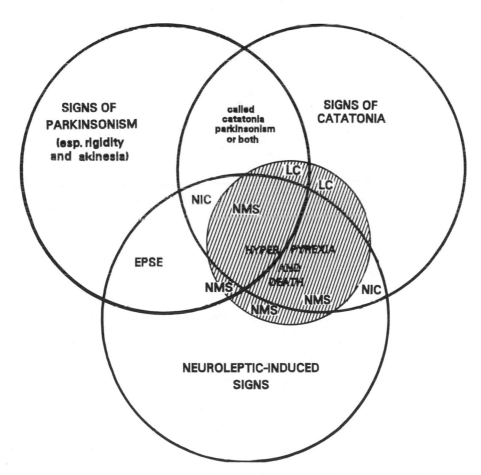

Figure 20-1. Overlapping characteristics of different parkinsonian, catatonic, and neuroleptic-induced extrapyramidal signs. Abbreviations: EPSE, neuroleptic-induced extrapyramidal side effects; NMS, neuroleptic malignant syndrome; NIC, neuroleptic-induced catatonia; LC, lethal catatonia.

ian features, and four different combinations of signs have been referred to as neuroleptic malignant syndrome.

The main problem here is the lack of a proper definition of catatonia. Cases are described as lethal catatonia because of severe rigidity, akinesia, and mutism, all of which may also be parkinsonian signs. In fact, it is rare to find reports of death from either neuroleptic malignant syndrome or lethal catatonia in which signs of parkinsonism were not in evidence. Yet, because psychiatric illness is usually present in these patients, these syndromes have been considered more frequently to be related to catatonia (a "psychiatric" condition) than to parkinsonism, even if the patients never had catatonic episodes before in their lives. In a substantial number of cases, the condition "lethal catatonia" could perhaps be called "lethal parkinsonism." Later in this chapter we offer tentative guidelines for the diagnosis of catatonia that we believe will aid in the description and differentiation of these syndromes. At this time, however, we would like to offer what we hope is a heuristically helpful approach to these disorders.

Basically, if a patient demonstrates parkinsonian signs (rigidity, tremor, hypokinesia, or postural instability), then the patient should be considered to have an "extrapyramidal syndrome." If the patient meets criteria for catatonia as well, then a "catatonic–extrapyramidal syndrome" may be diagnosed. A pure "catatonic syndrome" occurs when the patient meets criteria for catatonia without showing cogwheel rigidity, tremor, or postural instability. In addition, if severe autonomic dysfunction is present (including hyperpyrexia, hypertension, and others) then the syndrome is "malignant," and, if it occurs in the face of neuroleptics and responds to neuroleptic withdrawal, then it is "neuroleptic-associated." We believe these distinctions to be important ones, especially as regards potential treatment differences between the different syndromes.

The interrelatedness of all these different signs is perhaps a clue to understanding them, as they may all represent variations on a pathological theme. The primary candidate for an underlying pathology in these conditions is the dopamine system, and, more specifically, blockade in dopaminergic transmission in different areas of the brain (Henderson & Wooten, 1981).

It is well known that neuroleptic medications are dopamine receptor blockers and that Parkinson's disease is related to a hypodopaminergic state. Dopamine antagonism has been shown to be an important factor in the induction, using different drugs, of "catatonia" in animals (Gonzalez-Vegas, 1974). There is also a report of L-dopa relieving catatonia in a patient with catatonic schizophrenia (Garfinkel & Stancer, 1976). It is not clear exactly where in the brain the dopamine blockade that would account for the motor signs of catatonia occurs, but the striatum and anterior limbic area (in particular, the anterior cingulum) may be involved (Roberts, 1965; Ross &

Stewart, 1981; Fricchione, 1985). Finally, the autonomic disturbances have been proposed to be associated with dopaminergic blockade in the preoptic anterior hypothalamus (Cox & Lee, 1977; Cox et al., 1978; Fricchione, 1985).

Benzodiazepines have been reported to relieve both neuroleptic malignant syndrome and "psychogenic" catatonia (Fricchione et al., 1983; Lew & Tollefson, 1983; McEvoy & Lohr, 1984), which has led some investigators to propose that there may be a dopamine–γ-aminobutyric acid balance in the brain that is upset in these disorders (Lew & Tollefson, 1983; Fricchione, 1985).

Another theory that relates especially to the various malignant disorders involves calcium metabolism. In one patient with apparent neuroleptic malignant syndrome, salmon calcitonin aborted some of the hyperthermic episodes (Carman & Wyatt, 1977). Calcitonin has been reported to lower serum calcium and raise calcium in the cerebrospinal fluid (Carman & Wyatt, 1979). There is a variety of evidence indicating that calcium facilitates dopaminergic formation and release (Gutman & Segal, 1972; Morgenroth et al., 1975; Lane & Aprison, 1977).

Caution must be exercised in considering "psychogenic" catatonia as a state of dopaminergic reduction, however. It should be remembered that catatonic schizophrenia often responds very well to neuroleptics, and there are reports of catatonic patients who either did not change or who became worse after the administration of amphetamine and apomorphine, but who responded to barbiturates in a dramatic fashion (Elkes, 1957; Cervantes et al., 1977). Also, barbiturates, which are agents of known effectiveness in many cases of "psychogenic" catatonia, have not been shown to be effective in neuroleptic malignant syndrome (Lew & Tollefson, 1983).

DIAGNOSTIC CRITERIA

Although it is too early to offer definitive diagnostic criteria for catatonia, we would like to present some tentative guidelines for diagnosis that we believe are heuristically helpful. These are listed in Table 20-6.

It should be stressed that catatonic signs frequently need to be elicited, lest they be overlooked. For this reason it is important to assess patients carefully for the presence of mild cataleptic states or minimal negativism or automatic obedience. Holding out a hand to be shaken often elicits some of these signs, as a patient may reach to shake even when instructed not to, or may slightly pull away each time the hand is offered. Patients who respond too quickly with a yes or no to a question should be asked to fully explain their answers, as these may be subtle manifestations of negativism or automatic obedience. Such thorough clinical investigation can often help solidify the diagnosis in patients who present with unusual behavior.

Table 20-6. Tentative Criteria for the Diagnosis of Catatonia

1. At least one of the following should be present:
   a. Catalepsy
   b. Positivism (such as automatic obedience, *Mitmachen, Mitgehen*)
   c. Negativism
2. At least two of the following should also be present:
   a. Stereotypies
   b. Mannerisms or grimacing
   c. Bizarreries
   d. Posturing
   e. Echo phenomena
   f. Excessive muscular tension
   g. Mutism
   h. Staring
3. For a diagnosis of retarded or withdrawn catatonia, hypokinesia should dominate the clinical picture
4. For a diagnosis of excited catatonia, impulsiveness, combativeness, denudativeness, or other signs of excessive activity should dominate the clinical picture.

TREATMENT

There are few studies on which firmly to base treatment recommendations, so that most of our discussion in this section is based on case reports and our own clinical experience.

Basically, the underlying cause of the catatonic episode should be addressed first, and special attention should be given to the possible presence of a variety of medical and neurological illnesses.

If the catatonic episode occurs in the face of schizophrenia or affective disorder, then the usual treatments for these afflictions should be tried. In particular, if there is a periodic course to the illness, lithium may be effective and, this failing, a trial of thyroid hormone seems warranted. Care should be taken, however, in the administration of neuroleptics to patients with a history of catatonia, as there is a potential risk of causing a malignant syndrome.

If there is a question as to whether there is an underlying "functional" psychosis, an amytal interview may be helpful in differentiating these from "organic" disorders. Morrison (1975) reported that 71 out of 97 (73%) catatonic patients in whom the catatonia accompanied psychiatric illness responded favorably to amytal.

If treatment of the underlying or associated condition fails, a trial of benzodiazepines may be helpful. There is evidence that the therapeutic effect of benzodiazepines may be maintained with prolonged oral dosage (McEvoy & Lohr, 1984). Also, in severe cases when there may be a delay in obtaining consent for electroconvulsive therapy (ECT), benzodiazepines may keep a patient mobile enough so that life-threatening events (such as thromboembolic disease) associated with prolonged immobility can be forestalled in the interval.

Severe catatonia is probably best treated with ECT (Salzman, 1980).

The treatment of any of the malignant syndromes is complex. Most importantly, supportive care is necessary, including emergency techniques for reducing the fever and attending to proper fluid and electrolyte balance. Any neuroleptics or other dopamine-blocking or depleting drugs should be immediately discontinued. Myoglobinuria may be treated by diuresis and alkalinization of the urine. Finally, ECT or drugs such as benzodiazepines, dantrolene, bromocriptine, or L-dopa may be tried (Jessee & Anderson, 1983; Granato, et al., 1983; Stoudemire & Luther, 1984; Kurlan et al., 1984; Fricchione, 1985).

SUMMARY

In conclusion, we believe there is evidence that catatonia represents a distinct entity, but that it should be defined on the basis of motor signs alone, as it appears to accompany a variety of different conditions. We also believe that catatonia should be diagnosed separately from any coexisting psychiatric disorder, mainly because the signs and symptoms can fluctuate a great deal over time and because they can accompany medical and neurological, as well as psychiatric, conditions. Treatment should be initially geared toward the accompanying medical or psychiatric condition except in severe cases, in which ECT should be tried, or in malignant cases, in which supportive treatment and neuroleptic discontinuation are important, and a variety of somatic treatments may be effective.

CHAPTER TWENTY-ONE

Hysterical Conversion Disorders of Movement

INTRODUCTION

In this chapter we review selected aspects of a fascinating condition known as hysterical conversion disorder (HCD). HCD has also been called hysterical neurosis/conversion type or hysterical conversion reaction. In the first few sections we offer a brief overview of the concept of hysteria and its different forms, followed by a discussion of the clinical characteristics, pathophysiology, and differential diagnosis of HCD.

THE PROBLEM OF HYSTERIA

Conversion disorders have usually been considered to fall under the rubric of "hysteria." According to Chodoff (1974), the term "hysteria" has been used in the psychiatric literature to describe a polysymptomatic condition (Briquet's syndrome) and a pathological personality type, as well as to indicate the presence of certain physical signs or symptoms occurring without organic basis. This is in addition to the nonpsychiatric usages of the term, including behavior that appears to be out of control in the face of stress, and overly emotional or seductive behavior, occurring primarily in women. Also, dissociative conditions, such as psychogenic fugue states or multiple personality disorder, have been considered to be a part of hysteria as well.

Of course, the controversy extends beyond simply what should or should not be considered "hysteria." Slater (1965), among others, has noted the possibility that hysteria may be a myth, with its sufferers being merely a random selection of patients whose complaints in no way represent any single definable entity. Others have not gone so far as to suggest abandoning the concept of hysteria, but have advocated abandoning or limiting the word because it appears unclear or pejorative (Lewis, 1974; American Psychiatric Association, 1980). In addition, different aspects of hysteria have been broken off from the total concept and renamed, giving rise to a fairly large number of terms, including somatization disorder, Briquet's syndrome, psychophysiological disorder, conversion disorder or reaction, histrionic personality disorder, hysterical personality disorder, pseudoseizures, and psychogenic pain disorder, along with many others.

Although the word "hysteria" undoubtedly encompasses a number of different disorders, it is worth remembering that these disorders may be interconnected. This appears to be especially true for somatization disorder and HCD. HCD and somatization or Briquet's disorder probably represent the bulk of what was called hysteria in the past. An analysis of the *Diagnostic and Statistical Manual of Mental Disorders* (DSM-III) (American Psychiatric Association, 1980) definitions for these two disorders reveals an interesting difference between the two. Somatization disorder is defined in a way similar to most other mental disorders in the DSM-III—that is, according to the presence of certain basic observable or reported signs and symptoms. The diagnosis of conversion disorder is different, however, for it depends entirely on the following: "positive evidence that the symptom is a direct expression of a psychological conflict" (p. 247). This is profoundly different in terms of underlying diagnostic theory, for the DSM-III diagnosis of conversion disorder, unlike that of most other mental disorders, is totally dependent on an inferred pathogenic mechanism, rather than on descriptive parameters. This observation raises the question of whether these two disorders are more closely related than is apparent from their definitions, with the differences between them reflective more of differences in underlying diagnostic theories than of an actual separateness of the conditions.

Other findings support the idea that HCD and somatization disorder may be closely related. Among a group of different criteria for validating the diagnosis of conversion symptoms, Lazare (1981) lists the presence of an associated somatization disorder first in order of importance. A recent study of conversion symptoms in Vanderbilt hospital reported that over one-third of patients with conversion symptoms had somatization disorder (Folks *et al.*, 1984).

It may be that HCD is a more specific type of somatization disorder, involving distinct sensory or voluntary motor systems of an individual. HCD appears to be more "externally oriented," involving the sensorimotor interface of an individual with the rest of the world, whereas somatization disorder appears to be more "internally oriented," involving more the individual's relationship with his or her own body. Nevertheless, the two disorders appear to be intimately related. Hysteria was once called "nervous mimicry" (Paget, 1873), and such a conception ties conversion and somatization phenomena together.

The link between HCD and hysterical (or histrionic) personality disorder has come under scrutiny because of the many cases of HCD that occur without concomitant personality disorders. It should be kept in mind, however, that histrionic personality disorder strongly overlaps a number of other personality disorders, such as passive–aggressive, borderline, narcissistic, and antisocial personalities. Distinguishing among the different personality disorders often proves to be difficult, if not impossible. Some investigators have drawn special attention to the strong relatedness of hysterical personality and antisocial personality, the difference being that one primarily involves men and the other women (Cloninger, 1978; Spalt, 1980). All of the above personality disorders seem to involve more "affective" symptoms, in contrast to the more "schizophrenia-like" symptoms seen in personality disorders such as schizoid, schizotypal, and paranoid types. McKegney (1967) noted that 32% of 144 patients with HCD had character disorders, and Stefansson *et al.* (1976) reported that 51% of their 37 cases of HCD had character disorders. Bishop and Torch (1979) noted that 38.1% and 9.5% of patients with HCD had passive–aggressive and hysterical personalities, respectively, and in the Folks *et al.* (1984) study quoted earlier, personality disorder was the second-most-common associated psychiatric diagnosis in patients with HCD, the first being somatization disorder.

We do not disagree with efforts to subdivide hysteria into discrete diagnoses. The problem is that the diagnoses do not seem to be discrete, but rather continue to show considerable symptomatic overlap. Premature separation may prevent us from perceiving important clues for both understanding and treating hysterical disorders.

HCD: A DIAGNOSIS BY EXCLUSION?

Many physicians stress that a diagnosis of HCD is not to be made by mere exclusion of other disorders, but that there are actual positive diagnostic criteria that should also be met. Such criteria as primary gain (in which the symptom successfully serves as a symbolic representation of a repressed unconscious conflict), secondary gain (in which the symptom benefits the patient secondarily, either because the patient then receives more attention, or the symptom allows the patient to more effectively manipulate the environment), and *la belle indifférence* (in which the patient shows no interest in or concern for the symptom) are often mentioned. As Lazare (1981) points out, however, primary and secondary gain or *la belle indifférence* are of little value in making a diagnosis, and what is more helpful is the presence of certain associated symptoms and signs. In particular, the presence of somatization disorder, other associated psychopathology, a model for the symptom (such as a previous similar illness in either the patient's own life or in the life of someone important to him), and preexisting emotional stress appear to be better criteria for making a diagnosis of HCD. Nevertheless, even if all of the above are present, that is not unassailable evidence that a given sign or symptom represents HCD.

There are a number of tests and examination procedures designed to highlight the presence of HCD, some of which are discussed later in this chapter and elsewhere in this book. They mainly include techniques that demonstrate nonanatomical or nonphysiological characteristics of the sign or symptom. Although these tests are often helpful, many excellent physicians have been fooled into thinking either that something is HCD when it is not, or that it is not HCD when it is. Especially confusing are unusual presentations of known organic illnesses. Watson and Buranen (1979) noted that 25% of 40 patients diagnosed as having conversion reactions were later found to have a variety of physical illnesses, including degenerative diseases and structural problems of the spinal cord, peripheral nerves, bones, muscles, and connective tissue. This is in keeping with the observations of other investigators, who have reported a 21% to 30% incidence of organic disease in patients with HCD (Gatfield & Guze, 1962; Slater & Glithero, 1965). And it has been reported that between 22% and 62% of patients with HCD may suffer from organic disease as well (Slater & Glithero, 1965; Whitlock, 1967). These patients with combined HCD and organic illness can be very confusing, because their hysterical symptoms often very closely resemble the symptoms of the true organic impairment.

It appears that there is no set of criteria that, when present, are definitively diagnostic of HCD. The presence of associated psychopathology and nonanatomical or nonphysiological signs is helpful, but much of the time HCD remains a diagnosis by exclusion.

DEFINITION AND DESCRIPTION

An HCD is one marked by symptoms or signs that mimic known neurological symptoms or signs, without the presence of the associated underlying neuropathological conditions commonly thought necessary for those symptoms or signs to occur. It commonly occurs during times of great emotional stress and is often accompanied by other mental disorders, such as somatization disorder or personality disorder. Frequently, the characteristics of the signs or symptoms resemble those of an earlier condition of either the patient or someone close to the patient. The condition may last for variable periods of time, from minutes to years, and may cause permanent physical damage (such as atrophy and contractures resulting from hysterical paralysis).

The prevalence of the disorder in a general hospital population probably varies somewhere between 5% and 16% (Ziegler *et al.*, 1960; McKegney, 1967; Stefansson *et al.*, 1976; Hafeiz, 1980; Folks *et al.*, 1984), and the incidence in a medical hospital population may be as high as 20% to 25% (Engel, 1970). In the general population, the incidence has been estimated to be approximately 0.5% (Ljungberg, 1957). The disorder appears to be more common in women, with the female:male ratio reported to be in the range of 2:1 to 12:1 (Robbins *et al.*, 1952; McKegney, 1967; Stefansson *et al.*, 1976; Hafeiz, 1980; Folks *et al.*, 1984). Slater (1961) has reported that as many as 50% of patients retain their symptoms for 1 year, 30% for as long as 5 years, and 20% for up to 15 years. It appears that motor phenomena are relatively common, accounting for perhaps as much as 27% of conversion signs and symptoms (Stefansson *et al.*, 1976; Hafeiz, 1980).

PATHOPHYSIOLOGY

As we mentioned earlier, a diagnosis of HCD is often made by exclusion of other disorders, which is a reflection of the fact that its pathophysiological basis is largely unknown.

Freud's early theories of hysteria (Breuer & Freud, 1895/1957; Freud, 1909) centered around the idea of unconscious repression of unacceptable sexual impulses, with the resulting pent-up emotional energy being expressed through physical symptoms. The symptoms were thought to be in some way symbolic of the repressed conflict, or "phantasies translated into the motor sphere." Initially, Freud believed that the repression was of actual sexual experiences suffered by patients when they were children, but later, upon discovering that these sexual experiences were largely fabricated, he modified his theory by suggesting that the sexual trauma was imagined. Freud believed that these imagined experiences nonetheless exerted a very powerful influence on the patient's lives. Freud later considered hysteria as a model or basis for all neuroses, and formulated the concept of the Oedipus complex to account for his observations of repressed sexual conflict. Later analysts, such as Abraham (1960b) and Reich (1949), proposed that hysterical patients had become "fixated" at the fairly advanced "phallic" stage of development, which meant that the hysteric patient was relatively healthy in comparison with patients fixated at the earlier oral or anal phases. Marmor (1953) challenged the idea that hysteria is easy to treat, and pointed out the strong pregenital (mainly oral) component to the disorder. The rise of ego psychology and its influence on psychoanalysis eventually led to a synthesis of these two positions, with the result that hysteria was divided into two forms: the first, in which the symptomatology is flagrant and severe (the bad hysterics, hysteroid types, or infantile or borderline personalities), is more related to pregenital factors; the second, in which the symptomatology is more subtle (the good or true hysterics), is more related to Oedipal or genital factors (Lazare, 1971).

In keeping with the psychoanalytic tradition, some investigators have drawn attention to the similarities between HCD and signs and symptoms that may be produced with hypnosis (Sackeim *et al.*, 1979). Others have pointed out that patients with hysteria are readily hypnotizable (Spiegel & Fink, 1979; Bliss, 1984), although the underlying pathophysiological basis for hypnotic phenomena is poorly understood.

Some investigators have theorized that HCD represents a form of non-verbal communication (Ziegler & Imboden, 1962; Rabkin, 1964) that may be shaped by the environment through behavioral conditioning (Blanchard & Hersen, 1976; Munford, 1978). The phenomenon of secondary gain is proposed to be an important factor in the maintenance of HCD. One of the problems with this theory is that it does not take into account "symptom substitution," whereby the removal of one sign or symptom from the patient is later replaced by another. It is not clear, however, that this happens in most patients with HCD. Nevertheless, Blanchard and Hersen (1976) have offered an explanation for the fact that some patients suffer symptom substitution and others do not; the authors claim that this has to do with whether the symptom alone is the focus of therapy (which may result in substitution) or whether the patient's whole environment is addressed by means of reinforcement of positive behaviors and social-skills training.

Neurophysiologically, there have been reports of somatosensory evoked response abnormalities in patients with hysterical hemianesthesia, where the somatosensory evoked response was normal on the unaffected side, but abnormal on the affected side (Hernandez-Peon *et al.*, 1963; Levy & Behrman, 1970). Other investigators have not found this difference (Halliday & Mason, 1964). There have also been reports on laterality differences in HCD, which are discussed in more detail in Chapter 25 and which are also difficult to interpret. Horvath *et al.* (1980) reported that 11 patients with prolonged HCD suffered a relative inability to screen out irrelevant stimuli, compared with 10 patients with anxiety neuroses. This finding was taken to support Janet's (1901) hypothesis that a deficit in attention underlies the symptoms of hysteria. These findings, however, are not specific to HCD; they occur in other disorders, such as schizophrenia, and require replication and further investigation. There have been too few studies of the neurobiology of HCD to allow one to draw any firm conclusions about the underlying biological basis of the disorder.

DIAGNOSIS OF HCD OF THE MOTOR SYSTEM

We have described many of the various conversion motor symptoms separately in the individual chapters of Section II of this book. Table 21-1 lists a

Table 21-1. Conditions Sometimes Mistaken for HCD (Especially Motoric HCD)

Epilepsy	Structural diseases of bone, connective tissues, or muscles
Multiple sclerosis	Myasthenia gravis
Frontal-lobe lesions	Guillain–Barré syndrome
Brain tumor	Spinal cord disease, including transverse myelitis and syringo-
Stroke	myelia
Head injury	Peripheral-nerve disease
Encephalitis	Muscular dystrophies
Neurosyphilis	Dystonia musculorum deformans
Klinefelter's syndrome	Myositis
On–off syndrome	

number of different disorders that have been mistaken for HCD. In Table 21-2 we offer a listing of different hysterical motor symptoms that have been described, along with some simple (but often unsatisfactory) ways of determining their hysterical basis.

It is important to differentiate HCD from malingering, as these two conditions may often resemble one another superficially. Malingering is a conscious and voluntary presentation of false symptoms and signs, whereas in HCD the patient is not consciously aware of producing the condition. According to the DSM-III (American Psychiatric Association, 1980), malingering should be considered when there is (1) a medicolegal context, (2) considerable discrepancy between objective findings and claimed distress, (3) uncooperativeness with evaluation and treatment, (4) presence of antisocial personality disorder, (5) obvious recognizable goal of the condition, (6) lack of emotional context, and (7) lack of response to hypnosis or barbiturates. In spite of these helpful guidelines, the distinction between malingering and hysteria can be very difficult.

An interesting area that has received little attention is the relationship of hysteria to catatonia. There are many interesting parallels between these two, as both may present with unresponsiveness, catalepsy, and bizarre behavior, and both may respond to intravenous barbiturates. It is possible that at some level there are important neurobiological similarities between these two disorders. For example, Frumkin *et al.* (1981) proposed that one possible mechanism for the amelioration of psychogenic symptoms with amobarbital may involve changes in cerebral dominance, with amobarbital causing a shift toward greater left-hemisphere dominance. It is possible that laterality differences may play a role in a number of different psychiatric disorders, including

Table 21-2. Signs and Symptoms of Motoric HCD

Conversion symptom	Characteristics
Paralysis	Usually mono- or paraplegia, often with hypotonia, but *Gegenhalten* may be present. Nonanatomical distribution may be present. When supine, attempting to lift leg does not result in pressure being exerted onto bed by leg (Hoover test). Synergistic wrist extension observed when making a fist.
Tremor	Usually involves a single limb, most commonly an arm. The frequency, amplitude, and exact location may vary over time. Mental diversions (such as counting backward) may result in a decrease in tremor (parkinsonian tremor usually increases). Often disappears while eating. Tremor only of hip or shoulder speaks for hysterical basis.
Chorea	May resemble Sydenham's chorea. Usually asymmetrical, often with significant rhythmic component.
Dystonia	Torticollis may be most common form and may be very difficult to distinguish from nonhysterical torticollis.
Gait disorder	Often lurching, zig–zag gait. Patients may stumble from one position to another in which there is some support. Fewer injuries than would be expected, considering appearance of gait. Foot may be dragged, but sideways gait is equal toward both sides. Soles and heels of shoes may be equally worn in spite of asymmetric gait. Some patients promptly or slowly sink to floor when placed on their feet.
Ataxia	May be equally severe with eyes open or shut. When standing, patients may simply fall when eyes close, without initial swaying or attempts to break fall. May be able to eat, dress, tie shoes without difficulty.
Seizures (hystero-epilepsy, pseudoseizures)	May coexist with true seizures. Usually appear more like grand mal seizures. Little evidence of tongue-biting or incontinence. Deep tendon reflexes may be near normal without Babinski. Movements are often bizarre and nonphysiological. Absence of epileptiform activity on EEG and absence of postictal slow waves. Lack of relationship of seizures to anticonvulsant medication levels.

Note. Other forms of HCD include myoclonus (including hiccups), rigidity, catalepsy, stuttering and stammering, mutism, and tics.

hysteria, schizophrenia, and affective disorders (see Flor-Henry, 1983, and also see Chapter 25), and that laterality differences may be important for catatonia as well. Although the exact mechanisms of action of barbiturates in psychiatric illness are not known, this idea indicates the possibility that there are important underlying similarities between hysteria and catatonia.

TREATMENT

Treatment is often unsatisfactory, particularly in the case of psychogenic seizures. Amytal interviews have proven beneficial (see Perry & Jacobs, 1982). Different forms of psychotherapy have been reported to be of benefit (such as psychoanalysis and behavioral therapy; Kass *et al.*, 1972; Hersen *et al.*, 1972; Dickes, 1974; and see Chodoff, 1974), but further research is required to determine the long-term efficacy of these techniques.

CHAPTER TWENTY-TWO

Psychiatric Aspects of Neuromotor Dysfunction

INTRODUCTION

In this chapter we shall review the involvement of the two major cerebral motor control systems—the cerebellum and the basal ganglia—in psychiatric disturbances. The chapter is divided into two sections. In the first we present a brief review of the potential importance of cerebellar and basal-ganglia dysfunction in psychiatric disorders, and in the second we offer a discussion of psychiatric symptomatology in classical cerebellar and basal-ganglia disorders.

CEREBELLUM AND BASAL GANGLIA IN PSYCHIATRIC DISORDERS

Cerebellum

Within the last two decades there has been increasing interest in nonmotor functions of the cerebellum, a structure previously thought to be concerned solely with movement—in particular, coordinated movement. Investigators have begun looking into the role that the cerebellum may play in psychiatric disorders such as schizophrenia and affective disorders. The evidence for cerebellar involvement in psychiatric disorders may be divided into clinical, neuroradiological, and neuropathological evidence.

Clinical Evidence

There is very little clinical evidence for cerebellar dysfunction in either schizophrenia or affective disorders. There have been occasional case reports of the association of tumors of the cerebellum or of cerebellar atrophy with psychosis, mania, or depression, but there is no consistent pattern to the psychosis, and it is not clear whether the psychiatric symptomatology was the result of the cerebellar insult (see Lohr & Jeste, 1986). Further, there is little evidence for clinical signs of cerebellar dysfunction in patients with schizophrenia. We recently assessed 20 schizophrenic patients without tardive dyskinesia, 20 schizophrenic patients with tardive dyskinesia, and 5 affective-disorder patients with tardive dyskinesia for the presence of dysdiadocho-kinesis, dysrhythmokinesis, past-pointing, and a variety of other cerebellar signs, and found no significant differences between any of these groups and a group of 20 normal control patients with no evidence of neurological impairment (Lohr et al., 1985).

Neuroradiological Evidence

Most of the evidence for cerebellar involvement in either schizophrenia or affective disorders derives from CT-scan studies of the brain in these disorders. In most instances the cerebellar vermis was evaluated, mainly because this is the most readily visible cerebellar structure on CT scan. These studies are summarized in Table 22-1. Of the 15 studies listed, 10 compared schizophrenic patients with normal controls, and of these 10, five reported a significant difference between these two groups (Weinberger & Wyatt, 1981; Heath et al., 1982; Lippmann et al., 1982; Weinberger et al., 1982; Dewan et al., 1983), and five did not (Coffman et al., 1981; Tanaka et al., 1981; Nasrallah et al., 1981a; Boronow et al., 1985; DeLisi et al., 1986).

Of the eight studies that have looked at cerebellar vermian atrophy in affective disorders, four compared affective-disorder patients with controls (Nasrallah et al., 1981a; Heath et al., 1982; Lippmann et al., 1982; Weinberger et al., 1982), and in every case the affective-disorder group had more vermian abnormalities. All eight studies compared affective-disorder patients with schizophrenic patients (Weinberger et al., 1979; Heath et al., 1979; Nasrallah et al., 1981a; Pearlson & Veroff, 1981; Heath et al., 1982; Lippmann et al., 1982; Weinberger et al., 1982; Rieder et al., 1983), and in six studies the percentage of patients with vermian atrophy was approximately the same in both groups, with one study (Weinberger et al., 1979) reporting more vermian atrophy in schizophrenic patients and another study (Nasrallah et al., 1981a) reporting more in manic patients.

It can be seen that in the case of both schizophrenia and affective disorders there appears to be evidence for cerebellar vermis atrophy on CT scan, although it is not clear whether there is any significant difference between schizophrenia and affective disorders in this respect. However, it should be noted that CT scans are a less than ideal means of evaluating aspects of the cerebellum, including the cerebellar vermis, because of the large amount of artifact and noise caused by the bony encasement of the posterior fossa. Furthermore, the criteria for assessment of vermian atrophy have

Table 22-1. CT-Scan Studies of Cerebellar Vermis in Schizophrenia and Affective Disorders

Reference	Schizophrenia		Affective disorders[a]		Normal controls	
	n	%	*n*	%	*n*	%
Weinberger *et al.* (1979)	60	17	15	0	—	—
Heath *et al.* (1979)	85	40	31	29	—	—
Nasrallah *et al.* (1981a)	43	12	15	27	—	—
Coffman *et al.* (1981)	14	NS	—	—	21	NS
Tanaka *et al.* (1981)	49	2	—	—	39	0
Weinberger and Wyatt (1981)	100	13	—	—	66	5
Pearlson and Veroff (1981)	22	5	17	0?	—	—
Heath *et al.* (1982)	50	50	64	53	1,541	4
Lippmann *et al.* (1982)	54	17	18	28	79	4
Weinberger *et al.* (1982)	17	12	23	9	26	0
Dewan *et al.* (1983)	23	18	—	—	23	NS
Rieder *et al.* (1983)	28	7	19	11	—	—
Boronow *et al.* (1985)	30	3	—	—	26	8
DeLisi *et al.* (1986)	26	19	—	—	20	10

Note. %, percentage atrophied; NS, not stated.
[a]The affective-disorder patients of Heath *et al.* (1979, 1982) were mainly unipolar; those of Nasrallah *et al.* (1981a), Pearlson and Veroff (1981), Lippmann *et al.* (1982), and Rieder *et al.* (1983) were bipolar.

varied considerably from study to study, and are somewhat difficult to quantify. Also, a recent magnetic-resonance-imaging (MRI) study of the cerebellum in schizophrenia found no difference between schizophrenic patients and controls, and this technique is superior to CT scanning in terms of visualization of the cerebellum (Coffman *et al.*, 1985; Mathew & Partain, 1985).

Neuropathological Evidence

There have been few neuropathological studies of the cerebellum in either schizophrenia or affective disorders. Roizin *et al.* (1959) noted either a loss or an irregular arrangement of Purkinje cells in the cerebella of three schizophrenic and one bipolar patient who had been treated with neuroleptic medications, and these investigators attributed the pathological changes to the neuroleptics. Weinberger *et al.* (1980) measured the cross-sectional area of the anterior vermis (seen in midsagittal section) in the brains of 12 leukotomized schizophrenic patients, 12 leukotomized nonschizophrenic patients, and seven normal controls. When the age of the different patients was taken into account, four patients fell below the 95th percentile limit that was calculated from the 21 nonschizophrenic controls, and three of these were schizophrenic patients. However, there were no significant differences between the mean anterior vermian areas among any of the groups.

Reyes and Gordon (1981) measured cerebellar Purkinje cell density in the vermis of eight schizophrenic patients and 12 normal controls. They noted a significant decrease in the Purkinje cell linear density in the schizophrenic group compared with the control group, but they also noted a significant increase in surface density of the cerebellar folia. These two findings taken together may indicate no difference in the absolute Purkinje cell number between the two groups, although this is not clear.

Stevens (1982) reported gliosis or Purkinje cell loss qualitatively in at least eight out of 28 schizophrenic patients.

Finally, Lohr and Jeste (1986) found no difference in Purkinje cell density in the anterior vermis, posterior vermis, or cerebellar hemispheres among 23 leukotomized schizophrenic patients, 5 leukotomized unipolar patients, 7 leukotomized bipolar patients, 11 leukotomized controls, and 37 nonleukotomized normal controls.

In summary, the neuropathological evidence for involvement of the anterior vermis or other parts of the cerebellar cortex in either schizophrenia or affective disorders is contradictory, although there may be a subgroup of patients with schizophrenia or affective disorders who have cerebellar abnormalities, and there may be cerebellar abnormalities that are not detectable with the techniques being used.

Summary

It appears that there is little direct evidence for cerebellar dysfunction in either schizophrenia or affective disorders, with most of the evidence of cerebellar atrophy being based on CT-scan findings. Of course, it is possible that a small subgroup of psychiatric patients have cerebellar abnormalities, and also that cerebellar pathology of a more subtle nature that is difficult to discover using available neurobiological research techniques might exist in larger numbers of patients.

Basal Ganglia

In contrast with lack of evidence involving the cerebellum, there is considerable evidence that the basal ganglia are involved in psychiatric disorders—particularly, schizophrenia and, possibly, affective disorders as well. This section will again be divided into clinical, neuroradiological, and neuropathological categories of evidence.

Clinical Evidence

Extrapyramidal dysfunction in psychiatric disorders was proposed as early as 1899–1900 by Wernicke and later, in 1922, by Kleist. However, it was the advent of neuroleptic medications and their effects on both psychiatric symptoms and motor signs that generated considerable discussion of the possibility that the basal ganglia are related to schizophrenia—a discussion that is still going on today. Mettler (1955) and Mettler and Crandell (1959a, 1959b) were strong proponents of the idea that schizophrenia represents dysfunction of the basal ganglia. They noted, for example, reports by Lewy (1923) and Steck (1926) of alternating psychiatric and extrapyramidal signs in individuals, often involving catatonia and parkinsonism. Mettler (1955) proposed that "dysfunction of the striatum results in an inability on the part of an organism to maintain adequate contact with its environment (probably the only entirely satisfactory, irreducible characteristic of a psychotic process, though not of this alone)" (Mettler & Crandell, 1959b, p. 552). These latter authors reported an increased incidence of parkinsonism in a mental-hospital population, but it is not clear whether this may have been due to the increased age of the population or to the inclusion of patients with postencephalitic parkinsonism, up to half of whom may have psychiatric symptoms (Mettler & Crandell, 1959b).

Since Mettler and Crandell, many investigators have noted the presence of abnormal movements, frequently of a choreoathetoid nature, in patients with schizophrenia and other psychiatric disorders. This literature has recently been summarized by Casey and Hansen (1984), who reviewed the Mettler and Crandell study (1959b) as well as 28 additional studies performed from 1959 to 1984. From the Casey and Hansen review, it appears that the probable overall prevalence of spontaneous (i.e., not related to neuroleptic medications) movements is somewhere in the range of 4% to 7% of patients (most patients in the studies reviewed probably had schizophrenia, although there were undoubtedly a number with affective disorders and neurological disorders as well). Women, institutionalized patients, and patients with organic mental disorders appeared to be at greater risk for developing abnormal movements, and the movements themselves appeared to be clinically similar to movements described in tardive dyskinesia. The finding of spontaneous abnormal movements of a choreoathetoid nature in patients with schizophrenia implicates dysfunction of the basal ganglia in at least some patients with this disorder.

Earlier, in Chapter 12, we discussed the role of the basal ganglia in the initiation and speed of movement. The initiation of movement (as reflected in the reaction time, or RT) and the speed of movement (as reflected in the movement time, or MT) are known to be abnormal in Parkinson's disease, and abnormal RT and MT have been observed in monkeys with basal-ganglia lesions. Patients with schizophrenia have also been observed to have prolonged RT (Steffy & Galbraith, 1980; Schneider & Wilson, 1983), even before the advent of neuroleptic medications that cause drug-induced parkinsonism (Wells & Kelley, 1922). This, too, may be indicative of basal-ganglia pathology in schizophrenia.

Clinically, many physicians have noted that psychomotorically retarded depressed patients often have a parkinsonian appearance. One of the most careful observers of the movements of psychiatrically ill patients was William Stoddart, who documented a number of different motor abnormalities in schizophrenic, manic, and depressed patients. In depressed patients, he noted the following:

The attitude and general appearance of the melancholiac are quite characteristic. . . . The head and trunk are inclined forwards as in paralysis agitans and there is slight flexion of the hips and knees. There is also slight flexion of the shoulders; and the elbows, which are rigidly held to the side, are flexed to a right angle. In cases of agitated melancholia the fingers are in constant movement during waking hours. . . . [In] severe cases of stuporose melancholia . . . rigidity affects the large proximal joints most and the small peripheral joints least; for this reason I have called it "proximal rigidity," in contradistinction to "peripheral rigidity," such as that which occurs commonly in hemiplegia. . . . Melancholiacs can rarely hold their arms vertically above their heads and when they shake hands they do so from the wrist. (1909, pp. 179–180)

More recently, investigators such as Greden and Carroll (1981) have hypothesized that certain motor features of depressives, such as prolonged speech latency, may be due to "similar CNS [central nervous system] disturbance in mesolimbic–nigrostriatal functioning, as has been documented in patients with Parkinson's disease" (p. 1445).

In summary, there is clinical evidence of basal-ganglia dysfunction in some patients with schizophrenia and possibly in some with depression as well, but further work is necessary to clarify this issue.

Neuroradiological Evidence

The basal ganglia are poorly visualized on CT scan, although some of the more recent CT scanning equipment allows for better visualization of the striatum. Some investigators have taken the presence of lateral ventricular enlargement to be indicative of basal-ganglia atrophy, but this is certainly far from clear. Although striatal degeneration may cause ventricular enlargement, not all cases of ventricular enlargement are due to striatal atrophy. Thus, it is not clear whether the evidence for ventricular enlargement (especially as measured by the ventricular/brain ration, or VBR) in both schizophrenia and affective disorders reflects basal-ganglia pathology, as opposed to some other process. It is interesting to note, however, that a recent PET-scan study noted significantly lower metabolic rates in the basal ganglia of patients with affective disorders in comparison with normal control subjects (Buchsbaum *et al.*, 1986).

Neuropathological Evidence

A number of investigators have reported pathological changes in the basal ganglia in patients with schizophrenia and catatonia, most notably in the globus pallidus, but also in the striatum (Buscaino, 1920; Josephy, 1923; Nagasaka, 1925; Vogt & Vogt, 1952; Dom & DeSaedeleer, 1981; Stevens, 1982; Bogerts *et al.*, 1985), although some studies did not find any changes in these conditions (Arendt, 1983). The exact findings have differed in detail, which ranges from description of fatty degeneration of neurons to description of actual neuron loss, and very few studies relied on quantitative methodology. It remains to be determined which of the numerous findings, if any, is generally applicable to schizophrenic patients. There are too few neuropathological studies in affective disorders to allow one to draw any firm conclusions about basal-ganglia pathology in these conditions.

Summary

It appears from a clinical perspective that there is evidence for basal-ganglia involvement in schizophrenia and, to a lesser extent, in affective disorders. There is neuroradiological and neuropathological evidence that is consistent with basal-ganglia dysfunction in these conditions as well, but further work along these lines is needed.

PSYCHIATRIC PROBLEMS IN NEUROMOTOR DISORDERS

In this section we briefly review the evidence for psychiatric dysfunction in disorders of the basal ganglia, including Parkinson's disease, Huntington's disease, Sydenham's chorea, Wilson's disease, Meige's syndrome, progressive supranuclear palsy, and Hallervorden–Spatz disease.

Parkinson's Disease

Parkinson's disease is a chronic progressive disorder usually beginning in middle-aged or elderly individuals, and is characterized by tremor, rigidity, bradykinesia, a flexed posture, a festinating gait, and impaired postural reflexes. Pathologically, it is characterized by degeneration of pigmented neurons in the substantia nigra pars compacta, ventral tegmental area and locus ceruleus. Neurochemically, there is a decrease of dopamine and probably also of serotonin and norepinephrine. Parkinson's disease is only one cause of parkinsonism, and other causes are listed in Table 22-2. In this section, however, we shall concentrate on idiopathic Parkinson's disease, and the two most commonly reported psychiatric symptoms in this disorder are dementia and depression.

Dementia

Although James Parkinson (1817) did not believe that dementia occurred in Parkinson's disease, over the course of this century a number of investigators, such as Lewy (1923), have pointed out that a percentage of patients with Parkinson's disease do indeed become demented. In a recent review by Mayeux and Stern (1983) it was noted that perhaps somewhere between 30% and 80% of patients with Parkinson's disease suffer some form of intellectual impairment. However, some investigators have not reported mental deterioration in patients with true idiopathic Parkinson's disease. For example, Danielczyk (1983), in a study of 21 patients with advanced Parkinson's disease who were over 70 years old concluded that "Permanent dementia is not characteristic of patients with typical idiopathic PD [Parkinson's disease] even in advanced age" (p. 161). This investigator did note that a small subgroup of patients with Parkinson's disease did show moderate intellectual impairment, but this group also had focal neurological signs. Nevertheless, most researchers believe that a dementiform process occurs in at least a subgroup of patients with Parkinson's disease. It may be that patients with dementia and parkinsonism may be a distinct subgroup of patients with Parkinson's disease, as such patients have been noted to have greater brady-

Table 22-2. Conditions in Which Parkinsonism Occurs

Idiopathic Parkinson's disease: paralysis agitans, shaking palsy

Drug-induced: neuroleptics, reserpine, tetrabenazine, lithium, tricyclic antidepressants, metoclopramide, α-methyldopa, diazoxide, N-methylphenyltetrahydropyridine (MPTP)

Associated with encephalitis: encephalitis lethargica, Creutzfeldt–Jakob disease, neurosyphilis

Associated with heavy-metal toxicity: manganese, copper (Wilson's disease), iron (Hallervorden–Spatz disease)

Associated with carbon-based toxins: carbon monoxide, carbon tetrachloride, carbon disulfide, methanol, organophosphates, cyanide

Multisystem atrophies: striatonigral degeneration, progressive supranuclear palsy (Steele–Richardson–Olszewski syndrome), Shy–Drager syndrome, olivopontocerebellar atrophy

Associated with dementia: Alzheimer's disease, parkinsonism–dementia complex of Guam, normal pressure hydrocephalus, Huntington's disease

Other causes: brain tumors and trauma, hypoparathyroidism, typhoid, poliomyelitis, basal-ganglia calcifications

---

kinesia than do nondemented patients with Parkinson's disease (Piccirilli *et al.*, 1984). Also, Sroka *et al.* (1981) reported that patients with Parkinson's disease with an organic mental syndrome invariably had signs of cerebral atrophy on CT scan (much like patients with Alzheimer's disease), whereas those without organic mental syndrome had normal-appearing CT scans. This also tends to indicate that a subset of Parkinson's disease is related to Alzheimer's disease.

One question that has arisen is whether or not the dementia observed in Parkinson's disease is a result of L-dopa treatment. A study by Sweet *et al.* (1976) on 100 patients with parkinsonism appears to indicate that this is not the case, and that the dementia occurs as a part of the course of the illness itself.

In those patients with Parkinson's disease with evidence of dementia, it is not clear whether the dementia is of the same form in every patient. It has been proposed that there may be two types of dementia in Parkinson's disease, one that more closely resembles the dementia of Alzheimer's disease, and one that has been termed a "subcortical dementia" (see Jeste *et al.*, 1984c). As for the possibility of an Alzheimer's type of dementia in Parkinson's disease, investigators have noted not only clinical similarities, but neuropathological similarities as well, with reports of increased frequencies of senile plaques, neurofibrillary tangles, granulovacuolar degeneration, and increased neuronal loss in the brains of patients with Parkinson's disease (Hakim & Mathieson, 1979; Boller *et al.*, 1980).

The case for a subcortical dementia—that is, a dementia that is caused by damage to subcortical structures such as the basal ganglia or thalamus—is less clear. Cummings and Benson (1984) noted that subcortical dementia may be important in disorders such as Parkinson's disease, Wilson's disease, spinocerebellar degenerations, idiopathic basal-ganglia calcifications, and the dementia-like symptoms sometimes associated with depression. They state that subcortical dementia, unlike the typical "cortical" dementia of Alzheimer's disease, is marked not by aphasia, but, rather, by dysarthria and a lengthened information-processing time. Other investigators have questioned the usefulness of subcortical dementia as a concept, and noted the indistinct nature of the neuropsychological impairment (Mayeux *et al.*, 1983). Basically, further work is necessary to elucidate the presence and characteristics of dementia in Parkinson's disease (Huber & Paulson, 1985).

Depression

Like dementia, depression has been recognized in recent years to be a frequently encountered mental symptom in Parkinson's disease. Although depression was noted by Parkinson (1817) in his initial description of the disorder, he did not attribute any great significance to it. Mjones (1949) was one of the first to point out the importance of depression in cases of

Parkinson's disease, and how depression may be far out of proportion to the degree of neurological impairment. This finding has been confirmed by later investigators, and currently it is estimated that between 40% and 50% of patients with Parkinson's disease may have significant depressive symptomatology, even when there is no evidence of dementia (Warbuton, 1964; Mindham, 1970; Marsh et al., 1971; Horn, 1974; Robins, 1976; Vogel, 1982; see Jeste et al., 1984c). Investigators have reported a relationship between the motor signs of parkinsonism and the depression, although the relationship is not a particularly strong one, and it appears that the motor signs are probably most associated with the apathetic component of depressive illness (Mayeux et al., 1981; Vogel, 1982).

The pathophysiological mechanism of depression in Parkinson's disease is unclear. It has been proposed that depression, which has long been thought to reflect a hypocatecholaminergic state, may occur in cases of Parkinson's disease because Parkinson's disease represents just such state, being marked by hypodopaminergic and probably also hyponoradrenergic function. However, direct evidence for this notion is lacking. Also, a recent report by Mayeux et al. (1984) noted that the concentration of 5-hydroxyindoleacetic acid, the major metabolite of serotonin, was decreased in depressed compared to nondepressed patients with Parkinson's disease, thus implicating a role for serotonin in the etiology of the depression in cases of Parkinson's disease.

In depressed patients with Parkinson's disease, the adminstration of a tricyclic antidepressant may result in improvement of both the depression and the parkinsonian features. The treatment of depression in cases of Parkinson's disease is problematic at times, because most tricyclic antidepressants have significant anticholinergic activity. Recently, some investigators have reported results indicating that some of the new antidepressants, including nomifensine (Park et al., 1981) and trazodone (Ananth, 1983), which possess less anticholinergic activity, may be helpful in cases of Parkinson's disease.

Other Psychiatric Problems

Todes and Lees (1985) have noted that patients with Parkinson's disease may have characteristic personalities marked by "emotional and attitudinal inflexibility, a lack of affect and a predisposition to depressive illness, which may antecede the development of motor abnormalities by several decades." In the twin study of Ward et al. (1983) there appears to be evidence of lifelong personality differences between affected twin-pair members and their unaffected partners. This study is notable for demonstrating virtually no concordance for Parkinson's disease in 43 pairs of monozygotic twins, indicating that genetic or familial factors are of very little importance in the disorder. Another interesting finding of the study was that the members with Parkinson's disease had much less exposure to nicotine than did the unaffected members. The reasons for this are unclear, however.

Another question that has arisen concerns the notion of alcohol abuse in patients with Parkinson's disease. Carlen *et al.* (1981) reported heavy alcohol intake in seven patients with Parkinson's disease, and stressed the possible detrimental nature of alcohol in cases of Parkinson's disease. Lang *et al.* (1982), however, did not find a greater incidence of alcohol consumption in 125 patients with Parkinson's disease compared to a control population, and also observed only mild effects of alcohol on parkinsonian signs and symptoms. Ward *et al.* (1983), in the above-mentioned twin study, did not find a difference in alcohol intake between affected and unaffected members of discordant twin pairs.

Finally, the medications used to treat Parkinson's disease may cause psychiatric problems. L-Dopa has been reported to cause psychosis consisting of hallucinations and illusions as well as vivid dreams, confusional states and, paradoxically, depression. Psychosis may occur in as many as 60% of patients treated long-term with L-dopa (Sweet *et al.*, 1976), although the psychosis is usually relatively mild and benign. Moskovitz *et al.* (1978) have proposed that L-dopa-induced psychosis represents a kindling phenomenon, much as has been hypothesized for temporal-lobe seizures and bipolar affective disorder. Other drugs used in the treatment of Parkinson's disease including bromocriptine, pergolide, lisuride, and mesulergine, may also cause hallucinations, presumably because these drugs are dopaminergic agonists.

Huntington's Disease

Huntington's disease is a hereditary degenerative disease of unknown etiology that is marked by pathological changes in small to medium-sized neurons (spiny type I) in the basal ganglia (most notably in the caudate nucleus), and cortical atrophy (most severe in the frontal lobes). The disease has an autosomal dominant mode of inheritance, and the gene for the disorder has recently been found to be located on chromosome 4 (Gusella *et al.*, 1983). The most common form consists of progressive clumsiness and choreoathetoid movements usually beginning before age 30. Other signs of disordered movement, including tics, rigidity, and dystonia, may occur as well. There are two variants of the disorder that may occur in the same families as those suffering from the more typical form. The first is known as the Westphal variant, and is characterized by progressive rigidity, especially of the trunk and proximal limb musculature. It is more rapidly progressive than the typical form. A second form, known as the juvenile variant, resembles the Westphal variant but occurs in children and adolescents.

A wide range of psychiatric disorders have been reported in patients with Huntington's disease, and this literature has been reviewed by Jeste *et al.*

(1984c). In their analysis of the literature, it appears that over 90% of patients with Huntington's disease suffer some form of psychopathology, and that in 46% of patients, psychiatric symptoms are the reason for first admission. In 65% of cases psychopathology appears before the onset of movement disorder. Most commonly the initial psychiatric symptomatology consists of neurosis, personality disorder, or emotional instability, but over time it appears that the most common psychiatric diagnosis is dementia (89%), followed by affective disorder (42%, mainly depression) and schizophrenia-like psychosis (18%). Dementia itself occurs before the onset of movement disorder in approximately 10% of cases.

Josiassen et al. (1983) have presented evidence that the cognitive dysfunctions seen in Huntington's disease do not develop at a uniform rate, but, rather, that visuospatial and auditory memory deficits occur much earlier than deficits in cognitive flexibility. Visuospatial and memory impairments also appear to be strongly related to the degree of atrophy present on CT scan. The atrophy seen on CT scan begins in the neostriatal-frontal regions and spreads caudally over the cerebral cortex as the illness progresses (Sax et al., 1983).

Sydenham's Chorea

Sydenham's chorea is believed to be a delayed reaction to group-A streptococcal infection, which usually occurs in children and adolescents. It is closely linked to rheumatic fever, and the majority of patients with chorea also manifest other rheumatic conditions, such as arthritis, myocarditis, and endocarditis. As in Huntington's disease, a variety of different psychiatric symptoms have been reported, and in some cases are thought to last long beyond the choreiform stage of the illness. For example, Wertheimer (1963), in a study of over 2,500 patients who had earlier developed rheumatic fever, noted a four-fold increase of psychiatric disorders of various types compared to normal control population. This would be consistent with the fact that postchoreic patients often evidence continued abnormalities in basal-ganglia function, including a predilection to redevelop chorea after stimulants or estrogens or during pregnancy (chorea gravidarum; see Chapter 3).

The most commonly described psychopathological changes are neuroses and personality disorders, the latter having at times been called "postchoreic personality." Commonly described traits include fidgetiness, dizziness, shyness, irritability, and excitability, occurring in perhaps as many as 10% to 20% of patients and lasting long after the chorea has disappeared (Schwartzmann, 1950; Krauss, 1976). Freeman et al. (1965) noted that 83% of 40 postchoreic patients had neurosis or personality disorder 30 years after the rheumatic fever, in comparison with only 25% of control subjects. Other studies, however, have not confirmed these findings (Sacks *et al.*, 1962; Stehbens and Macqueen, 1972).

Some investigators have also proposed a link between Sydenham's chorea and schizophrenia (see Jeste *et al.*, 1985). Guttman (1936) noted that a history of chorea was reported twice as frequently by schizophrenic patients compared to bipolar patients, and Bruetsch (1940), in performing autopsies on 100 schizophrenic patients, noted that nine had rheumatic valvular lesions. Wertheimer (1957) noted that 8.2% of 147 schizophrenic patients had a history of rheumatic fever, as compared to only 2.4% of 420 age-matched controls. Thus, there is suggestive evidence of a link between rheumatic fever and at least some cases of schizophrenia, but no definite conclusions can be drawn at this time.

Wilson's Disease

Wilson's disease is a degenerative disorder of the central nervous system marked by an abnormality in copper metabolism, consisting of increased enteric absorption of copper and failure of copper to bind with apoceruloplasmin. This results in a decrease in the bound product of copper and apoceruloplasmin (the product is ceruloplasmin), which results in elevated free copper concentration in the blood, increased excretion of copper in the urine, and deposition of copper in the tissues, most notably the brain and the liver. The disease has an autosomal recessive mode of inheritance and commonly manifests with hepatic cirrhosis and jaundice, renal tubular damage, neuronal damage in a variety of brain areas (especially the basal ganglia), and Kayser–Fleischer rings, which are observed initially as brownish-red or green crescents in the superior and inferior aspects of the corneoscleral junction. The movement disorder usually consists of rigidity, coarse proximal tremor ("wing-beating"), choreoathetosis, and/or dystonia, usually accompanied by dysarthria and dysphagia. Many physicians have also drawn attention to a characteristic facial expression, often difficult to describe, but appearing to be one of silliness, vacuousness, or indifference, that does not necessarily reflect the actual affective state of the patient.

Martin (1968) has noted that Wilson's disease may be divided into two types, a juvenile form, which usually appears between ages 7 and 15, and a "late" form, which usually begins around age 30. Although both forms may be associated with psychiatric symptoms including impulsiveness, irritability, restlessness, and personality and affective changes, it is the late form that has been more associated with psychosis, usually of a paranoid type. In perhaps as many as 20% of patients, psychiatric symptoms precede the onset of other signs and symptoms (Scheinberg *et al.*, 1968). Occasionally, these presenting psychiatric symptoms, including paranoid delusions, hallucinations, or bizarre behavior, are severe. These psychiatric disturbances often improve after chelation therapy (Scheinberg et al., 1968). If untreated, patients develop dementia.

Meige's Syndrome

This condition is characterized by orofacial dystonia usually beginning after the fifth decade (see Chapter 15). Recent studies have reported that between one-third and one-half of patients suffer depressive symptoms before or at the onset of the disorder (Marsden, 1976; Tolosa, 1981; Jankovic & Ford, 1983).

Progressive Supranuclear Palsy

Progressive supranuclear palsy (also called Steele–Richardson–Olszewski syndrome) is a progressive condition that usually begins in the fifth to seventh decade and is characterized by supranuclear ophthalmoplegia, pseudobulbar palsy, and trunk and neck dystonias. Albert et al. (1974) have divided accompanying psychiatric symptoms into two broad groups consisting of (1) indifference, apathy, and depression, and (2) irritability and/or euphoria. There appears to be a dementia that occurs in the disorder (which stimulated the creation of the term "subcortical dementia"), consisting of forgetfulness, cognitive slowing, apathy, and impaired ability to manipulate information.

Hallervorden–Spatz Syndrome

Hallervorden–Spatz syndrome is a rare hereditary disorder that usually begins between the ages of 7 and 12 and is marked by the accumulation of a brown iron-containing pigment in the globus pallidus and substantia nigra reticulata, as well as neuronal degeneration. The disease is slowly progressive and consists of choreoathetosis, dystonia, and rigidity. Occasionally, there is spasticity, hyperreflexia, and dysarthria (Dooling et al., 1974). Psychiatric symptoms usually consist of either mental retardation or dementia.

CHAPTER TWENTY-THREE

Neuroleptic-Induced Movement Disorders, Including Tardive Dyskinesia

INTRODUCTION

Action of the Drug Used Alone

In doses of 50–100 mg intravenously, it provokes not any loss in consciousness, not any change in the patient's mentality but a slight tendency to sleep and above all "disinterest" for all that goes on around him. . . .

The curious central action reported above permits us to discern certain new relations between the pharmacodynamic deconditioning obtained with 4560 RP, already noticeable with diparcol and with phenergan, and the deconditioning technics dear to the Russian school in obstetric analgesia and in the treatment of many disease syndromes.

These facts let us foresee certain indications for this drug in psychiatry. . . . (Laborit *et al.*, 1952, translated in Caldwell, 1970, pp. 135–136)

The above selection is from an article entitled "Un nouveau stabilisateur végétatif (le 4560 RP)" by Laborit *et al.* (1952), the first article on chlorpromazine, a drug that was to herald a new age in psychiatry and rekindle interest in the neuropsychiatric aspects of movement disorders.

Drugs like chlorpromazine have been referred to using a variety of terms, such as "neuroplegic," "neurolytic," "tranquilizer," "ataraxic" (or "ataractic"), and "antipsychotic" (see Delay's comments on the etymology of these different terms in Kline, 1959, pp. 426–428), but the most widely accepted term for these drugs today is *neuroleptic*, meaning a reducing of nervous tension or a seizing or taking hold of nerves (depending on whether the Greek root is *leptos* or *lepsis*). The dual meaning of the term "neuroleptic" is interesting, for in spite of the ability of these drugs to reduce nervous tension, they were also noted to produce side effects that appeared to represent, if anything, an increase in nervous activity, such as akathisia.

251

Extrapyramidal reactions to the antipsychotic drug reserpine were known before the advent of chlorpromazine, but in the West it was chlorpromazine-induced reactions that drew attention to the effects of antipsychotics on the motor system (Caldwell, 1970). Delay and Denicker noted extrapyramidal signs as early as 1952 in their experiments with chlorpromazine (Deniker, 1960). Some investigators came to believe that extrapyramidal side effects were necessary for antipsychotic benefits (Haase, 1961), although other researchers disputed this idea (Cole & Clyde, 1961; Gunn, 1961; National Institute of Mental Health, 1964). (Indeed, this notion is still controversial, and has never been completely resolved.)

Approximately 5 years after the first reports of the efficacy of chlorpromazine in psychiatric disorders, Schönecker (1957) described three patients in Germany, all elderly women, who developed orobuccal dyskinesias following exposure to chlorpromazine. What was unusual about these patients was that in two of the cases the dyskinesia persisted for almost 3 months even after discontinuation of the neuroleptic, which was in marked contrast to the acute short-lived neuroleptic-induced movements described previously. Following Schönecker, reports of persistent neuroleptic-related dyskinesia appeared in France, England, Denmark, and America in the late 1950s and early 1960s (Sigwald et al., 1959; Kruse, 1960; Druckman et al., 1962; Uhrbrand & Faurbye, 1960; Hunter et al., 1964). The term "tardive dyskinesia" was first used in 1964 by Faurbye et al. to describe the syndrome. Although reports of tardive dyskinesia were rare at first, the number has grown over the years. In a 1973 review, Crane noted that reports of the prevalence of tardive dyskinesia ran as high as 40% among neuroleptic-treated patients. What makes tardive dyskinesia a particularly serious side effect of neuroleptics is the fact that the signs may persist for months to years after the drugs have been discontinued. At times, the dyskinesia can be physically disabling and, rarely, life-threatening (Casey & Rabins, 1978). Even when the dyskinesia is relatively mild, it may cause considerable embarrassment and social incapacitation in a population of patients who already have difficulties in social functioning.

This chapter is divided into two sections. In the first we discuss acute neuroleptic-induced extrapyramidal signs or side effects, including dystonic reactions, parkinsonism, and akathisia. In the second section we offer a discussion of tardive dyskinesia, focusing on description and epidemiology, neurochemical aspects, neuropathological studies, neuroradiological studies, psychological aspects, differential diagnosis, other tardive syndromes, and recent proposals of mechanisms for tardive dyskinesia.

Acute Neuroleptic-Induced Extrapyramidal Signs

Since their introduction over 30 years ago, neuroleptics have come to be used in many different conditions, psychiatric, neurologic, and others. Some of

Table 23-1. Conditions in Which Neuroleptic Medications Have Been Used[a]

Schizophrenia	Meige's syndrome
Paranoia	Dementia
Affective disorders	Delirium
(especially with psychosis)	Anxiety
Other psychoses	Nausea and vomiting
(drug-induced, toxic, metabolic)	Intractable hiccups
Huntington's disease	Pruritis
Senile chorea	Autism
Hemiballismus	Mental retardation
Tourette's syndrome	Organic behavioral problems
Other tic disorders	(secondary to brain trauma, brain tumors, etc.)
Torsion dystonias	

[a]The indication for neuroleptic treatment for some of these conditions is not clear.

these are listed in Table 23-1. There are a variety of different neurological signs that may be seen following neuroleptic administration. Most of these signs are believed to involve the extrapyramidal system (see Chapter 2) because they clinically resemble signs seen in patients with known diseases of the basal ganglia. For this reason, the signs are frequently termed neuroleptic-induced extrapyramidal signs (EPS) or extrapyramidal side effects (EPSE). These acute EPS are listed in Table 23-2. Different neuroleptics have different propensities to cause EPS, and, in general, higher-potency neuroleptics (such as haloperidol, fluphenazine, and thiothixene) are associated with more frequent and more severe EPS than are low-potency drugs (such as chlorpromazine and thioridazine).

Table 23-2. Acute Neuroleptic-Induced Extrapyramidal Signs

Parkinsonism, including:
  Tremor (including 4–7-cycle-per-second tremor-in-repose, 8–12-cycle-per-second postural tremor, and rabbit syndrome)
  Hypokinesia (including bradykinesia and akinesia)
  Rigidity (often with cogwheel phenomenon)
  Flexed posturing
  Postural instability
Akathisia (inability to sit still, accompanied by inner discomfort)
Tasikinesia (tendency to move)
Dystonia (including oculogyric crises, torticollis, etc.)
Acute choreoathetoid movements
Acute tics

Table 23-3 summarizes the findings of Ayd from his two large studies of neuroleptic-induced EPS. It can be seen that akathisia is the most common EPS, followed by drug-induced parkinsonism. Ayd (1983) noted that men are approximately twice as likely to develop dystonic reactions as are women, whereas women are twice as likely to develop akathisia and parkinsonism. Most EPS occur within 2 to 3 months of beginning neuroleptics, with dystonic reactions usually occurring before akathisia, which, in turn, usually precedes the development of parkinsonism. These are not hard and fast rules, however, because EPS can develop at almost any time in any form. High-potency neuroleptics, in addition to being associated with more severe parkinsonism, usually cause a more rapid appearance of EPS.

Dystonic reactions, which have been reported to occur in up to 50% of patients treated with neuroleptics, usually appear within 4 days of neuroleptic treatment, and almost all occur within 15 days (Swett, 1975; Winslow et al., 1986). Swett (1975) noted that the most common dystonic reactions were torticollis, trismus, and oculogyric crisis. Only a few patients had generalized dystonias or opisthotonos. Haloperidol and fluphenazine, both high-potency neuroleptics, were the most common associated medications. Drug-induced dystonic reactions may be dangerous, and in severe cases of pharyngeal dystonia, the patient's airway can be closed. (See also Chapter 15, on dystonia.)

In spite of the fact that neuroleptics, perhaps by blocking postsynaptic dopamine receptors, result in a condition similar to Parkinson's disease (where there is a loss of dopaminergic cells in the substantia nigra), there are some differences between neuroleptic-induced parkinsonism and Parkinson's disease. For example, EPS tends to be somewhat more symmetrical than Parkinson's disease (although EPS is also frequently asymmetrical). Akathisia is much more common in drug-induced states than in Parkinson's disease, and tremor is more common in Parkinson's disease than in neuroleptic-induced EPS.

Table 23-3. Frequencies of Neuroleptic-Induced Extrapyramidal Signs (EPS)[a]

	1961 survey	1981 survey
n	3,775	5,000
Some EPS	38.9%	61.9%
No EPS	61.1%	38.1%
Akathisia	21.2%	36.8%
Parkinsonism	15.4%	13.2%
Dystonic reactions	2.3%	11.9%
Type of neuroleptic	48.3% low potency 51.7% high potency	All high potency

[a]Based on Ayd (1983)

Treatment of EPS can prove difficult. If the neuroleptic can be discontinued, reduced in dosage, or changed, many patients will have an improvement in EPS, but often this is not feasible. Many patients with parkinsonism respond to anticholinergic and antihistaminic agents, such as benztropine, trihexyphenidyl, orphenadrine, and others. Anticholinergic therapy is associated with a number of risks, however, including urinary retention and memory loss. Direct dopaminergic stimulants, such as amantadine, may benefit patients who, for medical or other reasons, cannot tolerate anticholinergic medications. Amantadine, however, should be used with care, especially in the elderly, for it has a propensity to worsen psychosis. We recommend that patients receive as low a dosage of antiparkinsonian medications as possible. Patients with akathisia may respond poorly to antiparkinsonian medications, and, in these patients, propranolol or benzodiazepines may be helpful (see Chapter 4). Although amantadine has been used in the treatment of akathisia, there is evidence that tolerance develops, much as that seen when amantadine is used to treat the signs and symptoms of Parkinson's disease (Zubenko et al., 1984). Finally, in some patients methylphenidate or barbiturates may be of help when other agents fail.

The question of whether or not antiparkinsonian medications should be added prophylactically to the medication regimen of patients started on neuroleptics is still debated. Those in favor of adding prophylactic antiparkinsonian drugs point out that there is significantly less risk of developing side effects such as dystonia (Stern & Anderson, 1979; Winslow et al., 1986), which, in turn, leads to greater patient compliance, and that the development of acute EPS may be associated with later development of tardive dyskinesia. Those against adding prophylactic antiparkinsonian drugs note that these drugs have significant side effects of their own, that antiparkinsonian agents may increase the risk of tardive dyskinesia, that acute EPS is relatively uncommon, that prophylaxis is of questionable benefit, especially in older patients, and that treatment of parkinsonism after it develops is more effective than is prophylaxis (Baldessarini, 1977; Moleman et al., 1982). It is clear that many of these beliefs are contradictory, and that more investigative work is required in this area. Until further discoveries are made, our present approach is to use prophylactic antiparkinsonian drugs only in those cases in whom we have reason to believe there is high risk for developing EPS (such as young men being treated with high doses of high-potency neuroleptics) and in whom the development of EPS would probably adversely affect compliance. We should also mention that there is evidence that if neuroleptics are started at a low dose and the dose is slowly increased to a point at which mild extrapyramidal rigidity is detectable by the examiner, patients may experience good antipsychotic effects without as much risk for developing disturbing EPS (McEvoy et al., 1986).

Many patients are not aware of neuroleptic-induced movement disorders, including both acute neuroleptic-induced EPS (Freedman et al.,

1979) and tardive dyskinesia (Smith *et al.*, 1979; Alexopoulos, 1979; Rosen *et al.*, 1982). In the Freedman *et al.* study, only 1 out of 14 patients with acute EPS (including parkinsonism and dystonia) was totally aware of the side effects, and in the Rosen *et al.* study, only a third of the patients with tardive dyskinesia had any awareness of the abnormal movements. The reasons for this lack of perception are unknown, although Freedman *et al.* have conjectured that dopaminergic transmission in the brain is necessary for appropriate processing of sensory information, and that abnormalities in dopaminergic transmission may be associated with sensory neglect. Lohr *et al.* (1987) recently reported that two-thirds of 41 patients with tardive dyskinesia and one-third of 35 patients with neuroleptic-induced parkinsonism (mainly bradykinesia and rigidity) were aware of having a movement disorder, as compared to nearly 100% of 23 patients with Huntington's disease and 18 patients with Parkinson's disease accompanied by choreoathetoid movements. Furthermore, awareness of tardive dyskinesia was found to be associated with older age, a diagnosis of schizoaffective disorder, more severe orofacial dyskinesia, and more manic symtomatology, whereas awareness of neuroleptic-induced parkinsonism was also associated with older age and a diagnosis of schizoaffective disorder, but with more depressive symtomatology. These findings indicate that lack of self-awareness of movement disorders involves more than just sensory neglect associated with dopaminergic dysfunction, and that other clinical variables such as diagnosis and age are also important.

TARDIVE DYSKINESIA

Description and Epidemiology

Tardive dyskinesia is a neuroleptic-induced disorder consisting primarily of choreoathetoid movements affecting the orofacial region and upper limbs. The movements usually appear after at least 3 months of neuroleptic treatment. Although the orofacial and upper-extremity musculature is most commonly involved, the trunk, lower extremities, pharynx, and diaphragm are affected in some patients. Orobuccolingual movements occur in approximately 80% of patients, and approximately 10% of patients have abnormal movements in all the major body regions (Jeste & Wyatt, 1982). The orofacial movements usually consist of thrusting or protrusion of the tongue ("bonbon sign" or "fly-catcher's tongue") or vermicular tongue movements, chewing movements, and lip-smacking or pouting. Patients may blink, grimace, or frown repetitively. In the upper extremities, athetoid finger movements ("piano player's fingers") are commonly observed, and in the lower extremities athetosis of the toes is usually seen. Foot-stamping may occur, as well as inversion, eversion, and lateral movements of the foot. There may be rocking or twisting movements of the trunk and neck, and diaphragmatic, intercostal, and abdominal muscle contractions may cause respiratory or gastrointestinal symptoms.

The reported prevalence of tardive dyskinesia in psychiatric patients treated chronically with neuroleptics has increased progressively from approximately 5% (until 1965) to more than 25% (since 1976) (Jeste & Wyatt, 1981). The current reported prevalence of tardive dyskinesia has varied from 5% to 60% in certain subgroups of patients.

The course of the syndrome varies from fully reversible to persistent. About 33% of cases of tardive dyskinesia are reversible, with disappearance of the movements within 3 months of drug withdrawal (Jeste & Wyatt, 1982). A disorder probably related to tardive dyskinesia is "neuroleptic-withdrawal-emergent dyskinesia," which as a rule disappears within 1 to 3 weeks of discontinuing medications, and often occurs in children (Winsberg et al., 1977; Polizos & Engelhardt, 1978). This withdrawal-emergent dyskinesia may at times be a forerunner of the irreversible syndrome.

Neuroleptics are the only drugs that commonly produce a dyskinesia that persists after drug discontinuation. Although other drugs may cause choreoathetoid movements (see Table 23-4), there is no clear evidence that drugs other than neuroleptics produce an irreversible dyskinesia.

Age and gender are related to the prevalence and prognosis of tardive dyskinesia. Jeste and Wyatt (1981), based on a review of 19 studies, calculated that women have a 41% higher mean prevalence than do men, but the reasons are unknown. Also, patients aged 40 to 70 appear to have more severe dyskinesias, as well as a higher prevalence of tardive dyskinesia (Kane & Smith, 1982; Toenniessen et al., 1985) and a lower rate of remission than do younger patients (Smith & Baldessarini, 1980).

Tardive dyskinesia can occur in a number of different diagnostic categories outside of schizophrenia. Patients with unipolar depression (Rush et al., 1982) and bipolar affective disorder (Yassa et al., 1983) have been identified as high-risk groups for tardive dyskinesia. Other high-risk groups include retarded patients, especially those with phenylketonuria (Richardson et al., 1984). However, the issue of organicity and brain damage as a risk factor is controversial (Wolf et al., 1982).

Other factors that may be associated with tardive dyskinesia are high-dose neuroleptic treatment and high-potency neuroleptic medications, as well as depot neuroleptics (Jeste & Wyatt, 1982). Because the use of these agents may be reserved for special subgroups of patients who may be resistant to or show poor response to neuroleptics, the higher incidence of dyskinesia may be related to the underlying illness itself, rather than to the type of treatment. Finally, other factors that may be associated with tardive dyskinesia are parkinsonism, dental problems, and dentures (Jeste & Wyatt, 1982).

Variation in the anatomical distribution and in the course of illness has prompted investigators to propose subclassification schemes for tardive dyskinesia. Kidger et al. (1980) and Barnes et al. (1980, 1983), on the basis of studies of the somatic distribution of movements in tardive dyskinesia patients, proposed that tardive dyskinesia may occur in a central (i.e., orofacial) and a peripheral form. The peripheral syndrome may be more common in younger patients, whereas orofacial movements may occur more often in the elderly (Bucci, 1971; Barnes *et al.*, 1983; Lohr *et al.*, 1986a). The validity of such a classification scheme has not yet been established, however. Subtyping of tardive dyskinesia is discussed in more detail in the last section of this chapter.

Neurochemical Aspects

Neurochemical theories of tardive dyskinesia have generally involved the dopaminergic and cholinergic systems, although recent attention has been focused on abnormalities in the noradrenergic, GABA-ergic, and putative peptidergic neurotransmitter systems as well. In this section, we briefly review the evidence for the involvement of these systems in tardive dyskinesia.

Dopamine (DA)

For a number of years, investigators have proposed that dopaminergic overactivity is the primary mechanism of tardive dyskinesia. The evidence for this hypothesis derives from the following observations:

1. Neuroleptic withdrawal, presumably accompanied by a decrease in dopaminergic receptor blockade, causes worsening of dyskinesia.
2. L-Dopa and amphetamine, both of which are dopaminergic agonists, aggravate tardive dyskinesia.
3. DA-depleting agents (e.g., reserpine, tetrabenazine) and DA receptor blocking agents (e.g., neuroleptics) may decrease the movements.
4. Because DA is known to be reduced in Parkinson's disease, the fact that Parkinson's disease and tardive dyskinesia show opposite responses to dopaminergic agonists (Parkinson's disease improves, whereas tardive dyskinesia worsens) may indicate that there is a relative dopaminergic hyperactivity in tardive dyskinesia.

Although this evidence implicates dopaminergic hyperactivity in tardive dyskinesia, the exact mechanism is unclear. Some investigators (e.g., Klawans, 1973; Klawans & Rubovits, 1974) have proposed that supersensitivity of striatal postsynaptic dopaminergic receptors may be responsible for the dyskinetic movements. The concept of "denervation supersensitivity" probably originated in the 19th century, after it was observed that the heart and gut demonstrated increased responsiveness to specific agonists after being surgically denervated (see Langer, 1975). Denervation supersensitivity was first described in the central nervous system in 1961, by Stavraky, for acetylcholine, and later, in 1971, by Ungerstedt, for catecholamines. In the DA receptor supersensitivity model of tardive dyskinesia, neuroleptic medications (which are thought to result in chemical blockade of postsynaptic DA receptors; Snyder, 1976; Peroutka & Snyder, 1980) are believed to cause the chemical equivalent of surgical denervation. Long-term treatment with neuroleptics would then be followed by an increase in the number and/or the sensitivity of postsynaptic DA receptors, resulting in supersensitivity to DA. In the striatum, this supersensitivity could appear as dyskinetic movements. It is clear that animals treated with neuroleptic medications develop DA receptor supersensitivity (see Moore, 1981, for a review of the animal literature). However, in man the primary clinical evidence supporting this idea is indirect, and includes the following:

NEUROLEPTIC-WITHDRAWAL-EMERGENT DYSKINESIAS

Neuroleptic-withdrawal-emergent dyskinesias have been mentioned earlier in this chapter. In at least some cases it is possible that these dyskinesias may be the result of DA receptor supersensitivity (Baldessarini et al., 1980). However, it is not clear whether withdrawal dyskinesias are related to tardive dyskinesia.

L-DOPA-INDUCED DYSKINESIAS AND TARDIVE DYSKINESIA

Some investigators have proposed that L-dopa-induced dyskinesias in patients with Parkinson's disease result from denervation supersensitivity of striatal target neurons that lose dopaminergic input from the substantia nigra (Langer, 1975). Because L-dopa-induced dyskinesias and neuroleptic-induced tardive dyskinesia may appear clinically similar, similar pathophysiologic processes may be involved in the development of these two dyskinesias. However, there is no direct support for the idea that DA receptor supersensitivity underlies L-dopa-induced dyskinesias.

NEUROLEPTIC SUPPRESSION OF TARDIVE DYSKINESIA

Patients who develop tardive dyskinesia often benefit from an increase in neuroleptic dosage, at least initially, which has been thought to support the notion of DA receptor supersensitivity. Increasing the dose is believed to cause further blockade of the supersensitive DA receptors. Neuroleptics, however, have a number of different neurochemical actions, including blockade of noradrenergic receptors (Peroutka & Snyder, 1980), and it is not clear whether the suppression of dyskinesias is specifically the result of DA blockade.

There are a number of problems with the supersensitivity hypothesis (see

Kaufmann *et al.*, 1986). There is a lack of comparability of animal models of DA receptor supersensitivity and human tardive dyskinesia. Long-term administration of neuroleptics always produces supersensitivity in animals, but only occasionally produces dyskinesias in monkeys (Gunne *et al.*, 1984) and in humans (Simpson, 1980; Baldessarini *et al.*, 1980; Jeste & Wyatt, 1981; Kane & Smith, 1982). Also, supersensitive DA receptors demonstrate an increased responsiveness to DA agonists such as apomorphine in animals, but apomorphine does not exacerbate tardive dyskinesia (see Jeste & Wyatt, 1982). The risk for tardive dyskinesia appears to increase with age, whereas the number of striatal DA receptors decreases with age in both animals and man (Joseph *et al.*, 1978; Wong *et al.*, 1984). Finally, postmortem studies of patients or animals with neuroleptic-induced dyskinesias have reported no significant differences in the binding of the D_2 receptor marker [3H]spiperone when compared with nondyskinetic controls (Crow *et al.*, 1982; Waddington *et al.*, 1983).

Norepinephrine (NE)

Much of the evidence for dopaminergic hyperactivity in tardive dyskinesia may also be interpreted as indicating noradrenergic hyperactivity. Drugs, such as amphetamine and methylphenidate, that worsen tardive dyskinesia are both dopaminergic and noradrenergic stimulants. In addition, neuroleptics are thought to blockade noradrenergic receptors (Peroutka & Snyder, 1980).

There is also more direct evidence of noradrenergic hyperactivity in tardive dyskinesia. Jeste *et al.* (1979, 1982) and Arato *et al.* (1980) reported higher plasma dopamine β-hydroxylase (DBH, the enzyme that catalyzes the formation of NE from DA) activity in a subgroup of patients with tardive dyskinesia, which is consistent with reports of increased central noradrenergic activity following long-term adminstration of neuroleptics (Schelkunov, 1967), and of increased urinary excretion of NE in monkeys with neuroleptic-induced dyskinesias (Messiha, 1980). Some investigators have not reported a difference in plasma DBH activity between patients with and without tardive dyskinesia, however (Markianos *et al.*, 1983). Jeste *et al.* (1984d) also reported elevated cerebrospinal fluid NE in patients with tardive dyskinesia from Bombay, India. Drugs, such as fusaric acid, propranolol, and clonidine, that inhibit noradrenergic activity have been reported to be effective in the treatment of some patients with tardive dyskinesia (Viukari & Linnoila, 1977; Bacher & Lewis, 1980; Freedman *et al.*, 1980).

A recent report by Kaufmann *et al.* (1986) suggests that a subset of patients with tardive dyskinesia is characterized by large ventricles on CT scan, and that this subgroup is associated with low or normal noradrenergic activity (as indicated by low plasma DBH activity). Another subset of patients with tardive dyskinesia demonstrated elevated noradrenergic activity, and this subset was not associated with ventricular enlargement. These findings may indicate that certain biochemical abnormalities (such as increased noradrenergic activity) and structural abnormalities (such as enlarged ventricles) may be inversely related, a finding that has been noted by investigators in a number of different conditions, including schizophrenia, affective disorders, and alcoholism (VanKammen et al., 1983; Meltzer et al., 1984; Bridge et al., 1985).

Exactly how noradrenergic abnormalities relate to abnormal movements is unclear. Several different movement disorders thought to be related to basal-ganglia pathology have been associated with disturbances in NE metabolism or pathways, including Huntington's disease (Lieberman et al., 1972), Parkinson's disease (Lieberman et al., 1972; Hornykiewicz, 1976), autosomal dominant torsion dystonia (Wooten et al., 1973; Ebstein et al., 1974), and Tourette's syndrome (see Cohen et al., 1984). The relationship between noradrenergic hyper- or hypoactivity and dysfunction of striatal circuitry is unclear. Although there is very little striatal NE, the striatum contains large numbers of NE receptors (Alexander et al., 1975; Palacios & Kuhar, 1980), the functional role of which is unknown. Hornykiewicz (1976) has proposed that NE sets up the sensitivity of those neuronal systems on which DA acts in regulating locomotor activation, and has shown that DBH inhibitors reduce locomotor excitation caused by drugs such as L-dopa. The exact site or sites of DA–NE interaction remain to be determined. It has also been shown that stimulation of the locus ceruleus (the major NE-containing nucleus in the brainstem) results in a marked reduction of the excitatory response of neurons to substance P in the cingulate gyrus of the rat (Jones & Olpe, 1984). Because substance P may be an important transmitter in outflow tracts of the striatum (see Chapter 2), it is conceivable that a similar situation might obtain in efferent striatal pathways, as patients with elevated NE activity may effectively have a reduction of neuronal responsiveness to substance P, and thus manifest dysfunction related to abnormal basal-ganglia output.

γ-Aminobutyric Acid (GABA)

GABA is the most abundant neurotransmitter in the neostriatum (Pasik, et al., 1979; Ribak, 1981). GABA is an inhibitory neurotransmitter thought to be involved in the regulation of NE, DA, and acetylcholine activity (Scatton & Bartholini, 1982; Scatton et al., 1982). In rats, long-term neuroleptic treatment has been shown to cause a significant loss of neurons in the striatum (Pakkenberg et al., 1973; Nielsen & Lyon, 1978), as well as a reduction of glutamic acid decarboxylase (GAD, the enzyme that catalyzes the synthesis of GABA) activity in the substantia nigra, medial globus pallidus, and subthalamic nucleus (Gunne et al., 1984; Gunne & Haggstrom, 1985). It has been reported that, in monkeys given long-term neuroleptic treatment, only those animals that developed dyskinesias demonstrated a reduction in GAD activity, whereas similarly treated animals without dyskinesia did not (Gunne et al., 1984). GABA-ergic agonists, such as muscimol, γ-acetylenic GABA, and γ-vinyl GABA, have been shown to reduce the severity of dyskinesias in some patients with tardive dyskinesia (Tamminga et al., 1979, 1983; Casey et al., 1980; Stahl et al., 1985), although results have been conflicting in some cases. (For a recent review of GABA in movement disorders, see Scheel-Kruger, 1986.)

Neuropeptides

A number of different neuropeptides, including endorphins, enkephalins, substance P, somatostatin, and cholecystokinin, have been proposed to be important in dyskinetic disorders such as tardive dyskinesia, in part because most of these peptides are found in abundance in the striatum. However, there are few studies concerning the importance of neuropeptides in tardive dyskinesia, and the focus of most existing studies has been on the interactions of neuropeptides with dopaminergic mechanisms (see Tamminga & Frohman, 1979; Blum & Korczyn, 1983).

Neuropathological Studies

Few cases of tardive dyskinesia have been studied from a neuropathological perspective. Among the earliest reports is that of Grunthal and Walther-Buel (1960), who noted chromatolysis of neurons in the inferior olive in a patient who developed perioral dyskinesias after treatment with perphenazine. However, the duration of neuroleptic treatment was very short (13 days), raising the question of whether this patient truly had tardive dyskinesia.

Hunter et al. (1968) did not report any consistent neuropathological findings in three elderly patients who had been treated primarily with chlorpromazine and who exhibited mainly orofacial dyskinesias for 4 to 5 years before death. One patient who was assessed for metal content in the basal ganglia was noted to have increased iron in the globus pallidus and substantia nigra.

Gross and Kaltenback (1969), in three patients with persistent hyperkinesias following neuroleptics, reported pathological changes predominantly of large neurons in the medium portion of the caudate nucleus (patient #1), caudate atrophy and pathological changes in the "oral parts" of the substantia nigra (patient #2), and atrophy of the head of the caudate nucleus, putamen, and globus pallidus (patient #3). The third patient may have had Huntington's disease.

Christensen et al. (1970) in the first controlled study of neuropathological changes associated with tardive dyskinesia, reported midbrain and brainstem gliosis in 25 and degeneration of cells in the substantia nigra in 27 of the brains of 28 dyskinetic patients (these findings were noted in only four and seven of 28 control brains, respectively). However, when compared with the nondyskinetic patients, the dyskinetic patients were older (with a mean age of 74 years, as compared with 69 years in the control group), and all were women (the control group consisted of four women and 24 men). Also, the dyskinesias were believed to be related to neuroleptics in only 21 of the 28 cases.

Jellinger (1977) performed a controlled neuropathological study on the brains of 14 patients (mainly schizophrenic, ten men and four women) with drug-induced movement disorders (nine had developed perioral dyskinesias and five had drug-induced parkinsonism). The control group consisted of 14 nondyskinetic patients (again, mainly schizophrenic, six men and eight women). The two groups were comparable in terms of the amount of neuroleptic medication they had received. Five of the nine dyskinetic patients had pathology of the caudate nucleus (primarily involving swelling of large neurons and increased glial satellitosis bilaterally in the rostral two-thirds of the caudate nuclei) whereas none of the nondyskinetic control subjects had this condition. Few, if any, pathological changes were noted in the globus pallidus or other subcortical nuclei.

Other reports include that of Jamiety et al. (1976), who reported atrophic changes mainly in the substantia nigra of a 54-year-old man who was presumed to have tardive dyskinesia, and that of Ule and Struwe (1978), who described degenerative changes in the nigrostriatal area of a 66-year-old woman with abnormal movements. Recently, Campbell et al. (1985) reported extensive iron deposition in the caudate, putamen, globus pallidus, subthalamic nucleus, and substantia nigra pars reticulata of a 64-year-old man with bipolar affective disorder who developed tardive dyskinesia following an overdose of lithium and haloperidol.

In summary, it is possible that there may be pathology in the basal ganglia of patients with tardive dyskinesia, especially of the caudate nucleus and the substantia nigra, although the findings have not been consistent.

Neuroradiological Studies

There are a few CT-scan studies of tardive dyskinesia. Some reports indicate possible ventricular enlargement in tardive dyskinesia (Pandurangi et al., 1980; Bartels & Themelis, 1983), although other studies do not report any significant difference (Gelenberg, 1976b; Jeste et al., 1980; Brainin et al., 1983), and the results of some studies are difficult to interpret (Famuyiwa et al., 1979). It is possible that the studies that did not find significant differences looked at patients with less severe dyskinesia. Kaufmann et al. (1986) reported that enlarged ventricles occurred in a subgroup of patients with tardive dyskinesia with normal plasma activity of DBH, whereas patients with elevated DBH did not appear to have enlarged ventricles. This may indicate that only a subgroup of patients with tardive dyskinesia have enlarged ventricles.

In summary, although some of the results are conflicting, it appears that there is neuroradiological evidence for atrophy of the striatum and, particularly, of the caudate nucleus in a subset of patients with tardive dyskinesia. However, it should be noted that structures such as putamen and substantia nigra are not well visualized on CT scans.

Psychological Aspects

A number of investigators have recently reported an association of tardive dyskinesia with impaired cognitive functioning and so-called "negative symptoms" of schizophrenia, which include such symptoms as blunted affect and social withdrawal. Struve and Willner (1983) noted significantly greater impairment of patients with persistent tardive dyskinesia on the Conceptual Level Analogy Test, a neuropsychological measure of abstracting ability, when compared with a control group of patients without tardive dyskinesia who had also been treated with neuroleptics. Waddington et al. (1985) recently reported that schizophrenic patients with orofacial dyskinesia were older, more intellectually impaired, and more likely to show negative symptoms than schizophrenic patients without dyskinesia. Jeste et al. (1984b) also reported an association of tardive dyskinesia with negative symptoms of schizophrenia. Although the exact significance of these observations is unclear, they may indicate that areas of the basal ganglia that are dysfunctional in cases of tardive dyskinesia may be related to certain cognitive functions, an idea that is similar to the notion of "subcortical dementia," discussed in Chapter 22.

Differential Diagnosis

Although the movements of patients with tardive dyskinesia are usually choreoathetoid in nature, many different types of hyperkinetic motor signs, including hemiballismus, dystonia, tic, myoclonus, and tremor, have been reported to occur as a part of the syndrome. Some of these movements are discussed in more detail later in this chapter, in the section on other tardive syndromes. There have also been reports of persistent drug-induced parkinsonism lasting for up to 1 year following neuroleptic discontinuation (Aronson, 1985). The relationship of all these different tardive syndromes to one another is unclear.

There are a number of studies reporting the coexistence of tardive dyskinesia and acute EPS. The prevalence of the coexistence of the two disorders has been reported to be anywhere from 12% to 27% of patients treated with neuroleptic medications (Crane, 1972; Richardson & Craig, 1982; Wolf et al., 1983; Bitton & Melamed, 1984), and we have recently noted that the coexistence of rigidity and bradykinesia with tardive dyskinesia in a group of 60 institutionalized schizophrenic patients was greater than 40% (Lohr & Jeste, unpublished data). Tardive dyskinesia has also been reported to coexist with oculogyric crises (Nasrallah et al., 1980) as well as with blepharospasm–oromandibular dystonia or Meige's syndrome (Weiner et al., 1981). The coexistence of tardive dyskinesia and acute EPS can make the differential diagnosis difficult. Drug-induced parkinsonian tremor can be difficult to distinguish from tardive dyskinesia, because some patients with tardive dyskinesia have a significant rhythmical or stereotypical component to their movements. We have observed this component to be usually in the range of 2 cycles per second, which separates it from the coarse parkinsonian tremor that usually appears in the range of 4 to 7 cycles per second. This rhythmical component of tardive dyskinesia requires further investigation, but does appear to be similar to the rhythmical component described in other athetoid disorders, such as cerebral palsy. In this latter disorder, the rhythmical component has been noted to be in the 2.5-cycle-per-second range and to resemble clinically a rubral tremor (Lance & McLeod, 1981).

The differentiation between tardive dyskinesia and akathisia was discussed in Chapter 4.

Another acute drug-induced syndrome that involves primarily orofacial muscles is the *rabbit syndrome*, which is probably a parkinsonian tremor of the orofacial area. Although uncommon, it has been recently reported to have a prevalence of 4.4% in patients treated with neuroleptics alone (Yassa & Lal, 1986). The rabbit syndrome is marked by fine, rhythmic movements of the lips at about 5 cycles per second, sometimes accompanied by a popping sound when the lips are opened (Villeneuve, 1972; Todd et al., 1983). When the tongue is involved, there is usually a tremulous movement of the glossal muscles, which is different from the vermicular or thrusting movements seen in cases of tardive dyskinesia. Rabbit syndrome may respond to anticholinergic agents, whereas these agents usually make tardive dyskinesia worse. However, tardive dyskinesia and rabbit syndrome can coexist, and the combination may prove difficult to treat (Weiss et al., 1980).

Tardive dyskinesia tends to be more common in the elderly, and thus should be carefully differentiated from other senile buccolinguomasticatory (BLM) dyskinetic disorders (discussed in more detail in Chapters 3 and 26), which include the common spontaneous BLM dyskinesias of the elderly and edentulous dyskinesias. Meige's syndrome may also resemble tardive dyskinesia in the elderly, although Meige's syndrome is more dystonic in nature than is tardive dyskinesia. As mentioned in Chapter 3, a careful history of exposure to neuroleptics must be obtained from any geriatric patient, as some individuals do not remember taking these medications or simply consider them to be "sleeping pills," and therefore not important. Many geriatric patients have had antipsychotic medications (especially low-potency medications, such as thioridazine) prescribed for sleep disturbances or anxiety.

Disorders of the basal ganglia, such as Huntington's disease, Wilson's disease, and Sydenham's chorea, may present with psychiatric symptomatology in the early stages of the disorder, and a number of patients with these disorders are given neuroleptic medications for the psychiatric symptoms. Later, when abnormal movements appear, these patients may mistakenly be thought to have developed tardive dyskinesia. A positive family history for Huntington's disease, prior history of rheumatic fever, and appropriate laboratory tests, such as serum ceruloplasmin, serum, and urinary copper, antistreptolysin O (ASO) titers, etc., are necessary to make the correct diagnosis. Other neurological conditions to be considered in the differential diagnosis of tardive dyskinesia include Hallervorden–Spatz syndrome; dystonia musculorum deformans and other idiopathic dystonias; Tourette's syndrome and other idiopathic tic disorders; familial paroxysmal choreoathetosis; chorea-acanthocytosis; chorea gravidarum and chorea in association with oral contraceptives; hyperthyroidism; polycythemia; systemic lupus erythematosus; effects of stimulants (such as amphetamine, methylphenidate, and pemoline); and effects of L-dopa, as well as other drugs (Table 23-4).

Finally, tardive dyskinesia should be differentiated from stereotypies and mannerisms that occur in schizophrenia, catatonia, mental retardation, and autism, discussed earlier in Chapter 8 (see Table 8-4).

Table 23-4. Drugs Implicated in Dyskinetic Disorders, Including Tardive Dyskinesia

Neuroleptics, including:	Antiparkinsonian agents, including:
Phenothiazines	Amantadine
Thioxanthines	Bromocriptine
Butyrophenones	L-Dopa
Indolones	Antidepressants, including:
Dibenzazepines	Tricyclic antidepressants
Diphenylbutylpiperidines	Monoamine oxidase inhibitors
Stimulants, including:	Lithium
Amphetamines	Metoclopramide
Methylphenidate	α-Methyldopa
Fenfluramine	Anticonvulsants
Antihistamines	Estrogens

Other Tardive Syndromes

Movement disorders apart from choreoathetosis may occur after long-term administration of neuroleptic medications, including dystonia, tics, and akathisia. Like those in tardive dyskinesia, these movements may not disappear following cessation of neuroleptics. It is possible that these conditions may represent subtypes of tardive dyskinesia, but this is far from clear. Case reports of other tardive syndromes are listed in Tables 23-5 through 23-7, excluding the large number of cases of tardive dystonia reported by Burke *et al.* (1982). (For a recent review of tardive syndromes, see Jeste *et al.*, 1986a.)

Tardive Dystonia

Of the tardive syndromes apart from tardive dyskinesia, tardive dystonia has been the most commonly reported. The largest series is that of Burke *et al.* (1982), who reported 42 cases, aged 13 to 60. Tardive dystonia can occur in patients with a variety of diagnoses, including schizophrenia, depression, and anxiety, and may appear after months to years of exposure to neuroleptics, with the average duration of exposure in Burke *et al.*'s series being 3.7 years. In the Burke *et al.* series, only 5 out of the 42 patients had a spontaneous remission.

The dystonia may coexist with choreoathetoid movements, especially orofacial movements. The dystonia may be either generalized or focal, affecting the neck (torticollis, retrocollis), jaw, limbs, or back. Many different classes of neuroleptics have been implicated, and the dystonia has been reported to last up to 6 years after discontinuation of the neuroleptic, and may very well last longer. The pathophysiology is unknown, although it is likely that the basal ganglia are involved.

Treatment can often prove difficult. As with tardive dyskinesia, neuroleptic medication should be discontinued or reduced in dosage, if possible. Burke *et al.* reported that 68% of patients improved with tetrabenazine and 39% improved with anticholinergic drugs. This improvement with anticholinergic drugs is in contrast with tardive dyskinesia, in which there is usually a worsening of the movement disorder. Details of other cases of tardive dystonia are presented in Table 23-5.

Tardive Akathisia

To our knowledge, there have been seven case reports of tardive akathisia in patients ranging in age from 28 to 58 (Table 23-6). As in other tardive syndromes, different classes of neuroleptics have been implicated. Although cases have been too few to allow one to make any general recommendations

Table 23-5. Reports of Tardive Dystonia[a]

Reference	Age (yr)	Sex	Diagnosis	Medication[b] (duration)	Dystonia duration[c]	Treatment
Druckman et al. (1962)	46	F	Depression	CPZ (3 yr)	2 yr (+)	Meperidine Benztropine Phenobarbital Chlordiazepoxide Trihexyphenidyl Thalamotomy[d]
Dabbous and Bergman (1966)	5	M	Accidental exposure	PHE (NS)	2 yr (+)	Diphenhydramine Benztropine
Angle and McIntire (1968)	10	F	Mental retardation	PHE (NS)	7 mo	Diphenhydramine[d] Benztropine[d]
Keegan and Rajput (1973)	45	F	Schizophrenia	CPZ, TRI, THI (many years)	5 yr (+)	L-Dopa
Shields and Bray (1976)	5	F	Sydenham's chorea	HAL (1 mo)	5 mo (+)	Diphenhydramine Benztropine L-Dopa, deanol Reserpine Physostigmine
Kwentus et al. (1984)	42	F	Catatonia Depression	FLU (10 yr)	1 mo	Electroconvulsive therapy[d]
Gimenez-Roldan et al. (1985)	17	M	Schizophrenia	HAL, FLU (2 yr)	4 mo (+)	
	25	M	Schizophrenia	HAL (2 yr)	4.2 yr (+)	

	Age	Sex	Diagnosis	Drug (duration)	Outcome	
	26	F	Affective disorder / Mental retardation	HAL (2 yr)	2 yr (+)	Benztropine
	33	M	Schizophrenia	THI, PHE (15 yr)	4 mo (+)	Diphenhydramine
	34	M	Psychosis / Mental retardation	CPZ (4 yr)	2.7 yr (+)	Amantadine
	47	F	Psychosis / Mental retardation	THI, PRO (7 mo)	2.2 yr (+)	Diazepam
	42	F	Schizophrenia	HAL, THI, BUT (3 yr)	1.9 yr (+)	Phenobarbital
	39	F	Schizophrenia	CPZ (8 yr)	8 yr (+)	Carbamazepine
	61	M	Schizophrenia	FLU, THI (8 yr)	7 mo (+)	Bromocriptine[d]
Luchins and Goldman (1985)	27	M	Schizoaffective	CPZ, HAL, FLU, THX (8 yr)	10 mo	

[a] Excluding Burke et al. (1982), described in the text.

[b] Explanation of abbreviations: chlorpromazine, CPZ; fluphenazine, FLU; thioridazine, THI; thiothixene, THX; trifluoperazine, TRI; haloperidol, HAL; propericiazine, PRO; butaperazine, BUT; phenothiazine of unknown type, PHE; not stated, NS.

[c] (+) indicates a persistent condition.

[d] Treatment was believed to cause improvement in motor signs.

Table 23-6. Reports of Tardive Akathisia

Reference	Age (yr)	Sex	Diagnosis	Medication[a] (duration)	Akathisia duration[b]	Treatment
Kruse (1960)	55	F	Schizophrenia	CPZ, TRI (2 yr)	1.5 yr	Pentobarbital Chlordiazepoxide[c]
	58	F	Schizophrenia	FLU, TRI (NS)	3 mo (+)	Librium[c]
	50	F	Schizophrenia	THI (1 mo)	3 mo (+)	Chlordiazepoxide[c]
Weiner and Luby (1983)	50	F	Atypical psychosis	FLU (2 mo (+))	10 mo	Reserpine Procyclidine[c]
	43	M	Depression Catatonia	THI (1 yr)	6 mo (+)	Diazepam[c]
Braude and Barnes (1983)	42	F	Schizophrenia	FLU, CPZ (12 yr)	NS	Procyclidine
	28	M	Schizophrenia	FLU (5 yr)	NS	Anticholinergics

[a]For explanation of abbreviations, see Table 23-5.
[b](+) indicates a persistent condition.
[c]Treatment was believed to cause improvement in motor signs.

Table 23-7. Reports of Tardive Tourette's Syndrome

Reference	Age (yr)	Sex	Diagnosis	Medication[a] (duration)	Tic duration[b]	Treatment
Klawans et al. (1978)	28	F	Schizophrenia	CPZ (6 yr)	NS	Haloperidol[c]
DeVeaugh-Geiss (1980)	65	M	?	THI (6 yr)	6 mo	Spontaneous remission
Stahl (1980)	28	M	Mental	CPZ (13 yr)	2 yr (+)	Haloperidol[c] Physostigmine[c]
Seeman et al., (1981)	26	F	Schizophrenia	TRI, FLU (3 yr)	4 mo	Spontaneous remission
Mueller and Aminoff (1982)	27	M	Autism	THI (12 yr)	2 mo	Haloperidol[c]
Jeste et al. (1983)	44	M	Schizophrenia	PHE (24 yr)	1 yr (+)	Clonidine[c]
Munetz et al. (1985)	60	F	Schizophrenia	MES (many yr)	Months	Clonidine[c] Mesoridazine

[a]For explanation of abbreviations, see Table 23-5.
[b](+) indicates a persistent condition.
[c]Treatment was believed to cause improvement in motor signs.

for treatment, it appears that benzodiazepines such as diazepam and chlordiazepoxide may be helpful in some cases.

Tardive Tourette's Syndrome

Tardive Tourette's syndrome has been reported in seven patients, aged 22 to 60, who received a variety of different classes of neuroleptic medications (Table 23-7). In some cases the tics remitted spontaneously; in others, they were suppressed by neuroleptics. In two cases the tics were improved by clonidine, similar to idiopathic Tourette's syndrome. Tardive Tourette's syndrome may be more common than is appreciated, because stereotypies, noises, and other unusual behaviors seen in schizophrenic patients after neuroleptic treatment may possibly represent complex and simple tardive tic disorders.

Recent Proposed Mechanisms of Tardive Dyskinesia

Lohr *et al.* (1986b) proposed a possible mechanism for the pathogenesis of tardive dyskinesia, based on recent hypotheses concerning the functional circuitry of the striatum. Groves (1983), in what is probably the first comprehensive theory of striatal functioning, has hypothesized that the striatum may be composed of two basic types of circuits. The first circuit involves the abundant but small spiny type I (SI) neurons that appear to use GABA as a neurotransmitter. The second circuit involves the relatively uncommon but large spiny type II (SII) and aspiny type II (AspII) neurons, thought to use substance P (or possibly substance K) and acetylcholine, respectively. Lohr *et al.* (1986b) suggested that the manifestations of tardive dyskinesia may depend on which of these circuits is predominantly affected. Patients with damage primarily to the first circuit (SI neurons) might clinically resemble patients with Huntington's disease, in that they would have abnormalities in GABA-ergic activity and manifest more generalized choreoathetoid movements. This notion is supported by the finding that some patients with tardive dyskinesia affecting limbs and trunk resemble patients with Huntington's disease clinically (Lohr *et al.*, 1986a). Such generalized or limb–trunk tardive dyskinesia has been observed to be more common in younger persons (Kidger *et al.*, 1980; Barnes *et al.*, 1980, 1983; Lohr *et al.*, 1986a). Some patients with tardive dyskinesia also have enlarged ventricles on pneumoencephalography and on CT scan, possibly due to subcortical atrophy (Pandurangi *et al.*, 1980; Bartels & Themelis, 1983; Kaufmann *et al.*, 1986). In contrast, patients primarily with damage to the second circuit (SII and/or AspII neurons containing substance P [or K] and acetylcholine), who would comprise the majority of patients with tardive dyskinesia, would manifest orofacial dyskinesias. The findings of neuropathological damage to large neurons in localized portions of the striatum in some patients with tardive dyskinesia support this idea (Gross & Kaltenback, 1969; Jellinger, 1977). The second circuit, which represents a much smaller proportion of the striatum, may require less pathological insult to cause observable clinical signs than does the first circuit, and this could account for orofacial dyskinesias' being more common than generalized dyskinesias in cases of tardive dyskinesia.

The mechanisms of neuronal damage in persistent tardive dyskinesia are unknown. One possible mechanism, suggested by Cadet *et al.* (1986) involves the idea that damage to the striatum may result from production of cytotoxic free radicals during the metabolism of catecholamines, mainly DA and NE. Free radicals, which include such substances as molecular oxygen and hydroxyl radicals, are known cytotoxins and, in addition, cause membrane destabilization. They have been implicated in a number of different movement disorders, including Parkinson's disease, manganese-induced encephalopathy, and Hallervorden–Spatz disease (Perry *et al.*, 1982; Eriksson *et al.*, 1984; Perry *et al.*, 1985). The formation of free radicals is catalyzed by the presence of transition metals such as iron, manganese, cobalt, and copper. Free radicals are removed from the body by free-radical scavengers (such as vitamin E) and enzymes (such as glutathione peroxidase and superoxide dismutase). The evidence for the involvement of free radicals in tardive dyskinesia is indirect and includes the following:

1. The secondary increase in catecholamine turnover in the brain following treatment with neuroleptic medications (Korpi & Wyatt, 1984) as well as the increased noradrenergic activity in a subgroup of patients with tardive dyskinesia discussed earlier, could both be involved in the excessive production of free radicals over time, as increased catecholamine turnover may be associated with free-radical production (see Graham, 1979).
2. Long-term administration of neuroleptics causes increased manganese levels in the basal ganglia in animals (Bird *et al.*, 1967; Weiner *et al.*, 1980).
3. Postmortem studies of brains of patients with tardive dyskinesia have revealed increased iron content in the basal ganglia (Hunter *et al.*, 1968; Campbell *et al.*, 1985).
4. Acute methamphetamine administration causes the formation of the cytotoxin 6-hydroxydopamine (Seiden & Vosmer, 1984), which is believed to destroy cells through free-radical production.
5. Phenothiazines are readily oxidized to free radicals by metal ions (Lovstad, 1974).

Thus, excess free radicals may be produced directly from neuroleptics, via 6-hydroxydopamine or other metabolites of catecholamines, or because of excess deposition of transition metals in the brain. Excess free radicals may

Table 23-8. Possible Subtypes of Tardive Dyskinesia[a]

Orofacial	Generalized (limb–trunk)
Older (or throughout life)	Younger
Normal ventricles on CT scan	Enlarged ventricles on CT scan
Localized damage to the orofacial regions of striatum (especially large striatal neurons)	Generalized striatal damage (especially, medium-sized striatal neurons)
Increased NE activity	Normal NE activity
Associated with damage to circuit 2 of Groves (1983)	Associated with damage to circuit 1 of Groves (1983)

[a]See text. This is speculative.

also help explain the observed association of tardive dyskinesia with negative symptoms of schizophrenia (Cadet & Lohr, 1987). Furthermore, there may be a subgroup of patients with tardive dyskinesia who have impaired ability to metabolize free radicals, and, in this population, free-radical damage might be more extensive. These hypotheses remain highly conjectural, however.

It is possible that there may be subtypes of tardive dyskinesia that could be associated with some of the mechanisms discussed above. We have already noted the evidence for two clinical subgroups of tardive dyskinesia: an orofacial and a limb–trunk or generalized subgroup. Table 23-8 lists possible associated findings of these two subgroups, based on the available evidence presented in this chapter. This scheme is highly speculative, and much experimental work is required for verification. Also, it is likely that most patients with tardive dyskinesia represent an intermediate form between the two subgroups listed here. Exactly how free-radical damage would fit into this picture is unclear, but it is possible that the orofacial subgroup is associated with loss of large striatal neurons (especially, cholinergic neurons), as the result of years of exposure to increased DA and NE, whereas the generalized subgroup may represent a group of patients with deficient free-radical detoxifying mechanisms, and thus have more widespread and severe striatal damage.

CHAPTER TWENTY-FOUR

Sleep and Movement Disorders

INTRODUCTION

Sleep has a profound effect on almost all disorders of movement, especially hyperkinetic disorders. With rare exceptions, such as palatal myoclonus, paroxysmal choreoathetosis, or certain cases of hemiballismus, that may remain unchanged from wakefulness to sleep, most movement disorders either arise or attenuate with sleep. And in those movement disorders that abate during sleep, the architecture of sleep is frequently abnormal.

In this chapter we discuss three different aspects of the interaction of sleep and movement disorders. In the first section we present a brief review of sleep physiology, as well as a discussion of certain movement disorders that appear during sleep. In the second section we offer a discussion of sleep abnormalities associated with a number of different neuropsychiatric movement disorders. Finally, we consider some of the neuroanatomical and neurophysiological implications of the connections between sleep and movement.

SLEEP AND ASSOCIATED MOVEMENT DISORDERS

Sleep Physiology

Most of our knowledge about human sleep physiology derives from electroencephalographic studies, sometimes called *polysomnography*. Most sleep laboratories perform all-night electroencephalographic (EEG) recordings, along with measurements of physiological parameters such as respiratory rate, air flow, and oxygen content. Electromyographic and electrocardiographic measurements are also frequently made.

Using such techniques, investigators have divided sleep into a number of different stages. There are two basic kinds of sleep stages, called *rapid-eye-movement* or *REM* sleep (also called paradoxical, desynchronized, or "D-

state" sleep) and *non-rapid-eye-movement* or *NREM* sleep (also called ortho-
dox or "S-state" sleep). NREM sleep has been further divided into three to
four stages, usually called stage 1, stage 2, and delta or slow-wave sleep (delta
sleep is sometimes further subdivided into stage-3 and stage-4 sleep). All of
these different stages have certain special characteristics by which they are
recognized or defined, and these are summarized in Table 24-1.

Associated Movement Disorders

Periodic Movements of Sleep (PMS)

PMS is currently the most widely used term for what has also been called
periodic leg movements of sleep or nocturnal myoclonus. This condition was
initially described by Symonds in 1953, although he did not carefully distinguish it from disorders such as restless-legs syndrome. The movements are
usually highly stereotyped and rhythmic, and typically consist of dorsiflexion

Table 24-1. Stages of Sleep

Stage	Characteristics
Drowsy	Alpha waves present (8 to 12 cycles per second).
Non-rapid-eye-movement (NREM) (orthodox or "S-state" sleep)	
Stage 1	Low-voltage activity mainly in the 3-to-7-cycle-per-second (theta) range. Usually lasts from 0.5 to 7 minutes. Subjects may feel awake during this stage. Slow eye movements, no spindling seen.
Stage 2	Appearance of sleep spindles (12-to-14-cycle-per-second bursts lasting approximately 1 second) and K-complexes (large, slow EEG potentials that are intially negative, followed by a positive wave). Diffuse theta wave activity.
Stages 3 and 4 (delta or slow-wave sleep)	Predominance of delta-wave activity (0.5 to 2 cycles per second) with high-voltage (greater than 75-micro-volt) slow waves. Stage-3 sleep has delta activity 20% to 50% of the time, stage-4 sleep has delta activity $> 50\%$ of the time.
Rapid-eye-movement (REM) (paradoxical, desynchronized, "D-state" sleep)	Low-voltage, irregular, and fast, with sawtooth-shaped waves. Alternates with NREM sleep at approximately 90-minute intervals. Hypotonia is present, although small twitches may be seen. More than 80% of subjects awakened in this stage report dream phenomena. REM predominates during the last half of the sleep period.

of one or both feet, often with extension of the great toe and flexion of the knee or hip. Each movement is usually about 2 seconds in duration. The syndrome may occur in isolation, but often accompanies restless-legs syndrome, which was discussed in Chapter 4. PMS is almost always associated with NREM sleep, predominantly stages 1 and 2 (Lugaresi *et al.*, 1968; Bixler *et al.*, 1982).

PMS gained recognition because it was believed to be an important cause of insomnia (Guilleminault *et al.*, 1975), although doubt has recently been cast on this conjecture. Kales *et al.* (1982c), in a controlled study of 200 insomniac and 100 normal control subjects, reported the percentage of subjects with PMS to be almost identical in the two groups (around 5%). Coleman *et al.* (1980, 1982) discovered PMS in patients with a number of sleep disorders apart from insomnia, such as narcolepsy, sleep apnea, and excessive daytime sleepiness. Nevertheless, the relationship of PMS to sleep disorders is still a controversial one, as investigators continue to report sleep disturbances that appear to be related to PMS. Guilleminault and Flagg (1984) reported sleep fragmentation (short-lived EEG changes) to result from PMS, and Rosenthal *et al.* (1984) reported that PMS caused both insomnia and excessive daytime sleepiness. These latter investigators hypothesized that patients who react to PMS with either insomnia or excessive sleepiness may be on a continuum, with PMS initially causing prolonged awakenings and insomnia, and later in life producing chronic mild sleep loss associated with excessive daytime sleepiness. Indeed, in their study the patients with PMS and excessive sleepiness were older than those with insomnia.

Smith (1985) has recently proposed that PMS may be related to the Babinski sign, as the patterns of leg and toe movements in these two conditions are similar in appearance, and both occur during NREM sleep in a percentage of persons (a Babinski sign during sleep may occur in as much as 50% of normal persons). He speculated that PMS may be due to a loss of supraspinal inhibitory influences on the pyramidal tract during NREM sleep. Wechsler *et al.* (1986), in an electrophysiological study of patients with PMS, noted abnormal long-latency components in the blink reflexes and extremity reflexes, and also proposed that some disturbance in the central nervous system was producing increased excitability of brainstem and spinal cord reflexes.

Somnambulism (SA), or Sleep-Walking

In contrast with PMS, which occurs during stages 1 and 2, SA occurs during deeper NREM sleep—stages 3 and 4, delta or slow-wave sleep. Like other disorders that occur predominantly in delta sleep, such as nocturnal enuresis and pavor nocturnus (sleep terrors), SA is much more common in childhood and tends to disappear in adolescence, paralleling the decrease in slow-wave sleep that occurs during adolescence.

SA is a combination of waking and sleeping, and early in this century was thought to represent the acting out of dreams. This is now known not to be the case, as SA is almost never associated with REM sleep, in which most dreaming, and certainly most complex dreaming, occurs. Today, some investigators think of SA as being one of a group of disorders of arousal from sleep, where arousal is only partial or fragmented (Broughton, 1968).

Typically, the subject arises during the first several hours of sleep (when there is the greatest delta activity) and sits up quietly with eyes open, expressionless. After standing and beginning to move about in a slow uncoordinated manner, the patient may then start to perform fairly complex acts, such as going to the bathroom, dressing, or making a sandwich. Sometimes very complex activities, such as driving a car, may occur, but this is rare. Although patients may bump and bruise themselves, serious injury is usually not incurred (except in such cases as when a patient has recently moved to new living quarters with, say, a staircase where a bathroom used to be). Occasionally, patients may mumble, and in unusual cases are able to give one- or two-word replies to questions, which helps differentiate SA clinically from psychomotor seizures. The patients usually return to bed quietly, have little or no memory of the episode, and rarely have more than one episode per night.

It appears that there may be important psychological differences between those somnambulists whose nocturnal activities persist into adulthood and those who outgrow them. Kales et al. (1980) noted that, out of 50 adult subjects with a history of SA, the group with persistent SA ($n = 29$) differed from the group that outgrew SA ($n = 21$) by having a later age of onset and higher levels of psychopathology, particularly involving difficulties controlling aggression. In contrast, the group of "past sleepwalkers" was psychologically normal.

It should be mentioned that apart from idiopathic SA, other causes of SA have been reported. For example, febrile illness has been noted to be related to both SA and pavor nocturnus (Kales et al., 1979), and there are reports of SA possibly being caused by drugs such as neuroleptics, methaqualone, and antidepressants (Huapaya, 1979).

SA should be differentiated from dissociative states, complex partial seizures, and the nocturnal wanderings of patients with dementia or mental retardation. There is no generally accepted medical treatment, although arranging the furniture in the home to ensure clear walkways and double-locking the doors when away on trips or vacations is recommended to minimize injuries.

Nocturnal Paroxysmal Dystonia (NPD)

NPD is a very recently described clinical entity that also appears to occur during NREM sleep (Lugaresi et al., 1986). It consists of seizures characterized by dystonic, choreoathetoid, and ballismic movements, usually lasting less than a minute. Most affected patients have between 1 and 20 episodes every night, and the condition usually responds to treatment with carbamazepine. This disorder may last for years, during which time patients may also have episodes during the day or may have occasional epileptic seizures. Lugaresi *et al.* (1986) have also described two patients who had a similar condition, except that the attacks often lasted longer than a half hour and were not affected by treatment with carbamazepine. One of these latter patients went on to develop Huntington's disease.

Jactatio Capitis Nocturna (JCN)

JCN in a way completes the journey through the movement disorders associated with different stages of sleep, as JCN appears (in at least some cases) to be associated with REM sleep. The movements usually involve head-rocking or head-banging, sometimes accompanied by rolling body movements. They may begin at as early as 4 months of age and may last into adolescence or, rarely, into adulthood.

Before the advent of EEG sleep studies, a number of hypotheses were offered to explain the movements, such as their resulting from attempts to increase stimulation (especially erotic self-stimulation) or their being a reaction to maternal neglect or excessive restraint of movement (Levy, 1944; Spitz & Wolf, 1949; Lourie, 1956; Silberstein *et al.*, 1966). There is little or no experimental support for these ideas.

To our knowledge, Regestein *et al.* (1977b) were the first to perform electrophysiological studies on a patient with JCN. In a 25-year-old woman who would bruise herself and lacerate her scalp during sleep, these investigators noted that the head movements were specifically associated with desynchronized, or REM, sleep. This was a striking finding because ordinarily the body musculature (except the extraocular musculature) relaxes dramatically during REM sleep.

Following this study, other reports, which link JCN, not with REM, but with stages 1 and 2 sleep, have appeared (Freidin *et al.*, 1979; Walsh *et al.*, 1981). Recently, however, another report has again described an association of JCN with REM sleep (Gagnon & DeKoninck, 1985). Although the significance of these observations is unclear, it is possible that these investigators are dealing with two different forms of JCN. For instance, the reports of an association of JCN with REM were of adult patients (24 and 25 years old), whereas those of an association with stage-1 and stage-2 sleep were both of children (4 and 8 years old). This is a confusing area requiring further research. No medication has proved to be of consistent or lasting benefit in patients with JCN.

Cataplexy

For a discussion of cataplexy, see Chapter 10.

DISTURBANCE OF SLEEP IN MOVEMENT DISORDERS

There is a deep association between sleep and extrapyramidal disorders, as both hyperkinesias and rigidity tend to disappear with sleep, and many patients with basal-ganglia disorders complain of sleep disturbances.

Of all movement disorders, the sleep of Parkinson's disease has been most extensively studied, with investigations providing insight into both the nature of Parkinson's disease and the nature of sleep. Therefore, we shall first consider the sleep of parkinsonism in some detail, followed by briefer discussions of sleep in other movement disorders.

Parkinson's Disease

A wide variety of sleep abnormalities have been reported in patients with Parkinson's disease. A reduced number of sleep spindles (along with a reduction in stage-2 sleep) has been noted (Ferrari et al., 1964; Puca et al., 1973; Wein et al., 1979), as well as a reduction in REM sleep duration (Traczynska-Kubin et al., 1969; Kendel et al., 1972; Bergonzi et al., 1975; Mouret, 1975; Askenasy, 1981; Askenasy & Yahr, 1985), increased REM latency (Bergonzi et al., 1975), increased sleep latency (Kales et al., 1971; Kendel et al., 1972; Wein et al., 1979; Askenasy, 1981), increased slow-wave or delta sleep (Wein et al., 1979), decreased slow-wave sleep (Miele et al., 1970; Kales et al., 1971; Askenasy, 1981; Myslobodsky et al., 1982), blinking when the lights are turned off (Mouret, 1975), rapid eye movements and blepharospasm during slow-wave sleep (Mouret, 1975), persistent muscle activity during REM sleep (Traczynska-Kubin et al., 1969; Mouret, 1975), and increased fragmentation of sleep (Askenasy, 1981). This is quite a large number of sleep abnormalities for a single disorder. However, when these findings are considered together, certain general observations emerge:

1. The sleep of Parkinson's disease is lighter than normal, with greater time spent in the waking state and stages 1 and 2, less slow-wave and REM sleep, and increased sleep fragmentation.
2. A large number of patients with Parkinson's disease have abnormal movements (blinking, blepharospasm, tremor) or rigidity during NREM sleep (especially stage-2 sleep), and possibly during REM sleep as well.

In addition to these general observations, some investigators have proposed that there may be sleep differences between subtypes of Parkinson's disease. Mouret (1975) reported that patients with Parkinson's disease who have repetitive blinking at the onset of sleep may represent a separate group from those who have mentalis muscle rigidity during sleep, as he found no overlap between the two groups of patients with these signs. Further, he noted that the group with rigidity had significantly less REM sleep and significantly greater stage-1 and stage-2 sleep than did the "blinking" group. He proposed that the "rigid" group may have greater dysfunction of the locus ceruleus than does the "blinking" group. Later, Wein et al. (1979) noted that there were differences between patients with Parkinson's disease who predominantly had tremor, as compared to those largely with akinesia. These investigators reported that tremorous Parkinson's disease was associated with greater stage-2 sleep (and greater sleep-spindle activity) than noted in normal control subjects, whereas the akinetic group with Parkinson's disease was associated with less stage-2 sleep than were normals. As Parkinson's disease is known to involve pathological changes in more than just the substantia nigra, the differences between subgroups of patients with Parkinson's disease may reflect differences in pathology of other structures, such as the locus ceruleus. Interestingly, the two subgroups of Parkinson's disease, as described by Wein et al. (1979) on the basis of sleep studies, are very similar to a recent subdivision scheme proposed by Zetusky et al. (1985) based on a factor analysis of 334 patients with Parkinson's disease. These latter investigators noted two major subgroups of Parkinson's disease. The first was marked by tremor, preserved mental status, better prognosis, earlier age of onset, and family history of Parkinson's disease. The second was marked by bradykinesia, postural instability, and mental deterioration. It is possible that the first subgroup of Zetusky et al. may be similar in nature to the tremorous subgroup of Wein et al., and that the second subgroup of Zetusky et al. may be related to the akinetic subgroup of Wein et al.

The abnormalities of sleep in patients with Parkinson's disease raise the question of the exact role that dopamine (DA) plays in both the sleep disturbance and in sleep in general. The most convincing evidence that DA is involved in the sleep disturbance of Parkinson's disease derives from the reports of significant improvement in the sleep problems of patients with Parkinson's disease after treatment with L-dopa (Kendel et al., 1972; Mouret, 1975; Schneider et al., 1977; Askenasy, 1981; Myslobodsky et al., 1982; Askenasy & Yahr, 1985). Mouret (1975) observed that the most pronounced improvement with L-dopa occurred in the subgroup of patients with Parkinson's disease with reduced REM sleep. Myslobodsky et al. (1982) reported that, in patients with hemiparkinsonism, there was a small but significant reduction in delta-wave power over the "parkinsonian" hemisphere, in comparison with the "nonparkinsonian" hemisphere, and that this relative difference disappeared with L-dopa treatment.

Nevertheless, L-dopa does not appear to completely normalize the sleep of patients with Parkinson's disease (Wyatt et al., 1970), nor does bromocriptine, a direct dopaminergic agonist (Rabey et al., 1978). (Bromocriptine and

L-dopa appear to have similar effects on sleep.) In summary, although dopaminergic dysfunction does appear to be involved in the sleep disturbance of patients with Parkinson's disease, especially in the reduction of both REM and slow-wave sleep, dopaminergic mechanisms alone probably do not account for the entire sleep disturbance. The importance of disturbances in other neurotransmitters, particularly serotonin, in the sleep dysfunction of patients with Parkinson's disease is unclear (Askenasy & Yahr, 1985).

The reports of polysomnographic studies of patients with Shy–Drager syndrome and progressive supranuclear palsy have in general been similar to those of patients with Parkinson's disease. Briskin et al. (1978) noted decreased delta and REM sleep in two patients with Shy–Drager syndrome and Gross et al. (1978) reported a severe reduction of REM sleep and a decrease in spindling in patients with progressive supranuclear palsy.

Huntington's Disease

There have been few sleep studies of patients with Huntington's disease. Sishta et al. (1974) and Schlagenhauff and Sethi (1977) both reported low-amplitude delta waves in patients with Huntington's disease. Askenasy (1981) stated that the sleep findings of patients with Huntington's disease were similar to those of patients with Parkinson's disease. In particular, he noted a reduction of REM sleep in both these conditions. Also, Askenasy observed that choreiform movements continued through sleep, though at much lower intensity. Finally, Hansotia et al. (1985) noted decreased sleep efficiency, decreased delta sleep, increased REM sleep, and increased sleep-onset latency in five patients with moderately severe Huntington's disease, although two patients with mild Huntington's disease had normal sleep. Thus, the severity of sleep disturbance may parallel the severity of the movement disorder in Huntington's disease. Hansotia et al. also noted that medications for Huntington's disease improved the sleep disturbance to some extent.

Dystonia Musculorum Deformans

The most striking sleep abnormality in dystonia musculorum deformans, which has now been reported by two independent research teams, is that of "giant sleep spindles" (Wein & Golubev, 1979; Jankel et al., 1983, 1984). This spindling activity, excessive both in amplitude and duration, is in marked contrast to Parkinson's disease, in which spindling is reduced in most cases. The cause of this interesting finding is completely unknown, although it does lead one to consider the brainstem in a search for the neuropathological focus of dystonia musculorum deformans, about which very little is known.

Tourette's Syndrome

Sleep disturbances are commonly described by patients suffering from Tourette's syndrome, with as many as half of the patients with Tourette's syndrome who have a family history of the disorder reporting sleep continuity disturbances (Nee et al., 1980). The findings of sleep studies have been somewhat inconsistent. Mendelson et al. (1980) compared six patients with Tourette's syndrome, both on and off haloperidol, to nine normal control subjects on a variety of sleep parameters. They noted that there was 30% less delta sleep in the untreated patients with Tourette's syndrome in comparison with patients after treatment with haloperidol and with normal controls. In contrast, Glaze et al. (1983), who studied a group of 12 patients with Tourette's syndrome who had not received medication (group 1) and two patients with Tourette's syndrome who had been treated with haloperidol up to several weeks before their study (group 2), noted that group-1 patients had an *increased* percentage of delta sleep, but decreased REM sleep. Group-2 patients (who had been previously treated with haloperidol and who also were older than the nontreated patients by an average of 20 years) did not show these findings, and may, in fact, have had less delta sleep. Although it is difficult to reconcile the findings of these two studies, the patients studied by Mendelson et al. had been on neuroleptic medications in the past, whereas the group-1 patients in the Glaze et al. study had not. The idea of Glaze et al. that the discrepant findings could perhaps be accounted for by differences in patients' age between the two studies seems unlikely, as in both studies the mean age was 13 years. So, the exact nature of the sleep disturbance in patients with Tourette's syndrome, if indeed there is a consistent disturbance, remains to be elucidated.

An interesting observation in the Glaze et al. study concerns the persistence of tics during sleep. Tics were noted in all stages of sleep in the group-1 patients with Tourette's syndrome, and decreased significantly in the three patients who were treated with tetrabenazine. Also, 7 out of the 12 group-1 patients had paroxysmal episodes occurring in stage-4 sleep that consisted of sudden arousal, disorientation, confusion, and tics, and in general resembled pavor nocturnus. The exact nature and significance of these sudden episodes is unclear, although they may indicate disordered arousal in patients with Tourette's syndrome.

Catatonia

Takahashi and Gjessing (1972) reported the results of sleep studies in three cases of periodic catatonia. They noted increased sleep latency, a reduction in REM, no change or an actual prolongation of REM latency, and no change in delta sleep. The recent report of Linkowski *et al.* (1984) of a 31-year-old catatonic male patient differs from the above study, as these researchers noted reduced REM latency and an increase in REM activity, as well as a reduction in delta sleep, in comparison with a control subject. These latter findings are similar to those reported in depressive illness (Gillin *et al.*, 1984), and, in fact, this patient did have a depressive episode in the past. Although the characteristics of sleep in catatonia need to be more fully worked out, it is possible that sleep studies may offer a way of evaluating for a possible underlying or associated affective disorder.

Tardive Dyskinesia and Rabbit Syndrome

Villeneuve *et al.* (1973) studied the sleep of 21 chronic schizophrenic patients who had developed either tardive dyskinesia, rabbit syndrome, or both. They noted that the movements of tardive dyskinesia disappeared during all of the stages of sleep, but that rabbit syndrome persisted into stage 1. In patients with both tardive dyskinesia and rabbit syndrome, they noted that the rhythmical movements of rabbit syndrome (which they related to parkinsonism) were the last to disappear in the transition from wakefulness to sleep, and the first to reappear during the transition from sleep to wakefulness. These authors proposed that, since there are many transient erratic movements during the sleep of normal persons, rhythmicity of movements during sleep may be a useful guide for determining abnormality. Further studies are required in this area, as most other investigators of hyperkinetic movement disorders have reported persistence of the movements (in some form) during sleep.

GENERAL THOUGHTS ABOUT SLEEP AND MOVEMENT

In closing this review of sleep and movement disorders, we would like to offer a few general observations.

First, it appears that we must reevaluate the traditional clinical wisdom that states that most movement disorders disappear during sleep. It seems that not only do some forms of myoclonus and hemiballismus persist into sleep, but many other movement disorders do so as well, including tremors, tics, choreoathetoid movements, and even rigidity. It is clear that these movements are changed and usually reduced with sleep, but often do not disappear. Therefore, the connections between sleep and movement probably do not involve simple either/or mechanisms, but rather a much more complex process.

Second, the well-accepted association between the mechanisms of sleep and the brainstem (especially the locus ceruleus and the raphe nuclei) may provide clues to understanding the pathophysiological basis of certain movement disorders. We have already mentioned, for instance, the finding of giant sleep spindles in dystonia musculorum deformans. Also, the role of serotonin in movement disorders is poorly understood at this time, and sleep studies may be of help in this area. On the other hand, the disturbance of sleep in so many extrapyramidal disorders may indicate that the basal ganglia are important in sleep phenomena.

Finally, it is worth considering the nature of the different stages of sleep and the implications of these for various movement disorders. For example, it has recently been proposed that REM sleep represents a state of brain activation that is close to wakefulness and that is necessary for recovery from the deep hypnosis of sleep (Vertes, 1984). Here, then, is a state of brain activation without movement, yet we know that in some cases movements may occur during REM sleep, such as JCN and tics. Some investigators have speculated that the brainstem site governing the atonia of REM sleep is an area in the dorsolateral portion of the nucleus pontis oralis that lies adjacent to the locus ceruleus (see Vertes, 1984). If so, one may wonder what the significance of this site is for atonic and hypomotoric disorders (such as Parkinson's disease or cataplexy), or how experimental manipulation of this site might benefit hyperkinetic movement disorders.

All of these thoughts are highly speculative, but nevertheless serve to indicate the enormous heuristic potential of sleep studies in movement disorders.

CHAPTER TWENTY-FIVE

Handedness

WITH MELODIE A. LOHR

INTRODUCTION

Man possesses no instruments more versatile and powerful than his hands, for with them the face of the world has been changed. Yet all hands are not created equal, not even on a single individual, because one is usually alotted more skill and is used in preference to the other, and this phenomenon has been called "handedness."

In this chapter we shall describe the importance of the determination of handedness in neuropsychiatric disorders. As a manifestation of hemispheric differences in fine motor control, handedness may illuminate disorders in which hemispheric laterality is thought to be important. First, however, a brief account of the origin of handedness, along with a discussion of the measurement of handedness, will be presented.

THE ORIGIN OF HANDEDNESS

Some understanding of handedness in neuropsychiatric disorders may be gained by first considering the phenomenon of handedness from an evolutionary viewpoint.

"Handedness" refers to the preference and superior ability of one hand over the other in the execution of skilled motor tasks. This preference probably arose very early in man's development, and numerous evolutionary steps were required before its appearance—in particular, the development of hemispheric laterality. Table 25-1 offers a brief outline of the evolution of central-nervous-system laterality and hand preference.

In the evolution of handedness, as is evident from Table 25-1, there are two important and still unanswered questions which are of great significance

Table 25-1. Major Steps in the Evolution of Laterality and Handedness

Millions of years ago	Developments
> 500	Invertebrates develop bilateral symmetry (the nervous system may actually have been one of the earliest portions of invertebrates to develop bisymmetry).
> 500	Worms develop brains (which occurs in association with the general cephalization of sensory tissues taking place in forward-moving animals).
500	More advanced invertebrates develop crossed control (one side of the brain controls the opposite side of the body).
480	Earliest vertebrates appear (these also possess bilateral brain tissue, but it is not known whether this is homologous or analogous with the invertebrate-brain bisymmetry).
450	? Some arthropods develop significant nervous-system asymmetry.
300	Reptiles develop rudimentary cerebral cortex.
150	Primitive mammals (marsupials) develop rudimentary connections between the two cerebral hemispheres (to become the anterior commissure and corpus callosum in higher mammals).
100	? Some birds develop left-hemisphere dominance for song.
100	? Marsupials develop lateralized paw preference, equally divided between right and left (Megirian *et al.*, 1977).
70	? Rodents develop bilateral neurochemical asymmetry of the brain (Glick *et al.*, 1977), possibly related to lateral preference and greater learning ability.
50	Primates develop hand preferences, again approximately equally divided between left and right, with a large number showing no consistent preference. Also, there is evidence of lateralization of emotional systems in the brain (Doty *et al.*, 1973).
20	First manlike apes appear.
< 1	Early man develops language and consistent handedness, and becomes predominantly right-handed.

in any discussion of neuropsychiatric disorders. These are: (1) Why did handedness develop? and (2) Why is most of mankind right-handed? In the next sections we shall address these two questions.

Why Did Handedness Develop?

In attempting to answer this question, it may be helpful to address first the question of where in phylogeny hand preference arose.

In the course of the evolutionary development of animals, asymmetry in the nervous system appears to have arisen more than once—for example, in invertebrates, and then again in vertebrates. Another example is the development of left-brain control for song in canaries (Nottebohm, 1977) and the development of left-brain control for language in man. Although it is possible that these similar developments are merely analogous (Levy, 1977), they may reflect a common way in which organisms can deal with problems of integration and control (Dimond, 1977). Whatever the reason, bilateral nervous-system asymmetry, as is evident from Table 25-1, appears to have offered strong selective advantages for species along the entire phylogenetic spectrum.

Brain asymmetry and handedness, though related, are not the same, and in a search for the origins of true handedness it is best to look at the animals that possess structures that are nearest in kind to the hands of man: the primitive hands of primates.

Most studies on the distribution of handedness in monkeys report that at least 40% of the monkeys studied show no consistent hand preference, with the remainder being approximately equally divided between dextrals and sinistrals, with possibly a slight excess of sinistrals (Napier, 1980). There is also evidence that hand preference in monkeys is labile and highly sensitive to environmental conditions (Warren, 1977). Furthermore, there are indications that the preference of one hand over the other and the development of the corresponding cortical control occur together (Trevarthen, 1978), making hand preference in monkeys more an expression of learning and experience than an independent evolutionary development. In sum, if true handedness does exist in monkeys, it is certainly less fixed and more rudimentary than in humans, and is largely shaped by experience (Deuel & Dunlop, 1980).

The evidence for true handedness in very early man is not much more conclusive. A variety of studies analyzing Stone-Age tools and cave drawings have yielded equivocal results (Napier, 1980; Harris, 1980). Most of these studies indicate that, as in monkeys, a large percentage (perhaps the majority) of early men possessed ambiguous handedness, although there are hints of a possible right-hand preference in the remainder.

By the Bronze Age, however, it is much clearer that true handedness existed (Wile, 1934). For example, in a recent historical survey of art works depicting hand preferences, approximately 90% of the 12,000 works investigated (from 15,000 B.C. to the present time) depicted right-hand preference, and this percentage was stable over time and geographical area (Coren & Porac, 1977).

The bulk of the studies intimate that handedness developed slowly, possibly originating in the more advanced primates, and fully appearing in man during the Ice Age. The reasons for its development, however, remain uncertain. It has been suggested that the development of the *precision grip* (in which full opposability of the thumb is necessary in order to grasp objects precisely between the thumb and forefingers) was an important step, because the manipulative ability of primitive primate hands is so poor compared to man's that any manifestation of hand preference would have been largely irrelevant to survival (Napier, 1980). This does not explain the reason why handedness appeared, however.

The most reasonable hypothesis to us is that handedness and hemispheric specialization for language are intimately related. It has been proposed that linear/sequential information processing might, in a sense, "displace" spatial processing (Dimond, 1977), implying that the coexistence of the two different types of thinking in one hemisphere is less efficient than their separation (Whitaker & Ojemann, 1977). Because both language and sequential fine hand movements may depend on the same basic type of information-processing, as both of these phenomena grew in complexity their cortical control eventually settled together in one hemisphere. Handedness would thus have arisen in conjunction with the specialization of one side of the brain for language, which would account for the fact that more than 90% (and possibly close to 100%) of dextrals are left-hemisphere dominant for language, and more than 70% of sinistrals are right-hemisphere dominant. All of this is highly speculative, of course, but may be of some interest when we later address neuropsychiatric disorders, particularly in connection with the notions of "pathological left-handedness" and "cross-dominance."

Why Is Most of Mankind Right-Handed?

Estimates vary considerably, but probably somewhere between 70 and 95% of the people in the world are right-handed, and for unknown reasons. Many different hypotheses have been offered, but basically they all fall into one of two categories: (1) biological–genetic, and (2) cultural–environmental.

Biological–Genetic Hypotheses

The earlier biological hypotheses were based on the obvious asymmetries of the human viscera. It was proposed, for example, that the chest bulged on the right (the right lung being larger than the left) and the liver made the right side of the body heavier, so there was a shift of "the position of the centre of gravity of the body obliquely backward and to the right," thus leaving the right arm freer for motion (Buchanan, 1862, p. 153). Similar theories were based on other internal differences, such as the asymmetrical position of the heart and parts of the circulatory system (Harris, 1980).

Studies on the relationship of asymmetrical body structures and handedness are still being published, although there has been a shift in focus from the visceral organs to the brain. A recent review of the relationship of neuroanatomical asymmetries and handedness concludes:

Eight different large sets of data indicated that hand preference was correlated (sinistrals showed less or reversed asymmetry compared to dextrals) with right-left asymmetry in the parietal operculum, prefrontal region, occipital regions, venous drainage pattern, and blood volume supply. The neuroanatomical patterns associated with right- and left-hand preference are not diametrically opposed, which is consistent with the notion that dextrality and sinistrality form a dimension. . . . (Witelson, 1980, pp. 108–109)

In addition, because neonates show similar neuroanatomical asymmetry, Witelson postulates that the nervous-system asymmetry may be a substrate of handedness.

Other investigators, in keeping with this idea, have shown possible early evidence of right-dominance in infants, with infants being observed to turn their heads preferentially to the right side when lying down, which is thought to be related to the later development of handedness (Turkevich, 1977; Liederman & Coryell, 1981; Michel, 1981).

There have been several genetic hypotheses for right-hand predominance, but the most promising is that of Annett (1978), who postulates that in man there is a genetically controlled bias toward right-handedness only, with no corresponding genes governing sinistrality. Thus, without the "right-shift" genetic factor, an individual's handedness would be randomly developed according to environmental pressures, with potentially an equal chance for a person to become left- or right-handed.[1] This is supported by the finding that right-handers tend to be right-footed, whereas left-handers may be either right- or left-footed (Peters & Durding, 1978). Also, Annett believes that left-handedness occurs in two forms: that which results from an inherited deficiency in the "right-shift" factor, and that which develops as the result of perinatal difficulty or birth trauma (so-called "pathological left-handedness") (Annett, 1978).

Cultural–Environmental Hypotheses

The belief that culture is important in the determination of right-dominance has a long history. Plato, for example, held that ambidexterity is the natural order of things, and felt that the Athenians were to be blamed for training individuals to use one hand predominantly, especially in fighting (Jowett, 1953, p. 361).

Some proponents of the cultural hypothesis have proposed that it was the centralization of tool-making by artisans in the Bronze Age that coaxed men into becoming unimanual on the same side, so that everyone could use

---

[1]This is similar to the proposed reason for the approximately 50% incidence of *situs inversus* in Kartagener's syndrome, which is characterized by a defect in ciliary motility. Here, it is thought that visceral ciliary beating in early fetal development causes the normal left–right orientation of the visceral organs, and, when this is missing, the left–right orientation is random. We do not know whether this is related to handedness in these individuals.

the same tools (Wile, 1934). Others have claimed that right-preference was a consequence of combat, so that when the left hand held the shield to protect the heart and aorta, the right hand was free to wield the weapon, and those individuals who fought the other way around were less likely to survive (Harris, 1980).

Still others have pointed to the fact that most mothers carry their babies on the left, closer to the heart, leaving the right hand free to perform more complex tasks (Huheey, 1977), although it seems that this might actually cause a greater restriction of the freedom of right-sided movement in the infant.

The studies of infants do not uniformly show a greater predisposition to right-handedness. For example, in Watson's (1924) study of handedness in infants between 4 months and 1 year of age, no consistency in hand usage (in reaching for candy) was demonstrated. Watson therefore proposed that dextrality is purely environmentally determined. Also, in the study of Turkevich cited earlier it was found that the preferred direction of infant head-turning could easily be influenced by holding the head in the midline prior to testing.

Further evidence supporting the influence of culture on handedness may be found in Levy's (1976) report of the increase in left-handed writers from 2% in 1932 to 11% in the 1970s, possibly reflective of a greater social acceptance of sinistrality over the years.

Which is more important, biological or environmental factors, in accounting for right-predominance in man? The answer is not known, but probably both have contributed. The available evidence suggests that there is an innate tendency toward dextrality in man, which is further amplified by cultural and other environmental pressures in the same direction. And as for why the right side is the predominant one, perhaps some morphological asymmetry in man was just sufficient to tip the balance in the dextral direction (see Geschwind & Galaburda, 1985).

If this is so, then left-hand preference would exist in those with little genetic predisposition and little environmental pressure to become right-handed. But, it also might exist in those who would have been right-handed had early cerebral insult not caused a shift toward sinistrality; this will be an important consideration in our discussion later on. The basis of other important associations of handedness are discussed in the last section of this chapter.

THE MEASUREMENT OF HANDEDNESS

Left-handed individuals have suffered abuse and derision throughout history. Words such as "sinister" and "gauche" are associated with the left side, and even the word "left" originally meant weak or worthless. Left-handers have been associated with bad luck and the devil, and have been called names such as "cow-pawed" and "cack-handed," the word "cack" meaning "excrement." Indeed the idea of the left hand as "unclean" is a common one in many countries, the left hand being the one used for excretory functions, whereas the right is used for eating. In India, for example, it is extremely impolite even to place the left hand on the dining area.

The reasons for this disparagement of sinistrals are unknown. Perhaps it was their unusualness or their small numbers, or perhaps it was their inability to use certain right-handed implements. An interesting possibility, which relates to the final section of this chapter, is that it was observed that there were a significant number of retarded, epileptic, or otherwise mentally compromised individuals who were sinistral. Whatever the reason, the old biases are only now beginning to disappear, with the relatively recent advent of such items as left-handed scissors and golf clubs.

The unfortunate status of left-handers has, nevertheless, caused considerable problems in estimating their number. It has been reported that anywhere from 1% to 30% of the population is left-handed (Wile, 1934), and over this century it appears that the average percentage has risen from 4% or 5% to between 8% and 11%.

Estimates continue to vary, however, and this may be due in large part not only to the greater social acceptance of sinistrality, but also to (1) differences between the various methods employed to assess handedness, (2) the inconsistent inclusion of mixed-handed persons, and (3) whether or not certain complicating factors, such as eyedness, footedness, and age are taken into account.

Assessment Methods

The most commonly used method to assess handedness is by questionnaire, and the two most popular questionnaires in use today are the Annett Hand Preference Questionnaire (AHPQ) (Annett, 1970), and the Edinburgh Handedness Inventory (EHI) (Oldfield, 1971). Both of these require responses to a relatively simple set of questions regarding the preferred hand employed to perform certain common tasks, such as writing and throwing. There are some problems with questionnaires, however, relating to difficulties in understanding some of the questions (McMeekan & Lishman, 1975) and to poor factor stability of some of the items, such as those relating to using a broom or opening a box (McFarland & Anderson, 1980).

Another major assessment technique involves measuring manual performance on a variety of simple tasks, such as placing dots rapidly in a series of circles, tapping fingers, or squeezing a dynamometer. It appears that in the use of performance techniques, the critical component related to handedness is the precision required to accomplish the task. For example, dotting the centers of circles that have a diameter of 2 millimeters results in fewer individuals' being labeled left-handed than when 9-millimeter circles are used (Steingrueber, 1975).

The last and least common means of assessing handedness makes use of certain physical measurements. For example, the base of the thumbnail is, in general, larger on the dominant hand (Block, 1974; Pittsley & Shearn, 1975), which is perhaps related to the fact that the nails on the dominant hand usually grow faster than those on the nondominant one (Napier, 1980). Also, certain asymmetries of the brain and skull appear to be related to handedness, with a forward protrusion of the right frontal bone (corresponding to a larger right frontal lobe) and a backward protrusion of the left occipital bone (corresponding to a larger left occipital lobe) being characteristic of right-handers, and the reverse being true, although less markedly, in left-handers (LeMay, 1977). These physical measures appear to be only imperfectly related to handedness, however, and thus are of limited clinical value.[2]

Mixed-Handers

Persons with mixed-handedness (or ambidexterity) present a problem in assessment. Many studies on the distribution of handedness in various disorders have merely excluded such persons from consideration, and other studies have thrown them in with the left-handers and called the group "non-right-handers." Some studies have assigned them to a category all their own, regardless of whether some mixed-handers were more right-handed than left-handed, or whether some of them were truly ambidextrous, being able to use both hands with equal facility.

Other Complicating Factors

To confound matters further, some studies also measured footedness and eyedness in combination with handedness, and considered these three characteristics together, whereas there is some evidence to indicate that the three (and especially handedness and eyedness) are only incompletely related (Clyma, 1972; Coren & Porac, 1980).

Also, the age of a patient should be taken into account, for there is evidence that, in children, consistency in hand usage increases with age

---

[2]Another assessment technique that has been claimed to be related both to handedness (Demarest & Demarest, 1980) and to schizophrenic vulnerability (Blau, 1977) is the measurement of *torque*, in which the patient draws circles around three *X*'s with each hand, and torque is deemed present if any of the circles is drawn in a clockwise direction. Further research is needed to show the usefulness of this technique, however.

(Bruml, 1972), and that in adults increasing age is associated with a shift toward dextrality (Fleminger *et al.*, 1977).

In general it can be seen that the assessment of handedness is no easy undertaking. Our personal preference involves a combination of questionnaire and performance measures, with the questionnaire including an assemblage of items from the EHI and the AHPQ for the assessment of preferred hand usage in writing, drawing, throwing, using a spoon, using a toothbrush, and striking a match (these items being selected on the basis of the studies of McMeekan & Lishman, 1975; Bryden, 1977; and McFarland & Anderson, 1980). As for performance tests, we prefer a sample of writing from each hand, along with a measure of the time it takes to dot the center of a series of 2-millimeter circles with each hand when the task is performed as quickly as is possible (Steingrueber, 1975). Measures of eyedness and footedness should not be included directly in the handedness assessment. Finally, we believe that it is better to plot the handedness of individuals on a spectrum from pure sinistral to pure dextral than to polarize a population (Palmer, 1974).

HANDEDNESS AND NEUROPSYCHIATRIC DISORDERS

Before embarking on a discussion of disturbances in the manifestation and distribution of handedness among various neuropsychiatric disorders, we shall briefly discuss some interesting hypotheses concerning the significance of disturbed lateral motor dominance. In particular, the following will be considered: (1) pathological left-handedness; (2) cross-dominance; and (3) unequal lateral predisposition to disease.

Pathological Left-Handedness

The theory of pathological left-handedness holds that early insult to the left side of the brain in individuals originally destined to be dextrals results in a transfer of motor dominance to the right hemisphere, leading to sinistrality (Satz, 1972, 1973; Orsini & Satz, 1986). There is some empirical support for this idea: for example, children with a history of perinatal complications have been shown to lack the rightward head-turning bias reported earlier (Liederman & Coryell, 1982), and mentally retarded individuals with abnormal EEGs have been found to have approximately twice the incidence of left-handedness as those with normal EEGs (Silva & Satz, 1979).

Now, it may be claimed that pathological right-handers should also exist, which could very well be true, except that these people would be difficult to identify, considering the large percentage of right-handers in the general population. If one assumes that brain damage is randomly distributed across the two hemispheres, then the absolute number of pathological left- and right-handers would be the same. They would, however, constitute a larger percentage of the group of left-handers. This theory has been invoked (together with the idea that over the centuries it may have been noticed that many more cognitively impaired people are left-handed than would be expected), to help in understanding the historical disparagement of sinistrals.

Some investigators, such as Bakan (1975), have claimed that all left-handedness may be pathological, implying that all people are naturally predisposed to become dextral. There is an abundance of evidence against this idea, however (Leiber & Axelrod, 1981), and today it appears that nonpathological causes account for most sinistrality.

Several predictions naturally follow if pathological left-handedness really exists. The first is that, since the left hemisphere is dominant in most people not only for motor control but also for language, there should be a greater incidence of left-handedness in populations with some language disorders. Second, it is possible that pathological processes with diffuse, but sometimes asymmetrical, cerebral involvement could potentially decrease the consistency of handedness in persons with those diseases, resulting in more mixed-handers (which is a reason for considering handedness on a spectrum). Third, pathological processes involving the brain might not change the final distribution of handedness, but might retard its full development, so that patients with certain illnesses would develop hand preference much later than do their peers.

In support of these three conjectures are indications, to be considered in more detail later, of increased sinistrality and mixed dominance or delayed dominance in a variety of conditions, including autism, dyslexia, and stuttering.

Cross-Dominance

It has been proposed that man not only possesses handedness, but also eyedness, earedness, facedness (for expressions), and footedness (Subirana, 1969; Ladavas, 1982). If an individual appears to be dominant on one side for hands, but dominant on the other side for any of the others, then that individual is said to possess *cross-dominance*.

Usually, "cross-dominance" refers to hand and eye or, less commonly, hand and foot. However there have been some interesting studies on a different kind of cross-dominance involving what it called the "thumb-to-finger-opposition index." Here, a person touches the thumb-pad and finger-pad (usually, little finger) of one hand together, and the examiner looks end-on at the angle made between lines drawn through the nailbeds (Metzig *et al.*, 1975). If the thumb–finger nailbeds are closer to being parallel on one hand than the other, then the former hand is thumb-to-finger-opposition-dominant. It is not clear what this means in evolutionary or developmental terms, but perhaps it is a mark of greater dexterity to be able to bring the thumb and finger in contact with the largest amount of surface area between them. This could certainly be related to greater opposability of the thumb and to the precision grip. In any case, here a cross-dominant person is hand-dominant on one side and thumb-to-finger-opposition-dominant on the other.

The origin of any of the forms of cross-dominance is not clear, but perhaps is related to pathological left-handedness, in the sense that putative brain damage may cause only some dominant functions to jump hemispheres, and not others (Taylor & Heilman, 1980). Cross-dominance could therefore be potentially of more significance in indicating previous brain damage than mere sinistrality alone.

The notion of cross-dominance is also of interest when considering the relationship of handedness and hemispheric dominance for language. There are conflicting reports, but basically it appears that there is a strong, though not indissoluble, connection between these two phenomena (Taylor & Heilman, 1980; Eling, 1983). Cross-dominance of language and handedness might therefore be associated with the other forms of cross-dominance mentioned here. In keeping with this, crossed hand–eye dominance has been related to poorer verbal learning skills (Swiercinsky, 1977).

Unequal Lateral Predisposition to Disease

This idea has been proposed at various times in various conditions, although it has not previously been called by this name. In a way, this hypothesis is the opposite of the previous two, for instead of pathological cerebral processes leading to disturbances in handedness, unilateral motor dominance itself predisposes to the asymmetrical development or manifestation of disease. There are two possible ways this could occur. One is that the asymmetrical halves of the nervous system, either functionally or anatomically, in some way are differentially attacked by, or differentially responsive to, certain pathogenic processes. A second possibility is that the use of one side of the body more than the other predisposes to asymmetrical manifestation of some illnesses. There is some support for this idea—for example, in the asymmetrical manifestation of poliomyelitis—but it must be kept in mind that motor symptomatology may be perceived by the patient as being more severe on the dominant side even when, by objective measurement, the two sides are equally affected, as in Parkinson's disease.

Developmental Disorders

The most pervasive of all the developmental disorders is infantile autism, and in 1977 Colby and Parkison reported an increased frequency of non-right-handedness (65%) in autistic children, compared to normal children (12%).

Their assessment method was based on the performance of 14 tasks, which were then weighted according to differing importance (writing and drawing being weighted more than throwing, for example). Some later studies confirmed these findings (Tsai & Stewart, 1982; Tsai, 1982, 1983), but others did not (Boucher, 1977; Barry & James, 1978). The latter studies indicated instead a developmental lag in the manifestation of consistent handedness, rather than an increase in nondextrality.

At this time it is not clear whether there truly is a sinistral shift in autistic children, but there are some indications that autistic children with a clearly established hand preference by age 5 tend to function better in a variety of developmental areas, and that this may be of some prognostic importance (Tsai, 1983).

There is also a higher frequency of mixed- and left-handedness in less severe developmental disorders, such as *dyslexia* (Hecaen & DeAjuriaguerra, 1964; Geschwind & Behan, 1982). Another study (Zurif & Carson, 1970) did not find a difference between dyslexics and normal readers in the distribution of handedness, but did report that the dyslexics were clumsier in general and showed evidence of less complete hemispheric specialization for language. *Stuttering* and *stammering* have also been reported to be associated with a high frequency of nondextrality, with many studies showing almost twice the normal frequency of mixed- and left-handedness.

Finally, mental retardation has been reported to be associated with a significant excess of sinistrality, again with many studies reporting approximately twice the normal frequency of left-handedness (Hecaen & DeAjuriaguerra, 1964). It is, however, important to note that this does not imply that left-handers are in any way cognitively impaired compared to right-handers, an idea for which there is very poor evidence (Newcombe *et al.*, 1975; Bishop, 1980).

Focal Brain Damage

It is now widely accepted that almost all right-handers are left-hemisphere dominant for language, which results in a certain amount of predictability regarding the disturbances of higher cortical functions that occur when one hemisphere of a dextral is damaged. Thus, left-hemisphere damage leads primarily to aphasia, alexia, agraphia, color and finger agnosia, right–left confusion, and ideomotor apraxia. In contrast, right-hemisphere insult usually results in unilateral neglect and somatognosia, aprosodia, anosognosia, prosopagnosia, dressing apraxia, and topographical disorientation. In a sense, this is probably an oversimplification, because hemispheric specialization does not develop all at once but, rather, gradually over the years. In fact, there is evidence to suggest that hemispheric lateralization is a growth process that occurs over the entire life span (Brown & Grober, 1983), with the result that similar types of brain damage at different ages may cause different dysfunctions. For example, Brown and Jaffe (1975) concluded that "a lesion in Wernicke's area will produce motor aphasia in a child, conduction aphasia in middle age, and jargon aphasia in late life" (see Brown & Grober, 1983, p. 431).

Predicting consequences of focal damage is difficult in dextrals, and is even more complex in left-handers. It has been proposed that in some sinistals language and, presumably, other functions are more bilaterally represented, which is thought to account for the fact that unilateral hemisphere damage results in aphasia in a greater proportion of left- than right-handers (Carter et al., 1980).[3] The aphasia, apraxia, and agnosia of sinistrals do not appear, however, to be as severe or as long-lasting as those of dextrals. The reader is referred to Hecaen and DeAjuriaguerra (1964), who summarize some of the observed differences between left- and right-handers regarding the impact of focal brain damage on higher cortical functions.

Schizophrenia

It did not take long for the implications of the studies of Sperry and coworkers on split-brain individuals to reach the field of schizophrenia research. For years, schizophrenia had been thought to be related to a "splitting" of psychic functions (Bleuler, 1911/1950), and the idea that the two halves of the brain might function as individual entities offered a possible explanation for some of the schizophrenic psychopathology. The idea of laterality difficulties in both schizophrenia and affective disorders has become a promising one for research, and is extensively reviewed by Flor-Henry (1983).

As a consequence of the interest in anomolous or disturbed lateralization of functions in schizophrenia, many studies on handedness have been performed, almost all of them within the last 10 to 15 years. These are summarized in Table 25-2. If one divides the schizophrenic populations studied into dextral and nondextral groups (which can be done for all the studies except Dvirskii, 1976, and Nasrallah et al., 1982a) and adds them up separately, one finds that there are 1,209 dextral schizophrenics (73%), compared to 451 nondextrals (27%). A similar calculation done for the normal controls reported in the studies reveals 1,564 (71%) dextrals and 643 (29%) nondextrals. Thus, if most of the studies are taken together (ignoring differences in assessment techniques and patient populations), there appears to be a slightly higher incidence of right-handedness among schizophrenics than among controls. The very large range of reported distributions precludes any definite conclusions at this time, however, and in fact invites the question: Why is there such a large discrepancy in the reported results?

---

[3]However, it has been postulated that a greater susceptibility to aphasia in sinistrals could potentially account for these findings (Hammond & Kaplan, 1982).

Perhaps the answer to this question lies in the possibility that different types and mixtures of schizophrenia were studied, and each of the types has a different distribution of handedness. Support for this idea comes from the studies of Boklage (1977) and Luchins *et al.* (1980) on schizophrenic twins, and the study of Luchins *et al.* (1979), which was done on a general schizophrenic population. These report left-handedness to be associated with a milder form of schizophrenia. Along similar lines is the study of McCreadie *et al.* (1982), which shows greater mixed dominance and left-handedness in schizophrenics who did not fulfill Feighner criteria (and thus possibly suffered milder disease), and the study of Nasrallah *et al.* (1982a), which shows greater left-handedness in paranoid schizophrenics as opposed to nonparanoid schizophrenics (paranoid schizophrenia typically occurs later in life and is less incapacitating than other forms). Taken together, these studies imply that left-handedness may in some way be a marker for a milder form of schizophrenia.

Affective Disorders

There have been fewer studies on handedness in affective disorders than on handedness in schizophrenia. These are summarized in Table 25-3. An analysis similar to that done on the schizophrenic studies reveals that 247 (70%) of the affectively disordered patients were reported to be fully dextral, compared to 1,022 (65%) of the controls cited in these studies. None of these studies individually reported a significant difference between the patients and the controls in the distribution of handedness. Of interest, though, is the study of (Metzig *et al.* (1976) showing a significant difference in the percentage of hand/thumb-to-finger cross-dominance between unipolar and bipolar affective disorder patients, with a significantly larger percentage of cross-dominance found in unipolar depressives. These authors believe that this supports the idea of a true difference between these two types of affective disorders.

Basal-Ganglia Disorders

Although there is little evidence for a difference in the distribution of handedness in either Parkinson's disease or postencephalitic parkinsonism, a study of the side of onset of parkinsonian symptoms revealed an approximately equal distribution over the dominant and nondominant side in Parkinson's disease, whereas patients with postencephalitic parkinsonism appeared to develop symptoms much more frequently on the dominant side (Reynolds & Locke, 1971). A later study, however, reported that patients with Parkinson's disease also reported symptoms that began more frequently on their dominant side (Klawans, 1972). On further investigation, however, Klawans found that most of these results could be explained by the fact that parkinsonian patients

Table 25-2. Handedness in Schizophrenia

Study	n	Assessment method	Hand preference (%)		
			R	Mixed	L
Bolin (1953)	143 (schizophrenia)	Performance	94	1	5
	76 (epilepsy)		83	3	14
	76 (oligophrenia)		92	4	4
Walker and Birch (1970)	80 (schizophrenia) (aged 8–11)	Performance	32	55	12
Oddy and Lobstein (1972)	140 (schizophrenia)	Questionnaire	90	9	1
	497 (normal)		80	17	3
Metzig et al. (1975)	13 (schizophrenia)	Questionnaire	100	—	0
	27 (bipolar)		93	—	7
	17 (central-nervous-system disease)		88	—	12
	61 (normal)		89	—	11
Wahl (1976)	26 (schizophrenia)	Questionnaire	77	15	8
	21 (nonschizophrenia)		76	10	14
	18 (normal)		94	0	6
Dvirskii (1976)	1,270 (schizophrenia)	Questionnaire	—	—	6 (men)
			—	—	9 (women)
	4,330 (normal)		—	—	5 (normal men)
			—	—	3 (normal women)
Gur (1977)	200 (schizophrenia)	Questionnaire	84	—	16
	200 (normal)		94	—	6
Fleminger et al. (1977)	102 (schizophrenia)	AHPQ	68	22	10
	800 (normal)		49	42	9
Luchins et al. (1979)	66 (schizophrenia and schizoaffective)	Performance	83	17 (nondextral)	

Study	Sample	Method	Group			
Taylor et al. (1980, 1982)	232 (schizophrenia): 141 with formal thought disorder (+FTD), 91 without (−FTD)	AHPQ	Total +FTD −FTD	64 61 68	30 33 25	6 6 7
Chaugule and Master (1981)	93 (schizophrenia) 150 (normal)	AHPQ		32 50	68 50 (nondextral)	
Wyatt et al. (1981)	79 (schizophrenia)	Performance		84	16 (nondextral)	
Nasrallah et al. (1981b)	84 (schizophrenia)	Performance		43	40	17
McCreadie et al. (1982)	116 (schizophrenia): 85 who met Feighner criteria (F+), 31 who did not (F−)	AHPQ	Total F+ F−	73 78 61	23 19 32	4 3 7
Nasrallah et al. (1982a)	80 (schizophrenia): 27 paranoid (P+), 53 nonparanoid (P−), 83 (normal)	Performance	P+ P−	67 89 (nonsinistral) 94 (nonsinistral)		33 11 6
Merrin (1984)	52 (schizophrenia): 25 paranoid (P+), 27 nonparanoid (P−), 40 (affective), 49 (normal)	Performance and questionnaire	Total P+ P−	83 84 82 85 78	10 8 11 12 20	8 8 7 3 2
Shan-Ming et al. (1985)	225 (schizophrenia) 56 (bipolar) 432 (normal)	Performance		80 96 93	20 7 7 (nondextral)	

Table 25-3. Handedness in Affective Disorders

Study	n	Assessment method	Hand preference (%) R	Mixed	L
Metzig *et al.* (1975) (see Table 25-2)	27 (bipolar)	Questionnaire	93	—	7
Metzig *et al.* (1976)	27 (bipolar)	Questionnaire	93	—	7
	27 (unipolar)		96	—	4
	17 (central-nervous-system disease)		88	—	12
	61 (normal)		89	—	11
Fleminger *et al.* (1977) (see Table 25-2)	120 (affective psychosis)	AHPQ	62	34	4
	800 (normal		49	42	9
Chaugule and Master (1981) (see Table 25-2)	23 (affective psychosis)	AHPQ	40	60	
	150 (normal)		50	50 (nondextral)	
Nasrallah and McCalley-Whitters (1982)	88 (bipolar)	Performance	58	34	8
	86 (normal)		71	22	7
Merrin (1984) (see Table 25-2)	40 (21 bipolar, 12 unipolar)	Performance	85	12	3
	49 (normal)		78	20	2
Shan-Ming *et al.* (1985) (see Table 25-2)	56 (bipolar)	Performance	96	4	
	432 (normal)		93	7 (nondextral)	

report dominant-sided symptoms first because they are the most bothersome, even when the onset of the disease is symmetrical. Thus, there is no good evidence to suggest an association between side of onset of Parkinson's disease or postencephalitic parkinsonism and the dominant side.

Metzig and coworkers have applied their techniques for assessing thumb-to-finger cross-dominance to populations of patients with Parkinson's disease and with Huntington's disease. They found an increased incidence of cross-dominance in both of these conditions, with 90% of patients with Parkinson's disease and 100% of patients with Huntington's disease manifesting cross-dominance, compared to 50% of controls. Further, they found that only 12% of the unaffected siblings of the patients with Huntington's disease were cross-dominant (Ast *et al.*, 1976; Rosenberg *et al.*, 1977).

Other Disorders

Epilepsy has been reported to be associated with an excess of sinistrality, most studies reporting approximately twice the normal percentage of left-handers in epileptic populations (Bolin, 1953; Hecaen & DeAjuriaguerra, 1964).

A recent study of *spina bifida* involving 203 children, ages four to nine, revealed a significant increase in left- and mixed-handedness when the patients were compared with 200 age-matched controls (Lonton, 1976). The author suggested that handedness may not only be "determined by cortical factors but may also be influenced by asymmetrical motor or sensory dysfunction due to lesion of the thoracic cord."

Poliomyelitis has been claimed to be more severe on the dominant side, which finding has been related to a predisposing influence of physical exertion on the spinal site for viral incubation (Russel, 1956, referenced in Reynolds and Locke, 1971). Also, Trembly (1968) reported, in a study of 98 patients with poliomyelitis, that those who were hand/eye cross-dominant were more frequently paralyzed.

Two other disorders in which the increased use of the dominant side has been thought to relate to more severe involvement of that side are *carpal tunnel syndrome* (Reinstein, 1981) and the occurrence of *scoliosis* in Duchenne muscular dystrophy (Johnson & Yarnell, 1976).

Most of the reports of the distribution of right- and left-sided *torticollis* have indicated that patients suffering from the leftward-turning form outnumber patients with rightward-turning form almost 2 to 1 (Stejskal & Tomanek, 1981). A recent study of torticollis did not find an association between the dominant hand and the side of torticollis, although an association was found between the direction of torticollis and the preferred direction of postural turning. Postural turning was assessed with a variety of tasks, such as noting the direction of turning when the patient is asked to turn 180° while standing with eyes closed (Stejskal & Tomanek, 1981; Stejskal, 1983, personal communication). These investigators posited that torticollis might be due to "the release of a postural rotational laterality in predisposed subjects and not to a presumed asymmetric lesion of the brain-stem" (Stejskal & Tomanek, 1981, p. 1029).

Biary and Koller (1985) reported a higher incidence of left-handedness in patients with *essential tremor*, compared with controls. Also, these investigators found a direct relationship between hand dominance (whether right or left) and severity of tremor. The latter finding did not hold true for parkinsonian tremor.

McCreadie *et al.* (1982) found that 68% of nondextral Feighner-criteria-positive schizophrenics had *tardive dyskinesia*, compared to only 29% of the dextral group. This was not found for the Feighner-criteria-negative schizophrenics. These investigators postulated that possible brain damage in the nondextral group might not only have caused pathological left-handedness, but also have predisposed them to a higher incidence of tardive dyskinesia.

Seltzer *et al.* (1984) reported that patients with *Alzheimer's disease* who developed the illness in the presenium had a significantly higher prevalence of left-handedness than did those who developed it in the senium. The authors considered this finding to be consistent with their hypothesis that early-onset Alzheimer's disease is associated with left-hemisphere vulnerability to the condition, and that senile and presenile dementia may be different disorders.

Mention should be made of the reports indicating that *hysterical conversion disorders* (Stern, 1977; Galin *et al.*, 1977) and *psychogenic somatic symptoms* (Axelrod *et al.*, 1980) occur more frequently on the left side. It is not clear whether these observations relate to handedness (where it would be more "convenient" to be psychogenically incapacitated on the nondominant side) or to some underlying cerebral asymmetry. There is other evidence, however, that motor dominance and the side of psychogenic symptoms are largely independent phenomena (Stern, 1977; Fleminger *et al.*, 1980).

Finally, a number of studies have reported an anomalous distribution of handedness among patients with *sociopathy* and *alcoholism*. Fitzhugh (1973), in a study of 19 consecutive court-referred juveniles, found that 32% of the delinquents were left-handed. Similarly, Gabrielli and Mednick (1980), in a study of children of mentally ill or character-disordered parents, reported that the degree of sinistrality of the children was associated with the number of delinquent offenses within the following 6-year period. A number of studies have reported an association between alcoholism and sinistrality (Bakan, 1973; Lee-Feldstein & Harburg, 1982; Nasrallah *et al.*, 1983; Smith & Chyatte, 1983; London *et al.*, 1985), but further investigations are necessary to clarify this issue.

A COMPREHENSIVE HYPOTHESIS OF THE ASSOCIATION OF HANDEDNESS WITH CEREBRAL DOMINANCE AND DEVELOPMENTAL AND IMMUNOLOGICAL DISORDERS

Geschwind and Behan (1982) and Geschwind and Galaburda (1985) have formulated a comprehensive hypothesis that helps explain the relationship of handedness to a number of different conditions. These investigators noted that left-handedness, developmental disorders (such as dyslexia, stuttering, and autism), certain immune and atopic disorders, migraine, and other conditions are associated with each other and with the male gender. These observations, along with other findings, such as the superiority of women at verbal skills and men at spatial skills, and the superior spatial skills of some patients with developmental disorders, prompted Geschwind and coworkers to propose that a developmental process in the fetal brain might be responsible for these associations. In essence, the investigators proposed the following:

1. The right cerebral cortex develops earlier than the left in most people, due to some factor that slows the growth of the left hemisphere.

2. This factor is related to the male gender, and very likely involves higher testosterone levels in male fetuses.
3. The delay in growth on the left side of the brain allows for enlargement of the right side, through a number of different mechanisms.
4. This right-hemisphere enlargement, which is more marked in men, will manifest as greater right-hemisphere (spatial) skills in men, and the smaller, more poorly developed left hemisphere will manifest as poorer left-hemisphere (verbal) skills in men than in women, as well as a higher incidence of developmental learning disorders in boys.
5. The higher testosterone levels in male fetuses may also cause abnormal development of the immune system, resulting in a higher incidence of immunological and atopic disorders in boys later in life.

There are many other findings and conjectures that relate to this interesting hypothesis, for which the reader is referred to the original references by Geschwind and coworkers.

SUMMARY

It is important for a variety of reasons, to assess handedness. For example, the presence of mixed- or left-handedness may be a marker of more severe illness in autistic and mentally retarded children, and a marker for less severe pathology in schizophrenics. Sinistrality also has important implications for persons suffering focal brain lesions, developmental disorders, and, possibly, for delinquency and alcoholism as well. Finally, handedness may shed light not only on disturbances in functioning, but also on the characteristics of superior functioning. Handedness provides important clues about the organization of the cerebral cortex, which makes it a convenient window to brain function.

CHAPTER TWENTY-SIX

Movement and Aging

INTRODUCTION

Aging and movement disorders may be considered to be related in three ways. First, aging itself has an effect on movement, with alterations in the motor system reflecting more general biological changes occurring in senescence. Second, many movement disorders are relatively age-specific. For example, Tourette's syndrome usually appears in early childhood or adolescence, whereas Parkinson's disease usually begins in middle age. Also, there are a number of movement disorders that commonly appear in old age and are often termed "senile" disorders of movement. Finally, pathological mechanisms involved in the general aging process may also be instrumental in causing certain movement disorders. In this chapter we discuss these three aspects of the relationship of aging and movement.

NORMAL AGING AND MOVEMENT

During normal senescence, the performance of the human motor system changes. The effects of age on different individuals is highly variable, however, for some persons are severely affected, whereas others show very little motor deficit for 7 or 8 decades. Table 26-1 lists a number of commonly observed changes in motor functioning that occur with normal aging.

The etiological factors involved in these age-related motor changes are not completely clear, but in general it is likely that one of two mechanisms, or some combination of the two, is responsible: (1) the changes in motor performance are related to age-associated changes in the musculoskeletal system, and (2) the changes in performance are related to changes in the nervous system. It is not always easy to distinguish between these two different mechanisms, and it is probable that they both contribute. In the remainder of this section, we shall discuss these two different mechanisms of age-related

Table 26-1. Commonly Observed Age-
Related Changes in Motor Function[a]

Loss of strength (especially in hands and legs)
Bradykinesia
Restriction of upward gaze
Mild rigidity
Generalized flexion
Loss of postural stability
Poverty of movement
Prolonged reaction and movement time
Loss of leg-flexing ability
Orofacial choreoathetoid movements
Tremor

[a]Critchley (1956, 1965); Welford (1977); Wolfson
and Katzman (1983).

decrement in motor function, and then discuss falling in the elderly, which constitutes perhaps the most important medical aspect of age-related motor deficit.

Musculoskeletal Changes with Age

In the musculoskeletal system, it is clear that with age many different changes that affect motor performance occur. Degenerative changes, such as osteoporosis and osteoarthritis in bones and joints, are present to some extent in almost all elderly people (see Jowsey, 1984; Chrisman, 1984). Older women are especially prone to osteoporosis. Such pathological changes have an important effect on posture and gait, resulting in a stooped posture with lessened mobility and impaired extremity movements. Bone brittleness and an increased susceptibility to falls also indirectly affect gait, and the assumption of a wide-based bradykinetic gait may occur partially because the patient is afraid of injuries during a fall. This gait is sometimes called *fear of further falling* (triple-F or three-F's gait), or postfall syndrome (Murphy & Isaacs, 1981), and is quite common, particularly in elderly women. (Falling is discussed at greater length later in this chapter; see also Chapter 18.)

Pathological changes in tendons and muscles are also important. With age, there is a loss of muscle mass in both men and women that appears to occur in spite of exercise (Forbes & Reina, 1970). Accompanying this loss of muscle mass is a loss of strength (Welford, 1977; Jokl, 1984; Hagan, 1984). There are a large number of histopathological changes in muscle, including muscle-fiber atrophy, hypertrophy of the sarcoplasmic reticulum (which may contribute to contractile protein dysfunction), and thickening of muscle-fiber basement membranes (which may cause decreased depolarization sensitivity of muscle cell membranes) (see Jokl, 1984). The structural protein collagen, an important constituent of tendons, also demonstrates changes with age (Klein & Rajan, 1984). Collagen becomes less soluble and less susceptible to enzymatic digestion with age, and this process is thought to be secondary to cross-linking or stabilization of the collagen macromolecule, although the precise mechanism is not clear. Such changes may contribute to the progressive slowing of movements and loss of range of movement seen in the elderly.

McDonagh *et al.* (1984) have provided evidence indicating that not all muscle fibers may be affected to the same degree in normal senescence. It appears that, especially in the legs, type II muscle fibers appear to be reduced in number and size to a greater extent than are type I fibers. (Type II muscle fibers are found in fast glycolytic muscles that are more important for quick actions and less important for the maintenance of posture.)

Nervous-System Changes with Age

Age-associated changes in the nervous system are largely confined to the central nervous system. The peripheral nervous system is relatively unaffected by the process of aging. Although there is a slight slowing in nerve conduction velocity, it is not enough to account for the bradykinesia observed in the elderly (see Welford, 1977; Kimura, 1983). (For a review of peripheral-nervous-system changes with age, see Spencer & Schaumburg, 1984.) In the central nervous system, certain histopathological changes, such as accumulation of lipofuscin in cells, may contribute to age-related motor changes, but the exact significance of these changes is uncertain (Scheibel & Scheibel, 1975; Mann *et al.*, 1984). Other changes, such as neuron loss in the brain, may be more important. Central motor systems may be especially vulnerable to neuron loss with age. In the cerebral cortex, for instance, it appears that the most severe neuron loss occurs in the frontal lobes, including the motor cortices (primary and secondary), whereas the occipital and parietal lobes, which subserve mainly sensory functions, appear to demonstrate little if any neuron loss with age (see Jeste *et al.*, 1986b). Subcortically, the putamen has been reported to show a significant loss of neurons with age (Bugiani *et al.*, 1978). In the brainstem, the only two nuclei that have been consistently reported to lose neurons with age are the substantia nigra and the locus ceruleus, both of which are important for movement (Brody, 1978; Tomlinson *et al.*, 1981; McGeer *et al.*, 1984b; McGeer *et al.*, 1977). Finally, a number of different investigators have reported a loss of cerebellar Purkinje cells with age (Ellis, 1920; Hall *et al.*, 1975; Jeste *et al.*, 1986b). All of these observed pathological changes may contribute to age-related decrements in motor functioning and may be at least partially responsible for bradykinesia and difficulty in motor-planning and coordination. However, it should be noted that neuronal loss with age may not be related to motor performance deficits at all, and may instead actually be responsible for preserving motor function with age. Comfort (1971) and others have noted that a loss of neurons, such as occurs in early development (in which neuron fallout may be associated with the development of more specific and more efficient neuronal circuits and connections), may be beneficial (see Clarke, 1985). Such a process, in which unnecessary, redundant, defective, or otherwise less useful neurons die to improve brain function, may occur throughout life. Thus, the exact relationship of neuron loss to age-related changes remains to be elucidated.

A wide variety of neurochemical changes, some of which are listed in Table 26-2, occur in the aging brain. The significance of these findings to motor performance is unclear, but loss of dopamine and dopaminergic receptors has been proposed to be responsible for the "parkinson-like" or "pseudoparkinsonian" motor functioning seen in some older persons. It is now widely accepted that, with age, ascending dopaminergic neurons degenerate along with postsynaptic dopamine receptors (Severson & Finch, 1980; Hornykiewicz, 1983; Memo et al., 1980; Missale et al., 1983; Roth, 1983). This is accompanied by a decline in dopamine content in the striatum that may amount to as much as a 50% loss by age 65 (Carlsson & Winblad, 1976). Although these decrements in dopaminergic transmission may be responsible for some of the bradykinesis of old age (dysfunction of the nigrostriatal tract has been considered to relate primarily to akinesia, rather than to rigidity and tremor), there are important differences between aging and Parkinson's disease. For example, in Parkinson's disease the loss of dopaminergic neurons is accompanied, at least in the initial stages of the illness, by a compensatory *increase* in dopamine receptors, in contrast with the *decrease* in receptors reported in aging, a fact that has prompted some investigators to consider that dopamine has a "trophic" effect on postsynaptic dopamine receptors (and possibly on postsynaptic neurons as well) (Agnati & Fuxe, 1980, 1984; Fuxe et al., 1981). Also, Newman et al. (1985) recently reported that L-dopa had no effect on the mild extrapyramidal impairment of ten healthy elderly persons, aged 59 to 72.

Consistent with the notion of dopamine tropism in the brain are reports that L-dopa administration to short-lived strains of mice both prolonged life span by as much as 50% and decreased age-related deficits in motor function (Cotzias et al., 1977; Papavasiliou, 1981). Intrastriatal grafts of embryonic substantia-nigra cell suspensions have been demonstrated to dramatically improve motor coordination in aged rats (Gate et al., 1983), and swimming dysfunction in aged rats has been shown to be responsive to both apomorphine (a dopamine receptor stimulant) and L-dopa (Marshall & Berrios, 1979). We have proposed that the dopamine content of different areas of the brain may be related to neuron loss in those areas, because areas

Table 26-2. Changes in Selected Neurotransmitters, Enzymes, and Receptors with Age[a]

Neurotransmitters	
Neurotransmitter	Change
Dopamine (DA)	Decrease (especially in basal ganglia)
Norepinephrine (NE)	Decrease
Acetylcholine (ACh)	Decrease (but little decrease in basal ganglia)
Serotonin (5-HT)	Unclear
γ-Aminobutyric acid (GABA)	Decrease (especially thalamus, but little decrease in basal ganglia)

Neurotransmitter metabolic enzymes	
Enzyme	Change
Tyrosine hydroxylase and DOPA decarboxylase (synthesize catecholamines)	Decrease[b]
Dopamine β-hydroxylase (synthesizes NE)	No change[c]
Monoamine oxidase and catechol-O-methyltransferase (degrade catecholamines)	Increase[d]
Choline acetyltransferase (synthesizes ACh)	Decrease (especially cortex)[e]
Glutamic acid decarboxylase (synthesizes GABA)	Decrease (especially thalamus)[f]

Neurotransmitter receptors[g]		
Receptor	Number	Affinity
Dopamine		
D_1	Decrease	Decrease
D_2	Unclear	Decrease
Norepinephrine		
α	? Decrease	Unclear
β	Increase	Decrease
Acetylcholine (muscarinic)	Decrease	No change
Serotonin	Unclear	Unclear
GABA	Decrease (hippocampus) Increase (cortex)	Unclear

[a]See Samorajski (1977), McGeer (1981), Cote and Kremzner (1983), and Selkoe and Kosik (1984).

highest in dopamine lose the most neurons with age, which may be the result of the loss of some trophic influence of dopamine as dopaminergic tracts degenerate (Jeste *et al.*, 1986b). It is not clear, however, whether this reflects a trophic mechanism of action of dopamine, because it is also possible that dopamine or some aspect of its metabolism may be toxic to neurons. We shall return to this point later in this chapter, when we discuss free-radical mechanisms of aging.

AGE SPECIFICITY OF MOTOR DISORDERS

In this section we review various aspects of age specificity of movement disorders. We begin with a brief review of mechanisms of age specificity, followed by a discussion of certain so-called "senile" movement disorders. The association of movement disorders and Alzheimer's disease is then very briefly reviewed, and, finally, we offer a discussion of falling in the aged, which is an issue of critical clinical importance.

Mechanisms of Age Specificity of Movement Disorders

Different movement disorders characteristically appear at different ages, and it is unclear why this is so. A number of possible mechanisms may be involved, however. One possible mechanism is that during aging there are certain stages of increased vulnerability to attack by certain types of illness. For example, stages marked by major hormonal changes such as puberty, pregnancy, or menopause may be associated with increased vulnerability to disorders in which endocrine factors are important. It is possible, for example, that some motor disorders may be the result of faulty neuroendocrine transmitter mechanisms that become clinically evident only when the patient is faced with significant age-related alterations in the endocrine system that overpower adaptive feedback mechanisms.

Another possible mechanism is that degenerative immunological changes occurring over the life of an individual may eventually result in a lowering of some aspect of immune status to below an important threshold level, allowing specific motor disorders to appear. For example, it has been determined that with age there are changes such as a decrease in the response

---

[b]See Cote and Kremzner (1974) and McGeer (1978).

[c]See Grote *et al.* (1974).

[d]See Robinson *et al.* (1977) and Stramentinoli *et al.* (1977).

[e]See McGeer (1981).

[f]See Perry *et al.* (1979) and McGeer (1981).

[g]See Burchinsky (1984) and Wong *et al.* (1984).

of T-lymphocytes to mitogens and a decrease in the influence of T-suppressor lymphocytes on B-lymphocytes (Stefansson *et al.*, 1984). These changes are also seen in disorders such as Down's syndrome, which points out the possibility that immune alterations and brain dysfunction may be related. The importance of this idea for motor disorders is unknown.

A third possibility is that some movement disorders are the result of a slow buildup of pathology over time (the so-called "leaky mutation"), whereby the disease finally manifests after a crucial degree of pathology is reached. Also, repetitive structural damage may be responsible for degenerative changes in brain, joints, muscles, bones, heart, and other organs and structures.

There are many other possibilities, none of which has been conclusively proven to be important for any given movement disorders. The field is of considerable interest, for future investigations in this area may shed light on the underlying pathology of not only movement disorders, but any disorders that possess a characteristic age of onset.

"Senile" Movement Disorders

Senile disorders are usually defined as those that commonly occur after the age of 65. Although there are many movement disorders, such as Parkinson's disease, hemiballismus, and Meige's syndrome, that are more common in older people, "senile" disorders are usually considered to be those that are chronic after development, are only slowly progressive (if progressive at all), and cause very little incapacitation of the patient. The two most common are senile tremor and senile chorea.

Senile tremor appears to be very common, affecting perhaps as much as 50% to 60% of elderly persons in a hospital setting (Moretti *et al.*, 1983). Most patients with senile tremor appear to have a form of essential tremor. The tremor often involves the head (titubation) and the mouth and lips. The lip tremor resembles rabbit syndrome (which occurs after neuroleptic treatment) and was described as early as 1882 by Demange, who called it "old rabbit face" (Critchley, 1956; see also Chapter 5).

Senile chorea, which is predominately an oral–facial–lingual dyskinesia, is also very common in the elderly. Klawans and Barr (1982) estimated a prevalence of 0.8% between the ages of 50 and 59, 6% between ages 60 and 69, and 7.8% between 70 and 79. This prevalence is similar to that reported by Varga *et al.* (1982), who reported a prevalence of slightly more than 10% in patients over age 60. In both these groups the patients were believed never to have been treated with neuroleptic drugs. Some elderly patients probably develop an orofacial dyskinesia in association with an edentulous state (Koller, 1983b; see also Chapter 3).

Motor Dysfunction and Alzheimer's Disease

It is apparent from Table 26-1 that many of the commonly observed age-related changes in motor function fit into the concept of pseudo-parkinsonism. Although this parkinson-like state is fairly common in the normal elderly, it does appear to be more common in elderly patients with dementia (Koller et al., 1984; Molsa et al., 1984). Recently, two different groups of investigators have reported that disorders of movement, in particular extrapyramidal signs and myoclonus, are fairly common in Alzheimer's disease and appear to be associated with greater severity of dementia (Mayeux et al., 1985; Chui et al., 1985). Mayeux et al. (1985) divided Alzheimer's disease into four groups: (1) benign, in which there is little or no progression of illness, (2) myoclonic, in which there is a younger age of onset and more severe intellectual decline, (3) extrapyramidal, which is also marked by severe intellectual decline and frequent psychotic symptoms, and (4) typical, which is marked by gradually developing dementia without other features. At the initial evaluation of 121 patients with Alzheimer's disease, these investigators noted that 34 (28%) had extrapyramidal signs, including rigidity and bradykinesia unrelated to neuroleptic drugs, and that 11 (10%) had myoclonus. Chui et al. (1985), in their study of 146 patients with Alzheimer's disease, noted extrapyramidal signs in 65 patients (45%), myoclonus in nine patients (6%), and hyperactive muscle stretch reflexes in 27 patients (19%).

Falling

Increased falling is one of the most disturbing aspects of age-related changes in the motor system. It may result from many different processes, and is especially common in elderly patients who are medically ill. The most common causes of increased falling in the elderly are listed in Table 26-3. Patients who fall are often poor historians when it comes to remembering events antecedent to the fall. Sometimes the explanations given are vague, with complaints, such as "I was dizzy," or "I blacked out," that often carry meanings different from what one would expect. The word "dizzy" in particular is commonly used to signify a number of different subjective states, from vertigo to lightheadedness to a vague feeling of instability in the legs and trunk. Time and patience are usually required to understand the patient's symptoms.

The causes of falls have been grouped into those that are imposed upon the patient (i.e., they are relatively unsuspected and surprising and require quick adaptive responses if a fall is to be prevented) and those that are initiated by the patient (i.e., the patient embarks on an activity that is familiar and volitional, and for which the nervous system should be prepared) (Wild

Table 26-3. Important Causes of Falling in the Elderly

Neurological causes	Cardiovascular causes
Hemiparesis	Postural hypotension
Parkinson's disease	Vertebrobasilar ischemia
Cervical spondylosis	Cardiac dysrhythmia
Vestibular disorders	Carotid sinus syndrome
Epilepsy	Medications and drugs
Musculoskeletal causes	Tranquilizers
Muscular wasting	Sedatives
Osteoarthritis of hip	Antihypertensives
Joint replacement	Antiepileptics
Amputation	Alcohol

et al., 1981). Causes of falls have been further divided into *extraordinary* (in which the specific causative activity exceeds normal daily activity) and *ordinary* (in which the causative activity is a part of the daily routine). Anyone can suffer a fall from extraordinary imposed causes (such as strenuous competitive exercise), and some healthy persons may fall as a result of ordinary imposed causes (such as accidentally bumping into an object while walking). Extraordinary initiated causes (such as painting a ceiling) may be important when the patient carries out an activity imprudently or when there is an age-related impairment in response. Ordinary initiated causes (such as simply walking on a level surface) are usually associated with falls only when there are illnesses of some sort, many of which are listed in Table 26-3. Patients with a history of falling during ordinary initiated activity always deserve a full medical workup.

The treatment of falling can often prove problematic. Any medical or neurological causes should of course be treated first. Wandering in the confused or demented elderly, a phenomenon that was discussed in Chapter 4, may predispose to falling, and interventions geared toward reduction of wandering-related injuries are helpful. Physical therapy and the provision of external support such as canes or walkers may be beneficial, although any techniques that allow the patient to walk with as little support as possible are preferable, though usually more costly and time-consuming. Restructuring the patient's environment is an important measure, and removing sharp-cornered objects, placing furniture so that a support is always at hand, carpeting the floors, especially in areas of high risk, adding hand railings in the bathroom and along stairs, and other such measures are often beneficial. Alerting neighbors to the risk of the patient's falling, and training the patient and the patient's family in how to raise the patient after a fall are also important. Most families grab the patient under the arms and pull, which often results in more injuries than are incurred in the fall itself. The patient should instead be gently rolled to the right side, and then, bending the right knee, the patient can lever himself to the kneeling position, finally using the left arm to twist into a chair.

COMMON MECHANISMS OF AGING AND MOVEMENT DISORDERS

Because a number of different movement abnormalities are observed in the process of normal aging, many investigators have proposed that certain movement disorders may reflect a process of accelerated or abnormal aging in movement-related regions of the brain, especially the basal ganglia. This idea has been frequently proposed for Parkinson's disease (e.g., Rinne, 1982), but has also been proposed for Huntington's disease (Finch, 1980) and tardive dyskinesia (Cadet et al., 1986) as well.

One of the most important general theories of aging in recent years is the free-radical theory (see Armstrong et al., 1984). Free radicals (such as a superoxide radical or hydroxyl radical) are highly reactive chemical species that readily interact with many different types of biochemicals resulting in cell damage and membrane destabilization. Much of the damage related to free-radical formation is the result of their powerful oxidative potential. Human beings, like other animals, are bathed in an ocean of oxygen that provides energy through the combustion of foodstuffs. However, during this combustion process, cytotoxic free radicals may be formed, thus making all organisms dependent on free-radical detoxifying systems, such as free-radical scavengers (e.g., vitamin E, uric acid) or enzymes (e.g., catalase, superoxide dismutase). Nevertheless, in spite of these antioxidant mechanisms, free-radical damage accrues over an individual's lifetime. It is possible that free-radical damage to areas in the brain occurring throughout life may underlie some forms of senile movement disorder, such as senile bradykinesia, senile choreoathetosis, or senile tremor. Of interest is the fact that the basal ganglia contain large amounts of iron, which may predispose to greater free-radical damage in this area than in other brain areas, as transition metals are important in free-radical production (Floyd et al., 1984).

It has been proposed that some movement disorders, such as Parkinson's disease and tardive dyskinesia, may in some cases be related to free-radical damage (Perry et al., 1984; Cadet, 1986; Cadet et al., 1986). This may be due to the fact that free radicals are produced during the metabolism of catecholamines, especially dopamine (Graham, 1979), and that individuals who may be deficient in free-radical detoxifying mechanisms (such as has been proposed for patients with Parkinson's disease) or who may have increased amounts of dopamine, either as part of an illness process or secondary to neuroleptic drugs (such as has been proposed for some types of schizophrenia and for tardive dyskinesia), may be predisposed to develop movement disorders. Although these ideas require further experimental verification, they serve to highlight possible interconnections between mechanisms of aging and movement disorders.

CHAPTER TWENTY-SEVEN

The Interface of Thought and Movement: Future Directions

We would like to conclude this book with some thoughts about the connections between thought and movement. The great British neurologist Hughlings Jackson (1889) once commented "of these 'mental centres,' [I] say that they are motor too—that they are the highest motor centres." The psychiatrist Gadelius (1933) echoed these comments years later when he stated, "Just as a movement becomes firm and supple and a grip of the spade or plough gets its necessary strength by a functional interaction between flexors and extensors, thus also our conscious resolutions acquire due firmness by a peculiar interaction between ideas and contrasting ideas." Gadelius also used such terms as "psychical tremor" to describe certain kinds of emotional or cognitive states characterized by oscillation or fluctuation. More recently, Bruyn (1968) has commented on what has been called the "choreomania" observed in the 14th century.

Thus, for many years investigators have recognized the association of movement and cognition, an association more profound than the simple notion that cognition controls movement; for the patterns of function and dysfunction in these two realms of human existence appear to be related in an elemental way.

The nature of the deep connection between thought and movement is not clear, but certainly many interesting parallels may be seen. For example, the frontal lobes appear to be the prime repository of motor control, as well as of important aspects of intellectual functioning. Catecholaminergic (especially dopaminergic) transmission is important in movement disorders such as Parkinson's disease and in cognitive disorders such as schizophrenia. Movement disorders such as Parkinson's and Huntington's diseases are frequently associated with cognitive and emotional impairment, and researchers have proposed a role for the basal ganglia in cognition. Other examples could be given, many of which are scattered throughout this book, that strongly suggest common underlying mechanisms for thought and movement.

It seems likely that subcortical nuclei, such as the putamen, caudate, amygdala, and septal nuclei, may be important in the manifestation of both movement disorders and psychopathology. In a number of chapters in this book, structural and functional aspects of subcortical nuclei and their connections have been discussed, along with their possible relationship to movement and psychopathology. In Chapter 2 it was noted how the striatum is somatotopically organized as well as organized according to associated cortical areas. Thus, the putamen is more closely associated with the primary motor cortex, whereas the caudate is more closely associated with motor association cortices. Other subcortical nuclei, such as the amygdala and septal nuclei, usually considered components of the limbic system, are related to cortical areas such as the cingulate gyrus and the prefrontal cortex. All of these subcortical nuclei receive dopaminergic fibers, mainly from the substantia nigra or from the ventral tegmental area of Tsai.

In Chapters 3, 7, 8, 12, 15, 19, 20, 22, and 23 the relationships of these areas to specific motor disorders were discussed. For example, dystonia was noted to be frequently associated with putaminal or lenticular damage, and tardive dyskinesia and Huntington's disease to be more frequently associated with damage to the caudate nucleus. Complex movement disorders such as Tourette's syndrome and compulsive behavior have been related to dysfunction in the cingulum.

When these different observations are considered together, a possible pattern emerges, presented in Table 27-1. Movement disorders that are very simple in form (such as dystonias, which, at their simplest, appear as sustained contractions of a single muscle) may be more associated with the pathology in the putamen and its connections, including the primary motor cortex. Dystonic disorders are rarely accompanied by primary psychopathology. Somewhat more complex disorders (such as tardive dyskinesia and

Table 27-1. Psychiatric Symptoms, Movement Disorders, and the Basal Ganglia

Subcortical structure	Putamen	Caudate	Amygdala/septum
Cortical projection area	Primary motor cortex	Motor association cortex	Cingulum and premotor cortex
Type of associated abnormal movement	*Simple* .... *Complex* Dystonic disorders	Tardive dyskinesia, Huntington's disease	Complex tics, stereotypies, compulsions
Associated psychopathology	*Infrequent* .... *Common*		

Huntington's disease, which can be dystonic, ticlike, and/or choreoathetoid in nature) are associated more with caudate pathology, and are more frequently accompanied by psychopathology (often dementia or psychosis). Finally, complex movement disorders such as complex tics, compulsions, and, possibly, stereotypies, may be more associated with damage to or dysfunction of limbic structures (including the cingulum, prefrontal cortex, amygdala, and septal areas), and are usually associated with psychopathology. It is conceivable that excessive or disorganized subcortical output may account for characteristics of both the psychopathology and the movement disorder in these different hyperkinetic conditions. Thus, the subcortical nuclei and their associated circuits may form a "gradient" across the brain, in which disorders of movement of increasing complexity are associated with increasing amounts of psychopathology. It is possible that different abnormalities in subcortical output underlie the characteristics of psychopathology in hypokinetic disorders as well. For example, akinesia seen in parkinsonism is associated with depression, which may be related to striatal output, and negativism is associated with the so-called "negative" symptoms of schizophrenia (such as anhedonia, abulia, and social withdrawal), which may be related to limbic output.

It appears not only that the severity of psychopathology may be related to the complexity of movement disorder, but also that the form of the psychopathology and the motor dysfunction may be associated. For example, Parkinson's disease, basically a hypokinetic disorder, is often associated with depression, and major depressive disorder is often associated with hypokinesis (see Chapter 22). Huntington's disease, a condition marked by random choreoathetoid movements, may be associated with emotional instability and psychosis, and schizophrenia, a psychotic disorder, may be associated with random chorealike movements (Jeste *et al.*, 1984c). Compulsive traits are frequently seen in depression and paranoia, and depression and paranoia occur in obsessive–compulsive disorders. It is possible to divide motor and psychiatric disturbances into two groups, one marked by hypokinesia, depression, and paranoia, and another by hyperkinesia, emotional instability, and psychosis (see Table 27-2). These different groups of "psychomotor" dysfunctions may be related to the characteristics of the output of various subcortical structures.

Although the exact neurobiological mechanisms for different forms of psychomotor dysfunction are unknown, a theoretical model that may be relevant has been proposed. Based upon the pioneering work of mathematicians such as Thom (1972), a group of mathematicians have developed the basic principles of a new branch of mathematics called *qualitative* or *nonlinear dynamics* (Garfinkel, 1983; Abraham, 1983; Smith, 1983; Mandell, 1983). These investigators have proposed that this theory may be applied to many different areas of medicine, including psychopathology and motor disorders. In this mathematical theory, different systems of the brain are

Table 27-2. Neuropsychiatric Dysfunction Divided According to Hyperstability versus Hyperinstability

	Hyperstable	Hyperunstable
	Neuropsychiatric disorders	
Movement disorder	Parkinson's disease	Huntington's disease
Affective disorder	Unipolar (depression)	Bipolar (mixed state)
Character disorder	Obsessive–compulsive	Hysterical
	Paranoid	Borderline
		Antisocial
Cognitive disorder	Paranoia	Schizophrenia
	Motor signs	
	Hypokinesia	Chorea
	Tremor	Athetosis
	Rigidity	Mannerisms
	Complex tics	
	Compulsions	
	Neurochemical basis	
	Decreased catecholaminergic transmission?	Increased catecholaminergic transmission?

considered to possess normal modes of operation, such as steady-state, oscillatory, and chaotic modes. One particular brain system may function most efficiently in a steady-state mode (e.g., systems controlling brain temperature), whereas another brain system may function best in an oscillatory mode (e.g., systems demonstrating a circadian rhythm). With pathology, a system moves from a normal mode to a "pathological mode," sometimes called a "failure mode." Motor disorders such as Parkinson's disease and Huntington's disease are considered to represent motor systems functioning in pathological modes. It is possible that, in shifting to a pathological mode of functioning, many different brain systems may shift in the same direction—that is, they may all shift toward more regular or stable modes of motion (steady state or oscillation) when more irregular motions are warranted (*hyperstability*), or toward more irregular modes of motion (chaos) when regularity is required (*hyperinstability*). This may account for some of the observed parallels between thought and movement disorders, as the brain systems governing movement and thought may jointly move into pathological modes of functioning. Thus, the motor and cognitive–emotional states of an individual could become "hyperstable" or "hyperunstable" together.

In Table 27-2 we present a list of neuropsychiatric signs, symptoms, and disorders that may represent a pathological mode of functioning marked either by hyperstability (in which there is a lack of randomness and spontaneity, and the patient falls victim to excessive steady-state conditions or oscillations) or hyperinstability (in which the patient is subjected to excessive randomness and chaos that overwhelm normal oscillatory or steady-state conditions). Of course there are many exceptions to these generalizations (e.g., depression and rigidity are not uncommon in Huntington's disease), and there are many conditions that fall between the two extremes listed here. Nevertheless, we believe that such hypotheses concerning the interface of motor and cognitive–emotional control may, in the future, contribute to an understanding of the organization of brain function.

APPENDIX

Oscillating Systems

In a simple springlike mechanical oscillating system the position of the oscillating object varies as a function of time in a sinusoidal manner. Such ideal mechanical systems can be described in terms of a *natural frequency* (determined by the stiffness and mass of the system) and an *amplitude* of excursion. However, such systems do not exist in reality, for there is always some type of friction or viscosity that eventually reduces the oscillations to zero (assuming that energy is not continually added to the system). This effect is known as *damping*. Damping not only gradually reduces the amplitude of the oscillatory excursions over time, but it also reduces the frequency of the oscillations. With damping, the excursions around a certain point become gradually smaller with time until oscillations cease, a phenomenon sometimes called *hunting*. As damping is increased, a point is reached where no hunting occurs, and the system is said to be *critically damped*.

If one were to consider, say, the human arm to be a simple springlike mechanical system, and further consider it to be in a gravity-free environment, then a command to move the arm from one location to another would cause oscillations around the goal location that would gradually decrease over time, until the new position was reached. If the arm were critically damped, no oscillations would occur, and the second location would be reached in one smooth continuous motion. Oscillations are generally not desired in movement, and systems in which they occur are sometimes referred to as *underdamped*. Damping beyond the critical point is also usually not desired, for then the movement will fall short of the goal location. The system would then be *overdamped*.

So much for the purely mechanical aspects of oscillations in a limb. The scenario becomes more complicated when we consider the mechanisms by which limb movement is controlled. Oscillations can occur, not only as a result of the mechanical characteristics of the limb, but also as a result of characteristics of the neural control systems.

In order to understand this further, we must consider the nature of control systems in general. Control systems may be classed as either *open-loop* or *closed-loop* systems. We have already discussed open- versus closed-loop systems to some

323

extent in relation to ballistic versus ramp movements. Basically, closed-loop systems are those in which the control action is in some way dependent on the output, whereas the control of open-loop systems is independent of output. Closed-loop control systems are commonly called *feedback control systems*, because part of the output is fed back into the control action.

There are many advantages of a feedback control system over an open-loop system. These include increased accuracy of response of the system, reduced sensitivity to fluctuations in system characteristics, and reduced effects of distortion and nonlinearities on the system's performance. However, there is one characteristic that is frequently a disadvantage: all feedback control systems have a tendency toward oscillation.

Let us look at how this may occur. A signal is sent to a muscle through a control system that determines how far that muscle is to contract—that is, how far a part of the body is to move. In a system with negative feedback the position of the limb (or the amount of contraction of the muscle) is in some way fed back into the control action at a point called the *mixer* or *comparator*. At this point the current position of the limb is compared with the incoming signal (corresponding to the desired position of the limb) and an error signal that moves the limb closer to the desired position is generated. When the error signal is zero, the limb stops.

Now, in terms of oscillatory tendency, there are two important characteristics of control systems that must be considered. One of these involves the *latency* or *loop-time* of the feedback pathway. No pathway is instantaneous, so that the signal the comparator sees fed back from the output is always delayed from what is actually going on at the output. Thus, the comparator is comparing an output signal that represents a condition that has already occurred. If the loop-time is short compared to changes in the input, the system works quite well. If the loop-time is lengthened for some reason, then oscillations will occur as the comparator attempts to reduce the error signal to zero. The oscillations occur because the output signal is not a true reflection of the current state of the output.

The second important characteristic relating to oscillatory tendency in control systems is their ability to increase (or decrease) the amount and type of output in relationship to input, which is called the *gain* of the system. Here, if the gain is too high, the comparator may be unable to compare correctly the system's output to its input, again resulting in oscillations.

As mentioned in Chapter 2, there is a hierarchy of movement control systems in the brain. At the lowest level, segmental spinal neurons form closed-loop feedback control systems with muscles, one of which is the myotatic reflex. Muscles may also be involved in closed-loop feedback control systems with neurons at higher levels in the nervous system—so-called long-loop reflexes. There are also control systems that do not involve peripheral nerves or muscles, but in which similar oscillatory phenomena may occur. These are *central oscillators*. It is not clear whether all central oscillators involve closed-loop feedback mechanisms as just described, but probably many of them do.

References

Abraham K. Contributions to a discussion on tic. In: *Selected Papers on Psychoanalysis.* New York, Basic Books, 1960a, pp. 323–325.

Abraham K. A short study of the development of the libido, viewed in the light of mental disorders. In: *Selected Papers on Psychoanalysis.* New York, Basic Books, 1960b, pp. 418–501.

Abraham RH. Dynamical models for physiology. Am J Physiol 245: R467–R472, 1983.

Abrams A, Braff D, Janowsky D, *et al.* Unresponsiveness of catatonic symptoms to naloxone. Pharmakopsychiat 11: 177–179, 1978.

Abrams R, Taylor MA. Catatonia: A prospective clinical study. Arch Gen Psychiatry 33: 579–581, 1976.

Abrams R, Taylor MA. Response to letter to the editor, "Criteria for the diagnosis of catatonia," by Gelenberg AJ. Am J Psychiatry 134: 463, 1977.

Abrams R, Taylor MA, Stolurow KAC. Catatonia and mania: Patterns of cerebral dysfunction. Biol Psychiatry 14: 111–117, 1979.

Achte KA. *Der Verlauf der Schizophrenien und der Schizophreniformen Psychosen.* Copenhagen, Ejnar Munksgaard, 1961.

Ackerknecht EH. *A Short History of Psychiatry.* New York, Hafner, 1959.

Ackerknecht EH. *A Short History of Medicine.* Baltimore, Johns Hopkins University Press, 1982a.

Ackerknecht EH. The history of psychosomatic medicine. Psychol Med 12: 17–24, 1982b.

Adler L, Angrist B, Peselow E, *et al.* Efficacy of propanolol in neuroleptic-induced akathisia. J Clin Psychopharm 5: 164–166, 1985.

Agid Y, Bonnet A-M, Signoret J-L, *et al.* Clinical, pharmacological, and biochemical approach of "onset- and end-of-dose" dyskinesias. In: Poirier LJ, Sourkes TL, Bedard PJ (eds). *The Extrapyramidal System and Its Disorders. Advances in Neurology.* Vol. 24. New York, Raven Press, 1979, pp. 401–410.

Agnati LF, Fuxe K. On the mechanism of the antiparkinsonian action of L-DOPA and bromocriptine: A theoretical and experimental analysis of dopamine receptor sub- and supersensitivity. J Neural Trans Supp 16: 69–81, 1980.

Agnati LF, Fuxe K. Computer-assisted morphometry and microdensitometry of transmitter identified neurons with special reference to the mesostriatal dopamine pathway. Acta Physiol Scand Supp 532: 1984.

Albert ML, Feldman RG, Willis AL. The subcortical dementia of progressive supranuclear palsy. J Neurol Neurosurg Psychiatry 37: 121–130, 1974.

Alexander RW, Davis JN, Lefkowitz RJ. Direct identification and characterization of beta-adrenergic receptors in rat brain. Nature 258: 437–440, 1975.

Alexopoulos GS. Lack of complaints in schizophrenics with tardive dyskinesia. J Nerv Ment Dis 167: 125–127, 1979.

Allen N, Knopp W. Hereditary parkinsonism–dystonia with sustained control by L-DOPA and anticholinergic medication. In: Eldridge R, Fahn S (eds). *Dystonia. Advances in Neurology.* Vol. 14. New York, Raven Press, 1976, pp. 201–214.

Allum JHJ, Dietz V, Freund H-J. Neuronal mechanisms underlying physiological tremor. J Neurophys 41: 557–571, 1978.

Altrocchi PH. Spontaneous oral–facial dyskinesia. Arch Neurol 26: 506–512, 1972.

Altrocchi PH, Forno LS. Spontaneous oral–facial dyskinesia: Neuropathology of a case. Neurology 33: 802–805, 1983.

Amado H, Lustman PJ. Attention deficit disorders persisting in adulthood: A review. Comp Psychiatry 23: 300–314, 1982.

American Psychiatric Association. *Diagnostic and Statistical Manual of Mental Disorders.* Ed. 3. Washington, D.C., American Psychiatric Press, 1980.

Ananth J. Choosing the right antidepressant. Psych J Univ Ottawa 8: 20–26, 1983.

Anden N-E, Johnels B. Effect of local application of apomorphine to the corpus striatum and to the nucleus accumbens on the reserpine-induced rigidity in rats. Brain Res 133: 386–389, 1977.

Andermann F, Keene DL, Andermann E, *et al.* Startle disease or hyperekplexia: Further delineation of the syndrome. Brain 103: 985–997, 1980.

Andreasen NC, Olsen S. Negative vs positive schizophrenia: Definition and validation. Arch Gen Psychiatry 39: 789–794, 1982.

Angel RW, Hofmann WW, Eppler W. Silent period in patients with parkinsonian rigidity. Neurology 16: 529–532, 1966.

Angle CR, McIntire MS. Persistent dystonia in a brain-damaged child after ingestion of phenothiazine. J Pediatr 73: 124–126, 1968.

Angrist B, Sathananthan G, Gershon S. Behavioral effects of L-DOPA in schizophrenic patients. Psychopharmacologia (Berlin) 31: 1–12, 1973.

Annett M. A classification of hand preference by association analysis. Br J Psychol 61: 300–321, 1970.

Annett M. Genetic and nongenetic influences on handedness. Behav Genetics 8: 227–249, 1978.

Antelman SM, Caggiula AR. Norepinephrine–dopamine interactions and behavior. Science 195: 646–653, 1977.

Apte SN, Langston JW. Permanent neurological deficits due to lithium toxicity. Ann Neurol 13: 453–455, 1983.

Arato M, Perenyi A, Fekete M, *et al.* Neuroendocrine investigations in tardive dyskinesia. Neuroendocrinol Lett 6: 315–320, 1980.

Arendt T, Bigl Y, Arendt A, *et al.* Loss of neurons in the nucleus basalis of Meynert in Alzheimer's disease, paralysis agitans and Korsakoff's disease. Acta Neuropathol (Berlin) 61: 101–108, 1983.

Arieti S. Volition and value: A study based on catatonic schizophrenia. In: Post S (ed). *Moral Values and the Superego Concept in Psychoanalysis.* New York, International Universities Press, 1972, pp. 275–288.

Armstrong D, Sohal RS, Cutler RG, *et al.* (eds). *Free Radicals in Molecular Biology, Aging, and Disease. Aging.* Vol. 27. New York, Raven Press, 1984.

Arnold LE, Kirilcuk V, Corson SA, *et al.* Levoamphetamine and dextroamphetamine: Differential effect on aggression and hyperkinesis in children and dogs. Am J Psychiatry 130: 165–170, 1973.

Aronin N, Cooper PE, Lorenz LJ, *et al.* Somatostatin is increased in the basal ganglia in Huntington disease. Ann Neurol 13: 519–526, 1983.

Aronson TA. Persistent drug-induced parkinsonism. Biol Psychiatry 20: 795–798, 1985.

Ashcroft GW, Eccleston D, Waddell JL. Recognition of amphetamine addicts. Br Med J 1: 57, 1965.

Askenasy JJM. Sleep patterns in extrapyramidal disorders. Int J Neurology 15: 62–76, 1981.

Askenasy JJM, Yahr MD. Reversal of sleep disturbance in Parkinson's disease by antiparkinsonian therapy: A preliminary study. Neurology 35: 527–532, 1985.

Ast M, Rosenberg S, Metzig E. Constitutional predisposition to central nervous system (CNS) disease determined by tests of lateral asymmetry. Neuropsychobiology 2: 269–275, 1976.

Astrup C. The Chronic Schizophrenias. Oslo, Universitetsforlaget, 1979.

Axelrod S, Noonan M, Atanacio B. On the laterality of psychogenic somatic symptoms. J Nerv Ment Dis 168: 517–525, 1980.

Ayd FJ. A survey of drug-induced extrapyramidal reactions. J Am Med Assoc 175: 1054–1060, 1961.

Ayd FJ Jr. Early-onset neuroleptic-induced extrapyramidal reactions: A second survey, 1961 1981. In: Coyle JT, Enna SJ (eds). Neuroleptics: Neurochemical, Behavioral, and Clinical Perspectives. New York: Raven Press, 1983, pp. 75–95.

Bacher NM, Lewis HA. Low-dose propranolol in tardive dyskinesia. Am J Psychiatry 147: 495–497, 1980.

Bakan P. Left-handedness and alcoholism. Percept Motor Skills 36: 514, 1973.

Bakan P. Are left-handers brain damaged? New Scientist 67: 200–202, 1975.

Baldessarini RJ. Chemotherapy in Psychiatry. Cambridge, Harvard University Press, 1977.

Baldessarini RJ, Cole JO, Davis JM, et al. Tardive Dyskinesia: A Task Force Report of the American Psychiatric Association. Washington, D.C., American Psychiatric Press, 1980.

Barbeau A. Cholinergic treatment in the Tourette syndrome. N Engl J Med 302: 1310–1311, 1980.

Barnes TRE, Braude WM. Akathisia variants and tardive dyskinesia. Arch Gen Psychiatry 42: 874–878, 1985.

Barnes TRE, Kidger T, Trauer T, et al. Reclassification of the tardive dyskinesia syndrome. Adv Biochem Psychopharm 24: 565–568, 1980.

Barnes TRE, Rossor M, Trauer T. A comparison of purposeless movements in psychiatric patients treated with antipsychotic drugs, and normal individuals. J Neurol Neurosurg Psychiatry 46: 540–546, 1983.

Baroni A, Benvenuti F, Fantini L, et al. Human ballistic arm abduction movements: Effects of L-DOPA treatment in Parkinson's disease. Neurology 34: 868–876, 1984.

Barris RW, Schuman HR. Bilateral anterior cingulate gyrus lesions. Neurology 3: 44 52, 1953.

Barry RJ, James AL. Handedness in autistics, retardates, and normals of a wide age range. J Aut Child Schiz 8: 315–323, 1978.

Bartels M, Themelis J. Computerized tomography in tardive dyskinesia: Evidence of structural abnormalities in the basal ganglia system. Arch Psychiat Nervenkrank 233: 371–379, 1983.

Bauer G, Prugger M, Rumpl E. Stimulus evoked oral automatisms in the locked-in syndrome. Arch Neurol 39: 435–436, 1982.

Baumeister AA, Forehand R. Stereotyped acts. In: Ellis NR (ed). International Review of Research in Mental Retardation. Vol. 6. New York, Academic Press, 1973, pp. 55–96.

Bax M, McKeith R (eds). Minimal Cerebral Dysfunction. Little Club Clinics in Developmental Medicine. Vol. 10. London, Heinemann, 1963.

Baxter DW, Lal S. Essential tremor and dystonic syndromes. In: Poirier LJ, Sourkes TL, Bedard PJ (eds). The Extrapyramidal System and Its Disorders. Advances in Neurology. Vol. 24. New York, Raven Press, 1979, pp. 373–377.

Beard GM. Experiments with the "Jumpers" or "Jumping Frenchmen" of Maine. J Nerv Ment Dis 7: 487–490, 1880.

Beart PM. Transmitters and receptors in the basal ganglia. In: McKenzie JS, Kemm RE, Wilcock LN (eds). *The Basal Ganglia: Structure and Function.* New York, Plenum Press, 1984, pp. 261–296.

Behar D, Rapoport J, Berg CJ, *et al.* Computerized tomography and neuropsychological test measures in adolescents with obsessive–compulsive disorder. Am J Psychiatry 141: 363–369, 1984.

Bell C. *Essays on the Anatomy of the Expression in Painting.* Ed. 1. London, Murray, 1806.

Benson DF. *Aphasia, Alexia, and Agraphia.* New York, Churchill Livingstone, 1979.

Berardelli A, Sabra AF, Hallett M. Physiological mechanisms of rigidity in Parkinson's disease. J Neurol Neurosurg Psychiatry 46: 45–53, 1983.

Berardelli A, Rothwell JC, Day BL, *et al.* Pathophysiology of blepharospasm and oromandibular dystonia. Brain 108: 593–608, 1985.

Bergen D, Tanner CM, Wilson R. The electroencephalogram in Tourette syndrome. Ann Neurol 11: 382–385, 1982.

Berger W, Altenmueller E, Dietz V. Normal and impaired development of children's gait. Human Neurobiol 3: 163–170, 1984.

Bergonzi P, Chiurulla C, Gambi D, *et al.* L-DOPA plus DOPA-decarboxylase inhibitor: Sleep organization in Parkinson's syndrome before and after treatment. Acta Neurol Belg 75: 5–10, 1975.

Berkson G. Abnormal stereotyped motor acts. In: Zubin J, Hunt HF (eds). *Comparative Psychopathology: Animal and Human.* New York, Grune & Stratton, 1967, pp. 76–94.

Berkson G, Mason WA. Stereotyped movements of mental defectives: III. Situation effects. Amer J Ment Defic 68: 409–412, 1963.

Berrios GE. Stupor revisited. Comp Psychiatry 22: 466–478, 1981a.

Berrios GE. Stupor: A conceptual history. Psychol Med 11: 677–688, 1981b.

Biary N, Koller W. Handedness and essential tremor. Arch Neurol 42: 1082–1083, 1985.

Bing R. Uber einige bemerkenswerte Begleiterscheinungen der "extrapyramidalen Rigidität" (Akathisie-Micrographie-Kinesia Paradoxa). Schweiz Med Wochenschr 4: 167–171, 1923.

Bing R. *Textbook of Nervous Diseases.* Ed. 5. Haymaker W (trans). St. Louis, Mosby, 1939, pp. 758–759.

Bird ED, Collins GH, Dodson MH, *et al.* The effect of phenothiazine on the manganese concentration in the basal ganglia of sub-human primates. In: Barbeau A, Burnette J-R (eds). *Progress in Neuro-Genetics.* Proceedings of the 2nd International Congress in Neuro-Genetics and Neuro-Ophthalmology. Montreal/Amsterdam, Exerpta Medica, 1967, pp. 600–605.

Bishop DVM. Handedness, clumsiness and cognitive ability. Dev Med Child Neurol 22: 569–579, 1980.

Bishop ER, Torch EM. Dividing "hysteria": A preliminary investigation of conversion disorder and psychalgia. J Nerv Ment Dis 167: 348–356, 1979.

Bitton V, Melamed E. Coexistence of severe parkinsonism and tardive dyskinesia as side effects of neuroleptic therapy. J Clin Psychiatry 45: 28–30, 1984.

Bixler EO, Kales A, Vela-Bueno A, *et al.* Nocturnal myoclonus and nocturnal myoclonic activity in a normal population. Res Comm Chem Pathol Pharmacol 36: 129–140, 1982.

Bjorklund A, Divac I, Lindvall O. Regional distribution of catecholamines in monkey cerebral cortex: Evidence for a dopaminergic innervation of the primate prefrontal cortex. Neurosci Lett 7: 115–119, 1978.

Black DW. Pathological laughter: A review of the literature. J Nerv Ment Dis 170: 67–71, 1982.

Blanchard EB, Hersen M. Behavioral treatment of hysterical neurosis: Symptom substitution and symptom return reconsidered. Psychiatry 39: 118–129, 1976.

Blau TH. Torque and schizophrenic vulnerability: As the world turns. Am Psychologist 32: 997–1005, 1977.

Bleuler E. *Dementia Praecox or the Group of Schizophrenias.* Zinkin J (trans). New York, International Universities Press, 1911/1950.

Bleuler E. *The Theory of Schizophrenic Negativism.* White WA (trans). *Nervous and Mental Disease Monograph Series.* No. 11. New York, The Journal of Nervous and Mental Disease Publishing Co., 1912.

Bliss EL. Hysteria and hypnosis. J Nerv Ment Dis 172: 203–206, 1984.

Bliss J. Sensory experiences of Gilles de la Tourette syndrome. Cohen DJ, Freedman DX (eds). Arch Gen Psychiatry 37: 1343–1347, 1980.

Block JE. Thumbs down on left-handedness (letter to ed). N Engl J Med 291: 307, 1974.

Blum I, Korczyn AD. Peptide neurotransmitters and their implications for the treatment of tardive dyskinesia. Mod Prob Pharmacopsychiatry 21: 187–195, 1983.

Blumer D. Temporal lobe epilepsy and its psychiatric significance. In: Benson DF, Blumer D (eds). *Psychiatric Aspects of Neurologic Disease.* New York, Grune & Stratton, 1975, pp. 151–170.

Bockenheimer S, Lucius G. Zur Therapie mit Dimethylaminoethanol (Deanol) bei neurolepti-kainduzierten extrapyramidalen Hyperkinesen. Arch Psychiat Nervenkrank 222: 69–75, 1976.

Bogerts B, Meertz E, Schonfeldt-Bausch R. Basal ganglia and limbic system pathology in schizophrenia. Arch Gen Psychiatry 42: 784–791, 1985.

Boghen D. Successful treatment of restless legs with clonazepam. Ann Neurol 8: 341, 1980.

Boghen D, Peyronnard JM. Myoclonus in familial restless legs syndrome. Arch Neurol 33: 368–370, 1976.

Boklage CE. Schizophrenia, brain asymmetry development, and twinning: Cellular relationship with etiological and possibly prognostic implications. Biol Psychiatry 12: 19–35, 1977.

Bolin BJ. Left-handedness and stuttering as signs diagnostic of epileptics. J Ment Sci 99. 403–408, 1953.

Boller F, Mizutani T, Roessmann U, et al. Parkinson disease, dementia, and Alzheimer disease: Clinicopathological correlations. Ann Neurol 7: 329–335, 1980.

Bonduelle M. The myoclonias. In: Vinken PJ, Bruyn GW (eds). *Diseases of the Basal Ganglia. Handbook of Clinical Neurology.* Vol. 6. New York, American Elsevier, 1968, pp. 761–781.

Bonner CA, Kent GH. Overlapping symptoms in catatonic excitement and manic excitement. Am J Psychiatry 92: 1311–1322, 1936.

Borison RL, Ang L, Shang S. New pharmacological approaches in the treatment of Gilles de la Tourette syndrome. In: Friedhoff AJ, Chase TN (eds). *Gilles de la Tourette Syndrome. Advances in Neurology.* Vol. 35. New York, Raven Press, 1982, pp. 377–382.

Boronow J, Pickar D, Ninan PT, et al. Atrophy limited to the third ventricle in chronic schizophrenic patients. Arch Gen Psychiatry 42: 266–271, 1985.

Bort RF. Catatonia, gastric hyperacidity, and fatal aspiration: A preventable syndrome. Am J Psychiatry 133: 446–447, 1976.

Boucher J. Hand preference in autistic children and their parents. J Aut Child Schiz 7: 177–187, 1977.

Boyd IA, Gladden MH, McWilliam PN, et al. Control of dynamic and static nuclear bag fibres and nuclear chain fibres by gamma- and beta-axons in isolated cat muscle spindles. J Physiol (London) 265: 133–162, 1977.

Braff DL. Impaired speed of information processing in nonmedicated schizotypal patients. Schiz Bull 7: 499–508, 1981.

Brainin M, Reisner T, Zeitlhofer J. Tardive dyskinesia: Clinical correlation with computed tomography in patients aged less than 60 years. J Neurol Neurosurg Psychiatry 46: 1037–1040, 1983.

Bramwell MJ. *Hypnotism: Its History, Practice, and Theory.* Philadelphia, Lippincott, 1921.

Brandon S, McClelland HA, Protheroe C. A study of facial dyskinesia in a mental hospital population. Br J Psychiatry 118: 171–184, 1971.

Braude WM, Barnes TRE. Late-onset akathisia: An indicant of covert dyskinesia: Two case reports. Am J Psychiatry 140: 611–612, 1983.

Braude WM, Barnes TRE, Gore SM. Clinical characteristics of akathisia: A systematic investigation of acute psychiatric inpatient admissions. Br J Psychiatry 143: 139–150, 1983.

Brenner I, Rheuban WJ. The catatonic dilemma. Am J Psychiatry 135: 1242–1243, 1978.

Breuer J, Freud S. On the psychical mechanism of hysterical phenomena (1893). In: Breuer J, Freud S. *Studies on Hysteria.* New York, Basic Books, 1895/1957.

Brice J, McLellan L. Suppression of intention tremor by contingent deep-brain stimulation. Lancet I: 1221–1222, 1980.

Brickner RM, Rosner AA, Munro R. Physiological aspects of the obsessive state. Psychosom Med 2: 369–383, 1940.

Bridge TP, Parker ES, Soldo BJ, *et al.* Age, alcohol, catechols, memory, and neuroanatomic change. Presented at the 135th Annual Meeting of the American Psychiatric Association, Dallas, May 1985. New Research Abstract 156.

Briskin JG, Lehman KL, Guilleminault C. Shy-Drager syndrome and sleep apnea. In: Guilleminault C, Dement WC (eds). *Sleep Apnea Syndromes.* New York, A.R. Liss, 1978, pp. 317–322.

Brodal A. *Neurological Anatomy in Relation to Clinical Medicine.* Ed. 3. New York, Oxford University Press, 1981.

Brody H. Cell counts in cerebral cortex and brainstem. In: Katzman R, Terry RD, Bick KL, (eds). *Alzheimer's Disease, Senile Dementia and Related Disorders.* New York, Raven Press, 1978, pp. 345–351.

Broughton R. Sleep disorders: Disorders of arousal? Science 159: 1070–1078, 1968.

Brown JW, Grober E. Age, sex, and aphasia type: Evidence for a regional cerebral growth process underlying lateralization. J Nerv Ment Dis 171: 431–434, 1983.

Brown J, Jaffe J. Hypothesis on cerebral dominance. Neuropsychologia 13: 107–110, 1975.

Brown RM, Crane AM, Goldman PS. Regional distribution of monoamines in the cerebral cortex and subcortical structures of the rhesus monkey: Concentrations and in vivo synthesis rates. Brain Res 168: 133–150, 1979.

Bruetsch WL. Chronic rheumatic brain disease as a possible factor in the causation of some cases of dementia praecox. Am J Psychiatry 97: 276–296, 1940.

Bruml H. Age changes in preference and skill measures of handedness. Percept Motor Skills 34: 3–14, 1972.

Brumlick J, Yap CB. *Normal Tremor.* Springfield, IL, Charles C Thomas, 1970.

Bruyn GW. Huntington's chorea: Historical, clinical and laboratory synopsis. In: Vinken PJ, Bruyn GW (eds). *Diseases of the Basal Ganglia. Handbook of Clinical Neurology.* Vol. 6. New York, American Elsevier, 1968, pp. 298–378.

Bryden MP. Measuring handedness with questionnaires. Neuropsychologia 15: 617–624, 1977.

Bucci L. The dyskinesias: A new therapeutic approach. Dis Nerv Syst 32: 324–327, 1971.

Buchanan A. Mechanical theory of the predominance of the right hand over the left, or, more generally, of the limbs of the right side over those of the left side of the body. *Address to the Philosophical Society of Glasgow.* March 12, 1862. Glasgow, Bell & Bain, 1862, pp. 5–29.

Buchsbaum MS, Wu J, DeLisi LE, *et al.* Frontal cortex and basal ganglia metabolic rates assessed by positron emission tomography with [^{18}F]2-deoxyglucose in affective illness. J Affect Dis 10: 137–152, 1986.

Bugiani O, Salvarani S, Perdelli F, et al. Nerve cell loss with aging in the putamen. Eur Neurol 17: 286–291, 1978.

Bugiani O, Tabaton M, Cammarata S. Huntington's disease: Survival of large striatal neurons in the rigid variant. Ann Neurol 15: 154–156, 1984.

Burchinsky SG. Neurotransmitter receptors in the central nervous system and aging: Pharmacological aspects (review). Exp Geront 19: 227–239, 1984.

Burke D. Critical examination of the case for or against fusimotor involvement in disorders of muscle tone. In: Desmedt JE (ed). *Motor Control Mechanisms in Health and Disease. Advances in Neurology*. Vol. 39. New York, Raven Press, 1983, pp. 133–150.

Burke D, Hagbarth K-E, Wallin BG. Reflex mechanisms in parkinsonian rigidity. Scand J Rehabil Med 9: 15–23, 1977.

Burke RE, Fahn S, Jankovic J, et al. Tardive dystonia: Late-onset and persistent dystonia caused by antipsychotic drugs. Neurology 32: 1335–1346, 1982.

Burton K, Farrell K, Li D, et al. Lesions of the putamen and dystonia: CT and magnetic resonance imaging. Neurology 34: 962–965, 1984.

Buscaino VM. Le cause anatomo-patologiche delle manifestazioni schizophreniche nella demenza precoce. Riv Patol Nerv Ment 25. 197–226, 1920.

Butler IJ, Koslow S, Seifert WE Jr, et al. Biogenic amine metabolism in Tourette syndrome. Ann Neurol 6: 37–39, 1979.

Cadet JL. The potential use of vitamin E and selenium in parkinsonism. Med Hypoth 20: 87–94, 1986.

Cadet JL, Lohr JB. Free radicals and the developmental pathobiology of schizophrenic burnout. Integr Psychiatry 1987, in press.

Cadet JL, Lohr JB, Jeste DV. Free radicals and tardive dyskinesia (letter to ed). Trends Neurosci 9: 107–108, 1986.

Caine ED, Polinsky RJ. Tardive dyskinesia in persons with Gilles de la Tourette's disease (letter to ed). Arch Neurol 38: 471–472, 1981.

Caine ED, Shoulson I. Psychiatric syndromes in Huntington's disease. Am J Psychiatry 140: 728–733, 1983.

Caine ED, Margolin DI, Brown GL. Gilles de la Tourette's syndrome, tardive dyskinesia and psychosis in an adolescent. Am J Psychiatry 135: 241–243, 1978.

Cairns H, Oldfield RC, Pennybacker B, et al. Akinetic mutism with an epidermoid cyst of the 3rd ventricle. Brain 64: 273–290, 1941.

Caldwell AE. *Origins of Psychopharmacology: From CPZ to LSD*. Springfield, IL, Charles C Thomas, 1970.

Campbell WG, Raskind MA, Gordon T, et al. Iron pigment in the brain of a man with tardive dyskinesia. Am J Psychiatry 142: 364–365, 1985.

Caparulo BK, Cohen DJ, Rothman SL, et al. Computed tomographic brain scanning in children with developmental neuropsychiatric disorders. J Am Acad Child Psychiatry 20: 338–357, 1981.

Caprini G, Melotti J. Un grave sindrome ticcose guarito con haloperidol. Riv Sper Freniat 86: 191–196, 1962.

Carlen PL, Lee MA, Jacob M, et al. Parkinsonism provoked by alcoholism. Ann Neurol 9: 84–86, 1981.

Carlsson A, Winblad B. Influence of age and time interval between death and autopsy on dopamine and 3-methoxytyramine levels in human basal ganglia. J Neural Transm 38: 271–276, 1976.

Carman JS, Wyatt RJ. Calcium and malignant catatonia (letter to ed). Lancet II: 1124–1125, 1977.

Carman JS, Wyatt RJ. Calcium: Pacesetting the periodic psychoses. Am J Psychiatry 136: 1035–1039, 1979.

Carpenter MB. Interconnections between the corpus striatum and brain stem nuclei. In:

McKenzie JS, Kemm RE, Wilcock LN (eds). *The Basal Ganglia: Structure and Function*. New York, Plenum Press, 1984, pp. 1–68.

Carpenter MB, Sutin J. *Human Neuroanatomy*. Ed. 8. Baltimore, Williams & Wilkins, 1983.

Carpenter WY, Bartko JJ, Carpenter CL, *et al.* Another view of schizophrenia subtypes: A report from the international pilot study of schizophrenia. Arch Gen Psychiatry 33: 508–516, 1976.

Carter RL, Hohengger M, Satz P. Handedness and aphasia: An inferential method for determining the mode of cerebral speech specialization. Neuropsychologia 18: 569–574, 1980.

Casey DE. Tardive dyskinesia and affective disorders. In: Gardos G, Casey DE (eds). *Tardive Dyskinesia and Affective Disorders*. Washington, D.C., American Psychiatric Press, 1984, pp. 1–20.

Casey DE, Hansen TE. Spontaneous dyskinesias. In: Jeste DV, Wyatt RJ (eds). *Neuropsychiatric Movement Disorders*. Washington, D.C., American Psychiatric Press, 1984, pp. 67–96.

Casey DE, Rabins P. Tardive dyskinesia as a life-threatening illness. Am J Psychiatry 135: 486–488, 1978.

Casey DE, Gerlach J, Magelund G, *et al.* Gamma-acetylenic GABA in tardive dyskinesia. Arch Gen Psychiatry 37: 1376–1379, 1980.

Cervantes P, Lal S, Smith F, *et al.* Dopaminergic function in two patients with catalepsy. Acta Psych Scand 55: 214–219, 1977.

Chadwick D, Reynolds EH, Marsden CD. Anticonvulsant-induced dyskinesias: A comparison with dyskinesias induced by neuroleptic. J Neurol Neurosurg Psychiatry 39: 1210–1218, 1976.

Charcot JM. In: Melotti G. Itorno ad alcuni casi di tic convulsive con coprolalia ed ecolalia. Riforma Medica 2: 185–186, 1885.

Chaugule VB, Master RS. Impaired cerebral dominance and schizophrenia. Br J Psychiatry 139: 23–24, 1981.

Childers AT. Hyperactivity in children having behavior disorders. Am J Orthopsychiatry 5: 227–243, 1935.

Chodoff P. The diagnosis of hysteria: An overview. Am J Psychiatry 131: 1073–1078, 1974.

Chrisman OD. The aging of articular cartilage. In: Nelson CL, Dwyer AP (eds). *The Aging Musculoskeletal System*. Lexington, MA, Collamore Press, 1984, pp. 59–63.

Christensen E, Moller JE, Faurbye A. Neuropathological investigation of 28 brains from patients with dyskinesia. Acta Psych Scand 46: 14–23, 1970.

Chui HC, Teng EL, Henderson VW, *et al.* Clinical subtypes of dementia of the Alzheimer type. Neurology 35: 1544–1550, 1985.

Clarke E, O'Malley CD. *The Human Brain and Spinal Cord*. Los Angeles, University of California Press, 1968.

Clarke PGH. Neuronal death in the development of the vertebrate nervous system. Trends Neurosci 8: 345–349, 1985.

Cloninger CR. The link between hysteria and sociopathy: An integrative model of pathogenesis based on clinical, genetic and neuro-physiological observations. In: Akiskal HS, Webb WL (eds). *Psychiatric Diagnosis: Exploration of Biological Predictors*. New York, SP Medical & Scientific Books, 1978, pp. 189–218.

Clyma EA. Hand and eye dominance in schizophrenia (letter to ed). Br J Psychiatry 120: 576, 1972.

Cody FWJ, Macdermott N, Matthews PBC, *et al.* Observations on the genesis of the stretch reflex in Parkinson's disease. Brain 109: 229–249, 1986.

Coffman JA, Mefferd J, Golden CJ, *et al.* Cerebellar atrophy in chronic schizophrenia. Lancet I: 666, 1981.

Coffman JA, Nasrallah HA, Andreasen N, *et al.* Cerebellar atrophy in schizophrenia: A reassessment by NMR imaging technique. *Abstracts of the Annual Meeting of the American College of Neuropsychopharmacology.* Maui, Hawaii, December 1985, p. 152.

Cohen DJ, Shaywitz BA, Johnson WT, et al. Biogenic amines in autistic and atypical children: Cerebrospinal fluid measures of homovanillic acid and 5-hydroxyindoleacetic acid. Arch Gen Psychiatry 31: 845–853, 1974.

Cohen DJ, Caparulo BK, Shaywitz BA, et al. Dopamine and serotonin metabolism in neuro-psychiatrically disturbed children: CSF homovanillic acid and 5-hydroxyindoleacetic acid. Arch Gen Psychiatry 34: 545–550, 1977.

Cohen DJ, Shaywitz BA, Young JG. Central biogenic amine metabolism in children with the syndrome of chronic multiple tics of Gilles de la Tourette: Norepinephrine, serotonin and dopamine. J Am Acad Child Psychiatry 18: 320–341, 1979.

Cohen DJ, Detlor J, Young JG, et al. Clonidine ameliorates Gilles de la Tourette syndrome. Arch Gen Psychiatry 37: 1350–1357, 1980.

Cohen DJ, Detlor J, Shaywitz BA, et al. Interaction of biological and psychological factors in the natural history of Tourette syndrome: A paradigm for childhood neuropsychiatric disorders. In: Friedhoff AJ, Chase TN (eds). *Gilles de la Tourette Syndrome. Advances in Neurology.* Vol. 35. New York, Raven Press, 1982, pp. 31–40.

Cohen DJ, Riddle MA, Leckman JF, et al. Tourette's syndrome. In: Jeste DV, Wyatt RJ (eds). *Neuropsychiatric Movement Disorders.* Washington, D.C., American Psychiatric Press, 1984, pp. 19–52.

Colby KM, Parkison C. Handedness in autistic children. J Aut Child Schiz 7: 3–9, 1977.

Cole JO, Clyde DJ. Extrapyramidal side effects and clinical response to the phenothiazines. In: Bordeleau L-M (ed). *Système Extra-Pyramidal et Neuroleptiques (Extrapyramidal System and Neuroleptics).* Montreal, Editions Psychiatriques, 1961, pp. 469–478.

Coleman RM, Pollak CP, Weitzman ED. Periodic movements in sleep (nocturnal myoclonus): Relation to sleep disorders. Ann Neurol 8: 416–421, 1980.

Coleman RM, Bliwise DL, Sajben N, et al. Daytime sleepiness in patients with periodic movements in sleep. Sleep 5: S191–S202, 1982.

Comfort A. Neuromythology? Nature 229: 282, 1971.

Cools AR. Haloperidol and the significance of alpha-adrenergically mediated control of a subpopulation of dopamine receptors for concepts such as supersensitivity and tolerance. Life Sci 23: 2475–2484, 1978.

Cools AR, Jaspers R, Schwarz M, et al. Basal ganglia and switching motor programs. In: McKenzie JS, Kemm RE, Wilcock LN (eds). *The Basal Ganglia: Structure and Function.* New York, Plenum Press, 1984, pp. 513–544.

Cooper IS. *Involuntary Movement Disorders.* New York, Harper & Row, 1969.

Cooper IS. 20-year followup study of the neurosurgical treatment of dystonia musculorum deformans. In: Eldridge R, Fahn S (eds). *Dystonia. Advances in Neurology.* Vol. 14. New York, Raven Press, 1976, pp. 423–447.

Cooper IS, Cullinan T, Riklan M. The natural history of dystonia. In: Eldridge R, Fahn S (eds). *Dystonia. Advances in Neurology.* Vol. 14. New York, Raven Press, 1976, pp. 157–170.

Coren S, Porac C. Fifty centuries of right-handedness: The historical record. Science 198: 631–632, 1977.

Coren S, Porac C. Birth factors and laterality: Effects of birth order, parental age, and birth stress on four indices of lateral preference. Behav Genet 10: 123–138, 1980.

Costall B, Naylor RJ. Is there a relationship between the involvement of extrapyramidal and mesolimbic brain areas with the cataleptic action of neuroleptic agents and their clinical antipsychotic effect? Psychopharmacologia 32: 161–170, 1973.

Cote LJ, Kremzner LT. Changes in neurotransmitter systems with increasing age in human brain. Trans Am Soc Neurochem 5: 83, 1974.

Cote LJ, Kremzner LT. Biochemical changes in normal aging in human brain. In: Mayeux R, Rosen WG (eds). *The Dementias*. New York, Raven Press, 1983, pp. 19–30.

Cotzias GC, Miller ST, Tang LC, *et al*. Levodopa, fertility, and longevity. Science 196: 549–551, 1977.

Couch, JR. Dystonia and tremor in spasmodic torticollis. Adv Neurol 14: 245–258, 1976.

Cox B, Lee TF. Do dopamine receptors have a physiological role in thermoregulation? Br J Pharmacol 61: 83–86, 1977.

Cox B, Kerwin R, Lee TF. Dopamine receptors in the central thermoregulatory pathways of the rat. J Physiol 282: 471–483, 1978.

Crane GE. Pseudoparkinsonism and tardive dyskinesia. Arch Neurol 27: 426–430, 1972.

Crane GE. Persistent dyskinesia. Br J Psychiatry 122: 395–405, 1973.

Cravioto H, Silberman J, Feigin I. A clinical and pathologic study of akinetic mutism. Neurology 10: 10–21, 1960.

Critchley E. Clinical manifestations of essential tremor. J Neurol Neurosurg Psychiatry 35: 365–372, 1972.

Critchley M. Arteriosclerotic Parkinsonism. Brain 52: 23–83, 1929.

Critchley M (ed). *James Parkinson (1755–1824)*. London, Macmillan, 1955.

Critchely M. Neurological changes in the aged. In: Moore JE, Merritt HH, Masselink RJ (eds). *The Neurologic and Psychiatric Aspects of the Disorders of Aging. Research Publications of the Association for Research in Nervous and Mental Disease*. Vol. 35. Baltimore, Williams & Wilkins, 1956, pp. 198–223.

Critchley M. Neurological disabilities. In: Freeman JT (ed). *Clinical Features of the Older Patient*. Springfield, IL, Charles C Thomas, 1965, pp. 233–240.

Crow TJ. Molecular pathology of schizophrenia: More than one disease process? Br Med J 280: 66–68, 1980.

Crow TJ. Positive and negative schizophrenia symptoms and the role of dopamine. Br J Psychiatry 139: 251–254, 1981.

Crow TJ, Cross AJ, Johnstone EC, *et al*. Abnormal involuntary movements in schizophrenia: Are they related to the disease process or its treatment? Are they associated with changes in dopamine receptors? J Clin Psychopharm 2: 336–340, 1982.

Cummings JL, Benson DF. Subcortical dementia: Review of an emerging concept. Arch Neurol 41: 874–879, 1984.

Cutler NR, Post RM. State-related cyclical dyskinesias in manic–depressive illness. J Clin Psychopharm 2: 350–354, 1982.

Dabbous IA, Bergman AB, Neurologic damage associated with phenothiazine. Am J Dis Child 111: 291–296, 1966.

Daly DD, Mulder DW. Gelastic epilepsy. Neurology 7: 189–192, 1957.

Damasio AR, Maurer RG. A neurological model for childhood autism. Arch Neurol 35: 777–786, 1978.

Danielczyk W. Various mental behavioral disorders in Parkinson's disease, primary degenerative senile dementia, and multiple infarction dementia. J Neural Trans 56: 161–176, 1983.

Darwin C. *The Expression of the Emotions in Man and Animals*. Chicago, University of Chicago Press, 1872/1965.

Davis JM, Dysken MW. Naxolone in amylobarbitone-responsive catatonia (letter to ed). Br J Psychiatry 133: 476, 1978.

De UJ. Catatonia from fluphenazine (letter to ed). Br J Psychiatry 122: 240–241, 1973.

DeAjuriaguerra J. The concept of akinesia. Psychol Med 5: 129–137, 1975.

Deecke L, Scheid P, Kornhuber HH. Distribution of readiness potential, pre-motion positivity, and motor potential of the human cerebral cortex preceding voluntary finger movements. Exp Brain Res 7: 158–168, 1969.

DeJong HH. *Experimental Catatonia*. Baltimore, Williams & Wilkins, 1945.

DeJong HH. Experimental catatonia in animals and induced catatonic stupor in man. Dis Nerv Syst 17: 135–139, 1956.

DeJong RN. *The Neurologic Examination.* Ed. 4. Philadelphia, Harper & Row, 1979.

DeLisi LE, Goldin LR, Hamovit JR, *et al.* A family study of the association of increased ventricular size with schizophrenia. Arch Gen Psychiatry 43: 148–153, 1986.

DeLong MR, Georgopoulos AP. Motor functions of the basal ganglia. In: Brooks VB (ed). *Handbook of Physiology, Section 1, The Nervous System, Volume II, Motor Control, Part 1.* Bethesda, MD, American Physiological Society, 1981, pp. 1017–1061.

DeLong MR, Georgopoulos AP, Crutcher MD. Cortico–basal ganglia relations and coding of motor performance. In: Massion J, Paillard J, Schultz W, *et al.* (eds). *Neural Coding of Motor Performance.* Berlin/Heidelberg/New York, Springer-Verlag, 1983, pp. 30–40.

Demarest J, Demarest L. Does the "torque test" measure cerebral dominance in adults? Percept Motor Skills 50: 155–158, 1980.

Demars J-PCA. Neuromuscular effects of long-term phenothiazine medication, electroconvulsive therapy and leucotomy. J Nerv Ment Dis 143: 73–79, 1966.

Denckla MB, Heilman KM. The syndrome of hyperactivity. In: Heilman KM, Valenstein E (eds). *Clinical Neuropsychology.* New York, Oxford, 1979, pp. 574–597.

Deniker P. Experimental neurological syndromes and the new drug therapies in psychiatry. Comp Psychiatry 1: 92–102, 1960.

Denny-Brown D. Clinical symptomatology of diseases of the basal ganglia. In: Vinken PJ, Bruyn GW (eds). *Diseases of the Basal Ganglia. Handbook of Clinical Neurology.* Vol. 6. New York, American Elsevier, 1968, pp. 133–172.

Deuel RK, Dunlop NL. Hand preferences in the rhesus monkey: Implications for the study of cerebral dominance. Arch Neurol 37: 217–221, 1980.

DeVeaugh-Geiss J. Tardive Tourette syndrome. Neurology 30: 562–563, 1980.

Devinsky O. Neuroanatomy of Gilles de la Tourette's syndrome: Possible midbrain involvement. Arch Neurol 40: 508–514, 1983.

Dewan MJ, Pandurangi AK, Lee SH, *et al.* Cerebellar morphology in chronic schizophrenic patients: A controlled computer tomography study. Psychiatry Res 10: 97–103, 1983.

Dickes RA. Brief therapy of conversion reactions: An in-hospital technique. Am J Psychiatry 131: 584–586, 1974.

Dimond SJ. Introductory remarks. In: Dimond SJ, Blizard DA (eds), *Evolution and Lateralization of the Brain.* Ann NY Acad Sci 299: 1–3, 1977.

Dolaeus J. *Systema Medicinale: A Compleat System of Physick, Theoretical and Practical.* Salmon W (trans). London, T. Passinger, 1686.

Dom R. *Neostriatal and Thalamic Interneurons: Their Role in the Pathophysiology of Huntington's Chorea, Parkinson's Disease and Catatonic Schizophrenia.* Thesis, Catholic University of Leuven. Leuven, Acco, 1976.

Dom R, DeSaedeleer J. Quantitative cytometric analysis of basal ganglia in catatonic schizophrenia. Abstract of the IIIrd World Congress of Biological Psychiatry. Stockholm, 1981, p. 76.

Dom R, Baro F, Brucher JM. A cytometric study of the putamen in different types of Huntington's chorea. In: Barbeau A, Chase TN, Paulson GW (eds). *Huntington's Chorea 1872–1972. Advances in Neurology.* Vol. 1. New York, Raven Press, 1973, pp. 369–385.

Domino EF, Piggott L, Demetriou S, *et al.* Visually evoked response in Tourette syndrome. In: Friedhoff AJ, Chase TN (eds). *Gilles de la Tourette Syndrome. Advances in Neurology.* Vol. 35. New York, Raven Press, 1982, pp. 115–120.

Donaldson J. Movement disorders. In: *Neurology of Pregnancy.* Philadelphia, W. B. Saunders, 1978, pp. 74–87.

Donlon P. The therapeutic use of diazepam for akathisia. Psychosomatics 14: 222–225, 1973.

Dooling EC, Adams RD. The pathological anatomy of posthemiplegic athetosis. Brain 98: 29–48, 1975.

Dooling EC, Schoene WC, Richardson EP Jr. Hallervorden–Spatz syndrome. Arch Neurol 30: 70–83, 1974.

Doty RW, Negrao N, Yagama N. The unilateral engram. Acta Neurobiol Exp 33: 711–728, 1973.

Drake ME Jr, Coffey CE. Complex partial status epilepticus simulating psychogenic unresponsiveness. Am J Psychiatry 140: 800–801, 1983.

Druckman R, Seelinger D, Thubin B. Chronic involuntary movements induced by phenothiazines. J Nerv Ment Dis 135: 69–76, 1962.

Dupont E. Parkinson's disease and essential tremor: Differential diagnostic and epidemiological aspects. In: Rinne UK, Klinger M, Stamm G (eds). *Parkinson's Disease: Current Progress, Problems and Management.* Amsterdam, Elsevier/North-Holland, 1980, 165–179.

Duval AM. Clinical studies in schizophrenia. Med Ann Dist Columbia 17: 92–132, 1948.

Dvirskii AE. Functional asymmetry of the cerebral hemispheres in clinical types of schizophrenia. Neurosci Behav Physiol 7: 236–239, 1976.

Ebstein RP, Freedman LS, Leiberman A, et al. A family study of serum dopamine-beta-hydroxylase levels in torsion dystonia. Neurology 24: 684–687, 1974.

Eccles JC. The cerebellum as a computer: Patterns in space and time. J Physiol 229: 1–32, 1973.

Eidelberg E, Walden JG, Nguyen LH. Locomotor control in Macaque monkeys. Brain 104: 647–663, 1981.

Eisenberg L, Ascher E, Kanner L. A clinical study of Gilles de la Tourette's disease (maladie des tics) in children. Am J Psychiatry 115: 715–723, 1959.

Ekbom KA. Asthenia crurum paraesthetica ("irritable legs"). Acta Med Scand 118: 197–209, 1944.

Ekbom KA. Restless legs syndrome. Neurology 10: 868–873, 1960.

Ekman P, Friesen WV. *Unmasking the Face.* Englewood Cliffs, NJ, Prentice-Hall, 1975.

Ekman P, Levenson RW, Friesen WV. Autonomic nervous system activity distinguishes among emotions. Science 221: 1208–1210, 1983.

Eldridge R. The torsion dystonias: Literature review and genetics and clinical studies. Neurology 20: 1–78, 1970.

Eldridge R, Fahn S (eds). *Dystonia. Advances in Neurology.* Vol. 14. New York, Raven Press, 1976.

Eldridge R, Sweet RD, Shapiro A, et al. Clinical and genetic observations of 21 families with Gilles de la Tourette syndrome. Neurology 25: 379, 1975.

Eling P. Comparing different measures of laterality: Do they relate to a single mechanism? J Clin Neuropsychol 5: 135–147, 1983.

Elkes J. Effects of psychosomimetic drugs in animals and man. In: Abramson HA (ed). *Neuropharmacology. Transactions of the Third Conference, May 21, 22, and 23, 1956, Princeton, N.J.* New York, Josiah Macy, Jr., Foundation, 1957.

Ellinwood EH. Amphetamine psychosis: I. Description of the individuals and process. J Nerv Ment Dis 144: 273–283, 1967.

Ellis RS. Norms for some structural changes in the human cerebellum from birth to old age. J Comp Neurol 32: 1–33, 1920.

Endicott J, Nee J, Fleiss J, et al. Diagnostic criteria for schizophrenia: Reliabilities and agreement between systems. Arch Gen Psychiatry 39: 884–889, 1982.

Engel GL. Conversion symptoms. In: MacBryde CM, Blacklow RS (eds). *Signs and Symptoms.* Ed. 5. Philadelphia, Lippincott, 1970, pp. 650–668.

Enoch MD, Trethowan WH. *Uncommon Psychiatric Syndromes.* Bristol, Wright, 1979, pp. 95–115.

Eriksson H, Morath C, Heilbronn E. Effects of manganese on the nervous system. Acta Neurol Scand 70 (Supp 100): 89–93, 1984.

Evarts EV. Activity of pyramidal tract neurons during postural fixation. J Neurophysiol 32: 375–385, 1969.

Evarts EV, Teravainen HT, Beuchert DE, et al. Pathophysiology of motor performance in Parkinson's disease. In: Fuxe K, Calne DB (eds). Dopaminergic Ergot Derivatives and Motor Function. Oxford, Pergamon, 1979, pp. 45–59.

Evarts EV, Teravainen H, Calne DB. Reaction time in Parkinson's disease. Brain 104: 167–186, 1981.

Everett PW, Kemm RE, McKenzie JS. Neural activity in basal ganglia output nuclei and induced hypermotility. In: McKenzie JS, Kemm RE, Wilcock LN (eds). The Basal Ganglia: Structure and Function. New York, Plenum Press, 1984, pp. 235–245.

Fahn S. The clinical spectrum of motor tics. In: Friedhoff AJ, Chase TN (eds). Gilles de la Tourette Syndrome. Advances in Neurology. Vol. 35. New York, Raven Press, 1982, pp. 341–344.

Fahn S. High dosage anticholinergic therapy in dystonia. Neurology 33: 1255–1261, 1983.

Fahn S. The varied clinical expressions of dystonia. In: Jankovic J (ed). Movement Disorders. Neurologic Clinics. Vol. 2, No. 3. Philadelphia, W. B. Saunders, 1984, pp. 541–554.

Fahn S, Eldridge R. Definition of dystonia and classification of the dystonic states. In: Eldridge R, Fahn S (eds). Dystonia. Advances in Neurology. Vol. 14. New York, Raven Press, 1976, pp. 1–6.

Famuyiwa OO, Eccleston D, Donaldson AA, et al. Tardive dyskinesia and dementia. Brit J Psychiatry 135: 500–504, 1979.

Farran-Ridge C. Some symptoms referable to the basal ganglia occurring in dementia praecox and epidemic encephalitis. J Ment Sci 72: 513–523, 1926.

Faurbye A, Rasch P-J, Petersen PB, et al. Neurological symptoms in pharmacotherapy of psychoses. Acta Psych Scand 40: 10–27, 1964.

Feinberg HB. An unusual diagnostic problem in an adolescent patient (possible lethal catatonia). Psych Quart 42: 203–210, 1968.

Feinberg M, Carroll BJ. Effects of dopamine agonists and antagonists in Tourette's disease. Arch Gen Psychiatry 36: 979–985, 1979.

Feindel W, Penfield W. Localization of discharge in temporal lobe automatism. Arch Neurol Psychiatry 72: 605–630, 1954.

Fenichel O. The Psychoanalytic Theory of Neurosis. New York, Norton, 1945, pp. 415–452.

Ferenczi S. Psychoanalytical observations on tic. Int J Psychoanal 2: 1–30, 1921.

Ferrari E, Puca FM, Margherita G. Le anomalie dei fusi da sonno nei parkinsoniani. Riv Neurol 34: 48–55, 1964.

Ferraro A, Barrera SE. Experimental Catalepsy. Utica, NY, State Hospitals Press, 1932.

Filion M. Effects of interruption of the nigrostriatal pathway and of dopaminergic agents on the spontaneous activity of globus pallidus neurons in the awake monkey. Brain Res 178: 425–441, 1979.

Finch CE. The relationships of aging changes in the basal ganglia to manifestations of Huntington's chorea. Ann Neurol 7: 406–411, 1980.

Findley LJ, Gresty MA, Halmagyi GM. Tremor, cogwheel phenomenon and clonus in Parkinson's disease. J Neurol Neurosurg Psychiatry 44: 534–546, 1981.

Fish FJ. Fish's Clinical Psychopathology: Signs and Symptoms in Psychiatry. Hamilton M (ed). Bristol, Wright, 1974.

Fish FJ. Fish's Schizophrenia. Hamilton M (ed). Bristol, Wright, 1976.

Fitzhugh KB. Some neuropsychological features of delinquent subjects. Percept Motor Skills 36: 494, 1973.

Flatau E, Sterling W. Progressiver Torsionsspasmus bei Kindern. Z Ges Neurol Psychiatr 7: 586–612, 1911.

Fleminger JJ, Dalton R, Standage KF. Handedness in psychiatric patients. Br J Psychiatry 131: 448–452, 1977.

Fleminger JJ, McGlure GM, Dalton R. Lateral response to suggestion in relation to handedness and the side of psychogenic symptoms. Br J Psychiatry 136: 562–566, 1980.

Flor-Henry P. *Cerebral Basis of Psychopathology.* Boston, Wright/PSG, 1983.

Flor-Henry P, Yeudall L, Koles ZJ, *et al.* Neuropsychological and power spectral EEG investigations of the obsessive compulsive syndrome. Biol Psychiatry 14: 119–130, 1979.

Flowers KA. Ballistic and corrective movements on an aiming task: Intention tremor and parkinsonian movement disorders compared. Neurology 25: 413–421, 1975.

Flowers KA. Visual "closed-loop" and "open-loop" characteristics of voluntary movement in patients with parkinsonism and intention tremor. Brain 99: 269–310, 1976.

Floyd RA, Zaleska MM, Harmon HJ. Possible involvement of iron and oxygen free radicals in aspects of aging in brain. In: Armstrong D, Sohal RS, Cutler RG, *et al.* (eds). *Free Radicals in Molecular Biology, Aging, and Disease. Aging.* Vol. 27. New York, Raven Press, 1984, pp. 143–161.

Foerster O. Mobile spasm of the neck muscles and its pathologic basis. J Comp Neurol 58: 725–735, 1933.

Folks DG, Ford CV, Regan WM. Conversion symptoms in a general hospital. Psychosomatics 25: 285–295, 1984.

Forbes GB, Reina JC. Adult lean body mass declines with age: Some longitudinal observations. Metabolism 19: 653–663, 1970.

Forssberg H, Johnels B, Steg G. Is parkinsonian gait caused by a regression to an immature walking pattern? In: Hassler RG, Christ JF (eds). *Parkinson-Specific Motor and Mental Disorders.* New York, Raven Press, 1984, pp. 375–379.

Foutz AS, Delashaw JB Jr, Guilleminault C, *et al.* Monoaminergic mechanisms and experimental cataplexy. Ann Neurol 10: 369–376, 1981.

Frazer JG. *The Golden Bough.* Ed. 1. London, Macmillan, 1890.

Freedman R, Silverman MM, Schwab PJ. Patients' awareness of extrapyramidal reactions to neuroleptic drugs: Possible evidence for the role of catecholamines in perception. Psychiatr Res 1: 31–38, 1979.

Freedman R, Bell J, Kirch D. Clonidine therapy for coexisting psychosis and tardive dyskinesia. Am J Psychiatry 137: 629–630, 1980.

Freeman J, Aron A, Collard J, *et al.* The emotional correlates of Sydenham's chorea. Pediatrics 35: 42–49, 1965.

Freeman T. *Childhood Psychopathology and Adult Psychoses.* New York, International Universities Press, 1976.

Freidin MR, Jankowski JJ, Singer WD. Nocturnal head banging as a sleep disorder: A case report. Am J Psychiatry 136: 1469–1470, 1979.

Freud S. Some general remarks on hysterical attacks. In: *Collected Works.* Vol. IX. London, Hogarth Press, 1909.

Freyhan FA. Extrapyramidal symptoms and other side effects. In: *Trifluoperazine: Clinical and Pharmacological Aspects.* Philadelphia, Lea & Febiger, 1958.

Fricchione GL. Neuroleptic catatonia and its relationship to psychogenic catatonia. Biol Psychiatry 20: 304–313, 1985.

Fricchione GL, Cassem NH, Hooberman D, *et al.* Intravenous lorazepam in neuroleptic-induced catatonia. J Clin Psychopharm 3: 338–342, 1983.

Friedhoff AJ. Receptor maturation in pathogenesis and treatment of Tourette Syndrome. In: Friedhoff AJ, Chase TN (eds). *Gilles de la Tourette Syndrome. Advances in Neurology.* Vol. 35. New York, Raven Press, 1982, pp. 133–140.

Friedreich N. Neuropathologische Beobachtung beim Paramyoklonus Multiplex. Virch Archiv Path Klin Med 86: 421–434, 1881.

Friel PB. Familial incidence of Gilles da la Tourette syndrome with observations on aetiology and treatment. Br J Psychiatry 122: 655–658, 1973.

Frumkin LR, Ward NG, Grim PS. A possible cerebral mechanism for the clearing of psychogenic symptoms with amobarbital. Biol Psychiatry 16: 687–691, 1981.

Fuxe K, Agnati LF, Kohler C, et al. Characterization of normal and supersensitive dopamine receptors: Effects of ergot drugs and neuropeptides. J Neural Transm 51: 3–37, 1981.

Gabrielli WF Jr, Mednick SA. Sinistrality and delinquency. J Abn Psychol 89: 654–661, 1980.

Gadelius B. *Human Mentality in the Light of Psychiatric Experience: An Outline of General Psychiatry.* London, Oxford, 1933.

Gage FH, Dunnett SB, Stenevi V, et al. Aged rats: Recovery of motor impairments by intrastriatal nigral grafts. Science 221: 966–969, 1983.

Gagnon P, DeKoninck J. Repetitive head movements during REM sleep. Biol Psychiatry 20: 176–178, 1985.

Galin D, Diamond R, Braff D. Lateralization of conversion symptoms: More frequent on the left. Am J Psychiatry 134: 578–580, 1977.

Garcia-Albea E, Franch O, Munoz D, et al. Brucghel's syndrome: Report of a case with post-mortem studies. J Neurol Neurosurg Psychiatry 44: 437–440, 1981.

Gardos G, Cole JO, Tarsy D. Withdrawal syndromes associated with antipsychotic drugs Am J Psychiatry 135: 1321–1324, 1978.

Garfinkel A. A mathematics for physiology. Am J Physiol 245: R455–R466, 1983.

Garfinkel PE, Stancer HC. L-DOPA and schizophrenia. Can Psychiat Assoc J 21: 27–29, 1976.

Gascon CG, Lombroso CT. Epileptic (gelastic) laughter. Epilepsia 12: 63–76, 1971.

Gastaut H, Villeneuve A. The startle disease or hyperekplexia: Pathological surprise reaction. J Nerv Ment Dis 5: 523–542, 1967.

Gatfield P, Guze S. Prognosis and differential diagnosis of conversion reactions: A follow-up study. J Clin Psychol 22: 623–631, 1962.

Gelenberg AJ. The catatonic syndrome. Lancet I: 1339–1341, 1976a.

Gelenberg AJ. Computerized tomography in patients with tardive dyskinesia. Am J Psychiatry 133: 578–579, 1976b.

Gelenberg AJ, Mandel MR. Catatonic reactions to high-potency neuroleptic drugs. Arch Gen Psychiatry 34: 947–950, 1977.

Gelineau J. De la narcolepsie. Gaz d Hôpit (Paris) 53: 626–628, 54: 635–637, 1880.

Georgopoulos AP, Caminiti R, Kalaska JF, et al. Spatial coding of movement: A hypothesis concerning the coding of movement direction by motor cortical populations. In: Massion J, Paillard J, Schultz W, et al. (eds). *Neural Coding of Motor Performance.* Berlin/Heidelberg/New York, Springer-Verlag, 1983, pp. 327–336.

Geschwind N. Disconnexion syndromes in animals and man. Brain 88: 237–294, 585–644, 1965.

Geschwind N. The apraxias in phenomenology of will and action. In: Straus EW, Griffiths RM (eds). *The Second Lexington Conference on Pure and Applied Phenomenology.* Pittsburgh, Duquesne University Press, 1967.

Geschwind N. The apraxias: Neural mechanisms of disorders of learned movement. Am Scientist 63: 188–195, 1975.

Geschwind N, Behan P. Left-handedness: Association with immune disease, migraine, and developmental learning disorder. Proc Natl Acad Sci 79: 5097–5100, 1982.

Geschwind N, Galaburda AM. Cerebral lateralization: Biological mechanisms, associations, and pathology: I. A hypothesis and a program for research. Arch Neurol 42: 428–459, 1985.

Ghalioungui P. *Magic and Medical Science in Ancient Egypt.* New York, Barnes & Noble, 1963.

Ghez C. Cortical control of voluntary movement. In: Kandel ER, Schwartz JH (eds). *Principles of Neural Science.* New York, Elsevier/North-Holland, 1981a, pp. 323–333.

Ghez C. Introduction to the motor systems. In: Kandel ER, Schwartz JH (eds). *Principles of Neural Science.* New York, Elsevier/North-Holland, 1981b, pp. 271–283.

Giannini AJ, Tamulonis D, Giannini MC, *et al.* Defective response to social cues in Mobius' syndrome. J Nerv Ment Dis 172: 174–175, 1984.

Gilles de la Tourette, G. Jumping, latah, myriachit. Arch Neurol (Paris) 8: 68–74, 1884.

Gilles de la Tourette, G. Etude sur une affection nerveuse caracterisée par de l'incoordination motrice accompagnée d'écholalie et de coprolalie (jumping, latah, myriachit). Arch Neurol (Paris) 9: 19–42, 158–200, 1885.

Gillin JC, Sitaram N, Wehr T, *et al.* Sleep and affective illness. In: Post RM, Ballenger JC (eds). *Neurobiology of Mood Disorders.* Baltimore, Williams & Wilkins, 1984, pp. 157–189.

Gilman S. Significance of muscle receptor control systems in the pathophysiology of experimental postural abnormalities. In: Desmedt JE (ed). *New Developments in Electromyography and Clinical Neurophysiology.* Vol. 3. Basel, Karger, 1973, pp. 175–193.

Gimenez-Roldan S, Mateo D, Bartolome P. Tardive dystonia and severe tardive dyskinesia: A comparison of risk factors and prognosis. Acta Psych Scand 71: 488–494, 1985.

Gjessing LR. Studies of periodic catatonia. I. Blood levels of protein-bound iodine and urinary excretion of vanillyl-mandelic acid in relation to clinical course. J Psychiat Res 2: 123–134, 1964.

Gjessing LR. Studies on urinary phenolic compounds in man. II. Phenolic-acids and -amines during a load of alpha-methyl-dopa and disulfiram in periodic catatonia. Scand Clinic Lab Invest 17: 549–557, 1965.

Gjessing LR. Effects of thyroxine, pyridoxine, orphenadrine-HCl, reserpine and disulfiram in periodic catatonia. Acta Psych Scand 43: 376–384, 1967.

Gjessing LR. A review of periodic catatonia. Biol Psychiatry 8: 23–45, 1974.

Gjessing LR. The switch mechanism in periodic catatonia and manic–depressive disorder. In: Obiols J, Ballus C, Gonzalez Monclus E, *et al.* (eds). *Biological Psychiatry Today.* Vol. A. Amsterdam, Elsevier/North-Holland, 1979, pp. 307–316.

Gjessing LR, Harding GF, Jenner FA, *et al.* The EEG Society and the Electrophysiological Technologists' Association: The EEG in three of Gjessing's patients with periodic catatonia. EEG and Clin Neurophysiol 23: 490, 1967.

Glaros AG, Rao SM. Bruxism: A critical review. Psychol Bull 84: 767–781, 1977.

Glaze DG, Frost JD Jr, Jankovic J. Sleep in Gilles de la Tourette's syndrome: Disorder of arousal. Neurology 33: 586–592, 1983.

Glazer WM, Moore DC, Hansen TC, *et al.* Meige syndrome and tardive dyskinesia. Am J Psychiatry 140: 798–799, 1983.

Glick SD, Jerussi TP, Zummerberg B. Behavioral and neuropharmacological correlates of nigrostriatal asymmetry in rats. In: Harnard S, Doty RW, Goldstein L, *et al.* (eds). *Lateralization in the Nervous System.* New York, Academic Press, 1977, pp. 213–250.

Goetz CG, Tanner CM, Klawans HL. Fluphenazine and multifocal tic disorders. Arch Neurol 41: 271–272, 1984.

Gonzales-Vegas JA. Antagonism of dopamine-mediated inhibition in the nigro-striatal pathway: A mode of action of some catatonia-inducing drugs. Brain Res 80: 219–228, 1974.

Graham DG. On the origin and significance of neuromelanin. Arch Pathol Lab Med 103: 359–362, 1979.

Granato JE, Stern BJ, Ringel A, *et al.* Neuroleptic malignant syndrome: Successful treatment with dantrolene and bromocriptine. Ann Neurol 14: 89–90, 1983.

Granit R. *Receptors and Sensory Perception.* New Haven, Yale University Press, 1955.

Greden JF, Carroll BJ. Psychomotor function in affective disorders: An overview of new monitoring techniques. Am J Psychiatry 138: 1441–1448, 1981.

Greden JF, Genero N, Price HL. Agitation-increased electromyogram activity in the corrugator muscle region: A possible explanation of the "Omega sign"? Am J Psychiatry 142: 348–351, 1985.

Greden JF, Genero N, Price HL, et al. Facial electromyography in depression: Subgroup differences. Arch Gen Psychiatry 43: 269–274, 1986.

Green JR, Angevine JB, White JC Jr, et al. Significance of the supplementary motor area in partial seizures and in cerebral localization. Neurosurgery 6: 66–75, 1980.

Greenberg LB, Gujavarty K. The neuroleptic malignant syndrome: Review and report of three cases. Comp Psychiatry 26: 62–70, 1985.

Greenblatt DJ, DiMascio A, Harmatz JS, et al. Pharmacokinetics and clinical effects of amantadine in drug-induced extrapyramidal symptoms. J Clin Pharmacol 17: 704–708, 1977.

Greene PH. Why is it easy to control your arms? J Motor Behav 14: 260–286, 1982.

Griesinger W. Mental Pathology and Therapeutics. A facsimile of the English Edition of 1867. New York, Hafner, 1965.

Grillner S. Locomotion in vertebrates: Central mechanisms and reflex interaction. Physiol Rev 55: 247–304, 1975.

Grimshaw L. Obsessional disorder and neurological illness. J Neurol Neurosurg Psychiatry 27: 229–231, 1964.

Gross H, Kaltenback E. Neuropathological findings in persistent hyperkinesia after neuroleptic long-term therapy. In: Cerletti A, Bove FJ (eds). The Present Status of Psychotropic Drugs. Amsterdam, Excerpta Medica Foundation, 1969, pp. 474–476.

Gross RA, Spehlmann R, Daniels JC. Sleep disturbances in progressive supranuclear palsy. EEG Clin Neurophysiol 45: 16–25, 1978.

Grote SS, Moses SG, Robins E, et al. A study of selected catecholamine metabolizing enzymes: A comparison of depressive suicides and alcoholic suicides with controls. J Neurochem 25: 667–673, 1974.

Groves PM. A theory of the functional organization of the neostriatum and the neostriatal control of voluntary movement. Brain Res Rev 5: 109–132, 1983.

Grunthal E, Walther-Buel H. Uber Schadigung der Oliva inferior durch Chlorpromazin. Psychiatr Neurol (Basel) 140: 149–157, 1960.

Guggenheim FG, Babigian HM. Catatonic schizophrenia: Epidemiology and clinical course. J Nerv Ment Dis 1598: 291–305, 1974.

Guillain G, Mollaret P. Deux cas de myoclonies synchrones et rythmées velo-pharyngo-laryngo-oculo-diaphragmatiques. Le problème anatomique et physio-pathologique de ce syndrôme. Revue Neurol 2: 545–566, 1931.

Guilleminault C. Cataplexy. In: Guilleminault C, Dement WC, Passouant P (eds). Narcolepsy. New York, Spectrum, 1976, pp. 125–143.

Guilleminault C, Flagg W. Effect of baclofen on sleep-related periodic leg movements. Ann Neurol 15: 234–239, 1984.

Guilleminault C, Raynal D, Weitzman ED, et al. Sleep-related periodic myoclonus in patients complaining of insomnia. Trans Am Neurol Assoc 100: 19–21, 1975.

Guinon G. Sur la maladie des tics convulsifs. Rev Med 6: 50–80, 1886.

Gunn DR. Discussion. In: Bordeleau L-M (ed). Système Extra-Pyramidal et Neuroleptiques (Extrapyramidal System and Neuroleptics). Montreal, Editions Psychiatriques, 1961, pp. 365–367.

Gunne L-M, Haggstrom J-E. Experimental tardive dyskinesia. J Clin Psychiatry 46: 48–50, 1985.

Gunne L-M, Haggstrom J-E, Sjoquist B. Association with persistent neuroleptic-induced dyskinesia of regional changes in brain GABA synthesis. Nature 309: 347–349, 1984.

Gur RE. Motoric laterality imbalance in schizophrenia. Arch Gen Psychiatry 34: 33–37, 1977.

Gusella JF, Wexler NS, Conneally PM, et al. A polymorphic DNA marker genetically linked to Huntington's disease. Nature 306: 234–238, 1983.

Gutman Y, Segal J. Effect of calcium, sodium and potassium on adrenal tyrosine hydroxylase activity in vitro. Biochem Pharmacol 21: 2664–2666, 1972.

Guttman E. On some constitutional aspects of chorea and on its sequelae. J Neurol Psychopathol 17: 16–26, 1936.

Gybels JM, Meulders M, Callens M, et al. Disturbances of visuo-motor integration in cats with small lesions of the caudate nucleus. Arch Int Physiol Biochim 75: 283–302, 1967.

Haase H-J. Psychiatrische Erfahrungen mit Megaphen (Largactil) und dem Rauwolfiaalkaloid Serpasil unter dem Gesichtspunkt des psychomotorischen Parkinsonsyndroms. Nervenarzt 26: 507–510, 1955.

Haase H-J. Extrapyramidal modification of fine movements: A "conditio sine qua non" of the fundamental therapeutic action of neuroleptic drugs. In: Bordeleau L-M (ed). Système Extra-Pyramidal et Neuroleptiques (Extrapyramidal System and Neuroleptics). Montreal, Editions Psychiatriques, 1961, pp. 329–353.

Haerer AF, Anderson DW, Schoenberg BS. Prevalence of essential tremor: Results from the Copiah County study. Arch Neurol 39: 750–751, 1982.

Hafeiz HB. Hysterical conversion: A prognostic study. Br J Psychiatry 136: 548–551, 1980.

Hagan RD. The kinematics of aging. In: Nelson CL, Dwyer AP (eds). The Aging Musculoskeletal System. Lexington, MA, Collamore Press, 1984, pp. 91–102.

Hagbarth K-E, Young RR. Participation of the stretch reflex in human physiological tremor. Brain 102: 509–526, 1979.

Hajal F, Leach AM. Familial aspects of Gilles de la Tourette syndrome. Am J Psychiatry 138: 90–92, 1981.

Hakim AM, Mathieson G. Dementia in Parkinson's disease: A neuropathologic study. Neurology 29: 1209–1214, 1979.

Hall TC, Miller AKH, Corsellis JAN. Variations in the human Purkinje cell population according to age and sex. Neuropath Appl Neurobiol 1: 267–292, 1975.

Haller JS, Axelrod P. Minimal brain dysfunction syndrome: Another point of view. Am J Dis Child 129: 1319–1324, 1975.

Hallett M, Khoshbin S. A physiological mechanism of bradykinesia. Brain 103: 301–314, 1980.

Halliday AM. The neurophysiology of myoclonic jerking: A reappraisal. Excerpta Medica International Congress Series 307: 1–29, 1975.

Halliday AM, Mason AA. The effect of hypnotic anaesthesia on cortical responses. J Neurol Neurosurg Psychiatry 27: 300–312, 1964.

Hamilton M (ed). Fish's Schizophrenia. Bristol, Wright/PSG, 1984.

Hammond GR, Kaplan RJ. Language lateralization and handedness: Estimates based on clinical data. Brain Lang 16: 348–351, 1982.

Hammond WA. A Treatise on Diseases of the Nervous System. Ed. 1. New York, Appleton-Century-Crofts, 1871, pp. 655–662.

Hammond WA. Myriachit: Newly described disease of nervous system and its analogues. NY State J Med 39: 190–192, 1884.

Hanin I, Merikangas JR, Merikangas KR, et al. Red-cell choline and Gilles de la Tourette syndrome. N Engl J Med 301: 66¹ ⁶62, 1979.

Hansotia P, Wall R, Berendes J. Sleep disturbances and severity of Huntington's disease. Neurology 35: 1672–1674, 1985.

Harik SI, Morris PL. The effects of lesions in the head of the caudate nucleus on spontaneous and L-DOPA induced activity in the cat. Brain Res 62: 279–285, 1973.

Harris LJ. Left-handedness: Early theories, facts, and fancies. In: Herron J (ed). Neuropsychology of Left-Handedness. New York, Academic Press, 1980, pp. 3–78.

Haskovec L. Akathisie. Arch Bohemes Med Clin 3: 193–200, 1902.

Hays HR. In the Beginnings. New York, G. P. Putnam's Sons, 1963.

Hearst ED, Munoz RA, Tuason VB. Catatonia: Its diagnostic validity. Dis Nerv Syst 32: 453–456, 1971.

Heath RG, Franklin DE, Shraberg D. Gross pathology of the cerebellum in patients diagnosed and treated as functional psychiatric disorders. J Nerv Ment Dis 167: 585–592, 1979.

Heath RG, Franklin DE, Walker CF, et al. Cerebellar vermal atrophy in psychiatric patients. Biol Psychiatry 17: 569–583, 1982.

Hecaen H, DeAjuriaguerra J. Left-Handedness; Manual Superiority and Cerebral Dominance. Ponder E (trans). New York, Grune & Stratton, 1964.

Heilizer F. The effects of chlorpromazine upon psychomotor and psychiatric behavior of chronic schizophrenic patients. J Nerv Ment Dis 128: 358–364, 1959.

Heilman KM. Apraxia. In: Heilman KM, Valenstein E. Clinical Neuropsychology. New York, Oxford, 1979, pp. 159–185.

Heilman KM, Bowers D, Watson RT, et al. Reaction times in Parkinson disease. Arch Neurol 33: 139–140, 1976.

Heilman KM, Rothi LJ, Valenstein E. Two forms of ideomotor apraxia. Neurology 32: 342–346, 1982.

Held JM, Cromwell RM, Frank ET Jr, et al. Effect of phenothiazines on reaction time in schizophrenics. J Psychiat Res 7: 209–213, 1970.

Henderson VW, Wooten GF. Neuroleptic malignant syndrome: A pathogenetic role for dopamine blockade? Neurology 31: 132–137, 1981.

Henry GW. Catatonia in animals. Experimental studies of the effect of bulbocapnine and other drugs. Am J Psychiatry 88: 757–793, 1931.

Hepp-Reymond M-C, Diener R. Neural coding of force and of rate of force change in the precentral finger region of the monkey. In: Massion J, Paillard J, Schultz W, et al. (eds), Neural Coding of Motor Performance. Berlin/Heidelberg/New York, Springer-Verlag, 1983, pp. 315–326.

Hernandez-Peon R, Chavez-Ibarra G, Aguilar-Figueroa E. Somatic evoked potentials in one case of hysterical anaesthesia. EEG Clin Neurophysiol 15: 889–892, 1963.

Hersen M, Gullick EL, Maherne PM, et al. Instructions and reinforcement in the modification of a conversion reaction. Psychol Rep 31: 719–722, 1972.

Hetzler BE, Griffin JL. Infantile autism and the temporal lobe of the brain. J Aut Dev Dis 11: 317–330, 1981.

Hobson JA, McCarley RW, Wyzinski PW. Sleep cycle oscillation: Reciprocal discharge by two brainstem neuronal groups. Science 189: 55–58, 1975.

Hoder EL, Leckman JF, Ehrenkranz R, et al. Clonidine in neonatal narcotic abstinence syndrome (letter to ed). N Engl J Med 305: 1284, 1981.

Hogarty GE, Gross M. Preadmission symptom differences between first-admitted schizophrenics in the predrug and postdrug era. Comp Psychiatry 7: 134–140, 1966.

Holmes G. The clinical symptoms of cerebellar disease. Lancet I: 1177–1182, 1922.

Holzman PS. Smooth pursuit eye movements in psychopathology. Schiz Bull 9: 33–36, 1983.

Hoover CF, Insel TR. Families of origin in obsessive–compulsive disorder. J Nerv Ment Dis 172: 207–215, 1984.

Hopf A. Uber histopathologische Veranderungen im Pallidum und Striatum bei Schizophrenie. In: Proceedings of the First International Congress of Neuropathology. Vol. 3. Turin, Rosenberg & Sellier, 1952, pp. 629–635.

Horn S. Some psychological factors in parkinsonism. J Neurol Neurosurg Psychiatry 37: 27–31, 1974.

Hornykiewicz O. Neurochemical interactions and basal ganglia function and dysfunction. In: Yahr MD (ed). The Basal Ganglia. New York, Raven Press, 1976, pp. 269–280.

Hornykiewicz O. Dopamine changes in the aging human brain: Functional considerations. In: Agnoli A, Crepaldi G, Spano PF, et al. (eds). Aging Brain and Ergot Alkaloids. Aging. Vol. 23. New York, Raven Press, 1983, pp. 9–14.

Horrax G. *Neurosurgery: An Historical Sketch.* Springfield, IL, Charles C Thomas, 1952.

Horvath T, Friedman J, Meares R. Attention in hysteria: A study of Janet's hypothesis by means of habituation and arousal measures. Am J Psychiatry 137: 217–220, 1980.

Huapaya LVM. Seven cases of somnambulism induced by drugs. Am J Psychiatry 136: 985–986, 1979.

Huber SJ, Paulson GW. The concept of subcortical dementia. Am J Psychiatry 142: 1312–1317, 1985.

Huheey JE. Concerning the origin of handedness in humans. Behav Genetics 7: 29–32, 1977.

Hunker CJ, Abbs JH, Barlow SM. The relationship between parkinsonian rigidity and hypokinesia in the orofacial system: A quantitative analysis. Neurology 32: 755–761, 1982.

Hunter R, Earl CJ, Thornicroff S. An apparently irreversible syndrome of abnormal movements following phenothiazine medication. Proc Roy Soc Med 57: 758–762, 1964.

Hunter R, Blackwood W, Smith M, *et al.* Neuropathological findings in three cases of persistent dyskinesia following phenothiazine medication. J Neurol Sci 7: 263–273, 1968.

Huntington G. On chorea. Med Surg Rep Philadelphia 317–321, 1872.

Hussian RA. Stimulus control in the modification of problematic behavior in elderly institutionalized patients. Int J Behav Genet 1: 33–42, 1982.

Hutt SJ, Hutt C, Lee D, *et al.* A behavioral and electroencephalographic study of autistic children. J Psychiat Res 3: 181–197, 1965.

Ichikawa K, Kim RC, Givelber H, *et al.* Chorea gravidarum: Report of a fatal case with neuropathological observations. Arch Neurol 37: 429–432, 1980.

Insel TR, Donnelly EF, Lalakea ML, *et al.* Neurological and neuropsychological studies of patients with obsessive–compulsive disorder. Biol Psychiatry 18: 741–751, 1983a.

Insel TR, Murphy DL, Cohen RM, *et al.* Obsessive–compulsive disorder: A double-blind trial of clomipramine and clorgyline. Arch Gen Psychiatry 40: 605–612, 1983b.

Isler H. *Thomas Willis 1621–1675.* New York, Hafner, 1968.

Itard JMG. Mémoire sur quelques fonctions involontaires des appareils de la locomotion, de la préhension et de la voix. Arch Gen Med 8: 385–407, 1825.

Jackson DM, Anden NE, Dahlstrom A. A functional effect of dopamine in the nucleus accumbens and in some other dopamine-rich parts of the rat brain. Psychopharmacologia 45: 139–149, 1975.

Jacobs BL, Klemfuss H. Brain stem and spinal cord mediation of serotonergic behavioral syndrome. Brain Res 100: 450–457, 1975.

Jamielity F, Kosc B, Lukaszewicz A. Zmiany neuropatologiczne w dyskinezji twarzowojezykowej prawdopodobonie polekowej. Neurol Neurochir Pol 26: 399–402, 1976.

Janet P. *The Mental State of Hystericals.* New York, Putnam, 1901.

Jankel WR, Allen RP, Niedermeyer E, *et al.* Polysomnographic findings in dystonia musculorum deformans. Sleep 6: 281–285, 1983.

Jankel WR, Niedermeyer E, Graf M, *et al.* Polysomnography of torsion dystonia. Arch Neurol 41: 1081–1083, 1984.

Jankovic J, Ford J. Blepharospasm and orofacial-cervical dystonia: Clinical and pharmacological findings in 100 patients. Ann Neurol 13: 402–411, 1983.

Jankovic J, Glaze DG, Frost JD Jr. Effect of tetrabenazine on tics and sleep of Gilles de la Tourette's syndrome. Neurology 34: 688–692, 1984.

Jasper HH. Mechanisms of epileptic automatism. Epilepsia 3: 381–390, 1962.

Jasper K. *General Psychopathology.* Manchester, Manchester University Press, 1963.

Jastrow J. Catalepsy. In: Baldwin JM (ed). *Dictionary of Philosophy and Psychology.* New York, Peter Smith, 1940, p. 158.

Jayne D, Lees AJ, Stern GM. Remission in spasmodic torticollis. J Neurol Neurosurg Psychiatry 47: 1236–1237, 1984.

Jelliffe SE. The mental pictures in schizophrenia and in epidemic encephalitis: Their alliances, differences and a point of view. Am J Psychiatry 6: 413–465, 1927.

Jellinger K. Neuropathologic findings after neuroleptic long-term therapy. In: Roizin L, Shiraki H, Grcevic N (eds). *Neurotoxicology.* New York, Raven Press, 1977, pp. 25–42.

Jellinger K. Neuromorphological background of pathochemical studies in major psychoses. In: Beckman H, Riederer P (eds). *Pathochemical Markers in Major Psychoses.* Berlin, Springer-Verlag, 1985, pp. 1–23.

Jenike MA. Obsessive–compulsive disorder: A question of a neurologic lesion. Comp Psychiatry 25: 298–304, 1984.

Jenkins RL, Ashby HB. Gilles de la Tourette's syndrome in identical twins. Arch Neurol 40: 249–251, 1983.

Jessee SS, Anderson GF. ECT in the neuroleptic malignant syndrome: Case report. J Clin Psychiatry 44: 186–188, 1983.

Jeste DV, Wyatt RJ. Changing epidemiology of tardive dyskinesia: An overview. Am J Psychiatry 138: 297 309, 1981.

Jeste DV, Wyatt RJ. *Understanding and Treating Tardive Dyskinesia.* New York, Guilford, 1982.

Jeste DV, Phelps BH, Wagner RL, et al. Platelet monoamine oxidase and plasma dopamine-beta-hydroxylase in tardive dyskinesia. Lancet II: 850–851, 1979.

Jeste DV, Wagner RL, Weinberger DR, et al. Evaluation of CT scans in tardive dyskinesia. Am J Psychiatry 137: 247–248, 1980.

Jeste DV, Linnoila M, Fordis CM, et al. Enzyme studies in tardive dyskinesia. III. Noradrenergic hyperactivity in a subgroup of dyskinetic patients. J Clin Psychopharm 2: 318 320, 1982.

Jeste DV, Cutler NR, Kaufmann CA, et al. Low-dose apomorphine and bromocriptine in neuroleptic-induced movement disorders. Biol Psychiatry 18: 1085–1091, 1983.

Jeste DV, Barban L, Parisi J. Reduced Purkinje cell density in Huntington's disease. Exp Neurol 85: 78–86, 1984a.

Jeste DV, Karson CN, Iager A-C, et al. Association of abnormal involuntary movements and negative symptoms. Psychopharm Bull 20: 380–381, 1984b.

Jeste DV, Karson CN, Wyatt RJ. Movement disorders and psychopathology. In: Jeste DV, Wyatt RJ (eds). *Neuropsychiatric Movement Disorders.* Washington, D.C., American Psychiatric Press, 1984c, pp. 119–150.

Jeste DV, Doongaji DR, Linnoila M. Elevated cerebrospinal fluid noradrenaline in tardive dyskinesia. Am J Psychiatry 144: 177–180, 1984d.

Jeste DV, Grebb JA, Wyatt RJ. Psychiatric aspects of movement disorders and demyelinating diseases. In: Hales RE, Frances AJ (eds). *American Psychiatric Association Annual Review.* Vol. IV. Washington, D.C., American Psychiatric Press, 1985, pp. 159–188.

Jeste DV, Wisniewski A, Wyatt RJ. Neuroleptic-associated tardive syndromes. Psych Clin N Am 9:183–192, 1986a.

Jeste DV, Lohr JB, Mani R, et al. Neuronal loss in aging and neuropsychiatric dementias. In: Jeste DV (ed). *Neuropsychiatric Dementias: Current Perspectives.* Washington, D.C., American Psychiatric Press, 1986b, pp. 111–143.

Johnson EW, Yarnell SK. Hand dominance and scoliosis in Duchenne muscular dystrophy. Arch Phys Med Rehabil 57: 462–464, 1976.

Johnson GC, Manning DE. Neuroleptic-induced catatonia: Case report. J Clin Psychiatry 44: 310–312, 1983.

Jokl P. The biology of aging muscle: Quantitative versus qualitative findings of performance capacity and age. In: Nelson CL, Dwyer AP (eds). *The Aging Musculoskeletal System.* Lexington, MA, Collamore Press, 1984, pp. 49–58.

Jones IH. Observations on schizophrenic stereotypies. Comp Psychiatry 6: 323–335, 1965.

Jones M, Hunter R. Abnormal movements in patients with chronic psychiatric illness. In: Crane GE, Gardner R Jr. (eds). *Psychotropic Drugs and Dysfunctions of the Basal Ganglia: A Multidisciplinary Workshop.* Public Health Service Publication No. 1938. Chevy Chase, MD, National Institute of Mental Health, 1969, pp. 53–59.

Jones RSG, Olpe H-R. Activation of the noradrenergic projection from locus coeruleus reduces the excitatory responses of anterior cingulate cortical neurons to substance P. Neuroscience 13: 819–825, 1984.

Joseph JA, Berger RE, Engel BT, *et al.* Age-related changes in the nigrostriatum: A behavioral and biochemical analysis. J Gerontol 33: 643–649, 1978.

Josephy H. Beitrage zur Histopathologie der Dementia praecox. Z Ges Neurol Psychiatr 86: 391–485, 1923.

Josiassen RC, Curry LM, Mancall EL. Development of neuropsychological deficits in Huntington's disease. Arch Neurol 40: 791–796, 1983.

Joubert M, Barbeau A. Akinesia in Parkinson's disease. In: Barbeau A, Brunette J-R (eds). *Progress in Neuro-Genetics.* Amsterdam, Exerpta Medica, 1969, pp. 366–376.

Jowett B (trans). *The Dialogues of Plato.* Vol. IV. Ed. 4. Oxford, Oxford University Press, 1953.

Jowsey J. Osteoporosis. In: Nelson CL, Dwyer AP (eds). *The Aging Musculoskeletal System.* Lexington, MA, Collamore Press, 1984, pp. 75–90.

Joyce RP, Gunderson CH. Carbamazepine-induced orofacial dyskinesia. Neurology 30: 1333–1334, 1980.

Kahlbaum KL. *Catatonia, or the Insanity of Tension.* Levij Y, Pridan T (trans) (originally, *Die Katatonie, oder das Spannungsirresein*). Baltimore, Johns Hopkins University Press, 1874/1973.

Kales A, Ansel RD, Markham CH, *et al.* Sleep in patients with Parkinson's disease and normal subjects prior to and following levodopa administration. Clin Pharmacol Ther 12: 397–406, 1971.

Kales A, Soldatos CR, Caldwell AB, *et al.* Somnambulism: Clinical characteristics and personality patterns. Arch Gen Psychiatry 37: 1406–1410, 1980.

Kales A, Cadieux RJ, Soldatos CR, *et al.* Narcolepsy–cataplexy. I. Clinical and electrophysiologic characteristics. Arch Neurol 39: 164–168, 1982a.

Kales A, Soldatos CR, Bixler EO, *et al.* Narcolepsy–cataplexy. II. Psychosocial consequences and associated psychopathology. Arch Neurol 39: 169–171, 1982b.

Kales A, Bixler EO, Soldatos CR, *et al.* Biopsychobehavioral correlates of insomnia, part 1: Role of sleep apnea and nocturnal myoclonus. Psychosomatics 23: 589–600, 1982c.

Kales JD, Kales A, Soldatos CR, *et al.* Sleepwalking and night terrors related to febrile illness. Am J Psychiatry 136: 1214–1215, 1979.

Kamen S. Tardive dyskinesia, a significant syndrome for geriatric dentistry. Oral Surg Oral Med Oral Pathol 39: 52–57, 1975.

Kane JM, Smith JM. Tardive dyskinesia: Prevalence and risk factors, 1959–1979. Arch Gen Psychiatry 39: 473–481, 1982.

Kane JM, Woerner M, Weinhold P, *et al.* Incidence and severity of tardive dyskinesia in affective illness. In: Gardos G, Casey DE (eds). *Tardive Dyskinesia and Affective Disorders.* Washington, D.C., American Psychiatric Press, 1984, pp. 21–28.

Karson CN, Freed WJ, Kleinman JE, *et al.* Neuroleptics decrease blink rates in schizophrenic subjects. Biol Psychiatry 16: 679–682, 1981.

Karson CN, LeWitt PA, Calne DB, *et al.* Blink rates in parkinsonism. Ann Neurol 12: 580–583, 1982.

Karson CN, Jeste DV, LeWitt PA, *et al.* A comparison of two iatrogenic dyskinesias. Am J Psychiatry 140: 1504–1506, 1983.

Karson CN, Burns RS, LeWitt PA, *et al.* Blink rates and disorders of movement. Neurology 34: 677–678, 1984.

Kass D, Silvers F, Abrams G. Behavioral group treatment of hysteria. Arch Gen Psychiatry 26: 42–50, 1972.

Kaufmann CA, Jeste DV, Shelton RC, et al. Noradrenergic and neuroradiologic abnormalities in tardive dyskinesia. Biol Psychiatry 21: 799–812, 1986.

Keegan DL, Rajput AH. Drug induced dystonia tarda: Treatment with L-DOPA. Dis Nerv Syst 34: 167–169, 1973.

Kelman DH. Gilles de la Tourette's disease in children: A review of the literature. J Child Psychol Psychiatry 6: 219–226, 1965.

Kelso JAS, Holt KG, Kugler PN, et al. On the concept of coordinative structures as dissipative structures: II. Empirical lines of convergence. In: Stelmach GE, Requin J (eds). Tutorials in Motor Behavior. New York, North-Holland, 1980, pp. 49–70.

Kelwala S, Ban TA. Febrile catatonia sustained by neuroleptics (letter to ed). Psych J Univ Ottawa 6: 135, 1981.

Kendel K, Beck U, Wita C, et al. Der Einfluss von L-DOPA auf den Nachtschlaf bei Patienten mit Parkinson-Syndrom. Arch Psychiatr Nervenkrank 216: 82–100, 1972.

Kendler KS, Hays P. Schizophrenia subdivided by the family history of affective disorder: A comparison of symptomatology and course of illness. Arch Gen Psychiatry 40: 951–955, 1983.

Kenny MG. Paradox lost: The latah problem revisited. J Nerv Ment Dis 171: 159–167, 1983

Kertesz A. Paroxysmal kinesigenic choreoathetosis: An entity within the paroxysmal choreoathetosis syndrome. Description of 10 cases, including 1 autopsied. Neurology 17: 680–690, 1967.

Kidd KK, Prusoff BA, Cohen DJ. Familial pattern of Gilles de la Tourette syndrome. Arch Gen Psychiatry 37: 1336–1339, 1980.

Kidger T, Barnes TRE, Trauer T, et al. Sub syndromes of tardive dyskinesia. Psychol Med 10: 513–520, 1980.

Kimura J. Electrodiagnosis in Diseases of Nerve and Muscle: Principles and Practice. Philadelphia, Davis, 1983.

King R, Faull KF, Stahl SM, et al. Serotonin and schizophrenia: Correlations between serotonergic activity and schizophrenic motor behavior. Psychiatry Res 14: 235–240, 1985.

Kinross-Wright V. Complications of chlorpromazine treatment. Dis Nerv Syst 16: 114–119, 1955.

Kirby GH. The catatonic syndrome and its relation to manic-depressive insanity. J Nerv Ment Dis 40: 694–704, 1913.

Klawans HL Jr. Relation between handedness and side of onset of parkinsonism (letter to ed). Lancet I: 850, 1972.

Klawans HL. The Pharmacology of Extrapyramidal Movement Disorders. Chicago, Karger, 1973.

Klawans, HL, Barr A. Prevalence of spontaneous lingual-facial-buccal dyskinesia in the elderly. Neurology 32: 558–559, 1982.

Klawans HL, Falk DK, Nausieda PA, et al. Gilles de la Tourette's syndrome after long-term chlorpromazine therapy. Neurology 28: 1064–1068, 1978.

Klawans H, Rubovits R. Effect of cholinergic and anticholinergic agents on tardive dyskinesia. J Neurol Neurosurg Psychiatry 27: 941–947, 1974.

Klee A. Akinetic mutism: Review of the literature and report of a case. J Nerv Ment Dis 133: 536–553, 1961.

Klein L, Rajan JC. The biology of aging human collagen. In: Nelson CL, Dwyer AP (eds). The Aging Musculoskeletal System. Lexington, MA, Collamore Press, 1984, pp. 37–48.

Kleist K. Die psychomotorischen Storungen bei Geisteskranken und ihr Verhaltnis zu den Motilitätstorungen bei Erkrankung der Stammganglien. München Med Wochenschr 69: 412, 1922.

348   References

Kleist K. Schizophrenic symptoms and cerebral pathology. J Ment Sci 106: 246–255, 1960.
Kline NS (ed). *Psychopharmacology Frontiers. Proceedings of the Psychopharmacology Symposium, 2nd International Congress of Psychiatry, Zurich, 1957.* Boston, Little, 1959.
Knight B. *Discovering the Human Body.* New York, Lippincott & Crowell, 1980.
Kobayashi RM. Treatment of movement disorders. In: Wiederholt WC (ed). *Therapy for Neurologic Disorders.* New York, Wiley, 1982, pp. 183–216.
Kolbe H, Clow A, Jenner P, *et al.* Neuroleptic-induced acute dystonic reactions may be due to enhanced dopamine release onto supersensitive postsynaptic receptors. Neurology 31: 434–439, 1981.
Koller WC. Alcoholism in essential tremor. Neurology 33: 1074–1076, 1983a.
Koller WC. Edentulous orodyskinesia. Ann Neurol 13: 97–99, 1983b.
Koller WC. Pharmacologic trials in the treatment of cerebellar tremor. Arch Neurol 41: 280–281, 1984.
Koller WC, Biary N. Effect of alcohol on tremors: Comparison with propranolol. Neurology 34: 221–222, 1984.
Koller WC, Trimble J. The gait abnormality of Huntington's disease. Neurology 35: 1450–1454, 1985.
Koller WC, Weiner WJ, Nausieda PA, *et al.* Pharmacology of ballismus. In: Klawans HL (ed). *Clinical Neuropharmacology.* Vol. 4. New York, Raven Press, 1979, pp. 157–174.
Koller WC, Wilson RS, Glatt SL, *et al.* Senile gait: Correlation with computed tomographic scans. Ann Neurol 13: 343–344, 1983.
Koller WC, Wilson RS, Glatt SL, *et al.* Motor signs are infrequent in dementia of the Alzheimer type. Ann Neurol 16: 514–516, 1984.
Koller W, O'Hara R, Dorus W, *et al.* Tremor in chronic alcoholism. Neurology 35: 1660–1662, 1985.
Kooiker JC, Sumi SM. Movement disorder as a manifestation of diphenylhydantoin intoxication. Neurology 24: 68–71, 1974.
Korein J, Lieberman A, Kupersmith M, *et al.* Effect of L-glutamine and isoniazid on torticollis and segmental dystonia. Ann Neurol 10: 247–250, 1981.
Kornhuber HH, Deecke L. Hirnpotentialanderungen bei Willkurbewegungen und passiven Bewegungen des Menschen: Bereitshaftspotential und reafferente Potentiale. Pflugers Arch Ges Phys 284: 1–17, 1965.
Korpi ER, Wyatt RJ. Reduced haloperidol: Effects on striatal dopamine metabolism and conversion to haloperidol in the rat. Psychopharm 83: 34–37, 1984.
Kraepelin E. *One Hundred Years of Psychiatry.* Baskin W (trans). New York, Citadel, 1918/1962.
Kraepelin E. *Dementia Praecox and Paraphrenia.* Barclay RM (trans). Robertson GM (ed). New York, Robert E. Krieger, 1919/1971.
Kramer H, Sprenger J. *Malleus Maleficarum.* Summers M (trans). London, Pushkin Press, 1489/1948.
Krauss S. Post-choreic personality and neurosis. J Ment Sci 92: 75–95, 1946.
Krauss S. Post-choreic personality and neurosis. In: Krauss S (ed). *Encyclopaedic Handbook of Medical Psychology.* London, Butterworths, 1976, pp. 401–406.
Krumholz A, Singer HS, Niedermeyer E, *et al.* Electrophysiological studies in Tourette's syndrome. Ann Neurol 14: 638–641, 1983.
Kruse W. Persistent muscular restlessness after phenothiazine treatment: Report of three cases. Am J Psychiatry 117: 152–153, 1960.
Kugler PN, Kelso JAS, Turvey MT. On the concept of coordinative structures as dissipative structures: I. Theoretical lines of convergence. In: Stelmach GE, Requin J (eds). *Tutorials in Motor Behavior.* New York, North-Holland, 1980, pp. 3–47.
Kunkle EC. The "jumpers" of Maine: A reappraisal. Arch Intern Med 119: 355–358, 1967.

Kurczynski TW. Hyperekplexia. Arch Neurol 40: 246–248, 1983.

Kurlan R, Hamill R, Shoulson I. Neuroleptic malignant syndrome. Clin Neuropharmacol 7: 109–120, 1984.

Kwentus JA, Schulz SC, Hart RP. Tardive dystonia, catatonia, and electroconvulsive therapy. J Nerv Ment Dis 172: 171–173, 1984.

Laborit H, Huguenard P, Alluaume R. Un nouveau stabilisateur végétatif (le 4560 RP). Presse Med 60: 347, 1952.

Ladavas E. The development of facedness. Cortex 18: 535–545, 1982.

Lance JW. Familial paroxysmal dystonic choreoathetosis and its differentiation from related syndromes. Ann Neurol 2: 285–293, 1977.

Lance JW. Symposium synopsis. In: Feldman RG, Young RR, Koella WP (eds). *Spasticity: Disordered Motor Control.* Chicago, Year Book, 1980, pp. 485–494.

Lance JW, McLeod JG. *A Physiological Approach to Clinical Neurology.* Ed. 2. London, Butterworths, 1975.

Lance JW, McLeod JG. *A Physiological Approach to Clinical Neurology.* Ed. 3. London, Butterworths, 1981.

Lance JW, Schwab RS, Peterson EA. Action tremor and the cogwheel phenomenon in Parkinson's disease. Brain 86: 95–110, 1963.

Landis C, Hunt WA. *The Startle Pattern.* New York, Farrar & Rhinehart, 1939.

Lane JD, Aprison MH. Calcium-dependent release of endogenous serotonin, dopamine and norepinephrine from nerve endings. Life Sci 20: 665–672, 1977.

Lang AF. Dopamine agonists in the treatment of dystonia. Clinical Neuropharmacology 8: 38–57, 1985.

Lang AE, Marsden CD, Obeso JA, et al. Alcohol and Parkinson disease. Ann Neurol 12: 254–256, 1982.

Lange H, Thörner G, Hopf A, et al. Morphometric studies of the neuropathological changes in choreatic diseases. J Neurol Sci 28: 401–425, 1976.

Langer SZ. Denervation supersensitivity. In: Iversen LL, Iversen SD, Snyder SH (eds). *Handbook of Psychopharmacology.* Vol. 2. New York, Plenum Press, 1975, pp 245–280.

Langworthy OR. *The Sensory Control of Posture and Movement: A Review of the Studies of Derek Denny-Brown.* Baltimore, Williams & Wilkins, 1970.

Larsen TA, Dunn HG, Jan JE, et al. Dystonia and calcification of the basal ganglia. Neurology 35: 533–537, 1985.

Laskowska D, Urbaniak K, Jus A. The relationship between catatonic–delirious states and schizophrenia in the light of a follow-up study (Stauder's lethal catatonia). Br J Psychiatry 111: 599–612, 1965.

Lassek AM. The human pyramidal tract. II. A numerical investigation of the Betz cells of the motor area. Arch Neurol Psychiatry 44: 718–724, 1940.

Lassek AM. The human pyramidal tract. III. Magnitude of the large cells of the motor area (area 4). Arch Neurol Psychiatry 45: 964–972, 1941.

Laufer MW, Denhoff E. Hyperkinetic behavior syndrome in children. J Pediatrics 50: 463–474, 1957.

Laufer MW, Shetty T. Attention deficit disorders. In: Kaplan HI, Freedman AM, Sadock BJ (eds). *Comprehensive Textbook of Psychiatry.* Ed. 3. Baltimore, Williams & Wilkins, 1980, pp. 2538–2550.

Lazare A. The hysterical character in psychoanalytic theory. Arch Gen Psychiatry 25: 131–137, 1971.

Lazare A. Conversion symptoms. N Engl J Med 305: 745–748, 1981.

Leavitt S, Tyler HR. Studies in asterixis. Arch Neurol 10: 360–368, 1964.

Le Boë F de (Sylvius). *A New Idea of the Practice of Physic.* Gower R (trans) (contemporary translation of the first book of *Praxeos medicae idaea*). London, Brabazon Aylmer, 1675.

Leckman JF, Maas JW, Redmond DE Jr. Effects of oral clonidine on plasma MHPG in man. Life Sci 26: 2179–2185, 1980.

Lee LV, Pascasio FM, Fuentes FD, *et al.* Torsion dystonia in Panay, Philippines. In: Eldridge R, Fahn S (eds). *Dystonia. Advances in Neurology.* Vol. 14. New York, Raven Press, 1976, pp. 137–152.

Lee RG, Stein RB. Resetting of tremor by mechanical pertubations: A comparison of essential tremor and parkinsonian tremor. Ann Neurol 10: 523–531, 1981.

Lee RG, Tatton WG. Long loop reflexes in man: Clinical applications. In: Desmedt JE (ed). *Cerebral Motor Control in Man: Long Loop Mechanisms. Progress in Clinical Neurophysiology.* Vol. 4. Basel, Karger, 1978, pp. 320–334.

Lee-Feldstein A, Harburg E. Alcohol use among right- and left-handed persons in a small community. J Stud Alcohol 43: 824–829, 1982.

Leiber L, Axelrod S. Not all sinistrality is pathological. Cortex 17: 259–272, 1981.

LeMay M. Asymmetries of the skull and handedness: Phrenology revisited. J Neurol Sci 32: 243–253, 1977.

Leonhard K. *The Classification of Endogenous Psychoses.* Ed. 5. Robins E (ed), Berman R (trans). New York, Halsted Press, 1979.

Levenson JL. Neuroleptic malignant syndrome. Am J Psychiatry 142: 1137–1145, 1985.

Levin M. Cataplexy. Brain 55: 397–405, 1932.

Levin S. Smooth pursuit impairment in schizophrenia: What does it mean? Schiz Bull 9: 37–44, 1983.

Levy DM. On the problem of movement restraint: Tics, stereotyped movements, hyperactivity. Am J Orthopsychiatry 14: 644–671, 1944.

Levy J. A review of evidence for a genetic component in the determination of handedness. Behav Genetics 6: 429–453, 1976.

Levy J. The origins of lateral asymmetry. In: Harnad S, Doty RW, Goldstein L, *et al.* (eds). *Lateralization in the Nervous System.* New York, Academic Press, 1977, pp. 195–212.

Levy R, Behrmann I. Cortical evoked responses in hysterical hemianaesthesia. EEG Clin Neurophysiol 29: 400–402, 1970.

Lew T-Y, Tollefson G. Chlorpromazine-induced neuroleptic malignant syndrome and its response to diazepam. Biol Psychiatry 18: 1441–1446, 1983.

Lewis SA, Oswald I, Dunleavy DLF. Chronic fenfluramine administration: Some cerebral effects. Br Med J 4: 67–70, 1971.

Lewis WC. Hysteria: The consultant's dilemma. Twentieth century demonology, pejorative epithet, or useful diagnosis? Arch Gen Psychiatry 30: 145–151, 1974.

Lewy FH. *Die Lehre vom Tonus und der Bewegung.* Berlin, Springer, 1923.

Lidsky TI, Weinhold PM, Levine FM. Implications of basal ganglionic dysfunction for schizophrenia. Biol Psychiatry 14: 3–12, 1979.

Lieberman AN, Freedman LS, Goldstein M. Serum dopamine-beta-hydroxylase activity in patients with Huntington's chorea and Parkinson's disease. Lancet I: 153–154, 1972.

Liederman J, Coryell J. Right-hand preference facilitated by rightward turning biases during infancy. Dev Psychobiol 14: 439–450, 1981.

Liederman J, Coryell J. The origin of left hand preference: Pathological and non-pathological influences. Neuropsychologia 20: 721–725, 1982.

Liepmann H. Das Krankheitsbild der Apraxie (motorischen Asymbolie) auf Grund eines Falles von einseitiger Apraxie. Monatsschr Psychiatr Neurol 8: 15–40, 102–132, 182–197, 1900.

Liepmann H. Die linke Hemisphare und das Handeln. München Med Wochenschr 49: 2375–2378, 1905.

Liepmann H. *Drei Aufsätze aus dem Apraxiegebiet.* Berlin, Karger, 1908.

Liepmann H. Apraxia. Ergeb Ges Med 1: 516–543, 1920.

Linkowski P, Desmedt D, Hoffmann G, *et al.* Sleep and neuroendocrine disturbances in catatonia: A case report. J Affect Dis 7: 892, 1984.

Lipinski JF, Zubenko GS, Cohen BM, *et al.* Propranolol in the treatment of neuroleptic-induced akathisia. Am J Psychiatry 141: 412–415, 1984.

Lippmann S, Manshadi M, Baldwin H, *et al.* Cerebellar vermis dimensions on computerized tomographic scans of schizophrenic and bipolar patients. Am J Psychiatry 139: 667–668, 1982.

Lipton RB, Levy DL, Holzman PS, *et al.* Eye movement dysfunction in psychiatric patients: A review. Schiz Bull 9: 13–32, 1983.

Ljungberg L. Hysteria, a clinical, prognostic, and genetic study. Acta Psych Neurol Scand 32 (Supp 112): 1957.

Lohr JB. Transient grasp reflexes in schizophrenia. Biol Psychiatry 20: 172–175, 1985.

Lohr JB, Jeste DV. Cerebellar pathology in schizophrenia? A neuronometric study. Biol Psychiatry 21: 865–875, 1986.

Lohr JB, Folstein SE, Jeste DV. Cerebellar signs in Huntington's disease, tardive dyskinesia and other movement disorders. Presented at the IVth World Congress of Biological Psychiatry, Philadelphia, PA, September 1985.

Lohr JB, Folstein SE, Jeste DV. Tardive dyskinesia and Huntington's disease: A clinical comparison. Society for Biological Psychiatry Abstracts 1986a, #169.

Lohr JB, Wisniewski A, Jeste DV. Neurological aspects of tardive dyskinesia. In: Nasrallah HA, Weinberger DR (eds). *The Neurology of Schizophrenia.* Amsterdam, Elsevier, 1986b, pp. 97–120.

Lohr JB, Lohr MA, Wasli E, *et al.* Self-perception of tardive dyskinesia and neuroleptic-induced parkinsonism: A study of clinical correlates. Psychopharm Bull 1987, in press.

Loiseau P, Cohadon F, Cohadon S. Gelastic epilepsy: A review and report of five cases. Epilepsia 12: 313–323, 1971.

Loizzo A, Scotti deCarolis A, Longo VG. Studies on the central effects of bulbocapnine. Psychopharmacologia 22: 234–249, 1971.

London WP, Kibbee P, Holt L. Handedness and alcoholism. J Nerv Ment Dis 173: 570–572, 1985.

Lonton AP. Hand preference in children with myelomeningocele and hydrocephalus. Dev Med Child Neurol 18 (Supp 37): 143–149, 1976.

Lorenz K. Preface. In: Darwin C. *The Expression of the Emotions in Man and Animals.* Chicago, University of Chicago Press, 1872/1965, pp. ix–xiii.

Lourie RS. The role of rhythmic patterns in childhood. Am J Psychiatry 105: 653–660, 1956.

Lovstad RA. Interaction of phenothiazine derivatives with human ceruloplasmin. Biochem Pharmacol 23: 1045–1052, 1974.

Luchins DJ, Goldman M. High-dose bromocriptine in a case of tardive dystonia. Biol Psychiatry 20: 179–181, 1985.

Luchins DJ, Weinberger DR, Wyatt RJ. Anomalous lateralization associated with a milder form of schizophrenia. Am J Psychiatry 136: 1598–1599, 1979.

Luchins D, Pollin W, Wyatt RJ. Laterality in monozygotic schizophrenic twins: An alternative hypothesis. Biol Psychiatry 15: 87–93, 1980.

Lugaresi E, Coccagna G, Berti-Ceroni G, *et al.* Restless legs syndrome and nocturnal myoclonus. In: Gastaut H, Lugaresi E, Berti-Ceroni G, *et al.* (eds). *The Abnormalities of Sleep in Man. Proceedings of the 15th European Meeting on Electroencephalography, Bologna, 1967.* Bologna, Aulo Gaggi Editore, 1968, pp. 285–294.

Lugaresi E, Cirignotta F, Montagna P. Nocturnal paroxysmal dystonia. J Neurol Neurosurg Psychiatry 49: 375–380, 1986.

Lundborg H. *Die Progressive Myoklonus-Epilepsie (Unverricht's Myoklonie).* Uppsala, Almqvist & Wiksell, 1903.

Lundh H, Tunving K. An extrapyramidal choreiform syndrome caused by amphetamine addiction. J Neurol Neurosurg Psychiatry 44: 728–730, 1981.

Luria AR. *The Working Brain: An Introduction to Neuropsychology.* Haigh B (trans). New York, Basic Books, 1973.

MacLean WE Jr, Lewis MH, Bryson-Brockmann WA, *et al.* Blink rate and stereotyped behavior: Evidence for dopamine involvement? Biol Psychiatry 20: 1321–1325, 1985.

Magee KR. Bruxism related to levodopa therapy (letter to ed). J Am Med Assoc 214: 147, 1970.

Mahendra B. Where have all the catatonics gone? Psychol Med 11: 669–671, 1981.

Mahler MS, Luke JA, Daltroff W. Clinical and follow-up study of the tic syndrome in children. Am J Orthopsychiatry 15: 631–647, 1945.

Mandell AJ. From intermittency to transitivity in neuropsychobiological flows. Am J Physiol 245: R484–R494, 1983.

Mann DMA, Yates PO, Marcyniuk B. Relationship between pigment accumulation and age in Alzheimer's disease and Down syndrome. Acta Neuropath 63: 72–77, 1984.

Markianos M, Tripodianakis J, Garelis E. Neurochemical studies of tardive dyskinesia. II. Urinary methoxyhydroxyphenylglycol and plasma dopamine-beta-hydroxylase. Biol Psychiatry 18: 347–354, 1983.

Markland ON, Garg BP, Weaver DD. Familial startle disease (hyperexplexia): Electrophysiologic studies. Arch Neurol 41: 71–74, 1984.

Marmor J. Orality in the hysterical personality. J Am Psychoanal Assoc 1: 656–671, 1953.

Marsden CD. Blepharospasm–oromandibular dystonia syndrome (Breughel's syndrome). J Neurol Neurosurg Psychiatry 39: 1204–1209, 1976.

Marsden CD. The mysterious motor function of the basal ganglia: The Robert Wartenberg lecture. Neurology 32: 514–539, 1982a.

Marsden CD. Motor disorders in schizophrenia. Psychol Med 12: 13–15, 1982b.

Marsden CD, Jenner P. The pathophysiology of extrapyramidal side-effects of neuroleptic drugs. Psychol Med 10: 55–72, 1980.

Marsden CD, Foley TH, Owen DAL, *et al.* Peripheral beta-adrenergic receptors concerned with tremor. Clin Sci 33: 53–65, 1967a.

Marsden CD, Meadows JC, Lange GW, *et al.* Effects of deafferentation on human physiological tremor. Lancet II: 700–702, 1967b.

Marsden CD, Meadows JC, Lange GW, *et al.* The role of the ballistocardiac impulse in the genesis of physiological tremor. Brain 92: 647–662, 1969a.

Marsden CD, Meadows JC, Lowe RD. The influence of noradrenaline, tyramine and activation of sympathetic nerves on physiological tremor in man. Clin Sci 37: 243–252, 1969b.

Marsden CD, Tarsy D, Baldessarini RJ. Spontaneous and drug-induced movement disorders in psychotic patients. In: Benson DF, Blumer D (eds). *Psychiatric Aspects of Neurological Disease.* New York, Grune & Stratton, 1975, pp. 219–265.

Marsden CD, Merton PA, Morton HB. The sensory mechanism of servo-action in human muscle. J Physiol 265: 527–535, 1977.

Marsden CD, Hallett M, Fahn S. The nosology and pathophysiology of myoclonus. In: Marsden CD, Fahn S (eds). *Movement Disorders.* Boston, Butterworth Scientific, 1981a, pp. 196–248.

Marsden CD, Merton PA, Morton HB. Human postural responses. Brain 104: 513–534, 1981b.

Marsden CD, Obeso JA, Rothwell JC. Clinical neurophysiology of muscle jerks: Myoclonus, chorea, and tics. In: Desmedt JE (ed). *Motor Control Mechanisms in Health and Disease.* New York, Raven Press, 1983a, pp. 865–882.

Marsden CD, Rothwell JC, Day BL. Long-latency automatic responses to muscle stretch in man: Origin and function. In: Desmedt JE (ed). *Motor Control Mechanisms in Health and Disease.* New York, Raven Press, 1983b, pp. 509–540.

Marsden CD, Lang AE, Quinn NP, et al. Familial dystonia and visual failure with striatal CT lucencies. J Neurol Neurosurg Psychiatry 49: 500–509, 1986.

Marsh GG, Markham CM, Ansel R. Levodopa's awakening effect on patients with Parkinsonism. J Neurol Neurosurg Psychiatry 34: 209–218, 1971.

Marshall JF, Berrios N. Movement disorders of aged rats: Reversal by dopamine receptor stimulation. Science 206: 477–479, 1979.

Marti-Ibanez F. Foreword. In: Riese W. *A History of Neurology*. New York, M.D. Publications, 1959.

Martin JP. *The Basal Ganglia and Posture*. London, Pitman, 1967.

Martin JP. Wilson's disease. In: Vinken PJ, Bruyn GW (eds). *Diseases of the Basal Ganglia. Handbook of Clinical Neurology*. Vol. 6. New York, American Elsevier, 1968, pp. 267–277.

Martin JP. A short essay on posture and movement. J Neurol Neurosurg Psychiatry 40: 25–29, 1977.

Mathew RJ, Partain CL. Midsagittal sections of the cerebellar vermis and fourth ventricle obtained with magnetic resonance imaging of schizophrenic patients. Am J Psychiatry 142: 970–971, 1985.

Matthews PBC. Proprioceptors and the regulation of movement. In: Towe AL, Luschei ES (eds). *Motor Coordination*. New York, Plenum Press, 1981.

Mauritz KH, Schmitt C, Dichgans J. Delayed and enhanced long latency reflexes as the possible cause of postural tremor in late cerebellar atrophy. Brain 104: 97–116, 1981.

May JV. *Mental Diseases: A Public Health Problem*. Boston, R. G. Badger, 1922.

May RH. Catatonic-like states following phenothiazine therapy. Am J Psychiatry 115: 1119–1120, 1959.

Mayeux R, Stern Y. Intellectual dysfunction and dementia in Parkinson's disease. In: Mayeux R, Rosen WG (eds). *The Dementias*. New York, Raven Press, 1983, pp. 211–227.

Mayeux R, Stern Y, Rosen J, et al. Depression, intellectual impairment, and Parkinson disease. Neurology 31: 645–650, 1981.

Mayeux R, Stern Y, Rosen J, et al. Is "subcortical dementia" a recognizable clinical entity? Ann Neurol 14: 278–283, 1983.

Mayeux R, Stern Y, Cote L, et al. Altered serotonin metabolism in depressed patients with Parkinson's disease. Neurology 34: 642–646, 1984.

Mayeux R, Stern Y, Spanton S. Heterogeneity in dementia of the Alzheimer type: Evidence of subgroups. Neurology 35: 453–461, 1985.

McAllister RG Jr. Fever, tachycardia, and hypertension with acute catatonic schizophrenia. Arch Intern Med 138: 1154–1156, 1978.

McCreadie RG, Crorie J, Barron ET, et al. The Nithsdale schizophrenia survey: Handedness and tardive dyskinesia. Br J Psychiatry 140: 591–594, 1982.

McDonagh MJN, White MJ, Davies CTM. Different effects of ageing on the mechanical properties of human arm and leg muscles. Gerontology 30: 49–54, 1984.

McEvoy JP, Lohr JB. Diazepam for catatonia. Am J Psychiatry 141: 284–285, 1984.

McEvoy JP, Stiller RL, Farr R. Plasma haloperidol levels drawn at neuroleptic threshold doses: A pilot study. J Clin Psychopharm 6: 133–138, 1986.

McFarland K, Anderson J. Factor stability of the Edinburgh Handedness Inventory as a function of test–retest performance, age, and sex. Br J Psychol 71: 135–142, 1980.

McGeer EG. Neurotransmitter systems in aging and senile dementia. Prog Neuro-Psychopharmacol 5: 435–445, 1981.

McGeer PL, McGeer EG, Suzuki JS. Aging and extrapyramidal function. Arch Neurol 34: 33–35, 1977.

McGeer PL, Eccles JC, McGeer EG. *Molecular Neurobiology of the Mammalian Brain*. New York, Plenum Press, 1978.

McGeer PL, McGeer EG, Suzuki JS. Aging, Alzheimer's disease, and the cholinergic system of the basal forebrain. Neurology 34: 741–745, 1984a.

McGeer PL, McGeer EG, Suzuki JS. Cholinergic and noradrenergic systems in aging, Alzheimer's disease and Down's syndrome. Abstr Soc Neurosci, 1984b, p. 995.

McGuffin P, Mawson O. Obsessive–compulsive neurosis: Two identical twin pairs. Br J Psychiatry 137: 285–287, 1980.

McHenry LC. *Garrison's History of Neurology.* Springfield, IL, Charles C Thomas, 1969.

McHugh PR, Folstein MF. Psychiatric syndromes of Huntington's chorea: A clinical and phenomenologic study. In: Benson DF, Blumer D (eds). *Psychiatric Aspects of Neurological Disease.* New York, Grune & Stratton, 1975, pp. 267–286.

McKegney FP. The incidence and characteristics of patients with conversion reactions: I. A general hospital consultation service sample. Am J Psychiatry 124: 5421–545, 1967.

McKeon J, McGuffin P, Robinson P. Obsessive–compulsive neurosis following head injury. Br J Psychiatry 144: 190–192, 1984.

McLeod JG. H reflex studies in patients with cerebellar disorders. J Neurol Neurosurg Psychiatry 32: 21–27, 1969.

McMeekan ERL, Lishman WA. Retest reliabilities and interrelationship of the Annett Hand Preference Questionnaire and the Edinburgh Handedness Inventory. Br J Psychol 66: 53–59, 1975.

Meares R. Natural history of spasmodic torticollis and effect of surgery. Lancet II: 149–151, 1971.

Megirian D, Weller L, Martin GF, *et al.* Aspects of laterality in the marsupial *trichosurus vulpecula* (brush-tailed possum). In: Dimond SJ, Blizard DA (eds). *Evolution and Lateralization of the Brain.* Ann NY Acad Sci 299: 197–212, 1977.

Meige H. Les convulsions de la face, une forme clinique de convulsion faciale bilaterale et médiane. Rev Neurol (Paris) 21: 437–443, 1910.

Meige H, Feindel E. *Tics and their Treatment.* Wilson SAK (ed & trans). New York, William Wood, 1907.

Meinck HM, Benecke R, Kuster S, *et al.* Cutaneomuscular (flexor) reflex organization in normal man and in patients with motor disorders. In: Desmedt JE (ed). *Motor Control Mechanisms in Health and Disease.* New York, Raven Press, 1983, pp. 787–796.

Meltzer HY, Tong C, Luchins DJ. Serum dopamine-beta-hydroxylase activity and lateral ventricular size in affective disorders and schizophrenia. Biol Psychiatry 19: 1395–1402, 1984.

Memo M, Lucchi L, Spano PF, *et al.* Aging process affects a single class of dopamine receptors. Brain Res 202: 488–492, 1980.

Mendelson WB, Caine ED, Goyer P, *et al.* Sleep in Gilles de la Tourette syndrome. Biol Psychiatry 15: 339–343, 1980.

Merikangas JR, Merikangas KR, Kopp U, *et al.* Blood choline and response to clonazepam and haloperidol in Tourette's syndrome. Acta Psych Scand 72: 395–399, 1985.

Merrin EL. Motor and sighting dominance in schizophrenia and affective disorder: Evidence for right-hand grip strength prominence in paranoid schizophrenia and bipolar illness. Br J Psychiatry 146: 539–544, 1984.

Messiha FJ. Biochemical studies after chronic administration of neuroleptics to monkeys. In: Fahn WE, Smith RC, Davis JM, *et al.* (eds). *Tardive Dyskinesia: Research and Treatment.* New York, SP Medical and Scientific Books, 1980, pp. 13–25.

Mettler FA. Effects of bilateral simultaneous subcortical lesions in the primate. J Neuropath Exp Neurol 4: 99–122, 1945.

Mettler FA. Perceptual capacity, functions of the corpus striatum and schizophrenia. Psych Quart 29: 89–111, 1955.

Mettler FA, Crandell A. Neurologic disorders in psychiatric institutions. J Nerv Ment Dis 128: 148–159, 1959a.

Mettler FA, Crandell A. Relation between parkinsonism and psychiatric disorder. J Nerv Ment Dis 129: 551–563, 1959b.

Metzig E, Rosenberg S, Ast M. Lateral asymmetry in patients with nervous and mental disease. Neuropsychobiology 1: 197–202, 1975.

Metzig E, Rosenberg S, Ast M, et al. Bipolar manic–depressives and unipolar depressives distinguished by tests of lateral asymmetry. Biol Psychiatry 11: 313–323, 1976.

Meyers R. Ballismus. In: Vinken PJ, Bruyn GW (eds). *Disorders of the Basal Ganglia. Handbook of Clinical Neurology.* Vol. 6. New York, American Elsevier, 1968, pp. 476–490.

Michel GF. Right-handedness: A consequence of infant supine head-orientation preference? Science 212: 685–687, 1981.

Miele V, Proli F, Salzarulo P. Aspetti elettropoligrafici del sonno nei malati parkinsoniani. Riv Sper Freniat 204: 69–82, 1970.

Mikkelsen EJ, Detlor J, Cohen DJ. School avoidance and social phobia triggered by haloperidol in patients with Tourette's disorder. Am J Psychiatry 138: 1572–1576, 1981.

Mindham RHS. Psychiatric symptoms in Parkinsonism. J Neurol Neurosurg Psychiatry 33: 188–191, 1970.

Missale C, Govoni S, Castelleti I., et al. Brain neurotransmitter changes in the brains of aged rats. In: Agnoli A, Crepaldi G, Spano PF, et al. (eds). *Aging Brain and Ergot Alkaloids. Aging.* Vol. 23. New York, Raven Press, 1983, pp. 15–22.

Mjones H. Paralysis agitans: A clinical and genetic study. Acta Psych Neurol Scand Supp 54, 1949.

Moleman P, Schmitz PJM, Ladee GA. Extrapyramidal side effects and oral haloperidol: An analysis of explanatory patient and treatment characteristics. J Clin Psychiatry 43: 492–496, 1982.

Molsa PK, Marttila RJ, Rinne UK. Extrapyramidal signs in Alzheimer's disease. Neurology 34: 1114–1116, 1984.

Monrad-Krohn GH. *The Clinical Examination of the Nervous System.* London, H. K. Lewis, 1964.

Monsour N, Robb SS. Wandering behavior in old age: A psychosocial study. Social Work September: 411–416, 1982.

Moore KE. Dyskinesia: Animal experimental correlates. Acta Psych Scand 63 (supp 291): 88–102, 1981.

Moore RY. Catecholamine neuron systems in brain. Ann Neurol 12: 321–327, 1982.

Moretti G, Calzetti S, Quartucci G, et al. Studio epidemiologico sul tremore della terza età. Min Med 74: 1701–1705, 1983.

Morgenroth VH, Boadle-Biber MC, Roth RH. Activation of tyrosine hydroxylase from central noradrenergic neurons by calcium. Mol Pharmacol 11: 427–435, 1975.

Morrison JR. Catatonia: Retarded and excited types. Arch Gen Psychiatry 28: 39–41, 1973.

Morrison JR. Changes in subtype diagnosis of schizophrenia: 1920–1966. Am J Psychiatry 131: 674–677, 1974.

Morrison JR. Catatonia: Diagnosis and management. Hosp Comm Psychiatry 26: 91–94, 1975.

Mortimer JA, Webster DD. Evidence for a quantitative association between EMG stretch responses and Parkinsonian rigidity. Brain Res 162: 169–173, 1979.

Moskovitz C, Moses H III, Klawans HL. Levodopa-induced psychosis: A kindling phenomenon. Am J Psychiatry 135: 669–675, 1978.

Mouret J. Differences in sleep in patients with Parkinson's disease. EEG Clin Neurophysiol 38: 653–657, 1975.

Mueller J, Aminoff MJ. Tourette-like syndrome after long-term neuroleptic drug treatment. Br J Psychiatry 141: 191–193, 1982.

Munetz MR, Cornes CL. Distinguishing akathisia and tardive dyskinesia: A review of the literature. J Clin Psychopharm 3: 343–350, 1983.

Munetz MR, Slawsky RC, Neil JF. Tardive Tourette's syndrome treated with clonidine and mesoridazine. Psychosomatics 26: 254–257, 1985.

Munford PR. Conversion disorder. Psych Clin N Am 1: 377–390, 1978.

Munro A. Monosymptomatic hypochondriacal psychosis. Br J Hosp Med 24: 34–38, 1980.

Murphy HBM. Commentary on "The resolution of the Latah paradox." J Nerv Ment Dis 171: 176–177, 1983.

Murphy J, Isaacs B. The post-fall syndrome: A study of 36 elderly patients. Referenced in: Isaacs B. The clinical aspects of falling. *Roche Seminars on Aging.* No. 6. 1981.

Myslobodsky M, Mintz M, Ben-Mayor V, et al. Unilateral dopamine deficit and lateral EEG asymmetry: Sleep abnormalities in hemi-Parkinson's patients. EEG Clin Neurophysiol 54: 227–231, 1982.

Nagasaka G. Zur Pathologie der extrapyramidalen Zentren bei Schizophrenie. Arb Neurol Inst Univ Wien 27: 363–396, 1925.

Nakra BRS, Hwu H-G. Catatonic-like syndrome during neuroleptic therapy. Psychosomatics 23: 769–770, 1982.

Napier J. *Hands.* New York, Pantheon, 1980.

Narbona J, Obeso JA, Tunon T, et al. Hemi-dystonia secondary to localised basal ganglia tumour. J Neurol Neurosurg Psychiatry 47: 704–709, 1984.

Nashner LM. Adapting reflexes controlling the human posture. Exp Brain Res 26: 59–72, 1976.

Nashner LM. Analysis of stance posture in humans. In: Towe AL, Luschei ES (eds). *Motor Coordination. Handbook of Behavioral Neurobiology.* Vol. 5. New York, Plenum Press, 1981, pp. 527–565.

Nasrallah HA, McCalley-Whitters M. Motor lateralization in manic males. Br J Psychiatry 140: 521–522, 1982.

Nasrallah HA, Pappas NJ, Crowe RR. Oculogyric dystonia in tardive dyskinesia. Am J Psychiatry 137: 850–851, 1980.

Nasrallah HA, Jacoby CG, McCalley-Whitters M. Cerebellar atrophy in schizophrenia and mania. Lancet I: 1102, 1981a.

Nasrallah HA, Keelor K, vanShroeder C, et al. Motoric lateralization in schizophrenic males. Am J Psychiatry 138: 1114–1115, 1981b.

Nasrallah HA, McCalley-Whitters M, Kuperman S. Neurological differences between paranoid and nonparanoid schizophrenia: Part I. Sensory–motor lateralization. J Clin Psychiatry 43: 305–306, 1982a.

Nasrallah HA, Schroeder D, Petty F. Alcoholism secondary to essential tremor. J Clin Psychiatry 43: 163–164, 1982b.

Nasrallah HA, Keelor K, McCalley-Whitters M. Laterality shift in alcoholic males. Biol Psychiatry 18: 1065–1067, 1983.

National Institute of Mental Health. Psychopharmacology Service Center. Collaborative Study Group. Phenothiazine treatment in acute schizophrenia. Arch Gen Psychiatry 10: 246–261, 1964.

National Institute of Mental Health. Abnormal Involuntary Movement Scale. In: Guy W (ed). *ECDEU Assessment Manual.* Rockville, MD, US Department of Health, Education and Welfare, 1976, pp. 534–537.

Nausieda PA, Koller WC, Weiner WJ, et al. Chorea induced by oral contraceptives. Neurology 29: 1605–1609, 1979.

Nausieda PA, Koller WC, Weiner WJ, et al. Pemoline-induced chorea. Neurology 31: 356–360, 1981.

Nausieda PA, Bieliauskas LA, Bacon LD, et al. Chronic dopaminergic sensitivity after Sydenham's chorea. Neurology 33: 750–754, 1983.

Nauta WJH. Limbic innervation of the striatum. In: Friedhoff AJ, Chase TN (eds). *Gilles de la*

Tourette Syndrome. Advances in Neurology. Vol. 35. New York, Raven Press, 1982, pp. 41–48.

Nee LE, Caine ED, Polinsky RJ, *et al.* Gilles de la Tourette syndrome: Clinical and family study of 50 cases. Ann Neurol 7: 41–49, 1980.

Nemiah JC. Phobic disorder (phobic neurosis). In: Kaplan HI, Freedman AM, Sadock BJ (eds). *Comprehensive Textbook of Psychiatry/III.* Baltimore, Williams & Wilkins, 1980a, pp. 1493–1504.

Nemiah JC. Obsessive–compulsive disorder (obsessive–compulsive neurosis). In: Kaplan HI, Freedman AM, Sadock, BJ (eds). *Comprehensive Textbook of Psychiatry/III.* Baltimore, Williams & Wilkins, 1980b, pp. 1504–1517.

Newcombe FG, Ratcliff GG, Carrivick PJ, *et al.* Hand preference and I.Q. in a group of Oxfordshire villages. Ann Human Biol 2: 235–242, 1975.

Newman RP, LeWitt PA, Jaffe M, *et al.* Motor function in the normal aging population: Treatment with levodopa. Neurology 35: 571–573, 1985.

Nielsen EB, Lyon M. Evidence for cell loss in corpus striatum after long-term treatment with a neuroleptic drug (flupenthixol) in rats. Psychopharm 59: 85–89, 1978.

Noth J, Friedemann H-H, Podoll K. Long latency reflexes in patients with basal ganglia disorders. In: McKenzie JS, Kemm RE, Wilcock LN (eds). *The Basal Ganglia: Structure and Function.* New York, Plenum Press, 1984, pp. 343–353.

Nottebohm F. Asymmetries in neural control of vocalization in the canary. In: Harnad S, Doty RW, Goldstein L, *et al.* (eds). *Lateralization in the Nervous System.* New York, Academic Press, 1977, pp. 23–44.

Nunberg H. On the catatonic attack. In: *Practice and Theory of Psychoanalysis.* Nervous and Mental Disease Monograph. New York, Coolidge Foundation, 1948, pp. 3–23.

Nutt JG. Abnormalities of posture and movement. In: Cassel CK, Walsh JR (eds). *Geriatric Medicine.* Vol. 1. *Medical, Psychiatric and Pharmacological Topics.* New York, Springer-Verlag, 1984, pp. 50–60.

Obeso JA, Rothwell JC, Marsden CD. The neurophysiology of Tourette syndrome. In: Friedhoff AJ, Chase TN (eds). *Gilles de la Tourette Syndrome. Advances in Neurology.* Vol. 35. New York, Raven Press, 1982, pp. 105–114.

Obeso JA, Rothwell JC, Lang AE, *et al.* Myoclonic dystonia. Neurology 33: 825–830, 1983.

O'Conner DC, Walker AE. Prologue. In: Walker AE (ed). *A History of Neurological Surgery.* Baltimore, Williams & Wilkins, 1951.

Oddy HC, Lobstein TJ. Hand and eye dominance in schizophrenia. Br J Psychiatry 120: 331–332, 1972.

Ohye C, Imai S, Nakajima H, *et al.* Experimental study of spontaneous postural tremor induced by a more successful tremor-producing procedure in the monkey. In: Poirier LJ, Sourkes TL, Bedard PJ (eds). *The Extrapyramidal System and Its Disorders. Advances in Neurology.* Vol. 24. New York, Raven Press, 1979, pp. 83–91.

Oldfield RC. The assessment and analysis of handedness: The Edinburgh Inventory. Neuropsychologia 9: 97–113, 1971.

Olkinuora M. A psychosomatic study of bruxism with emphasis on mental strain and familiar disposition. Suomen Hammaslaakariseuran Toimituksia 65: 312–324, 1972a.

Olkinuora M. A factor-analytic study of psychosocial background in bruxism. Suomen Hammaslaakariseuran Toimituksia 68: 184–199, 1972b.

Olkinuora M. Psychosocial aspects in a series of bruxists compared with a group of non-bruxists. Suomen Hammaslaakariseuran Toimituksia 68: 200–208, 1972c.

Olkon DM. *Essentials of Neuro-Psychiatry: A Textbook of Nervous and Mental Disorders.* Philadelphia, Lea & Febiger, 1945, pp. 101–105.

Oppenheim H. Uber eine eigenartige Krampfkrankheit des kindlichen und jugenlichen Alters (Dysbasia lordotica progressiva, Dystonia musculorum deformans). Neurol Centrabl 30: 1090–1107, 1911.

Orlovsky GN, Shik ML. Standard elements of cyclic movement. Biophysics 10: 935–944, 1965.

Ornitz EM. The functional neuroanatomy of infantile autism. Int J Neurosci 19: 85-124, 1983.

Orsini DL, Satz P. A syndrome of pathological left-handedness: Correlates of early left hemisphere injury. Arch Neurol 43: 333-337, 1986.

Ounsted D. The hyperkinetic syndrome in epileptic children. Lancet 269: 303-311, 1955.

Owens DGC, Johnstone EC, Frith CD. Spontaneous involuntary disorders of movement in neuroleptic treated and untreated chronic schizophrenics: Prevalence, severity and distributions. Arch Gen Psychiatry 39: 452-461, 1982.

Paget J. Nervous mimicry. In: Paget J. *Clinical Lectures and Essays*. New York, Appleton, 1875 (originally published in Lancet, 1873).

Pakkenberg B, Regeur L, Fog R, et al. CT scans in 12 patients with Gilles de la Tourette syndrome. Proceedings of the Danish Neurological Society. Act Neurol Scand 65: 234-235, 1982.

Pakkenberg H, Fog R, Nilakatan B. The long-term effect of perphenazine enanthate on the rat brain: Some metabolic and anatomical observations. Psychopharmacologia 29: 329-336, 1973.

Palacios JM, Kuhar MJ. Beta-adrenergic-receptor localization by light microscopic autoradiography. Science 208: 1378-1380, 1980.

Palmer RD. Dimensions of differentiation in handedness. J Clin Psychol 30: 545-552, 1974.

Pandurangi AK, Devi V, Channabasavanna S. Caudate atrophy in irreversible tardive dyskinesia (a pneumoencephalographic study). J Clin Psychiatry 41: 229-231, 1980.

Pao P-N. *Schizophrenic Disorders: Theory and Treatment from a Psychodynamic Point of View*. New York, International Universities Press, 1979.

Papavasiliou PS, Miller ST, Thal LJ, et al. Age-related motor and catecholamine alterations in mice on levodopa supplemented diet. Life Sci 28: 2945-2952, 1981.

Park DM, Findley LJ, Hanks G, et al. Nomifensine: Effect in parkinsonian patients not receiving levodopa. J Neurol Neurosurg Psychiatry 44: 352-357, 1981.

Parkinson J. *An Essay on the Shaking Palsy*. London, Sherwood, Neely & Jones, 1817.

Pasik PK, Pasik T, DiFiglia M. The internal organization of the neostriatum in mammals. In: Divac I, Oberg RGE (eds). *The Neostriatum*. Oxford, Pergamon Press, 1979, pp. 5-36.

Passouant P. The history of narcolepsy. In: Guilleminault C, Dement WC, Passouant P (eds). *Narcolepsy*. New York, Spectrum, 1976, pp. 1-14.

Paulson GW. Meige's syndrome: Dyskinesia of the eyelids and facial muscles. Geriatrics 27: 69-73, 1972.

Pearlson GD, Veroff AE. Computerized tomographic scan changes in manic-depressive illness. Lancet II: 470, 1981.

Peele R, VonLoetzen IS. Phenothiazine deaths: A critical review. Am J Psychiatry 130: 306-309, 1973.

Penfield W. Epileptic automatism and the centrencephalic integrating system. Assoc Res Nerv Ment Dis Proc (1950) 30: 513-528, 1952.

Penfield W, Jasper H. *Epilepsy and the Functional Anatomy of the Human Brain*. London, Churchill, 1954.

Penn H, Racy J, Lapham L, et al. Catatonic behavior, viral encephalopathy, and death. Arch Gen Psychiatry 27: 758-761, 1972.

Penry JK, Dreifuss FE. Automatisms associated with the absence of petit mal epilepsy. Arch Neurol 21: 142-149, 1969.

Perlmutter JS, Raichle ME. Pure hemidystonia with basal ganglion abnormalities on positron emission tomography. Ann Neurol 15: 228-233, 1984.

Peroutka SJ, Snyder SH. Relationship of neuroleptic drug effects at brain dopamine, serotonin, alpha-adrenergic and histamine receptors to clinical potency. Am J Psychiatry 137: 1518-1522, 1980.

Perry JC, Jacobs D. Overview: Clinical applications of the amytal interview in psychiatric emergency settings. Am J Psychiatry 139: 552-559, 1982.

Perry TL, Kish SJ, Buchanan J, *et al.* Gamma-aminobutyric-acid deficiency in brain of schizophrenic patients. Lancet I: 237–239, 1979.

Perry TL, Godin DV, Hansen S. Parkinson's disease: A disorder due to nigral glutathione deficiency? Neurosci Lett 33: 305–310, 1982.

Perry TL, Yong VW, Ito M, *et al.* Nigrostriatal dopaminergic neurons remain undamaged in rats given high doses of L-DOPA and carbidopa chronically. J Neurochem 43: 990–993, 1984.

Perry TL, Norman MG, Yong VW, *et al.* Hallervorden–Spatz disease: Cysteine accumulation and cysteine dioxygenase deficiency in the globus pallidus. Ann Neurol 18: 482–489, 1985.

Peters M, Durding BM. Handedness measured by finger tapping: A continuous variable. Can J Psychol 32: 257–261, 1978.

Petursson H. Lithum treatment of a patient with periodic catatonia. Acta Psych Scand 54: 248–253, 1976.

Piccirilli M, Piccinini GL, Agostini L. Characteristic clinical aspects of Parkinson patients with intellectual impairment. Eur Neurol 23: 44–50, 1984.

Piggott LR. Overview of selected basic research in autism. J Aut Dev Dis 9: 199–218, 1979.

Pijnenburg AJJ, VanRossum JM. Stimulation of locomotor activity following injection of dopamine into the nucleus accumbens. J Pharm Pharmacol 25: 1003–1005, 1973.

Pinel P. *A Treatise on Insanity.* Davis DD (trans). New York, Hafner, 1962.

Pittsley RA, Shearn MA. Nail down handedness (letter to ed). J Am Med Assoc 236: 819, 1975.

Plotkin D, Halaris A, DeMet EM. Biological studies in adult attention deficit disorder: Case report. J Clin Psychiatry 43: 501–502, 1982.

Plum F, Posner JB. *The Diagnosis of Stupor and Coma.* Ed. 3. Philadelphia, Davis, 1980.

Polinsky RJ, Ebert MH, Caine ED, *et al.* Cholinergic treatment in the Tourette syndrome. N Engl J Med 302: 1310, 1980.

Polizos P, Engelhardt DM. Dyskinetic phenomena in children treated with psychotropic medications. Psychopharm Bull 14(4): 65–68, 1978.

Pollock LJ, Davis L. Muscle tone in parkinsonian states. Arch Neurol Psychiatry 23: 303–319, 1930.

Porter R. Neuronal activities in primary motor area and premotor regions. In: Massion J, Paillard J, Schultz W, *et al.* (eds). *Neural Coding of Motor Performance.* Berlin/Heidelberg/New York, Springer-Verlag, 1983a, pp. 23–29.

Porter R. Functional organization of the motor cortex. In: Desmedt JE (ed). *Motor Control Mechanisms in Health and Disease.* New York, Raven Press, 1983b, pp. 301–320.

Powers P, Douglass TS, Waziri R. Hyperpyrexia in catatonic states. Dis Nerv Syst 37: 359–361, 1976.

Price RA, Kidd KK, Cohen DJ, *et al.* A twin study of Tourette syndrome. Arch Gen Psychiatry 42: 815–820, 1985.

Puca FM, Bricolo A, Turella G. Effect of L-DOPA or amantadine therapy on sleep spindles in parkinsonism. EEG Clin Neurophysiol 35: 327–330, 1973.

Pycock CJ, Kerwin RW, Carter CJ. Effect of lesion of cortical dopamine terminals on subcortical dopamine receptors in rats. Nature 286: 74–77, 1980.

Rabey J, Vardi J, Glaubman H, *et al.* EEG sleep study in parkinsonian patients under bromocryptine treatment. Eur Neurol 17: 345–350, 1978.

Rabkin R. Conversion hysteria as social maladaptation. Psychiatry 27: 349–363, 1964.

Rack PMH, Ross HF. The role of reflexes in the resting tremor of Parkinson's disease. Brain 109: 115–141, 1986.

Raichman JA, Martin RL, Stillings WA. Catatonic stupor: A diagnostically non-specific but distinct syndrome. J Clin Psychiatry 42: 477–478, 1981.

Ramsay Hunt J. Basal ganglia group: Striatal and thalamic types. In: *Acute Epidemic*

Encephalitis (*Lethargic Encephalitis*): *An Investigation by the Association for Research in Nervous and Mental Diseases.* New York, Hoeber, 1921, pp. 29–44.

Randrup A, Munkvad I. Stereotyped activities produced by amphetamine in several animal species and man. Psychopharmacologia 11: 300–310, 1967.

Read DJ, Feest TG, Nassim MA. Clonazepam: Effective treatment for restless legs in uremia. Br Med J 283: 885–886, 1981.

Reding GR, Zepelin H, Robinson JE, et al. Nocturnal teeth-grinding: All-night psychophysiologic studies. J Dent Res 47: 786–797, 1968.

Regestein QR, Kahn CB, Siegel AJ, et al. A case of catatonia occurring simultaneously with severe urinary retention. J Nerv Ment Dis 152: 432–435, 1971.

Regestein QR, Alpert JS, Reich P. Sudden catatonic stupor with disastrous outcome. J Am Med Assoc 238: 618–620, 1977a.

Regestein QR, Hartmann E, Reich P. A head movement disorder occurring in dreaming sleep. J Nerv Ment Dis 164: 432–436, 1977b.

Reich W. *Character-Analysis.* New York, Orgone Institute Press, 1949.

Reinstein L. Hand dominance in carpal tunnel syndrome. Arch Phys Med Rehabil 62: 202–203, 1981.

Reyes MG, Gordon A. Cerebellar vermis in schizophrenia. Lancet II: 700–701, 1981.

Reynolds LM, Locke S. Relation between handedness and side of onset of parkinsonism (letter to ed). Lancet II: 714, 1971.

Ribak CE. The GABAergic neurons of the extrapyramidal system as revealed by immunocytochemistry. In: DiChiara G, Gessa GL (eds). *GABA and the Basal Ganglia.* New York, Raven Press, 1981, pp. 23–36.

Ribstein M. Hypnagogic hallucinations. In: Guilleminault C, Dement WC, Passouant P (eds). *Narcolepsy.* New York, Spectrum, 1976, pp. 145–160.

Richards RN, Barnett HJM. Paroxysmal dystonic choreoathetosis. Neurology 18: 461–469, 1968.

Richardson MA, Craig TJ. The coexistence of parkinsonism-like symptoms and tardive dyskinesia. Am J Psychiatry 139: 341–343, 1982.

Richardson MA, Pass R, Craig TJ, et al. Factors influencing the prevalence and severity of tardive dyskinesia. Psychopharm Bull 20(1): 33–38, 1984.

Rickland D, Breakfield X, Roth R. High affinity choline uptake by fibroblasts from patients with dystonia and Tourette syndrome. In: *Third International Symposium on Dystonia.* Vancouver, Canada, 1980.

Rieder RO, Mann LS, Weinberger DR, et al. Computed tomographic scans in patients with schizophrenia, schizoaffective, and bipolar affective disorder. Arch Gen Psychiatry 40: 735–739, 1983.

Riese W. *A History of Neurology.* New York, M.D. Publications, 1959.

Riley T, Brannon WL, Davis W. Phenothiazine reaction simulating acute catatonia. Postgrad Med 60: 171–173, 1976.

Rinne UK. Parkinson's disease as a model for changes in dopamine dynamics with aging. Gerontology 28 (Supp 1): 35–52, 1982.

Robbins E, Purtell JJ, Cohen ME. Hysteria in men. N Engl J Med 246: 677–685, 1952.

Roberts DR. Catatonia in the brain: A localization study. Int J Neuropsychiatry 1: 395–403, 1965.

Robins AH. Depression in patients with parkinsonism. Br J Psychiatry 128: 141–145, 1976.

Robinson DS, Sourkes TL, Nies A, et al. Monoamine metabolism in human brain. Arch Gen Psychiatry 34: 89–92, 1977.

Rodnick EH, Shakow D. Set in the schizophrenic as measured by a composite reaction time index. Am J Psychiatry 97: 214–225, 1940.

Roizin L, True C, Knight M. Structural effects of tranquilizers. Res Publ Assoc Res Nerv Ment Dis 17: 285–324, 1959.

Rolls ET. The initiation of movements. In: Massion J, Paillard J, Schultz W, *et al.* (eds). *Neural Coding of Motor Performance.* Berlin/Heidelberg/New York, Springer-Verlag, 1983, pp. 97–113.

Rosanoff AJ (ed). *Manual of Psychiatry.* Ed. 6. New York, Wiley, 1927, pp. 106–112.

Rosen AM, Mukherjee S, Olarte S, *et al.* Perception of tardive dyskinesia in outpatients receiving maintenance neuroleptics. Am J Psychiatry 139: 372–374, 1982.

Rosenberg S, Metzig E, Snider SR, *et al.* Detection of presymptomatic carriers of Huntington's chorea. Neuropsychobiology 3: 144–152, 1977.

Rosenthal L, Roehrs T, Sicklesteel J, *et al.* Periodic movements during sleep, sleep fragmentation, and sleep–wake complaints. Sleep 7: 326–330, 1984.

Ross ED. The aprosodias: Functional–anatomic organization of the affective components of language in the right hemisphere. Arch Neurol 38: 561–569, 1981.

Ross ED, Rush AJ. Diagnosis and neuroanatomical correlates of depression in brain-damaged patients. Arch Gen Psychiatry 38: 1344–1354, 1981.

Ross ED, Stewart RM. Akinetic mutism from hypothalamic damage: Successful treatment with dopamine agonists. Neurology 31: 1435–1439, 1981.

Roth GS. Brain dopaminergic and opiate receptors and responsiveness during aging. In: Agnoli A, Crepaldi G, Spano PF, *et al.* (eds). *Aging Brain and Ergot Alkaloids. Aging.* Vol. 23. New York, Raven Press, 1983, pp. 53–60.

Rothwell JC, Obeso JA, Day BL, *et al.* Pathophysiology of dystonias. In: Desmedt JE (ed). *Motor Control Mechanisms in Health and Disease.* New York, Raven Press, 1983a, pp. 851–864, 1983.

Rothwell JC, Obeso JA, Traub MM, *et al.* The behaviour of the long-latency stretch reflex in patients with Parkinson's disease. J Neurol Neurosurg Psychiatry 46: 35–44, 1983b.

Rush M, Diamond F, Alpert M. Depression as a risk factor in tardive dyskinesia. Biol Psychiatry 17: 387–392, 1982.

Rushworth G. Spasticity and rigidity: An experimental study and review. J Neurol Neurosurg Psychiatry 23: 99–118, 1960.

Rutter M, Graham P, Yule W. *A Neuropsychiatric Study in Childhood. Clinics in Developmental Medicine.* Nos. 35/36. London, Spastics International and Heinemann, 1970.

Sackeim HA, Nordlie JW, Gur RC. A model of hysterical and hypnotic blindness: Cognition, motivation, and awareness. J Abn Psychology 88: 474–489, 1979.

Sackeim HA, Greenberg MS, Weiman AL, *et al.* Hemispheric asymmetry in the expression of positive and negative emotions. Arch Neurol 39: 210–218, 1982.

Sacks L, Feinstein AR, Taranta A. A controlled psychologic study of Sydenham's chorea. J Pediatrics 61: 714–722, 1962.

Sacks O. *Awakenings.* New York, Dutton, 1983.

Saenz-Lope E, Herranz-Tanarro FJ, Masden JC, *et al.* Hyperekplexia: A syndrome of pathological startle responses. Ann Neurol 15: 36–41, 1984.

Said G, Bathien N, Cesaro P. Peripheral neuropathies and tremor. Neurology 32: 480–485, 1982.

Sakuma M. A comparative study by the behavioral observation for stereotypy in the exceptional children. Folia Psychiatr Neurol Japon 29: 371–391, 1975.

Salisach P. Charcot–Marie–Tooth disease associated with "essential tremor." J Neurol Sci 28: 17–40, 1976.

Salzman C. The use of ECT in the treatment of schizophrenia. Am J Psychiatry 137: 1032–1041, 1980.

Samorajski T. Central neurotransmitter substances and aging: A review. J Am Geriatr Soc 25: 337–348, 1977.

Sandyk R. Baclofen in hemifacial spasm. Eur Neurol 23: 163–165, 1984.

Sanes JN, Evarts EV. Motor psychophysics. Human Neurobiol 2: 217–225, 1984.

Sanes JN, Mauritz K-H, Evarts EV, *et al.* Motor deficits in patients with large-fiber sensory neuropathy. Proc Natl Acad Sci USA 81: 979–982, 1984.

Satoh T, Harada Y. Electrophysiological study on tooth-grinding during sleep. EEG Clin Neurophys 35: 267–275, 1973.

Satterfield JH. EEG issues in children with minimal brain dysfunction. In: Haber S, Wolff PH (eds). *Minimal Cerebral Dysfunction in Children.* New York, Grune & Stratton, 1973, p. 35.

Satz P. Pathological left-handedness: An explanatory model. Cortex 8: 121–135, 1972.

Satz P. Left-handedness and early brain insult. Neuropsychologia 11: 115–117, 1973.

Sax DS, O'Donnell B, Butters N, *et al.* Computed tomographic, neurologic, and neuropsychological correlates of Huntington's disease. Int J Neurosci 18: 21–36, 1983.

Scatton B, Bartholini G. Gamma-aminobutyric acid (GABA) receptor stimulation. IV. Effect of progabide (SL 76002) and other GABAergic agents on acetylcholine turnover in rat brain areas. J Pharmacol Exp Therap 220: 689–695, 1982.

Scatton B, Zivkovic B, Dedek J, *et al.* Gamma-aminobutyric acid (GABA) receptor stimulation. III. Effect of progabide (SL 76002) on norepinephrine, dopamine and 5-hydroxytryptamine turnover in rat brain areas. J Pharmacol Exp Therap 220: 678–688, 1982.

Scheel-Kruger J. Dopamine–GABA interactions: Evidence that GABA transmits, modulates and mediates dopaminergic functions in the basal ganglia and the limbic system. Acta Neurol Scand 73 (Supp 107): 1986.

Scheibel ME, Scheibel AB. Structural changes in the aging brain. In: Brody H, Harman D, Ordy JM (eds). *Clinical, Morphologic, and Neurochemical Aspects in the Aging Central Nervous System. Aging.* Vol. 1. New York, Raven Press, 1975, pp. 11–37.

Scheinberg IH, Sternlieb I, Richman J. Psychiatric manifestations in patients with Wilson's disease. Birth Def Orig Art Ser 4: 85–87, 1968.

Schelkunov EL. Adrenergic effect of chronic administration of neuroleptics. Nature 214: 1210–1212, 1967.

Schilder P. The organic background of obsessions and compulsions. Am J Psychiatry 94: 1397–1413, 1938.

Schlagenhauff RE, Sethi PK. Electro-clinical findings in Huntington's chorea. Clin Electroenceph 8: 100–108, 1977.

Schneck JM. *A History of Psychiatry.* Springfield IL, Charles C Thomas, 1960.

Schneider E, Ziegler B, Maxion H, *et al.* Sleep in parkinsonian patients under levodopa: Results of a long-term follow-up study. In: Koella WP, Levin P (eds). *Sleep 1976: Memory, Environment, Epilepsy, Sleep Staging.* Proceedings of the Third European Congress on Sleep Research, Montpellier, September 6–10 1976. Basel, Karger, 1977, pp. 447–450.

Schneider SJ, Wilson CR. Perceptual discrimination and reaction time in hallucinatory schizophrenics. Psych Res 9: 243–253, 1983.

Schönecker M. Ein eigentumliches Syndrom im oralen Bereich bei Megaphenapplikation. Nervenarzt 28: 35, 1957.

Schopler E, Dalldorf J. Autism: Definition, diagnosis, and management. Hosp Prac 15: 64–73, 1980.

Schultz W, Aebischer P, Ruffieux A. The encoding of motor acts by the substantia nigra. In: Massion J, Paillard J, Schultz W, *et al.* (eds). *Neural Coding of Motor Performance.* Berlin/Heidelberg/New York, Springer-Verlag, 1983, pp. 171–180.

Schwab RS, Chafetz ME, Walker S. Control of two simultaneous voluntary motor acts in normals and in parkinsonism. Arch Neurol Psychiatry 75: 591–598, 1954.

Schwalbe W. *Eine Eigentumliche Tonische Krampfform mit Hysterischen Symptomen.* Inaug Diss. Berlin, G. Schade, 1908. (Referenced in Zeman W. Dystonia: An overview. In: Eldridge R, Fahn S (eds). *Dystonia. Advances in Neurology.* Vol. 14. New York, Raven Press, 1976, pp. 91–103.)

Schwartz GE, Fair PL, Salt P, *et al*. Facial muscle patterning to affective imagery in depressed and nondepressed subjects. Science 192: 489–491, 1976.

Schwartzmann J. Chorea minor: Review of 175 cases with reference to etiology, treatment and sequelae. Rheumatism 6: 89–95, 1950.

Seeman MJ, Patel J, Pyke J. Tardive dyskinesia with Tourette-like syndrome. J Clin Psychiatry 42: 357–358, 1981.

Seeman P, Lee T. Antipsychotic drugs: Direct correlations between clinical potency and presynaptic action on dopamine neurons. Science 188: 1217–1219, 1975.

Segawa M, Hosaka A, Miyagawa F, *et al*. Hereditary progressive dystonia with marked diurnal fluctuation. In: Eldridge R, Fahn S (eds). *Dystonia. Advances in Neurology*. Vol. 14. New York, Raven Press, 1976, pp. 215–234.

Seiden LS, Vosmer G. Formation of 6-hydroxydopamine in caudate nucleus of the rat brain after a single dose of methylamphetamine. Pharmacol Biochem Behav 21: 29–31, 1984.

Siegnot MJ-N. Un cas de maladie des tics de Gilles de la Tourette quéri par le R. 1625. Ann Med Psychol 119(1): 578–579, 1961.

Sclkoe D, Kosik K. Neurochemical changes with aging. In: Albert ML (ed). *Clinical Neurology of Aging*. New York, Oxford, 1984, pp. 53–94.

Scltzer B, Burres MJK, Sherwin I. Left-handedness in early and late onset dementia. Neurology 34: 367–369, 1984.

Severson JA, Finch CE. Age changes in human basal ganglion dopamine receptors. Fec Proc 39: 508, 1980.

Seyffarth H, Denny-Brown D. The grasp reflex and the instinctive grasp reaction. Brain 71: 109–183, 1948.

Shahani B, Burrows P, Whitty SWM. The grasp reflex and perseveration. Brain 93: 181–192, 1970.

Shan-Ming Y, Flor-Henry P, Dayi C, *et al*. Imbalance of hemispheric functions in the major psychoses: A study of handedness in the People's Republic of China. Biol Psychiatry 20: 906–917, 1985.

Shapiro AK, Shapiro E. Tourette syndrome: History and present status. In: Friedhoff AJ, Chase TN (eds). *Gilles de la Tourette Syndrome. Advances in Neurology*. Vol. 35. New York, Raven Press, 1982a, pp. 17–23.

Shapiro AK, Shapiro E. Clinical efficacy of haloperidol, pimozide, penfluridol, and clonidine in the treatment of Tourette's syndrome. In: Friedhoff AJ, Chase TN (eds). *Gilles de la Tourette Syndrome. Advances in Neurology*. Vol. 35. New York, Raven Press, 1982b, pp. 383–386.

Shapiro AK, Shapiro E, Wayne HL, *et al*. Tourette's syndrome: Summary of data on 34 patients. Psychosom Med 35: 419–435, 1973.

Shapiro AK, Shapiro E, Bruun RD, *et al*. *Gilles de la Tourette Syndrome*. New York, Raven Press, 1978.

Shapiro AK, Shapiro ES. *Tics, Tourette Syndrome and other Movement Disorders: A Physician's Guide*. Bayside, NY, Tourette Syndrome Association, 1980.

Shapiro AK, Shapiro E, Eisenkraft GJ. Treatment of Gilles de la Tourette syndrome with pimozide. Am J Psychiatry 140: 1183–1186, 1983.

Shear MK, Frances A, Weiden P. Suicide associated with akathisia and depot fluphenazine treatment. J Clin Psychopharm 3: 235–236, 1983.

Sheehy MP, Marsden CD. Writer's cramp: A focal dystonia. Brain 105: 461–480, 1982.

Shekim WO, Dekirmenjian H, Chapel JL. Urinary MHPG excretion in the hyperactive child syndrome and the effects of dextroamphetamine. Psychopharm Bull 14(2): 42–44, 1978.

Shetty T, Chase TN. Central monoamines and hyperkinesis of childhood. Neurology 26: 1000–1002, 1976.

Shields WB, Bray PF. A danger of haloperidol therapy in children. J Pediatr 88: 301–303, 1976.

Shik ML, Orlovsky GN. Neurophysiology of locomotor automatism. Physiol Rev 56: 465–501, 1976.

Shuttleworth E, Wise G, Paulson G. Choreoathetosis and diphenylhydantoin intoxication. J Am Med Assoc 230: 1170–1171, 1974.

Sigwald J, Bouttier D, Raymondeaud C, et al. Quatre cas de dyskinésie facio-bucco-lingui-masticatrice à évolution prolongée secondaire à un traitement par les neuroleptiques. Rev Neurol (Paris) 100: 751–755, 1959.

Silberstein RM, Blackman S, Mandell W. Autoerotic head banging: A reflection on the opportunism of infants. J Am Acad Child Psychiatry 5: 235–242, 1966.

Silva DA, Satz P. Pathological left-handedness: Evaluation of a model. Brain Lang 7: 8–16, 1979.

Simons RC. The resolution of the Latah paradox. J Nerv Ment Dis 168: 195–206, 1980.

Simpson GM. The current status of tardive dyskinesia. Int Drug Ther Newsl 15: 22–24, 1980.

Simpson GM, Shrivastava RK. Abnormal gaits in tardive dyskinesia (letter to ed). Am J Psychiatry 135: 865, 1978.

Singer HS, Oshida L, Coyle JT. CSF cholinesterase activity in Gilles de la Tourette's syndrome. Arch Neurol 41: 756–757, 1984.

Sishta SK, Troupe A, Marszalek KS, et al. Huntington's chorea: An electroencephalographic and psychometric study. EEG Clin Neurophysiol 36: 387–393, 1974.

Slater E. "Hysteria 311." J Ment Sci 107: 359–381, 1961.

Slater E. Diagnosis of "hysteria." Br Med J 1: 1395–1399, 1965.

Slater E, Glithero E. Follow-up of patients diagnosed as suffering from "Hysteria." J Psychosom Res 9: 9–13, 1965.

Smego RA Jr, Durack DT. The neuroleptic malignant syndrome. Arch Intern Med 142: 1183–1185, 1982.

Smith JM, Baldessarini RJ. Changes in prevalence, severity and recovery in tardive dyskinesia with age. Arch Gen Psychiatry 37: 1368–1373, 1980.

Smith JM, Kucharski LT, Oswald WT, et al. A systematic investigation of tardive dyskinesia in inpatients. Am J Psychiatry 136: 918–922, 1979.

Smith RC. Relationship of periodic movements in sleep (nocturnal myoclonus) and the Babinski sign. Sleep 8: 239–242, 1985.

Smith V, Chyatte C. Left-handed versus right-handed alcoholics: An examination of relapse patterns. J Stud Alcohol 44: 553–555, 1983.

Smith WR. Qualitative mathematical models of endocrine systems. Am J Physiol 245: R473–R477, 1983.

Snyder LH, Rupprecht P, Pyrek J, et al. Wandering. Gerontologist 18: 272–280, 1978.

Snyder SH. The dopamine hypothesis of schizophrenia: Focus on the dopamine receptor. Am J Psychiatry 133: 197–202, 1976.

Spalt L. Hysteria and antisocial personality: A single disorder? J Nerv Ment Dis 168: 456–464, 1980.

Spencer PS, Schaumburg HH. Experimental models of primary axonal disease induced by toxic chemicals. In: Dyck PJ, Thomas PK, Lambert EH, et al. Peripheral Neuropathy. Vol. 1. Ed. 2. Philadelphia, Saunders, 1984, pp. 636–649.

Spiegel D, Fink R. Hysterical psychosis and hypnotizability. Am J Psychiatry 136: 777–781, 1979.

Spitz RA, Wolf KM. Autoeroticism: Some empirical findings and hypotheses on three of its manifestations in the first year of life. Psychoanal Study Child. 3/4: 85–120, 1949.

Sripada P. Catatonia: A nonspecific syndrome. Res Staff Phys April: 41–44, 1982.

Sroka H, Elizan TS, Yahr MD, et al. Organic mental syndrome and confusional states in Parkinson's disease: Relationship to computerized tomographic signs of cerebral atrophy. Arch Neurol 38: 339–342, 1981.

Stahl S. Tardive Tourette syndrome in an autistic patient after long-term neuroleptic administration. Am J Psychiatry 137: 1267–1269, 1980.

Stahl SM. Akathisia and tardive dyskinesia: Changing concepts. Arch Gen Psychiatry 42: 915–917, 1985.

Stahl SM, Berger PA. Cholinergic treatment in the Tourette syndrome (reply to letter to ed). N Engl J Med 302: 1311, 1980.

Stahl SM, Berger PA. Bromocriptine, physostigmine, and neurotransmitter mechanisms in the dystonias. Neurology 32: 889–892, 1982.

Stahl SM, Layzer RB, Aminoff MJ, et al. Continuous cataplexy in a patient with a midbrain tumor: The limp man syndrome. Neurology 30: 1115–1118, 1980.

Stahl SM, Thornton JE, Simpson ML, et al. Gamma-vinyl-GABA treatment of tardive dyskinesia and other movement disorders. Biol Psychiatry 20: 888–893, 1985.

Stark L. *Neurological Control Systems.* New York, Plenum Press, 1968.

Stark L. Abnormal patterns of normal eye movements in schizophrenia. Schiz Bull 9: 55–72, 1983.

Stavraky GW. *Supersensitivity following Lesions of the Nervous System.* Toronto, University of Toronto Press, 1961.

Steck H. Les syndromes extrapyramidaux dans les maladies mentales. Arch Suiss Neurol Psychiatr 19: 195–233, 20: 92–136, 1926.

Stefansson JG, Messina JA, Meyerowitz S. Hysterical neurosis, conversion type: Clinical and epidemiological considerations. Acta Psychiat Scand 53: 119–138, 1976.

Stefansson K, Antel J, Arnason BGW. Neuroimmunology of aging. In: Albert ML (ed). *Clinical Neurology of Aging.* New York, Oxford University Press, 1984, pp. 76–94.

Steffy RA, Galbraith K. A comparison of segmental set and inhibitory deficit explanations of the crossover pattern in process schizophrenic reaction time. J Abnorm Psychol 83: 227–233, 1974.

Steffy RA, Galbraith KJ. Relation between latency and redundancy-associated deficit in schizophrenic reaction time performance. J Abnorm Psychol 89: 419–427, 1980.

Stehbens JA, Macqueen JC. The psychological adjustment of rheumatic fever patients with and without chorea. Clin Pediatrics 11: 638–640, 1972.

Stein RB, Lee RG. Tremor and clonus. In: Brooks VB (ed). *Handbook of Physiology, Section 1, The Nervous System, Volume II, Motor Control, Part 1.* Bethesda, MD, American Physiological Society, 1981, pp. 325–343.

Steingrueber HJ. Handedness as a function of test complexity. Percept Motor Skills 40: 263–266, 1975.

Stejskal L, Tomanek Z. Postural laterality in torticollis and torsion dystonia. J Neurol Neurosurg Psychiatry 44: 1029–1034, 1981.

Stern DB. Handedness and the lateral distribution of conversion reactions. J Nerv Ment Dis 164: 122–128, 1977.

Stern TA, Anderson WH. Benztropine prophylaxis of dystonic reactions. Psychopharm 61: 261–262, 1979.

Stern Y, Mayeux R, Cote L. Reaction time and vigilance in Parkinson's disease: Possible role of altered norepinephrine metabolism. 41: 1086–1089, 1984.

Stevens H. Jumping Frenchmen of Maine. Arch Neurol 12: 311–314, 1965.

Stevens JR. An anatomy of schizophrenia? Arch Gen Psychiatry 29: 177–189, 1973.

Stevens JR. Disturbances of ocular movements and blinking in schizophrenia. J Neurol Neurosurg Psychiatry 41: 1024–1030, 1978.

Stevens JR. Neuropathology of schizophrenia. Arch Gen Psychiatry 39: 1131–1139, 1982.

Stevens JR. Psychosis and epilepsy (letter to ed). Ann Neurol 14: 347–348, 1983.

Stevens JR, Sachdev K, Milstein V. Behavior disorders of childhood and the electroencephalogram. Arch Neurol 18: 160–177, 1968.

Still GF. The Coulstonian Lectures on some abnormal physical conditions in children. Lancet I: 1008–1012, 1077–1082, 1163–1168, 1902.

Stoddart WHB. *Mind and its Disorders: A Text-Book for Students and Practitioners.* Philadelphia, P. Blakiston's Son, 1909.

Stoessl AJ, Martin WRW, Clark C, *et al.* PET studies of cerebral glucose metabolism in idiopathic torticollis. Neurology 36: 653–657, 1986.

Stoudemire A, Luther JS. Neuroleptic malignant syndrome and neuroleptic-induced catatonia: Differential diagnosis and treatment. Int J Psych Med 14: 57–63, 1984.

Stramentinoli G, Gualano M, Catto E, *et al.* Tissue levels of S-adenosylmethionine in aging rats. J Gerontol 32: 392–394, 1977.

Straus EW, Griffith RM. Pseudoreversibility of catatonic stupor. Am J Psychiatry 111: 680–685, 1955.

Strauss AA, Lehtinen V. *Psychopathology and Education of the Brain-Injured Child.* Vol. 1. New York, Grune & Stratton, 1947.

Strecker EA, Ebaugh FG. *Practical Clinical Psychiatry for Students and Practitioners.* Ed. 4. Philadelphia, P. Blakiston's Son, 1935, pp. 387–393.

Struve FA, Willner AE. A long term prospective study of electroencephalographic and neuropsychological correlates of tardive dyskinesia: Initial findings at five year followup. Clin Electroenceph 14: 186–201, 1983.

Subirana A. Handedness and cerebral dominance. In: Vinken PJ, Bruyn GW (eds). *Disorders of Speech, Perception and Symbolic Behavior. Handbook of Clinical Neurology.* Vol. 4. New York, American Elsevier, 1969, pp. 248–272.

Suhren O, Bruyn GW, Tuynman JA. Hyperexplexia: A hereditary startle syndrome. J Neurol Sci 3: 577–605, 1966.

Sukov RJ. Thrombophlebitis as a complication of severe catatonia (letter to ed). J Am Med Assoc 220: 587–588, 1972.

Sunohara N, Mano Y, Ando K, *et al.* Idiopathic dystonia–parkinsonism with marked diurnal fluctuation of symptoms. Ann Neurol 17: 39–45, 1985.

Sevensson TH, Bunney BS, Aghajanian GK. Inhibition of both noradrenergic and serotonergic neurons in brain by the alpha-adrenergic agonist clonidine. Brain Res 92: 291–306, 1975.

Sweet RD, McDowell FH, Feigenson JS, *et al.* Mental symptoms in Parkinson's disease during chronic treatment with levodopa. Neurology 26: 305–310, 1976.

Swett C Jr. Drug-induced dystonia. Am J Psychiatry 132: 532–534, 1975.

Swiercinsky DP. Significance of crossed eye–hand dominance for the adult neuropsychological evaluation. J Nerv Ment Dis 165: 134–138, 1977.

Symonds CP. Nocturnal myoclonus. J Neurol Neurosurg Psychiatry 16: 166–171, 1953.

Takahashi S, Gjessing LR. Studies of periodic catatonia: III. Longitudinal sleep study with urinary excretion of catecholamines. J Psychiat Res 9: 123–139, 1972.

Talairach J, Bancand J, Geier S, *et al.* The cingulate gyrus and human behavior. EEG Clin Neurophysiol 34: 45–52, 1973.

Tamminga CA, Frohman LA. Neuroendocrine approach to the study and treatment of tardive dyskinesia. In: Muller EE, Agnoli A (eds). *Neuroendocrine Correlates in Neurology and Psychiatry.* Amsterdam, Elsevier/North-Holland, 1979, 139–149.

Tamminga CA, Crayton JW, Chase TN. Improvement in tardive dyskinesia after muscimol therapy. Arch Gen Psychiatry 36: 595–598, 1979.

Tamminga CA, Thaker GK, Ferraro TN, *et al.* GABA agonist treatment improves tardive dyskinesia. Lancet II: 97–98, 1983.

Tanaka Y, Hazama H, Kawahara R, *et al.* Computerized tomography of the brain in schizophrenic patients: A controlled study. Acta Psych Scand 63: 191–197, 1981.

Tanner CM, Goetz CG, Klawans HL. Cholinergic mechanisms in Tourette syndrome. Neurology 32: 1315–1317, 1982.

Tatton WG, Lee RG. Evidence for abnormal long-loop reflexes in rigid Parkinsonian patients. Brain Res 100: 671–676, 1975.

Tatton WG, Bawa P, Bruce IC. Altered motor cortical activity in extrapyramidal rigidity. In: Poirier LJ, Sourkes TL, Bedard PJ (eds). *The Extrapyramidal System and Its Disorders. Advances in Neurology* Vol. 24. New York, Raven Press, 1979, 141–160.

Tatton WG, Bedingham W, Verrier MC, *et al.* Characteristic alterations in responses to imposed wrist displacements in parkinsonian rigidity and dystonia musculorum deformans. Can J Neurol Sci 11: 281–287, 1984.

Taylor HG, Heilman KM. Left-hemisphere motor dominance in righthanders. Cortex 16: 587–603, 1980.

Taylor J. *Selected Writings of John Hughlings Jackson.* London, Hodder & Stoughton, 1932.

Taylor MA, Abrams R. Catatonia: Prevalence and importance in the manic phase of manic-depressive illness. Arch Gen Psychiatry 34: 1223–1225, 1977.

Taylor PJ, Dalton R, Fleminger JJ. Handedness and schizophrenia. Br J Psychiatry 136: 375–383, 1980.

Taylor PJ, Dalton R, Fleminger JJ, *et al.* Differences between two studies of hand preference in psychiatric patients. Br J Psychiatry 140: 166–173, 1982.

Temkin, O. *The Falling Sickness.* Baltimore, Johns Hopkins University Press, 1971.

Templer DI, Veleber DM. The decline of catatonic schizophrenia. Orthomol Psychiatry 10: 156–158, 1981.

Teravainen H, Evarts E, Calne D. Effects of kinesthetic inputs on parkinsonian tremor. In: Poirier LJ, Sourkes TL, Bedard PJ (eds). *The Extrapyramidal System and Its Disorders. Advances in Neurology.* Vol. 24. New York, Raven Press, 1979, pp. 161–173.

Thom R. *Stabilité structurelle et morphogénèse; essai d'une théorie générale des modèles.* Reading, MA, W. A. Benjamin, 1972.

Thomas GCG, Wilson DC. The recognition of pre-schizophrenic states. Virg Med Monthly. 76: 405–410, 1949.

Todd R, Lippmann S, Manshadi M, *et al.* Recognition and treatment of rabbit syndrome, an uncommon complication of neuroleptic therapies. Am J Psychiatry 140: 1519–1520, 1983.

Todes CJ, Lees AJ. The pre-morbid personality of patients with Parkinson's disease. J Neurol Neurosurg Psychiatry 48: 97–100, 1985.

Toenniessen LM, Casey DE, McFarland BH. Tardive dyskinesia in the aged. Arch Gen Psychiatry 42: 278–287, 1985.

Tolosa ES. Clinical features of Meige's disease (idiopathic orofacial dystonia). Arch Neurol 38: 147–151, 1981.

Tomlinson BE, Irving D, Blessed G. Cell loss in the locus coeruleus in senile dementia of Alzheimer type. J Neurol Sci 49: 419–428, 1981.

Torrey EF. *Schizophrenia and Civilization.* New York, Aronson, 1980.

Traczynska-Kubin D, Atzef E, Petre Quadens O. Le sommeil dans la maladie de Parkinson. Acta Neurol Belg 69: 727–733, 1969.

Tredgold AF. *Mental Deficiency (Amentia).* Ed. 1. New York, Wook, 1908.

Trembly D. Crossed dominance of hand and eye in relation to poliomyelitis. Percept Motor Skills 26: 231–234, 1968.

Trevarthen C. Manipulative strategies of baboons and origins of cerebral asymmetry. In: Kinsbourne M (ed). *Asymmetrical Function of the Brain.* Cambridge, Cambridge University Press, 1978, pp. 329–391.

Tsai LY. Brief report: Handedness in autistic children and their families. J Aut Dev Dis 12: 421–423, 1982.

Tsai LY. The relationship of handedness to the cognitive, language, and visuo-spatial skills of autistic patients. Br J Psychiatry 142: 156–162, 1983.

Tsai LY, Stewart MA. Handedness and EEG correlation in autistic children. Biol Psychiatry 17: 595–598, 1982.

Turkewitz G. The development of lateral differences in the human infant. In: Harnad S, Doty RW, Goldstein L, et al. (eds). Lateralization in the Nervous System. New York, Academic Press, 1977, pp. 251–260.

Udaka F, Yamao S, Nagata H, et al. Pathologic laughing and crying treated with levodopa. Arch Neurol 41: 1095–1096, 1984.

Uhrbrand L, Faurbye A. Reversible and irreversible dyskinesia after treatment with perphenazine, chlorpromazine, reserpine, and electroconvulsive therapy. Psychopharmacologia 1: 408–418, 1960.

Ule G, Struwe O. Hirnveranderungen bei Dyskinesie nach Neuroleptika-Medikation. Nervenarzt 49: 268–270, 1978.

Ungerstedt U. Postsynaptic supersensitivity after 6-hydroxydopamine-induced degeneration of the nigro-striatal dopamine system. Acta Physiol Scand 367 (Supp): 69–93, 1971.

Unverricht H. Die Myoklonie. Leipzig, Deuticke, 1891.

Vanasse M, Bedard P, Andermann F. Shuddering attacks in children: An early clinical manifestation of essential tremor. Neurology 26: 1027–1030, 1976.

Van Kammen DP, Mann LS, Sternberg DE, et al. Dopamine-beta-hydroxylase and homovanillic acid in spinal fluid of schizophrenics with brain atrophy. Science 220: 974–977, 1983.

VanPutten T. The many faces of akathisia. Comp Psychiatry 16: 43–47, 1975.

VanPutten T, Menkes JH. Huntington's disease masquerading as chronic schizophrenia. Dis Nerv Syst 34: 54–56, 1973.

VanWoert MH, Hwang EC. Biochemistry and pharmacology of myoclonus. In: Klawans HL (ed). Clinical Neuropharmacology. Vol. 3. New York, Raven Press, 1978, pp. 167–184.

VanZandycke M, Martin J-J, Gaer LV, et al. Facial myokymia in the Guillain-Barré syndrome: A clinicopathologic study. Neurology 32: 744–748, 1982.

Varga E, Sugerman AA, Varga V, et al. Prevalence of spontaneous oral dyskinesia in the elderly. Am J Psychiatry 139: 329–331, 1982.

Vertes RP. Brainstem control of the events of REM sleep. Prog Neurobiol 22: 241–288, 1984.

Vilensky JA, Damasio AR, Maurer RG. Gait disturbances in patients with autistic behavior: A preliminary study. Arch Neurol 38: 646–649, 1981.

Villeneuve A. The rabbit syndrome, a peculiar extrapyramidal reaction. Can Psychiat Assoc J 17(SS-II): SS69–SS72, 1972.

Villeneuve A, Jus K, Jus A. Polygraphic studies of tardive dyskinesia and of the rabbit syndrome during different stages of sleep. Biol Psychiatry 6: 259–274, 1973.

Visser H. Gait and balance in senile dementia of Alzheimer's type. Age Aging 12: 296–301, 1983.

Viukari M, Linnoila M. Effect of fusaric acid on tardive dyskinesia and mental state in psychogeriatric patients. Acta Psych Scand 56: 57–61, 1977.

Vizioli R. Les bases neurophysiologiques de la cataplexie. EEG Clin Neurophysiol 16: 191–193, 1964.

Vogel H-P. Symptoms of depression in Parkinson's disease. Pharmacopsychiatry 15: 192–196, 1982.

Vogt C, Vogt O. Altérations anatomiques de la schizophrenia et d'autres psychoses dites fonctionelles. In: Proceedings of the First International Congress of Neuropathology. Vol. 1. Torino, Rosenberg & Sellier, 1952, pp. 515–532.

VonMonakow C. Die Lokalisation im Grosshirn und der Abbau der Funktionen durch corticale Herde. Wiesbaden, Bergmann, 1914.

Waddington JL, Cross AJ, Gamble SJ, et al. Spontaneous orofacial dyskinesia and dopaminergic function in rats after six months of neuroleptic treatment. Science 220: 530–532, 1983.

Waddington JL, Youssef HA, Molloy AF, et al. Association of intellectual impairment, negative symptoms, and aging with tardive dyskinesia: Clinical and animal studies. J Clin Psychiatry 46: 29–33, 1985.

Wald D, Lerner J. Lithium in the treatment of periodic catatonia: A case report. Am J Psychiatry 135: 751–752, 1978.

Wahl OF. Handedness in schizophrenia. Percept Motor Skills 42: 944–946, 1976.

Walker HA, Birch HG. Lateral preference and right–left awareness in schizophrenic children. J Nerv Ment Dis 151: 341–351, 1970.

Walsh GO, Delgado-Escueta AV. Type II complex partial seizures: Poor results of anterior temporal lobectomy. Neurology 34: 1–13, 1984.

Walsh JK, Kramer M, Skinner JE. A case report of jactatio capitis nocturna. Am J Psychiatry 138: 524–526, 1981.

Walsh KW. Neuropsychology: A clinical approach. Edinburgh, Churchill Livingstone, 1978.

Warburton JW. Depressive symptoms in Parkinsonism patients referred for thalamotomy. J Neurol Neurosurg Psychiatry 30: 368–370, 1964.

Ward CD, Duvoisin RC, Ince SE, et al. Parkinson's disease in 65 pairs of twins and in a set of quadruplets. Neurology 33: 815–824, 1983.

Warren JM. Handedness and cerebral dominance in monkeys. In: Harnad S, Doty RW, Goldstein L, et al. (eds). Lateralization in the Nervous System. New York, Academic Press, 1977, pp. 151–162.

Watson CG, Buranen C. The frequency and identification of false positive conversion reactions. J Nerv Ment Dis 167: 243–472, 1979.

Watson JB. Behaviorism. New York, The People's Institute Publishing Co., 1924.

Webster DD, Mortimer JA. Failure of L-DOPA to relieve activated rigidity in Parkinson's disease. In: Messiha FS, Kenny AD (eds). Parkinson's Disease: Neurophysiological, Clinical, and Related Aspects. New York, Plenum Press, 1977, pp. 297–313.

Wechsler IS. Clinical Neurology. Philadelphia, Saunders, 1963.

Wechsler LR, Stakes JW, Shahani BT, et al. Periodic leg movements of sleep (nocturnal myoclonus): An electrophysiological study. Ann Neurol 19: 168–173, 1986.

Weddington WW, Marks RC, Verghese JP. Disulfiram encephalopathy as a cause of the catatonia syndrome. Am J Psychiatry 137: 1217–1219, 1980.

Wein A, Golubev V. Polygraphic analysis of sleep in dystonia musculorum deformans. Waking Sleeping 3: 41–50, 1979.

Wein A, Golubev V, Yakhno N. Polygraphic analysis of sleep and wakefulness in patients with Parkinson's syndrome. Waking Sleeping 3: 31–40, 1979.

Weinberger DR, Kelly MJ. Catatonia and malignant syndrome: A possible complication of neuroleptic administration: Report of a case involving haloperidol. J Nerv Ment Dis 165: 263–268, 1977.

Weinberger DR, Wyatt RJ. Structural pathology of the cerebellum in schizophrenia: CT and post-mortem studies. In: Perris C, Struwe G, Jansson B (eds). Biological Psychiatry 1981. Amsterdam, Elsevier/North-Holland, 1981, pp. 272–275.

Weinberger DR, Torrey EF, Wyatt RJ. Cerebellar atrophy in chronic schizophrenia. Lancet I: 718–719, 1979.

Weinberger DR, Kleinman JE, Luchins DJ, et al. Cerebellar pathology in schizophrenia: A controlled postmortem study. Am J Psychiatry 137: 359–361, 1980.

Weinberger DR, DeLisi LE, Perman GP, et al. Computed tomography in schizophreniform disorder and other acute psychiatric disorders. Arch Gen Psychiatry 39: 778–783, 1982.

Weiner WJ, Luby ED. Persistent akathisia following neuroleptic withdrawal. Ann Neurol 13: 466–467, 1983.

Weiner WJ, Nausieda PA. Meige's syndrome during long-term dopaminergic therapy in Parkinson's disease. Arch Neurol 39: 451–452, 1982.

Weiner WJ, Nausieda PA, Klawans HL. Methylphenidate-induced chorea: Case report and pharmacologic implications. Neurology 28: 1041–1044, 1978.

Weiner WJ, Nausieda PA, Klawans HL. Regional brain manganese levels in an animal model of tardive dyskinesia. In: Fann WE, Smith RC, Davis JM, et al. (eds). Tardive Dyskine-

sia: Research and Treatment. New York, SP Medical and Scientific Books, 1980, pp. 159–163.

Weiner WJ, Nausieda PA, Glantz RH. Meige syndrome (blepharospasm–oromandibular dystonia) after long-term neuroleptic therapy. Neurology 31: 1555–1556, 1981.

Weiner WJ, Nora LM, Glantz RH. Elderly inpatients: Postural reflex impairment. Neurology 34: 945–947, 1984.

Weingarten K. Tics. In: Vinken PJ, Bruyn GW (eds). *Diseases of the Basal Ganglia. Handbook of Clinical Neurology.* Vol. 6. New York, American Elsevier, 1968, pp. 782–808.

Weintraub MI. *Hysterical Conversion Reactions: A Clinical Guide to Diagnosis and Treatment.* New York, SP Medical and Scientific, 1983.

Weintraub S, Mesulam M-M, Kramer L. Disturbances in prosody: A right-hemisphere contribution to language. Arch Neurol 38: 742–744, 1981.

Weiss G, Hectman L, Perlman T, *et al.* Hyperactives as young adults: A controlled prospective ten-year follow-up of 75 children. Arch Gen Psychiatry 36: 675–681, 1979.

Weiss KJ, Ciraulo DA, Shader RI. Physostigmine test in the rabbit syndrome and tardive dyskinesia. Am J Psychiatry 137: 627–628, 1980.

Welford AT. Motor performance. In: Birren JE, Schaie KW. *Handbook of the Psychology of Aging.* New York, Van Nostrand Reinhold, 1977, pp. 450–496.

Wells FL, Kelley CM. The simple reaction in psychosis. Am J Psychiatry 79: 53–59, 1922.

Wender Ph, Reimherr FW, Wood DR. Attention deficit disorder ("minimal brain dysfunction") in adults. Arch Gen Psychiatry 38: 449–456, 1981.

Wernicke C. *Krankenvorstellungen aus der psychiatrischen Klinik in Breslau.* Breslau, Schletter, 1899–1900.

Wertheimer N. The differential incidence of rheumatic fever in the histories of paranoid and non-paranoid schizophrenics. J Nerv Ment Dis 125: 637–641, 1957.

Whatmore GB, Ellis RM. Some neurophysiological aspects of depressed states: An electromyographic study. Arch Gen Psychiatry 1: 70–80, 1959.

Whitaker HA, Ojemann GA. Lateralization of higher cortical functions: A critique. In: Dimond SJ, Blizard DA (eds). *Evolution and Lateralization of the Brain.* Ann NY Acad Sci 299: 459–473, 1977.

Whitlock FA. The aetiology of hysteria. Acta Psych Scand 43: 144–162, 1967.

Wiesendanger M. Cortico-cerebellar loops. In: Massion J, Paillard J, Schultz W, *et al.* (eds). *Neural Coding of Motor Performance.* Berlin/Heidelberg/New York, Springer-Verlag, 1983, pp. 41–53.

Wild D, Nayak USL, Isaacs B. Description, classification and prevention of falls in old people. Rheumatol Rehabil 20: 153–159, 1981.

Wilder J, Silbermann J. *Beitrage zum Ticproblem.* Berlin, Karger, 1927.

Wile IS. *Handedness: Right and Left.* Boston, Lothrop, Lee & Shepard, 1934.

Williams P. An unusual response to chlorpromazine therapy. Br J Psychiatry 121: 439–440, 1972.

Wilson RL, Waziri R, Nasrallah HA, *et al.* The lateralization of tardive dyskinesia. Biol Psychiatry 19: 629–635, 1984.

Wilson RS, Garron DC, Klawans HL. Significance of genetic factors in Gilles de la Tourette syndrome: A review. Behav Genet 8: 503–510, 1978.

Wilson SAK. Some problems in neurology: II. Pathological laughing and crying. J Neurol Psychopathol 4: 299–333, 1924.

Wilson SAK. Disorders of motility and muscle tone, with special reference to the striatum. Lancet II: 1–53, 169, 215, 268, 1925.

Wilson SAK. *Neurology.* Ed. 2. Bruce AN (ed). Baltimore, Williams & Wilkins, 1955.

Wing L. Asperger's syndrome: A clinical account. Psychol Med 11: 115–129, 1981.

Winsberg BG, Hurwic MJ, Perel J. Neurochemistry of withdrawal emergent symptoms in children. Psychopharm Bull 13: 38–40, 1977.

Winslow RS, Stillner V, Coons DJ, *et al.* Prevention of acute dystonic reactions in patients beginning high-potency neuroleptics. Am J Psychiatry 143: 706–710, 1986.

Witelson SF. Neuroanatomical asymmetry in left-handers: A review and implications for functional asymmetry. In: Herron J (ed). *Neuropsychology of Left-Handedness.* New York, Academic Press, 1980, pp. 79–114.

Wolf ME, Ryan JJ, Mosnaim AD. Organicity and tardive dyskinesia. Psychosomatics 23: 475–480, 1982.

Wolf ME, Chevesich J, Lehrer E, *et al.* The clinical association of tardive dyskinesia and drug-induced parkinsonism. Biol Psychiatry 18: 1181–1188, 1983.

Wolfson LI, Katzman R. The neurologic consultation at age 80. In: Katzman R, Terry R (eds). *The Neurology of Aging.* Philadelphia, Davis, 1983, pp. 221–244.

Wong DF, Wagner HN Jr, Dannals RF, *et al.* Effects of age on dopamine and serotonin receptors measured by positron tomography in the living human brain. Science 226: 1393–1396, 1984.

Wood DR, Reimherr FW, Wender PH, *et al.* Diagnosis and treatment of minimal brain dysfunction in adults. Arch Gen Psychiatry 33: 1453–1460, 1976.

Woollam DHM. Concepts of the brain and its functions in classical antiquity. In: *The History and Philosophy of Knowledge of the Brain and Its Functions.* Springfield, IL, Charles C Thomas, 1958, pp. 5–18.

Wooten GF, Eldridge R, Axelrod J, *et al.* Elevated plasma dopamine-beta-hydroxylase in autosomal dominant torsion dystonia. N Engl J Med 288: 284–287, 1973.

Wyatt RJ, Chase TN, Scott J, *et al.* Effect of L-DOPA on the sleep of man. Nature 228: 999–1001, 1970.

Wyatt RJ, Potkin SG, Kleinman JE, *et al.* The schizophrenia syndrome: Examples of biological tools for subclassification. J Nerv Ment Dis 169: 100–111, 1981.

Yap P-M. Mental diseases peculiar to certain cultures: A survey of comparative psychiatry. J Ment Sci 97: 313–327, 1951.

Yarden PE, Discipio WJ. Abnormal movements and prognosis in schizophrenia. Am J Psychiatry 128: 317–323, 1971.

Yassa R, Lal S. Prevalence of the rabbit syndrome. Am J Psychiatry 143: 656–657, 1986.

Yassa R, Ghadirian AM, Schwartz G. Prevalence of tardive dyskinesia in affective disorder patients. J Clin Psychiatry 44: 410–412, 1983.

Young AB, Penney JB. Neurochemical anatomy of movement disorders. In: Jankovic J (ed). *Movement Disorders.* Philadelphia, W. B. Saunders, 1984, pp. 417–434.

Young JG, Kavanagh ME, Anderson GM, *et al.* Clinical neurochemistry of autism and associated disorders. J Aut Dev Dis 12: 147–165, 1982.

Young RR, Shahani BT. Pharmacology of tremor. In: Klawans HL (ed). *Clinical Neuropharmacology.* Vol. 4. New York, Raven Press, 1979, pp. 139–156.

Young RR, Growdon JH, Shahani BT. Beta-adrenergic mechanisms in action tremor. N Eng J Med 293: 950–953, 1975.

Zeman W. Dystonia: An overview. In: Eldridge R, Fahn S (eds). *Dystonia. Advances in Neurology.* Vol. 14. New York, Raven Press, 1976, pp. 91–104.

Zeman W, Dyken P. Dystonia musculorum deformans: Clinical, genetic and patho-anatomical studies. Psychiat Neurol Neurochir (Amsterdam) 70: 77–112, 1967.

Zetusky WJ, Jankovic J, Pirozzolo FJ. The heterogeneity of Parkinson's disease: Clinical and prognostic implications. Neurology 35: 522–526, 1985.

Ziegler DK. Prolonged relief of dystonic movements with diazepam. Neurology 31: 1457–1458, 1981.

Ziegler DK, Imboden JB. Contemporary conversion reactions. Arch Gen Psychiatry 6: 37–45, 1962.

Ziegler DK, Imboden JB, Meyer E. Contemporary conversion reactions: A clinical study. Am J Psychiatry 116: 901–910, 1960.

Ziehen T. Hysteria. In: Church A, Salinger JL (eds). *Diseases of the Nervous System.* New York, Appleton, 1910, pp. 1045–1097.

Ziehen T. Ein Fall von tonischer Torsionsneurose. Neurol Centrabl 30: 109–110, 1911.

Zilboorg G. *A History of Medical Psychology.* New York, W. W. Norton, 1941.

Zorumski CF, Bakris GL. Choreoathetosis associated with lithium: Case report and literature review. Am J Psychiatry 140: 1621–1622, 1983.

Zubenko GS, Barreira P, Lipinski JF Jr. Development of tolerance to the therapeutic effect of amantadine on akathisia. J Clin Psychopharm 4: 218–220, 1984.

Zurif EB, Carson G. Dyslexia in relation to cerebral dominance and temporal analysis. Neuropsychologia 8: 351–361, 1970.

Index

Belle indifférence, la, 230
Benzodiazepines
  akathisia treatment, 67, 272
  catalepsy diagnosis, 142
  catatonia treatment, 225–227
Benztropine, 255
Bereitschaftspotential (*see* Readiness potential)
Berger, Hans, 14
Beta-adrenergic system, 73, 75
Betz cells, 16
Biasing circuits, 34
Bimanual tasks, 18
Bipolar disorder
  handedness, 299, 302
  tardive dyskinesia, 257
Bizarreries, 95, 96, 104, 105
Blepharospasm, 158, 159, 206, 265
Bleuler, Eugen, 14, 203
Blind children, stereotypies, 108
Blink reflex, Meige's syndrome, 159
Blinking abnormalities
  Parkinson's disease, sleep, 280, 281
  schizophrenia, 174
"Bonbon sign," 256
Brachium conjunctivum, 29
Brachium pontis, 29
Bradykinesia, 131–137
  description, 132
  differential diagnosis, 133
  pathophysiology, 133–137
  and tardive dyskinesia, 265
Brain damage
  and handedness, 297, 298
  and hyperactivity, 58, 59
  and tardive dyskinesia, 257
Brainstem
  exaggerated startle response role, 119
  pathological laughter, 176
Briquet's disorder, 228, 229
Broca, Paul, 11
Brodmann's area *4*, 178
Bromocriptine
  in akinetic mutism, 133
  in catatonia, 227
  and sleep, Parkinson's disease, 281, 282
Bruxism, 81–83
  description, 81
  differential diagnosis, 81, 82
  treatment, 83
Buccolinguomasticatory disorders, 265
Bulbocapnine, 141, 204

Calcitonin, 225
Calcium, 225
Camptocormia, 185

Carbamazepine
  choreoathetoid movements, 56
  in complex partial seizures, 106
  in nocturnal paroxysmal dystonia, 278, 279
Carpal tunnel syndrome, 303
Catalepsy, 138–142
  description, 139, 140
  differential diagnosis, 140, 141
  pathophysiology, 141
  syndromes, 141, 142
Cataplectic atonia, 119
Cataplexy, 114–122
  description, 116
  differential diagnosis, 117, 118
  and narcoleptic syndrome, 116, 120
  pathophysiology, 118, 119
  treatment, 121
Catatonia, 201–227
  and catalepsy, 138, 139, 141, 142
  diagnostic criteria, 225, 226
  and gait, 184
  grasp reflexes, 112
  history, 202–204
  hysteria relationship, 234, 235
  Kahlbaum's theory, 13, 202
  neurological etiology, 218, 219
  "positivism," 112, 113
  prevalence, 219–222
  psychological theories, 216–218
  and schizophrenia, 203, 204, 210–216
  signs and symptoms, 205–210
  sleep studies, 283, 284
  syndromes, 148, 210–216
  treatment, 226, 227
"Catatonic–extrapyramidal syndrome," 224
Catatonic gait, 184
Catatonic schizophrenia, 211, 217–222
Catecholamines (*see also* Dopamine; Norepinephrine)
  hyperactivity, 62, 63
  tremor physiology, 73
Caudate nucleus
  anatomy, 24–26
  catalepsy, 141
  and movement disorder complexity, 318, 319
  tardive dyskinesia, 262–264
Central nervous system
  and aging, 308–311
  tremor origin, 70, 74, 75
Central oscillation, 70, 74, 75, 324
Cerea flexibilitas, 139
"Cerebellar catalepsy," 140
Cerebellar peduncles, 29, 30
Cerebellar tremor, 71
Cerebellar vermis, 238–240

tremor characteristics, 71, 72
Right hemisphere
  and handedness, hypothesis, 304, 305
  pathological laughter, 176
"Right-shift" factor, 290
Righting reflex, 38
Rigidity, 161–167
  description, 161, 162
  differential diagnosis, 163
  versus dystonia, 153
  and hypokinesia, 135
  pathophysiology, 163, 164
  syndromes, 164
  and tardive dyskinesia, 265
Rochester, New York, catatonia incidence,
  220
Rocking, pathophysiology, 100
Roentgen, Wilhelm Konrad, 14
Roman physicians, 6, 7
Rubral tremor, 76

Saccades, schizophrenia, 173, 174
Schizophrenia
  akathisia, 66
  basal ganglia, 29, 240–243
  and catalepsy, 142
  and catatonia, 203, 204, 210–216
  cerebellum role, 237–240
  choreoathetoid movements, 53, 54
  facial expression, 173, 174
  handedness, 298–301
  history, 14
  reaction time, 136, 137
  and Sydenham's chorea, 249
Schleiden, Matthias, 12
Schnauzkrampf, 173, 206
Schwann, Theodor, 12
"Scissors" gait, 184
Scoliosis, 303
Secondary gain, hysteria, 230, 233
Secondary motor cortex, 308
Segmental myoclonus, 125, 126
Segmental spinal reflexes, 166, 167
Seizures
  and automatisms, 99
  as conversion symptom, 235
Self-stimulation, 200
Senile chorea, 52, 312
"Senile" gait, 186, 187
Senile plaques, 245
Senile tremor, 312
Sensorimotor cortex, 18
Sensory cortex, 18
Sensory neglect, 256
Serotonin
  and aging, 310
  in depression, Parkinson's disease, 246
  extrapyramidal system, 27, 28

hyperekplexia mechanism, 119, 120
mannerisms mechanism, 104, 105
myoclonus, 126
Tourette's syndrome, 196
Sex hormones, 51
Short-latency spinal reflexes, 22, 23
Short-loop reflexes, 70
Shuddering attacks, 72
Shy–Drager syndrome, 282
"Side impulses," 147
Silok, 115
Simple negativism, 144, 145
Simple tics, 199
Sinistrality, 286–305
Sleep, 275–285
  and bruxism, 83
  and movement disorders, 275–285
  physiology, 274, 275
Sleep apnea, 277
Sleep latency
  catatonia, 283, 284
  Parkinson's disease, 280
Sleep spindles
  dystonia musculorum deformans, 282
  Parkinson's disease, 280
  physiology, 276
Sleep-walking, 277, 278
Sleeping sickness, 14
Slow-wave sleep (see Delta sleep)
Smooth-pursuit eye movements, 173, 174
Snout spasm, 206
Sociopathy, handedness, 304
Soft signs, 64
Somatization disorder, 229, 230
Somatosensory evoked potentials, 233
Somnambulism, 277, 278
Spasme facial median, 158
Spasticity
  description, 162
  differential diagnosis, 87, 163
  pathophysiology, 166, 167
Speech-inactive catatonia, 208
Speech latency, 242
Speech-prompt catatonia, 208
Speed of movement (see Movement time)
Spina bifida, 302
Spinal accessory nerve, 20
Spinal loop, cerebellum, 30, 31
Spinal myoclonus, 125, 126
Spinal reflexes
  and hierarchical motor system, 34
  pyramidal tract, 20–23
  spasticity, 166, 167
  tremor, 73
Spiny cells, 46, 47
Spiperone, 260
St. Vitus's dance, 8
Staggering reflex, 38